Panza's story in this volume deals a bit
with, well, feelings. People's feelings are so
complex, and their ways of showing them
even more so—I get lost sometimes just
thinking what to show and how.

– Yoshiyuki Nishi

Yoshiyuki Nishi was born in Tokyo. Two of
his favorite manga series are *Dragon Ball* and
the robot-cat comedy *Doraemon*. His latest
series, *Muhyo & Roji's Bureau of Supernatural
Investigation*, debuted in Japan's *Akamaru
Jump* magazine in 2004 and went on to be
serialized in *Weekly Shonen Jump*.

MUHYO & ROJI'S
BUREAU OF SUPERNATURAL INVESTIGATION

VOL. 9
The SHONEN JUMP Manga Edition

STORY AND ART BY
YOSHIYUKI NISHI

Translation & Adaptation/Alexander O. Smith
Touch-up Art & Lettering/Brian Bilter
Cover Design/Izumi Hirayama
Interior Design/Yukiko Whitley
Editor/Amy Yu

Editor in Chief, Books/Alvin Lu
Editor in Chief, Magazines/Marc Weidenbaum
VP, Publishing Licensing/Rika Inouye
VP, Sales & Product Marketing/Gonzalo Ferreyra
VP, Creative/Linda Espinosa
Publisher/Hyoe Narita

Printed in Canada

Published by VIZ Media, LLC
P.O. Box 77010
San Francisco, CA 94107

SHONEN JUMP Manga Edition
10 9 8 7 6 5 4 3 2 1
First printing, February 2009

www.viz.com   www.shonenjump.com

THE WORLD'S MOST POPULAR MANGA

SHONEN JUMP MANGA EDITION

Muhyo & Roji's Bureau of Supernatural Investigation

BSI

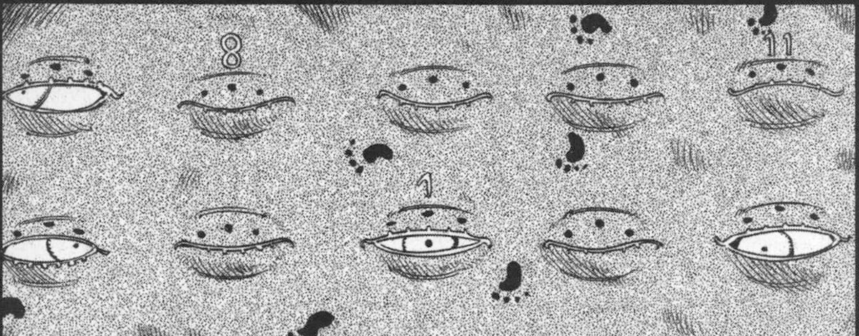

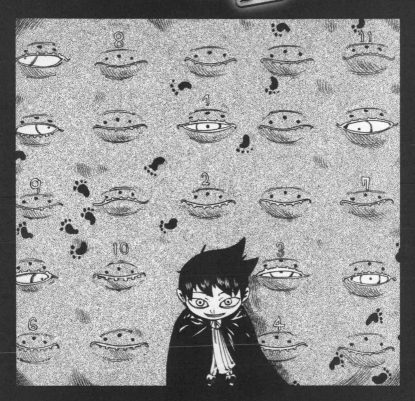

Vol. 9 Pansies

Story & Art by **Yoshiyuki Nishi**

Dramatis Personae

Jiro Kusano (Roji)

Assistant at Muhyo's office, recently promoted from the lowest rank of "Second Clerk" to that of (provisional) "First Clerk." Roji has a gentle heart and has been known to freak out in the presence of spirits. Lately, he has been devoting himself to the study of magic law so that he can pull his own weight someday.

Toru Muhyo (Muhyo)

Young, genius magic law practitioner with the highest rank of "Executor." Always calm and collected (though sometimes considered cold), Muhyo possesses a strong sense of justice and even has a kind side. Sleeps a lot to recover from the exhaustion caused by his practice.

Yu Abiko (Biko)

Muhyo's classmate and an Artificer. Makes seals, pens, magic law books, and other accoutrements of magic law.

Yoichi Himukai (Yoichi)

Judge and Muhyo's former classmate. Expert practitioner of all magic law except execution.

Rio Kurotori (Rio)

Charismatic Artificer who turned traitor when the Magic Law Association stood by and let her mother die.

Soratsugu Madoka (Enchu)

Muhyo's former classmate and Executor-hopeful until one event turned him onto the traitor's path.

Reiko Imai

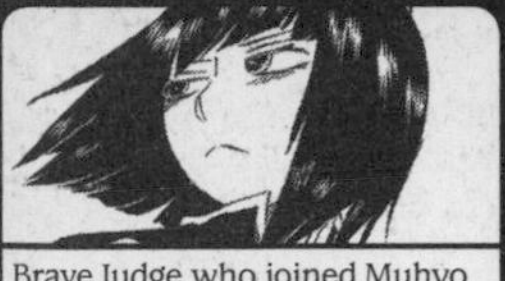

Brave Judge who joined Muhyo and gang during the fight against Face-Ripper Sophie.

Hanao Ebisu (Ebisu)

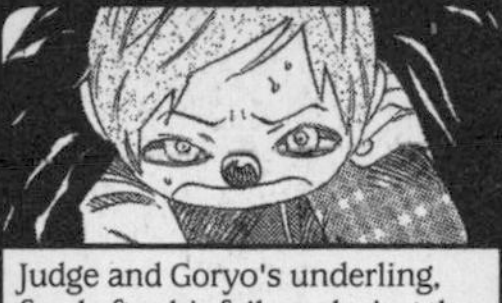

Judge and Goryo's underling, fired after his failure during the showdown against Muhyo.

Daranimaru Goryo (Goryo)

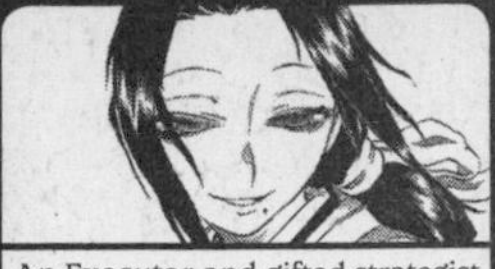

An Executor and gifted strategist who considers Muhyo his rival. Head of the Goryo Group syndicate.

Page Klaus

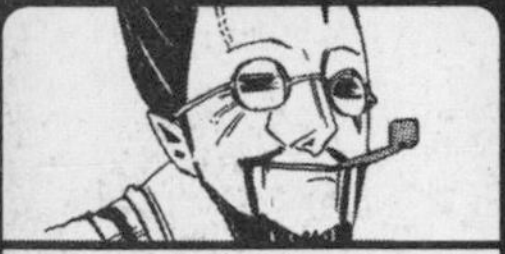

Chief Investigator for the Magic Law Association, Yoichi's boss, and Muhyo and Enchu's former instructor.

Tomas

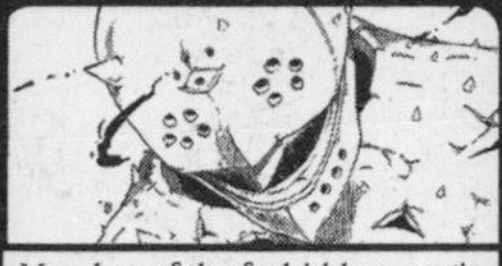

Member of the forbidden magic law group "Ark." He has a twisted appreciation for beauty.

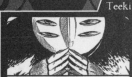

Teeki

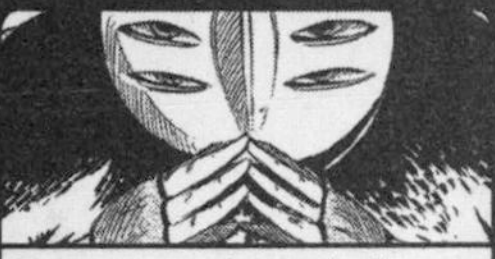

Dangerous entity marked as a traitor to the Magic Law Association for 800 years.

The Story

Magic law is a newly established practice for judging and punishing the increasing crimes committed by spirits; those who use it are called "practitioners."

Goryo has been taken captive by Tomas (a member of the Forbidden Magic Law group known as "Ark") and turned into a half-ghast. No longer in control of his own actions, Goryo grievously wounds Ebisu, who had come to save him. However, thanks to Kiriko, Goryo's spectralization is halted, and the real fight with Tomas begins. Unfortunately, Muhyo and the gang are helpless against Tomas's all-absorbing forbidden magic law, the "Armor of Flies." The only way to break through it is to destroy Tomas's book of forbidden magic law that is concealed within the armor. Now it's up to Roji to dive into Tomas's "Styxsand" and find it!

Nana Takenouchi (Nana)

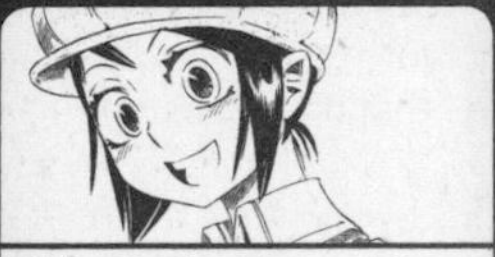

High school student, spirit medium, and aspiring photographer. Working as an assistant photographic investigator.

Kiriko

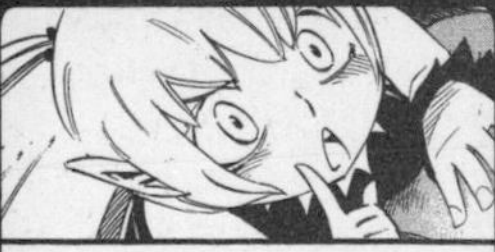

Envoy summoned to break Muhyo's contract with Pluto (which didn't end up happening).

Kenji Sato (Kenji)

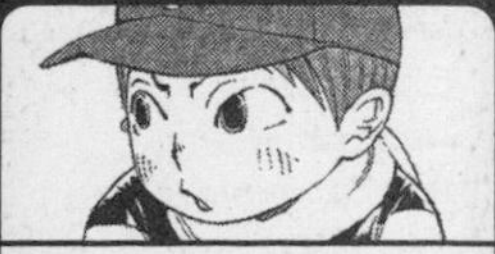

Friend of Muhyo and Roji since they saved him from a marauding ghost. A bit of a troublemaker.

Muhyo & Roji's Bureau of Supernatural Investigation BSI

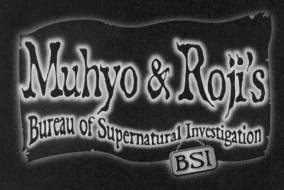

CONTENTS

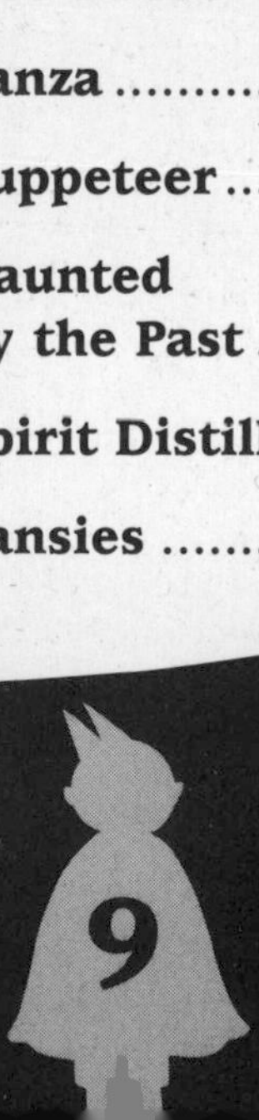
9

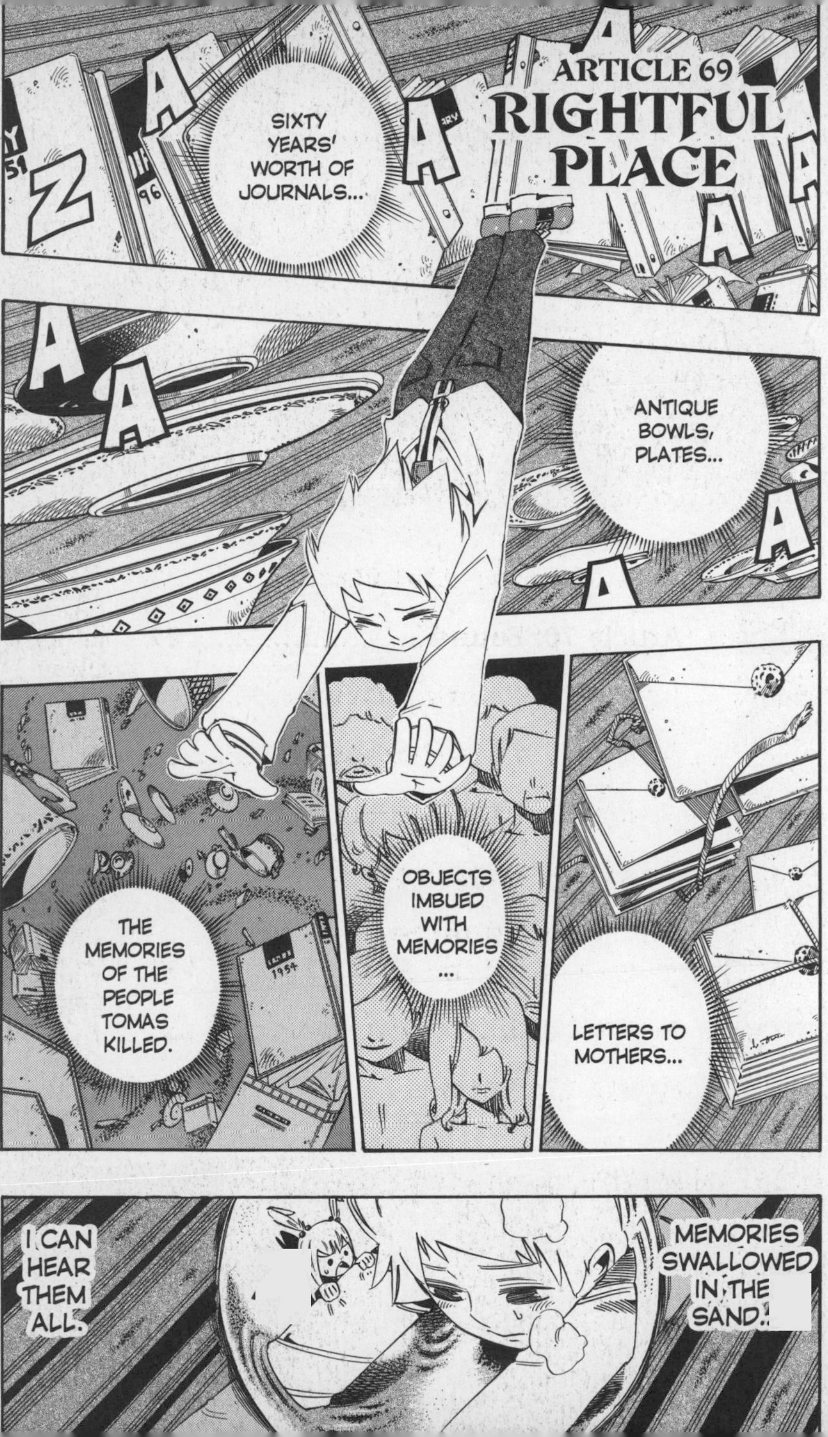
ARTICLE 69
RIGHTFUL PLACE
SIXTY YEARS' WORTH OF JOURNALS...
ANTIQUE BOWLS, PLATES...
LETTERS TO MOTHERS...
OBJECTS IMBUED WITH MEMORIES ...
THE MEMORIES OF THE PEOPLE TOMAS KILLED.
MEMORIES SWALLOWED IN THE SAND...
I CAN HEAR THEM ALL.

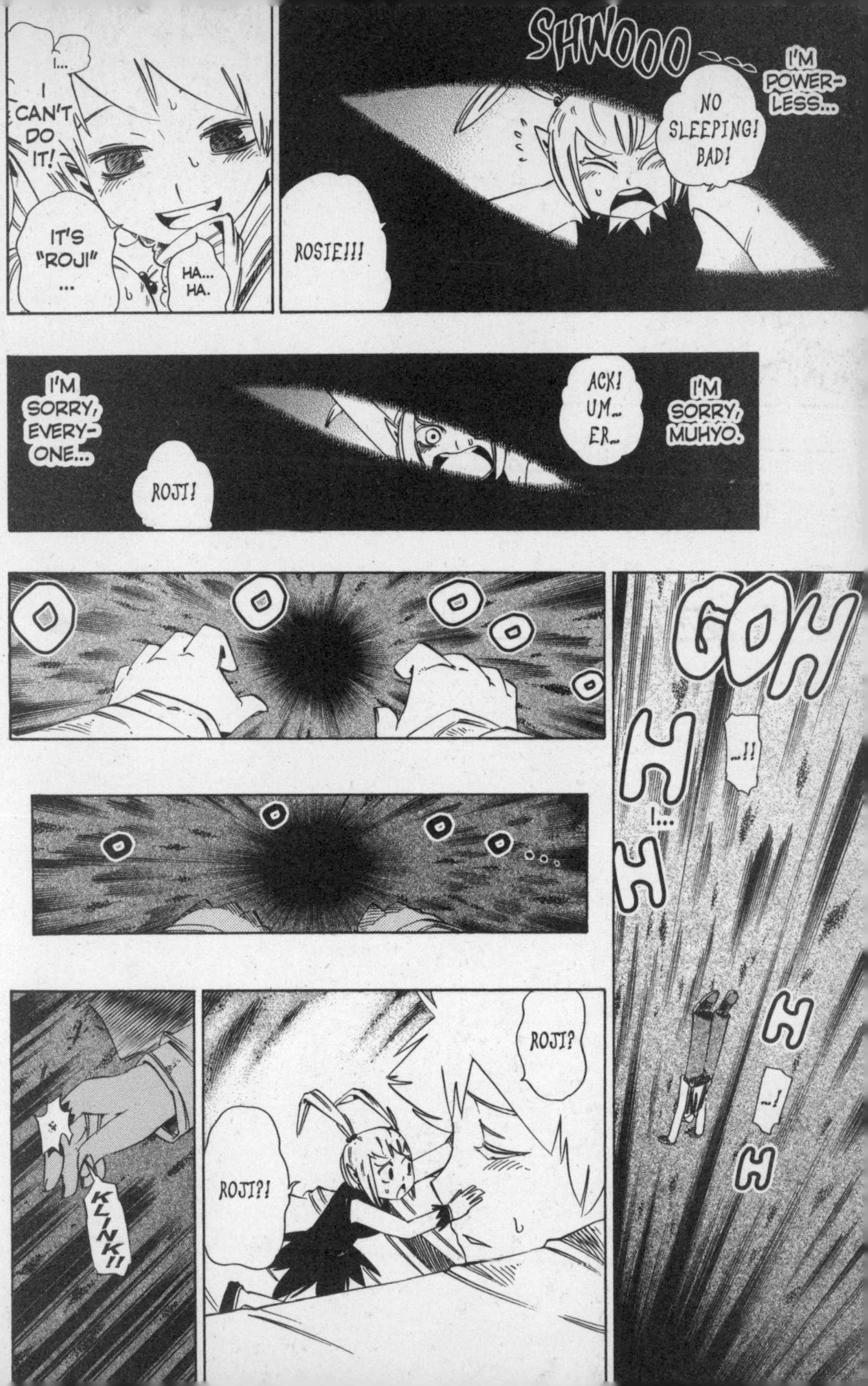
SHWOOO
I'M POWER-LESS...
NO SLEEPING! BAD!
ROSIE!!!
I...
I CAN'T DO IT!
IT'S "ROJI"...
HA... HA.
I'M SORRY, MUHYO.
ACK! UM... ER...
ROJI!
I'M SORRY, EVERY-ONE...
GOH
HH
...!!
I...
HHH
...!
ROJI?
ROJI?!
KLINK!!

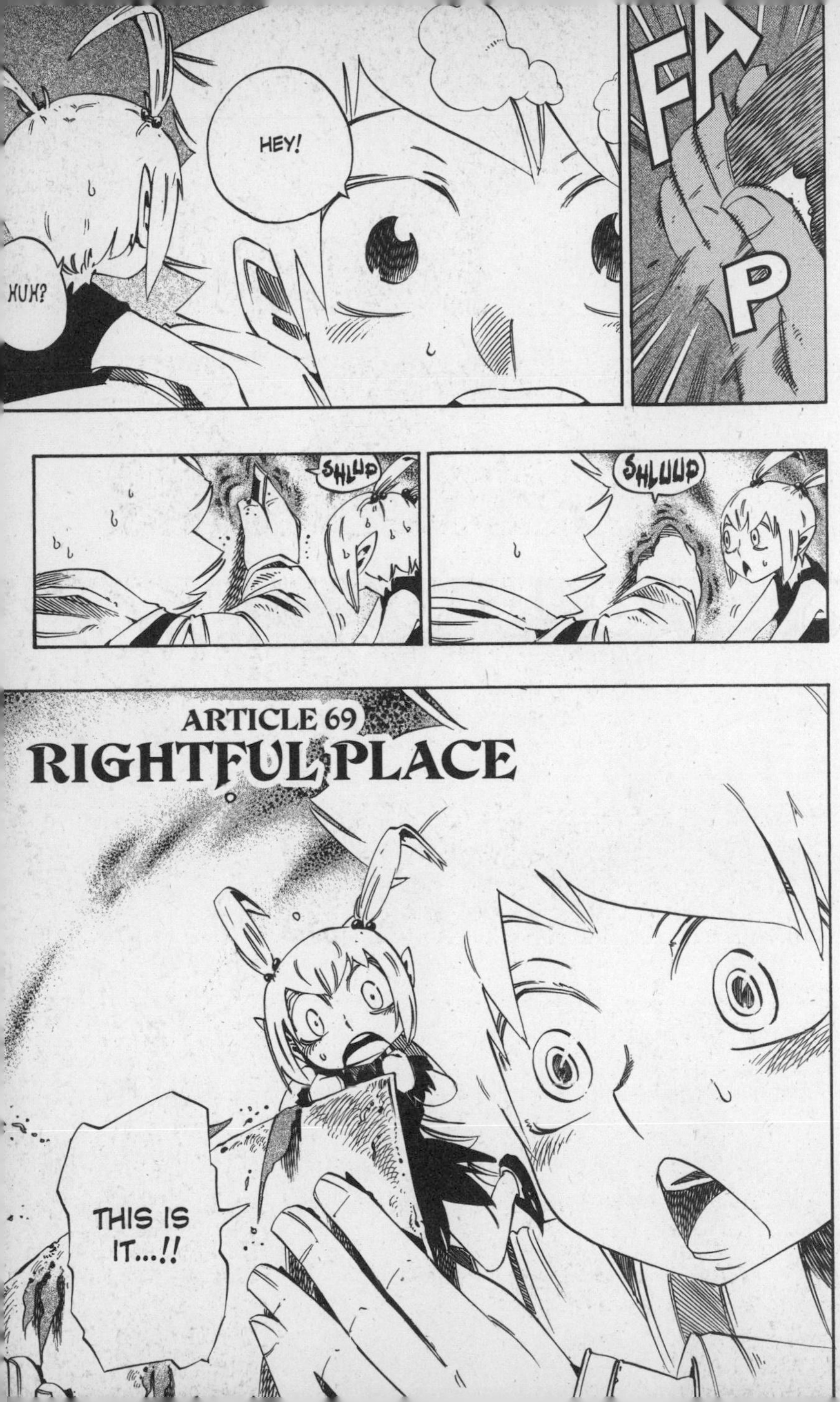
FAP
HEY!
HUH?
SHLUUP
SHLUP
ARTICLE 69
RIGHTFUL PLACE
THIS IS IT...!!

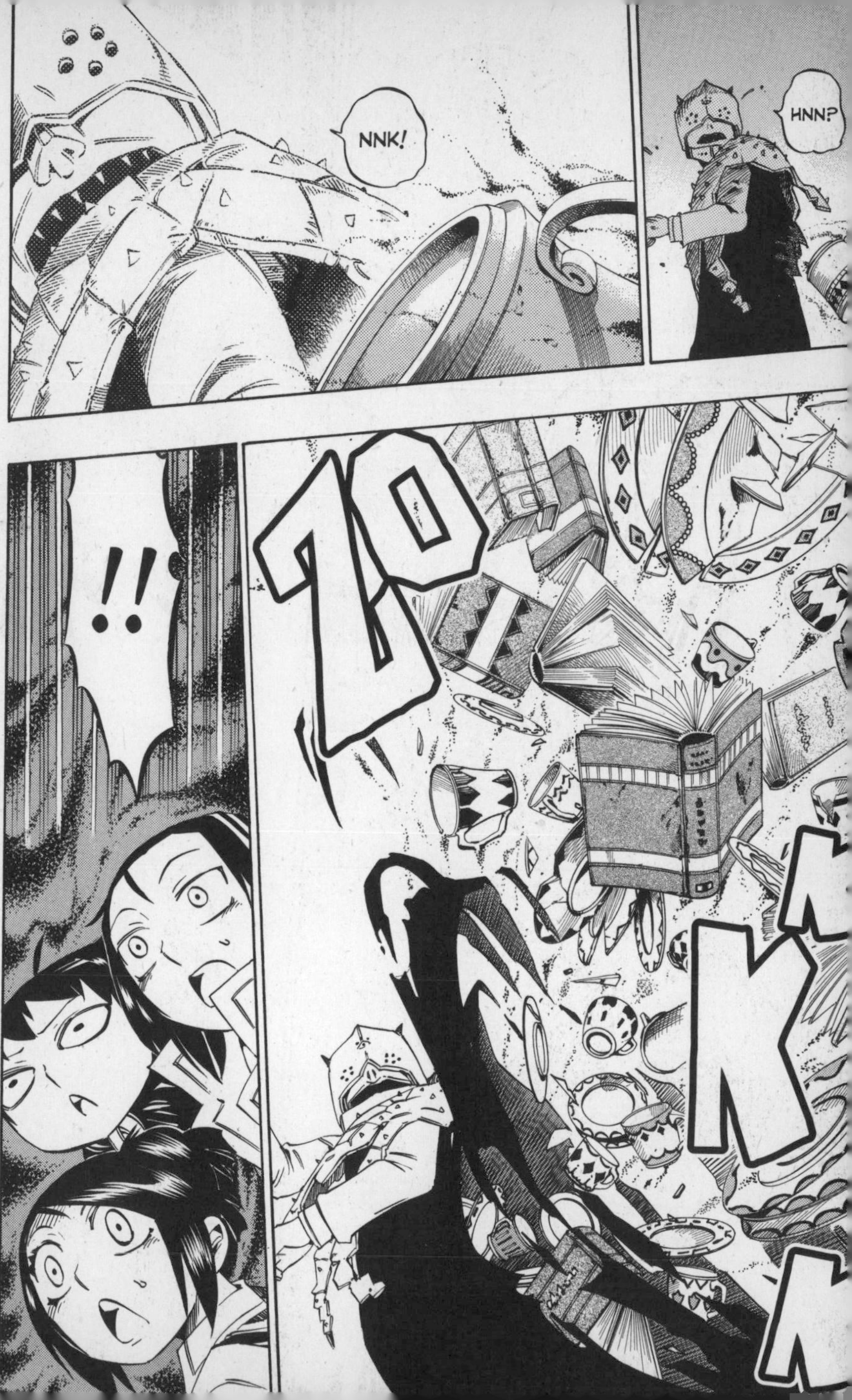
HNN?
NNK!
!!

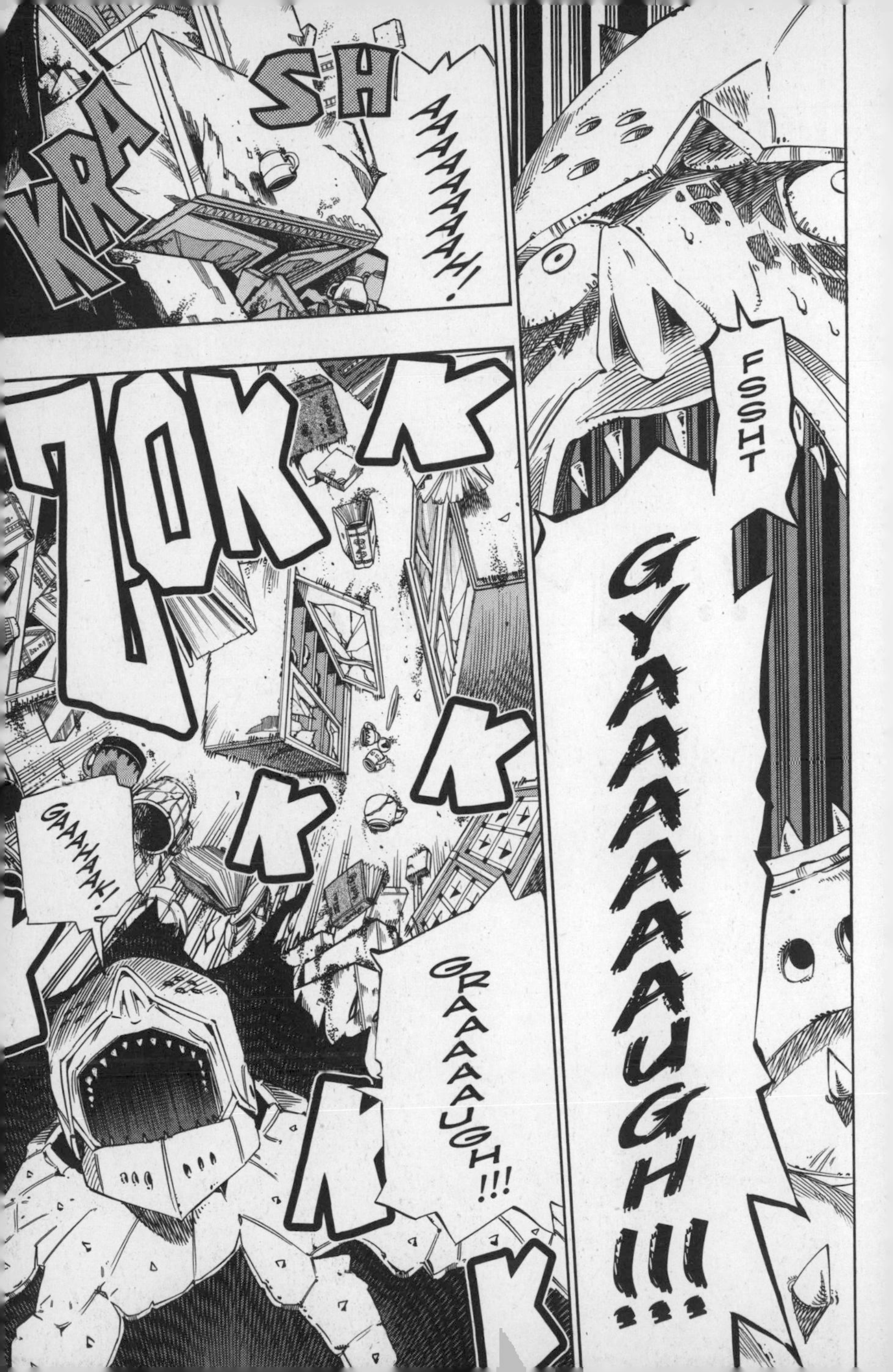
FSSHT
GYAAAAAAUGH!!!
KRASH
AAAAAAAAAH!
TOKKKKKK
GAAAAAAK!
GRAAAAAUGH!!!

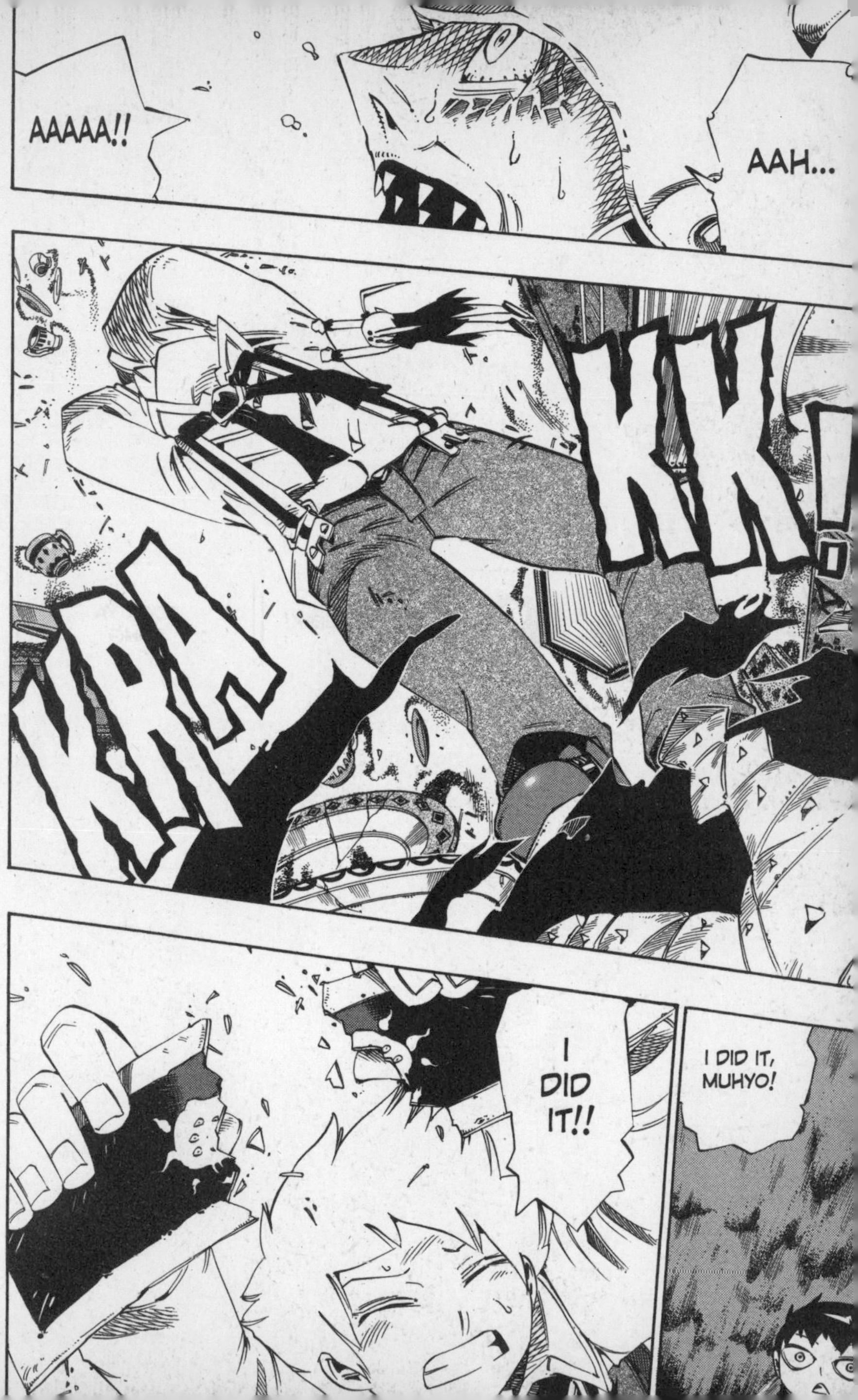
AAH...
AAAAA!!
KRAKK!
I DID IT, MUHYO!
I DID IT!!

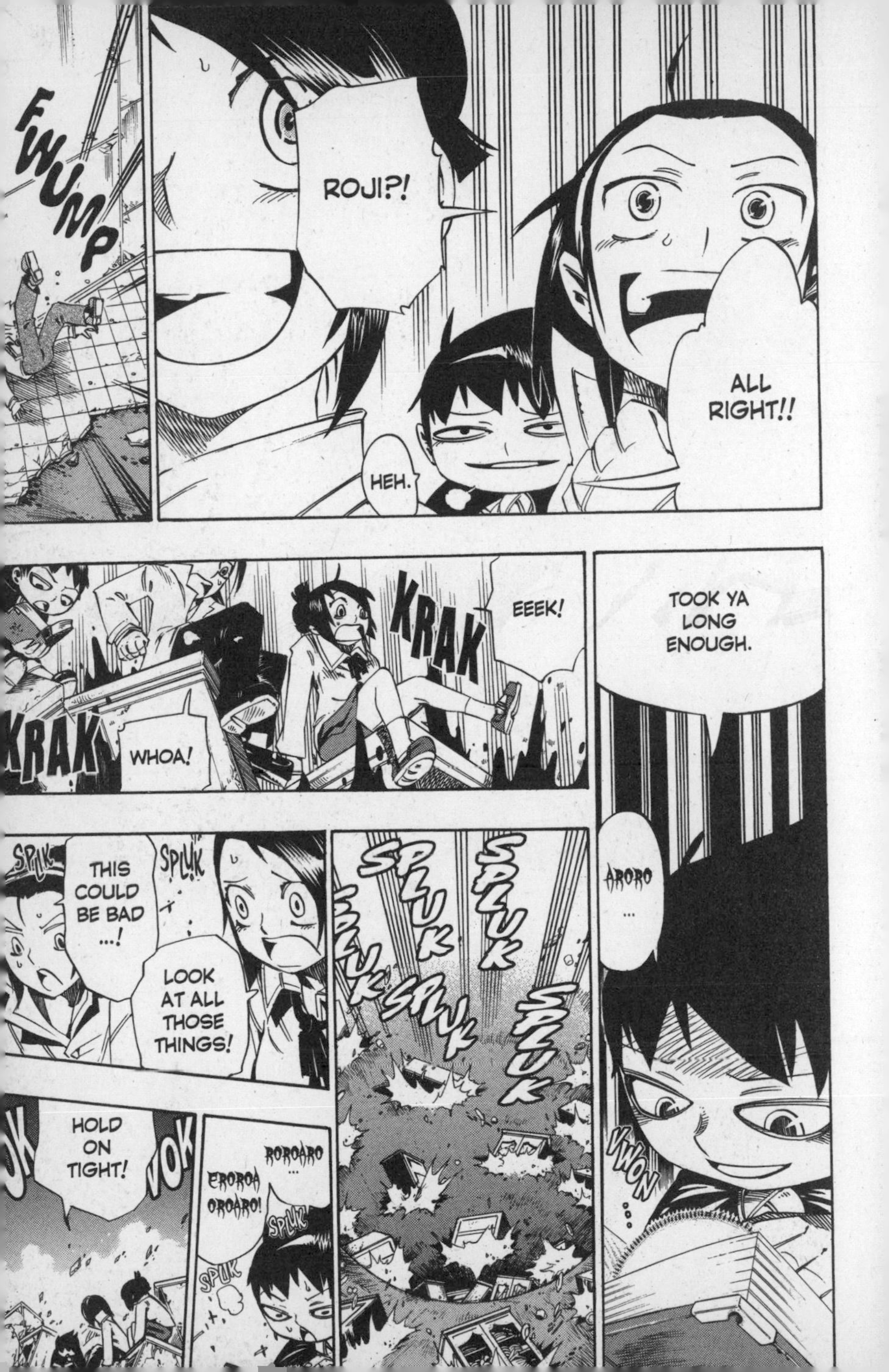

ROJI?!
ALL RIGHT!!
HEH.
FWUMP
TOOK YA LONG ENOUGH.
ARORO ...
VWON
KRAK
EEEK!
KRAK
WHOA!
SPLUK SPLUK SPLUK SPLUK SPLUK
SPLUK
THIS COULD BE BAD ...!
LOOK AT ALL THOSE THINGS!
SPLUK
VOK
ROROARO ...
EROROA OROARO!
SPLUK
SPLUK
HOLD ON TIGHT!

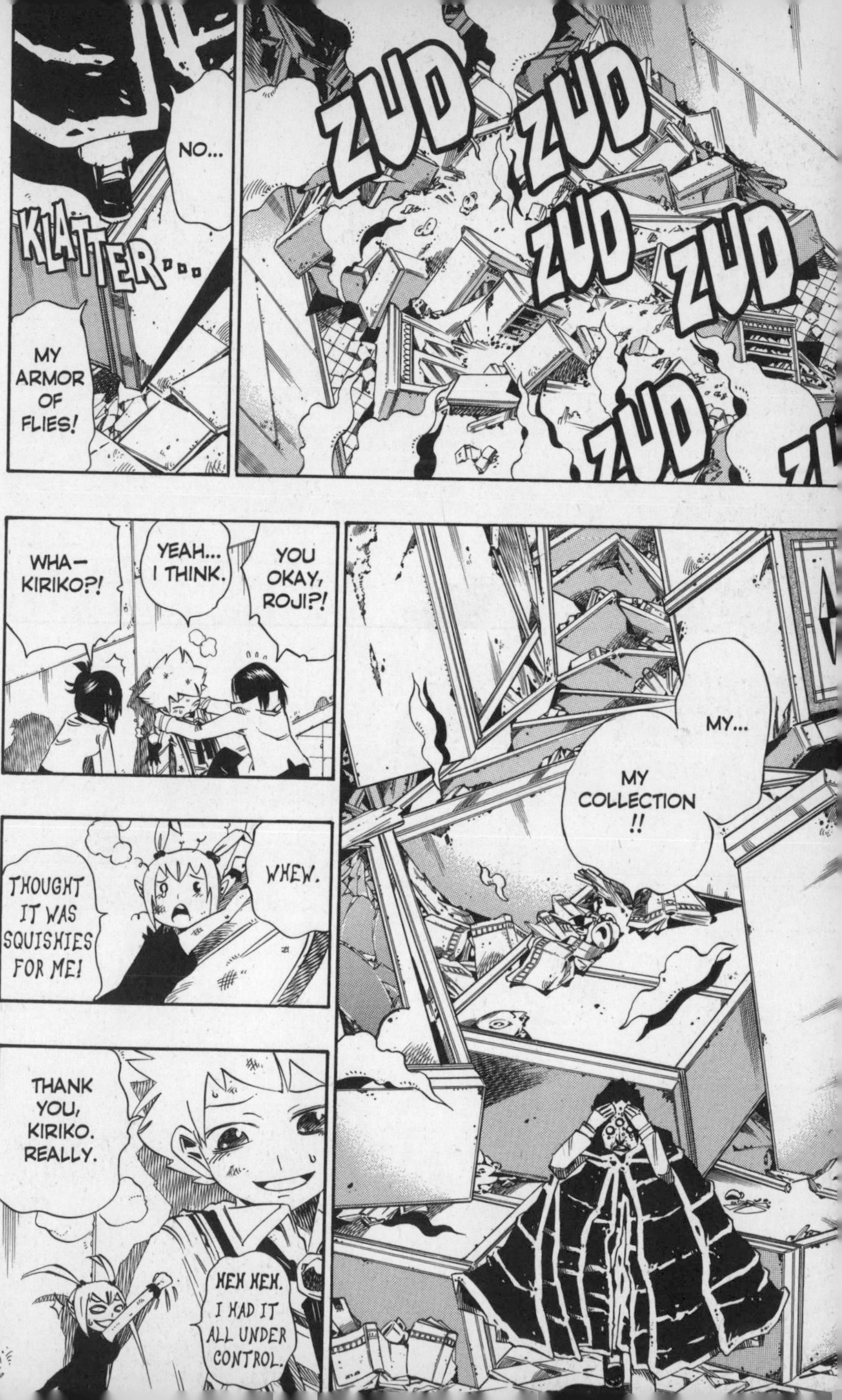
ZUD ZUD ZUD ZUD ZUD
NO...
KLATTER...
MY ARMOR OF FLIES!
MY...
MY COLLECTION !!
YOU OKAY, ROJI?!
YEAH... I THINK.
WHA- KIRIKO?!
WHEW.
THOUGHT IT WAS SQUISHIES FOR ME!
THANK YOU, KIRIKO. REALLY.
HEH HEH. I HAD IT ALL UNDER CONTROL.

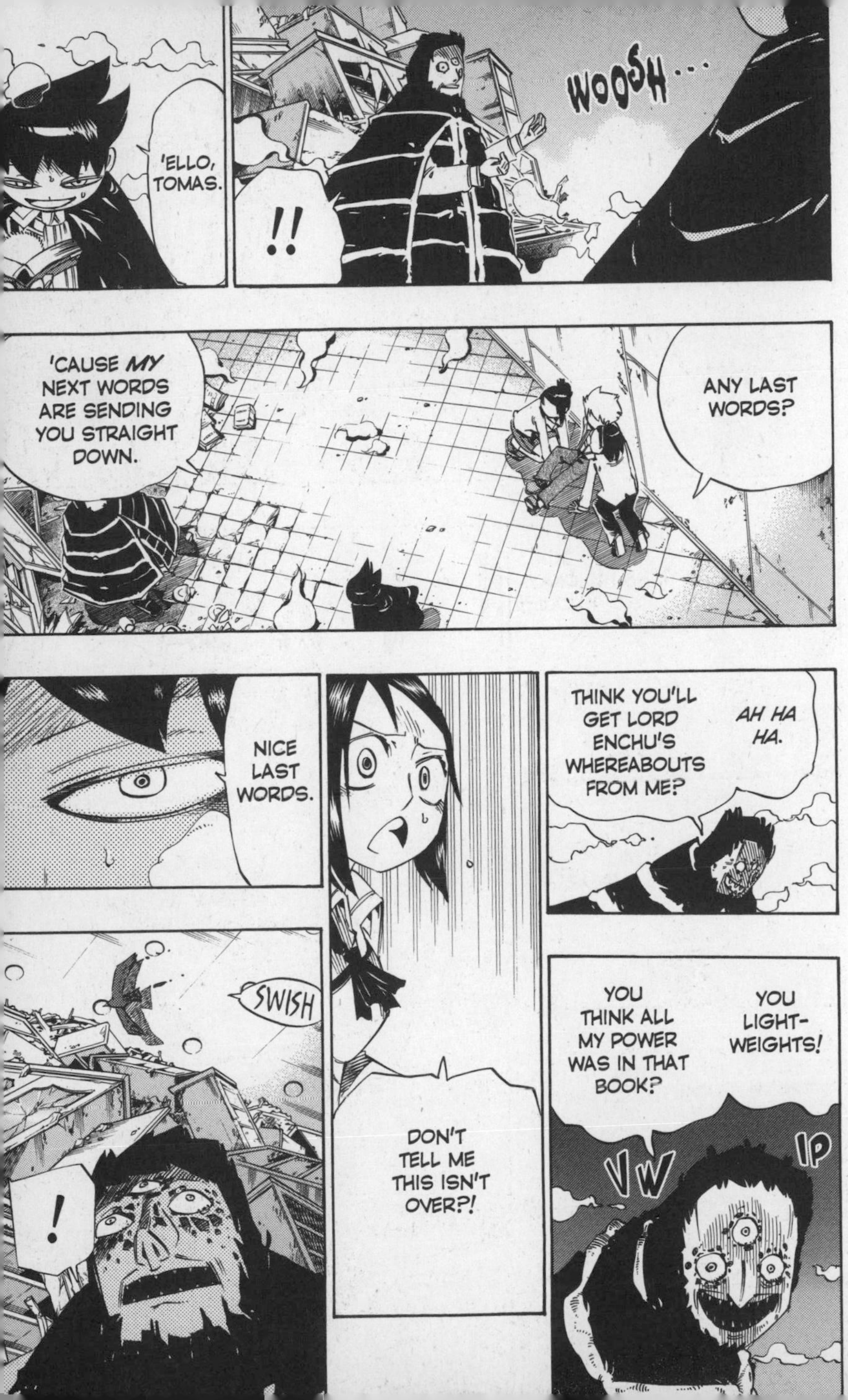
WOOSH...
'ELLO, TOMAS.
!!
ANY LAST WORDS?
'CAUSE *MY* NEXT WORDS ARE SENDING YOU STRAIGHT DOWN.
THINK YOU'LL GET LORD ENCHU'S WHEREABOUTS FROM ME?
AH HA HA.
YOU LIGHT-WEIGHTS!
YOU THINK ALL MY POWER WAS IN THAT BOOK?
VWIP
DON'T TELL ME THIS ISN'T OVER?!
NICE LAST WORDS.
SWISH
!

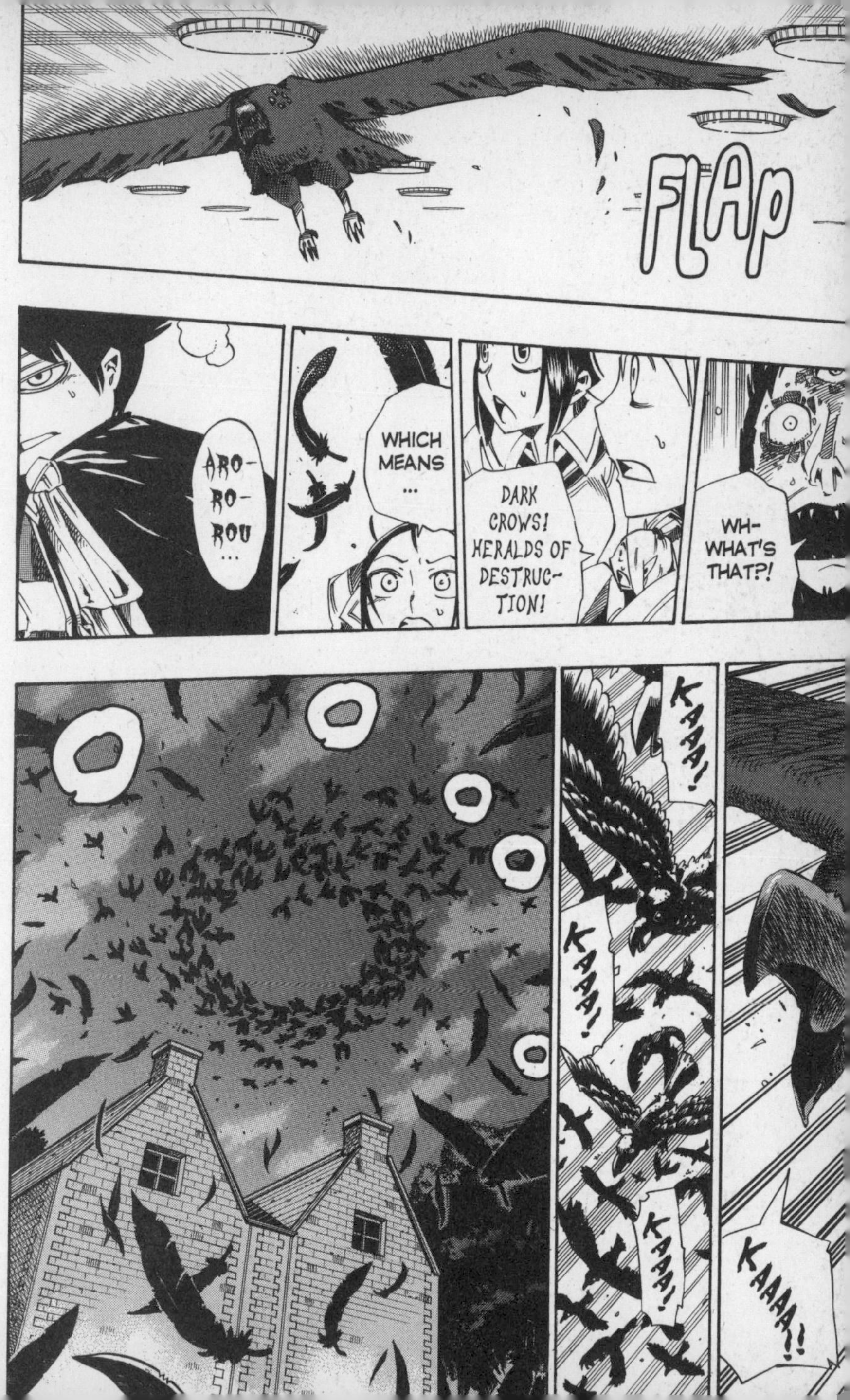
FLAP
WH- WHAT'S THAT?!
DARK CROWS! HERALDS OF DESTRUC-TION!
WHICH MEANS ...
ARO-RO-ROU ...
KAAAA!!
KAAA!
KAAA!
KAAA!

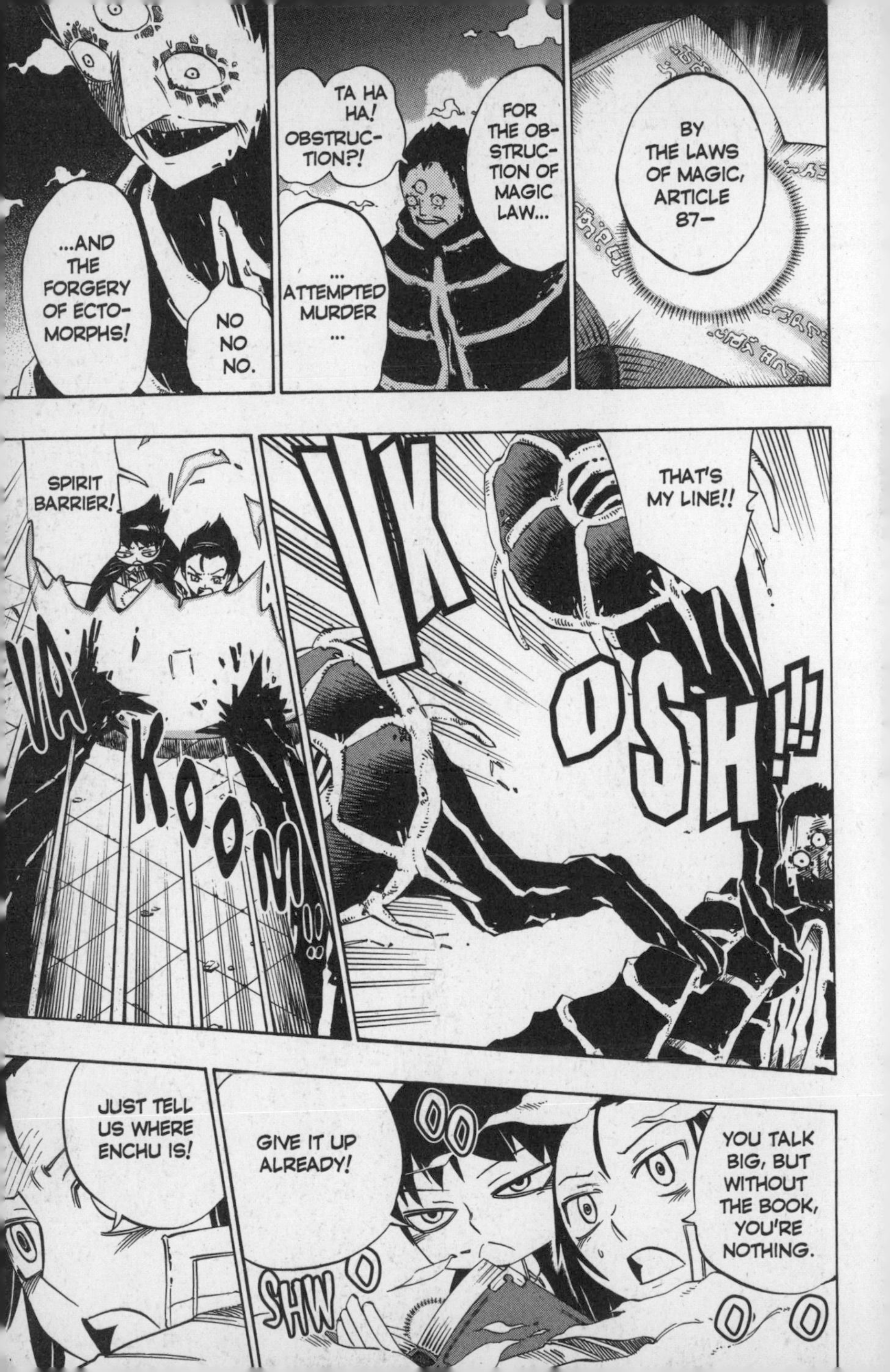
BY THE LAWS OF MAGIC, ARTICLE 87—
FOR THE OB-STRUC-TION OF MAGIC LAW...
TA HA HA! OBSTRUC-TION?!
...ATTEMPTED MURDER...
NO NO NO.
...AND THE FORGERY OF ECTO-MORPHS!
THAT'S MY LINE!!
VK
OSH!!
SPIRIT BARRIER!
KA
KOOM!!
YOU TALK BIG, BUT WITHOUT THE BOOK, YOU'RE NOTHING.
GIVE IT UP ALREADY!
SHW
JUST TELL US WHERE ENCHU IS!

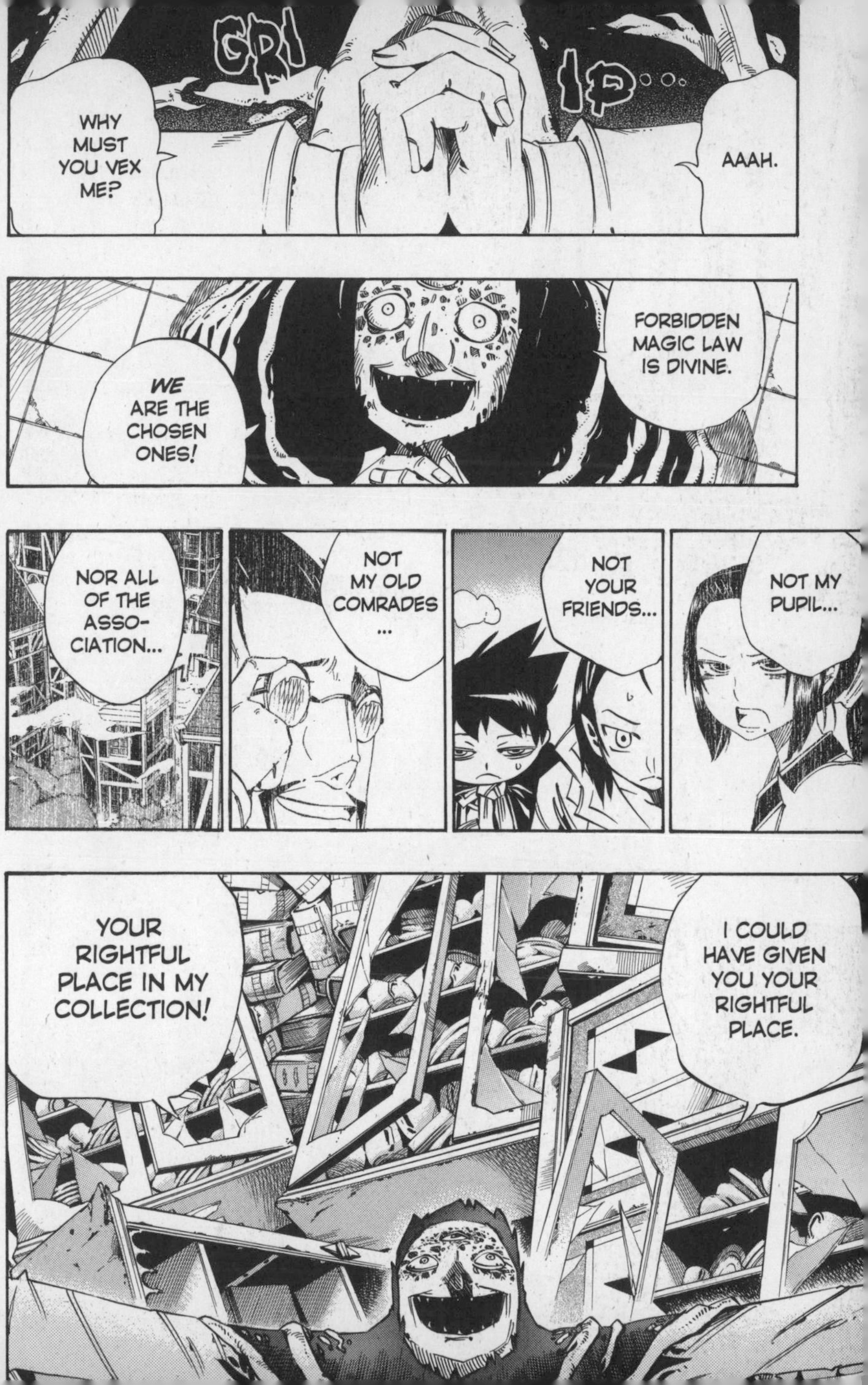
GRI IP...
AAAH.
WHY MUST YOU VEX ME?
FORBIDDEN MAGIC LAW IS DIVINE.
WE ARE THE CHOSEN ONES!
NOT MY PUPIL...
NOT YOUR FRIENDS...
NOT MY OLD COMRADES...
NOR ALL OF THE ASSO-CIATION...
I COULD HAVE GIVEN YOU YOUR RIGHTFUL PLACE.
YOUR RIGHTFUL PLACE IN MY COLLECTION!

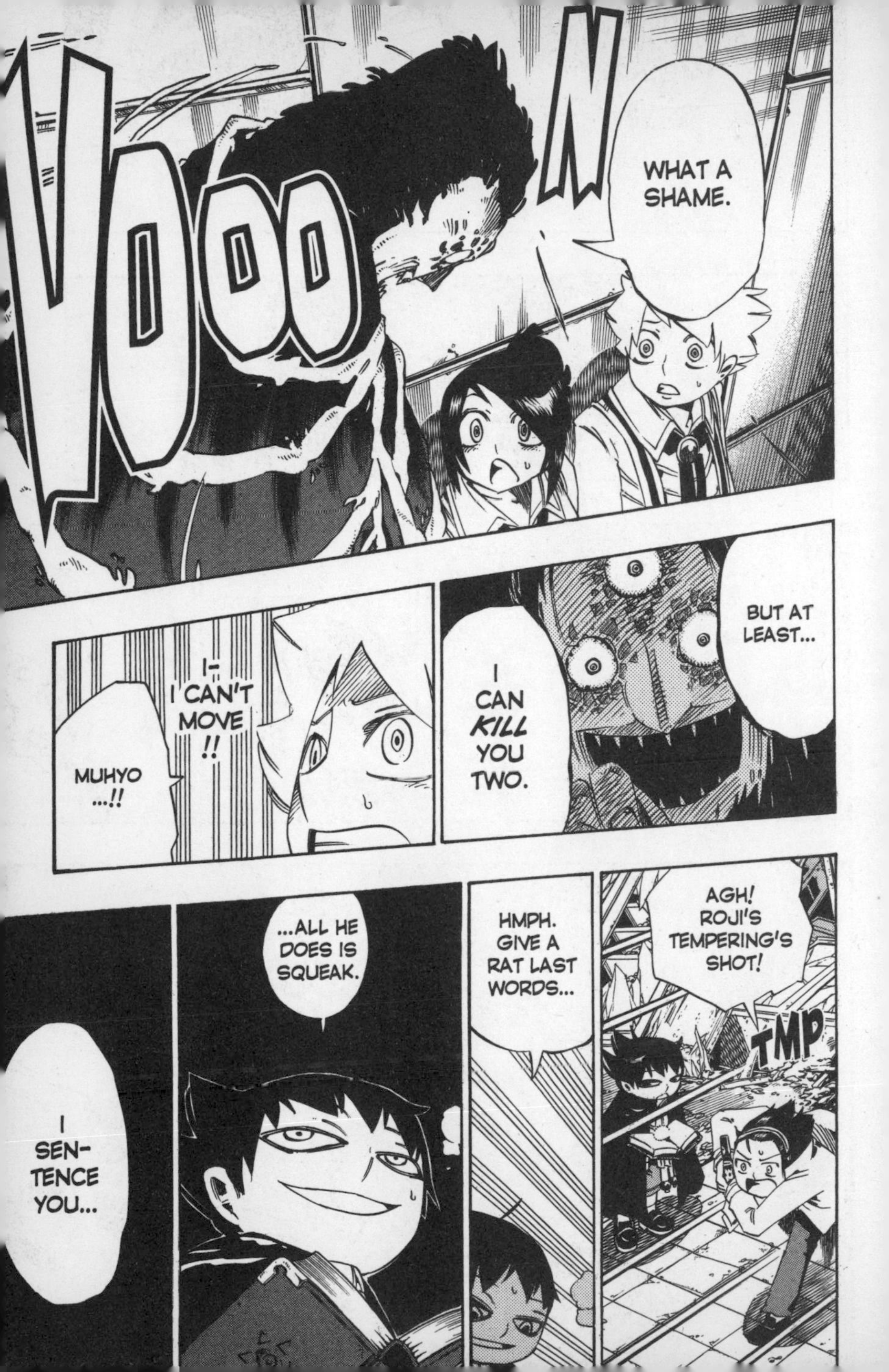
WHAT A SHAME.
VOOON
BUT AT LEAST...
I CAN *KILL* YOU TWO.
I- I CAN'T MOVE!!
MUHYO...!!
AGH! ROJI'S TEMPERING'S SHOT!
TMP
HMPH. GIVE A RAT LAST WORDS...
...ALL HE DOES IS SQUEAK.
I SENTENCE YOU...

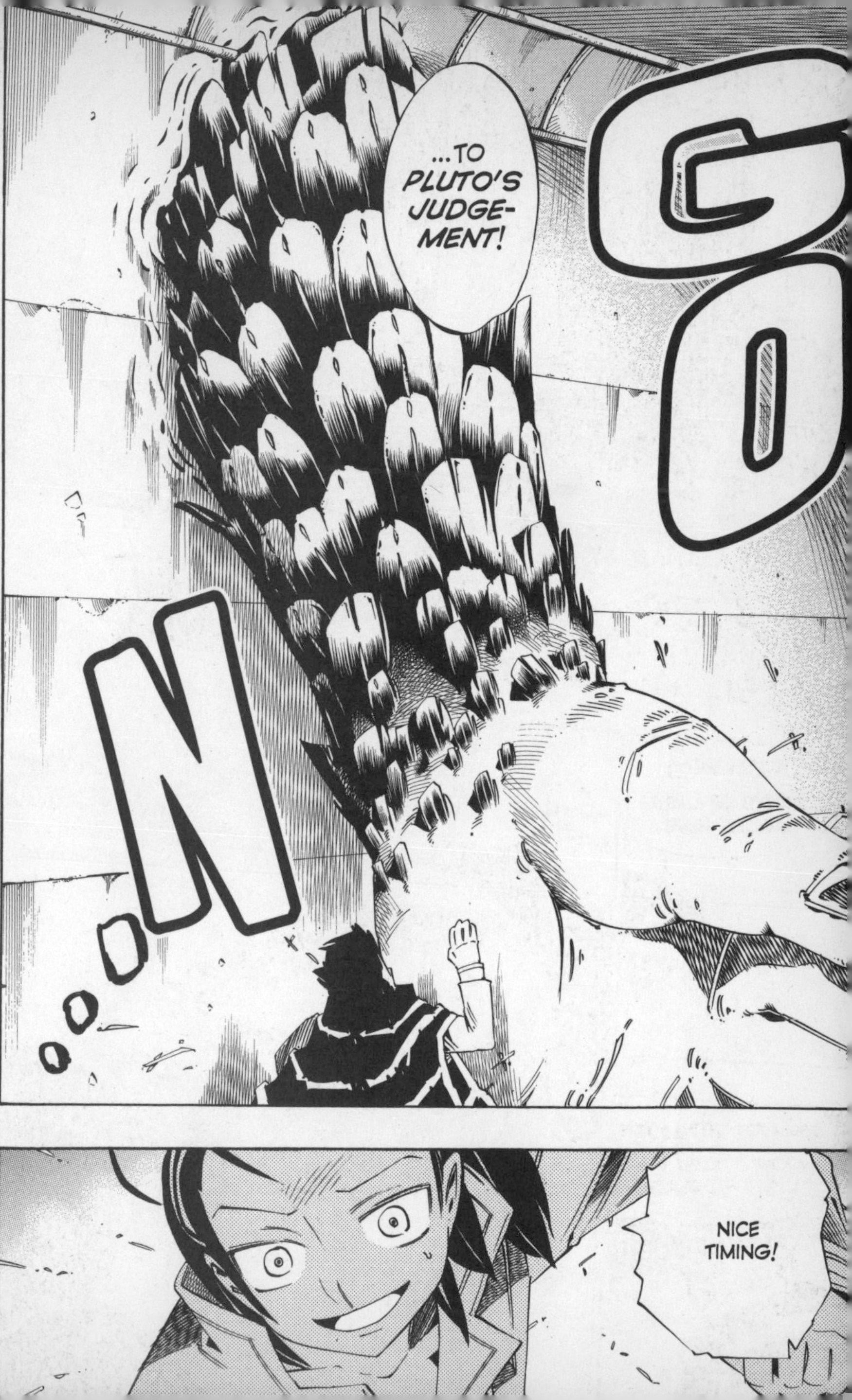
...TO PLUTO'S JUDGEMENT!
GON
NICE TIMING!

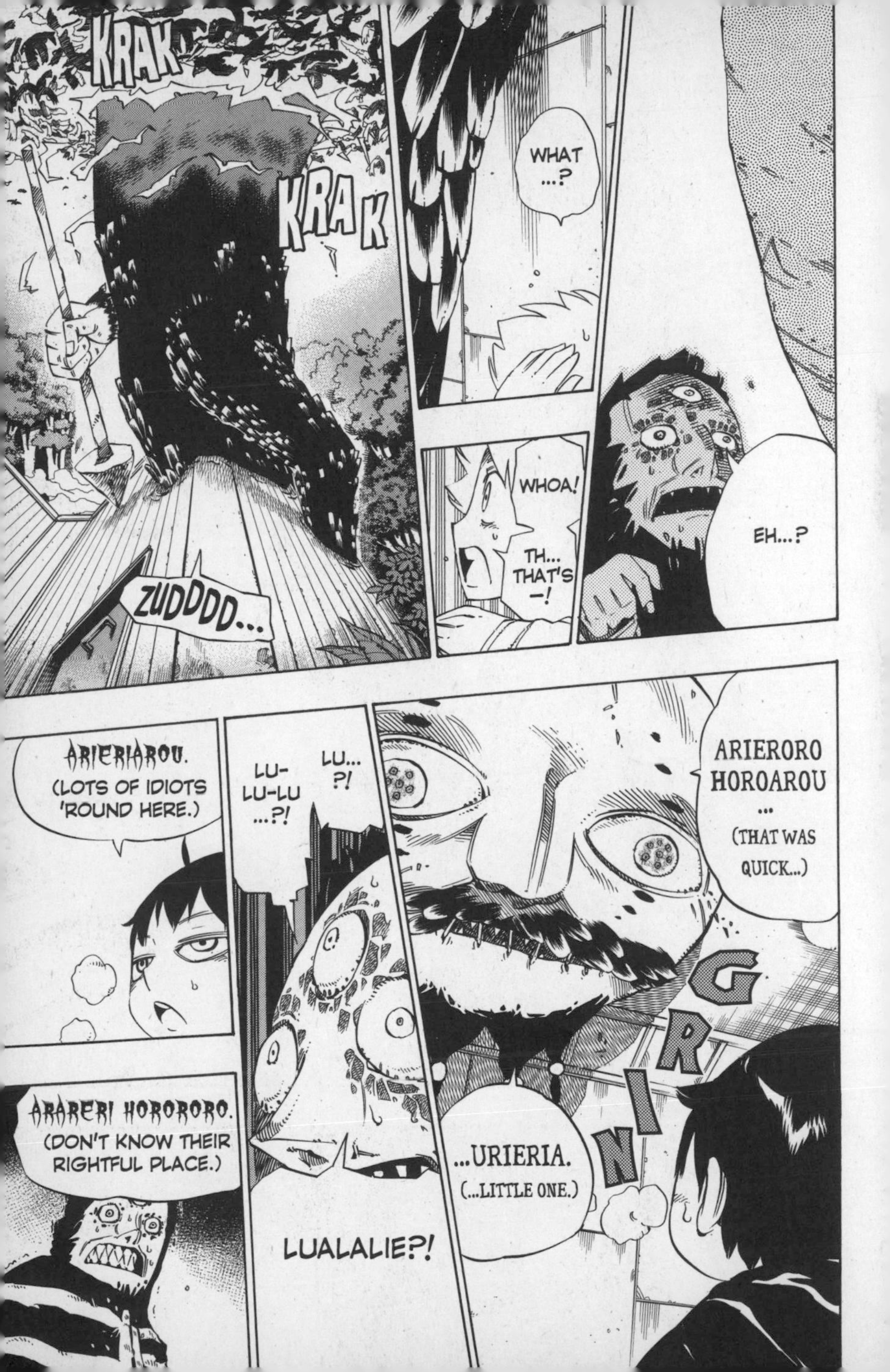
EH...?
WHAT ...?
WHOA!
TH... THAT'S —!
KRAK
KRAK
ZUDDDD...
ARIERORO HOROAROU ... (THAT WAS QUICK...)
GRIN
...URIERIA. (...LITTLE ONE.)
LU... ?!
LU- LU-LU ...?!
LUALALIE?!
ARIERIAROU. (LOTS OF IDIOTS 'ROUND HERE.)
ARARERI HORORORO. (DON'T KNOW THEIR RIGHTFUL PLACE.)

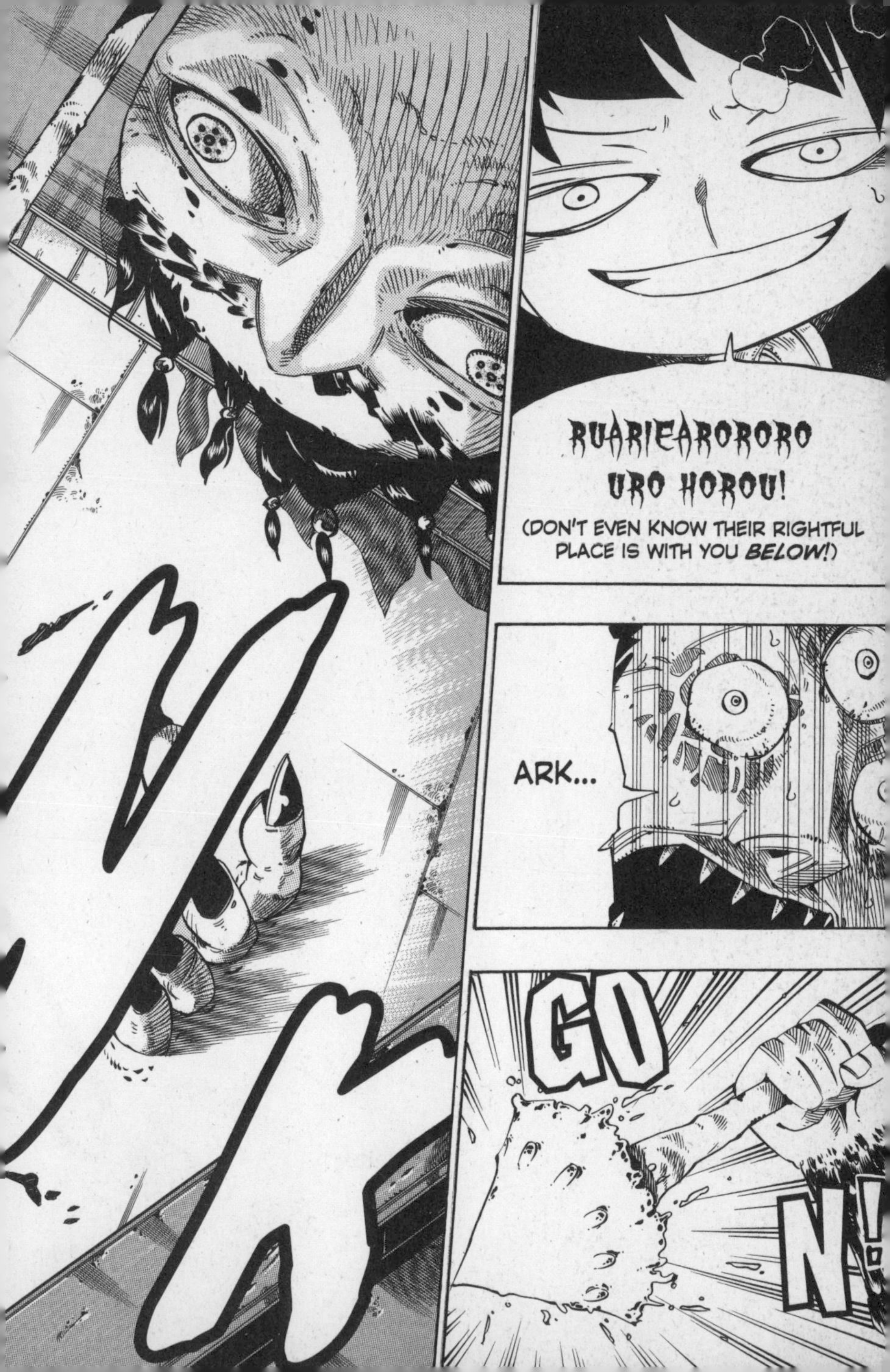
RUARIEARORORO
URO HOROU!
(DON'T EVEN KNOW THEIR RIGHTFUL PLACE IS WITH YOU *BELOW!*)
ARK...
GO
N!

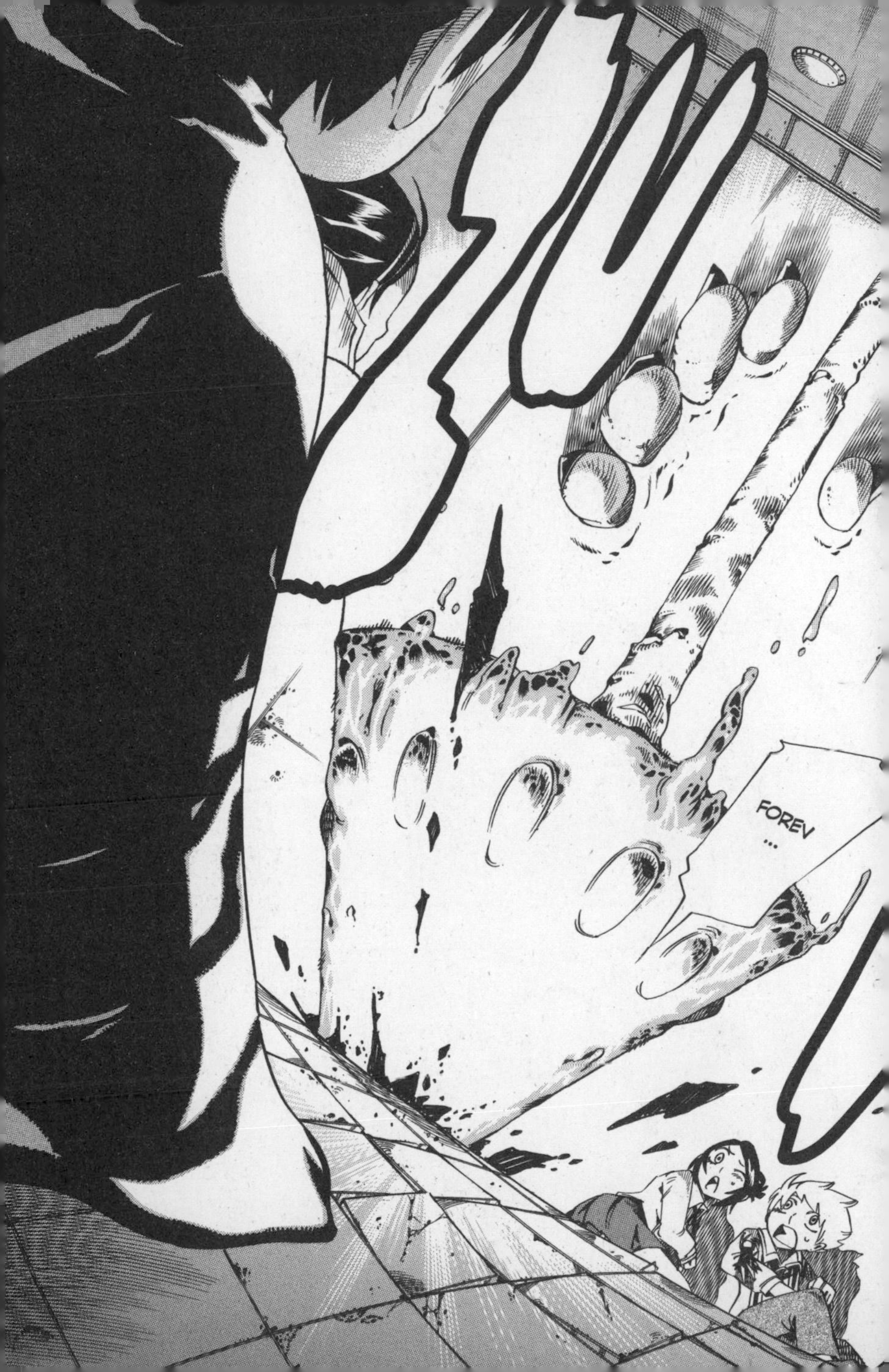
FOREV
...

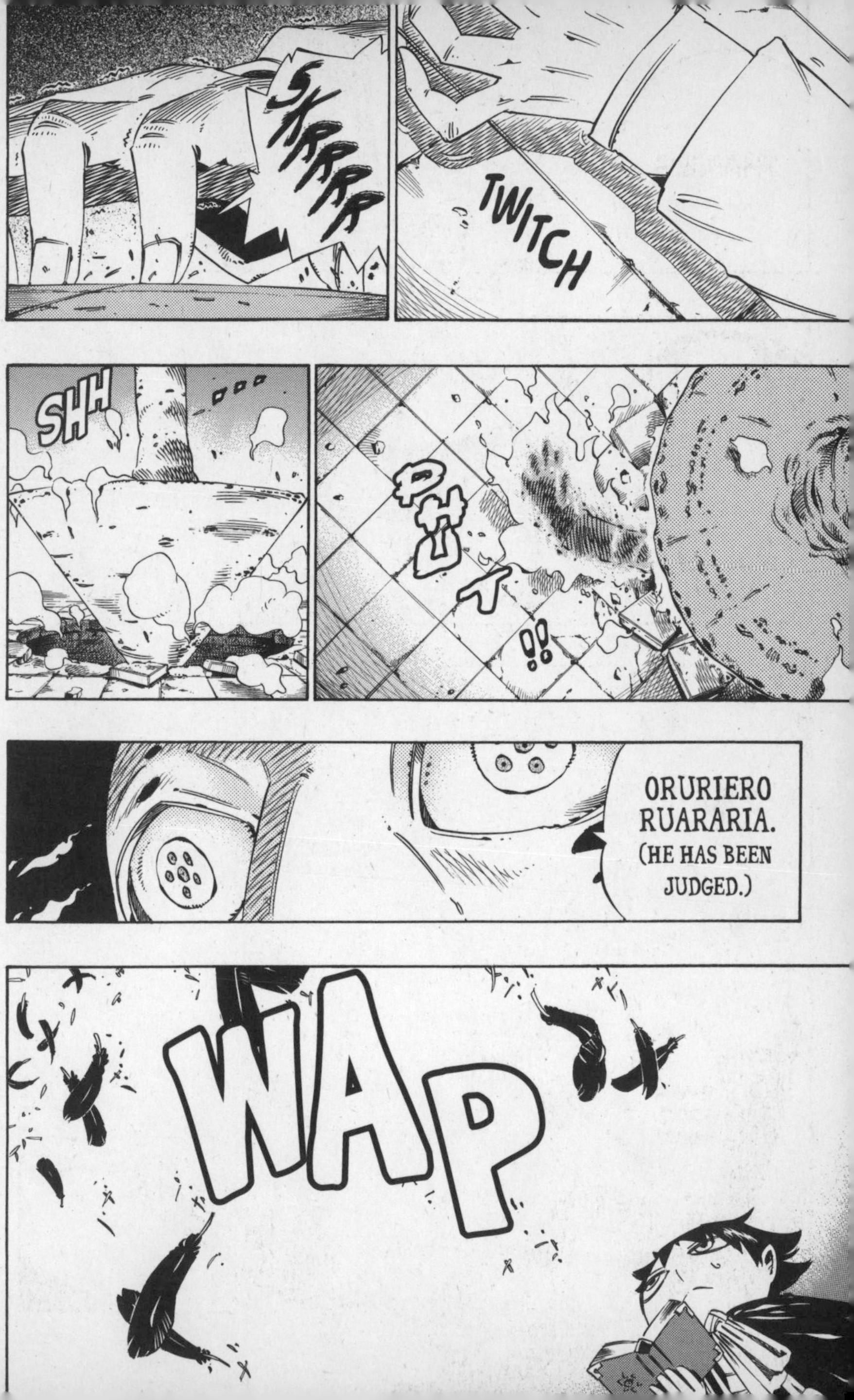

TWITCH
SKRRRR
PHUT
!!
SHH
...
ORURIERO RUARARIA. (HE HAS BEEN JUDGED.)
WAP

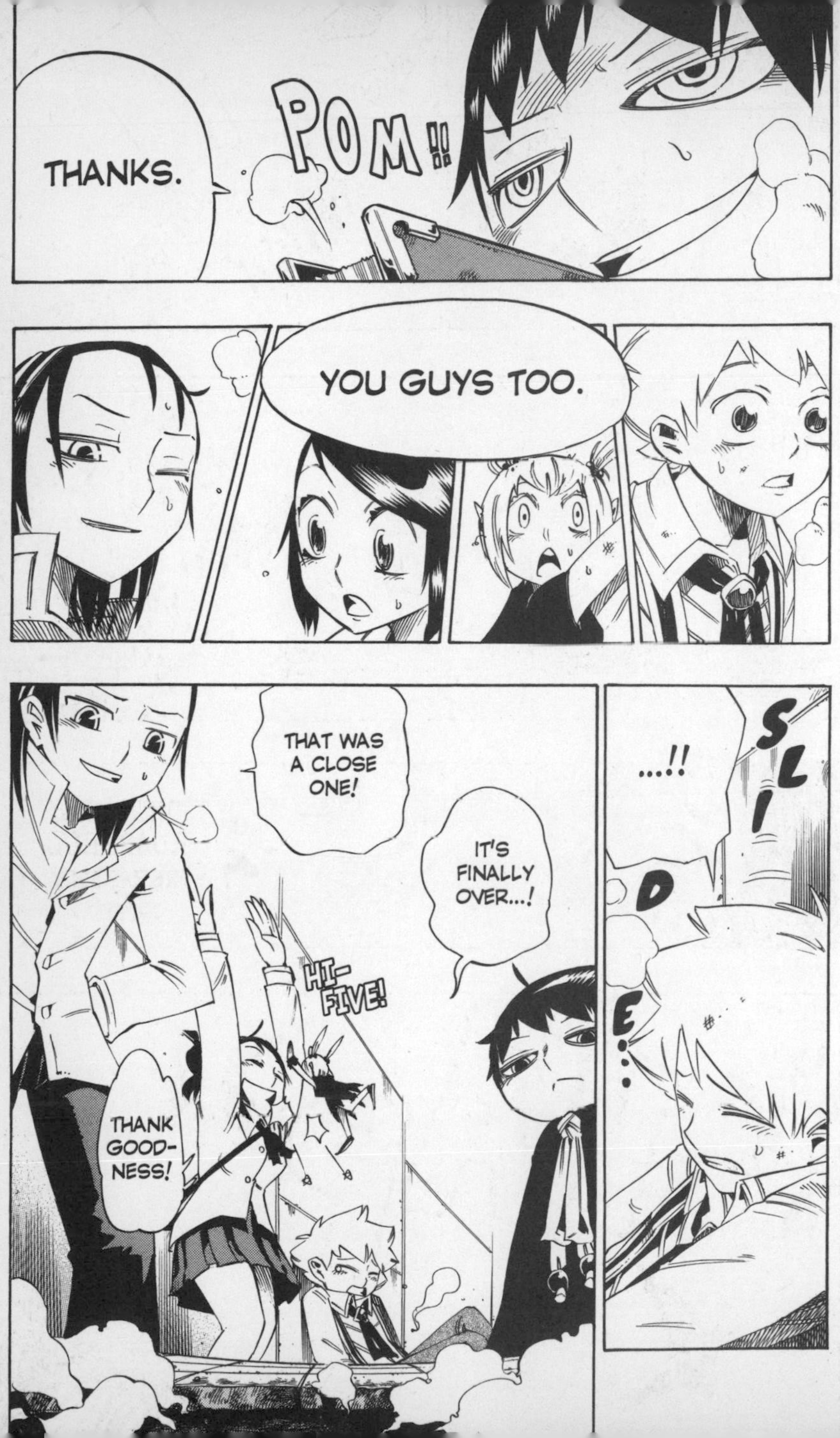
POM!!
THANKS.
YOU GUYS TOO.
SLIDE...
...!!
THAT WAS A CLOSE ONE!
IT'S FINALLY OVER...!
HI-FIVE!
THANK GOODNESS!

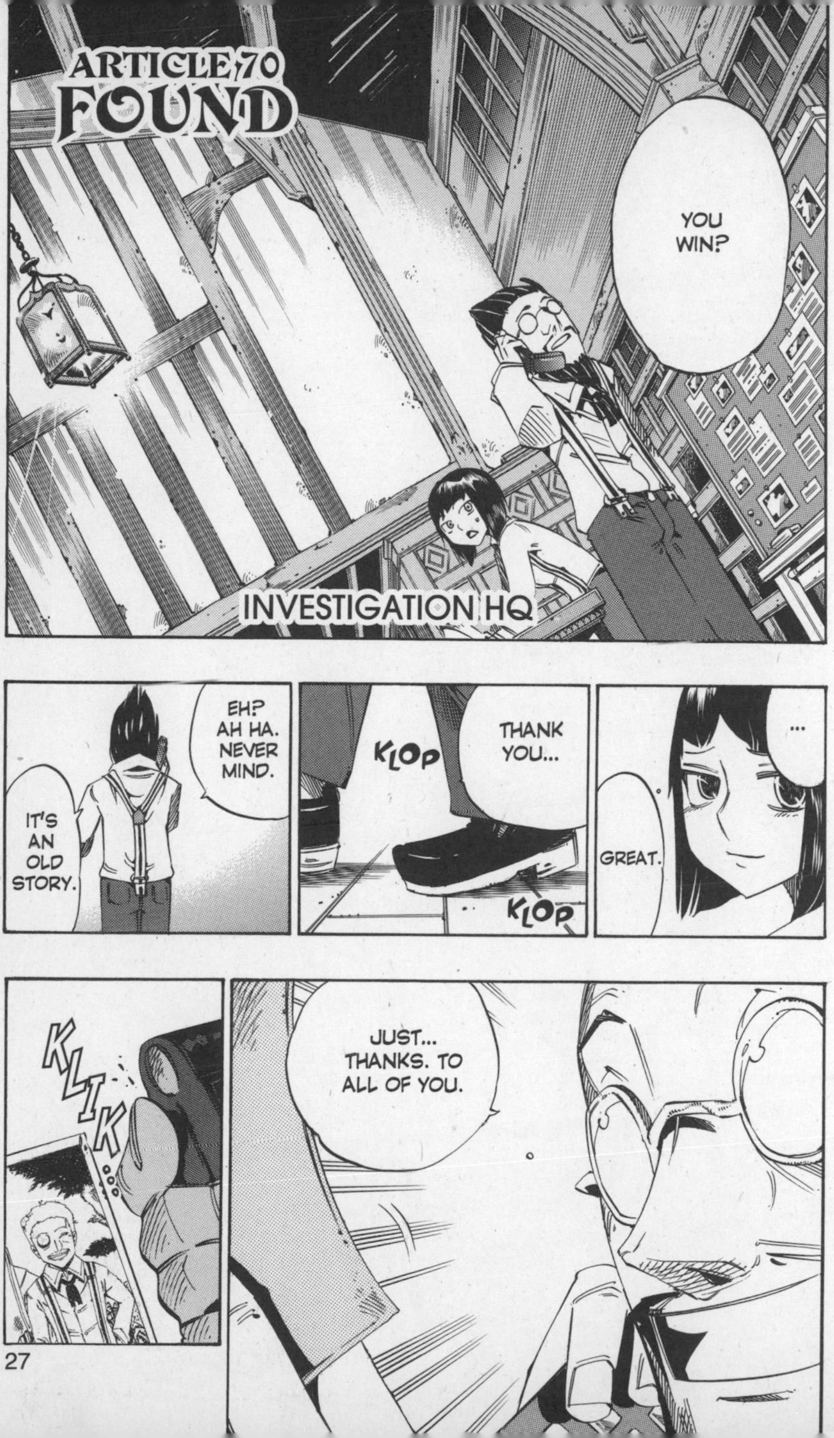
ARTICLE 70
FOUND
YOU WIN?
INVESTIGATION HQ
...
GREAT.
THANK YOU...
KLOP
KLOP
EH? AH HA. NEVER MIND.
IT'S AN OLD STORY.
JUST... THANKS. TO ALL OF YOU.
KLIK

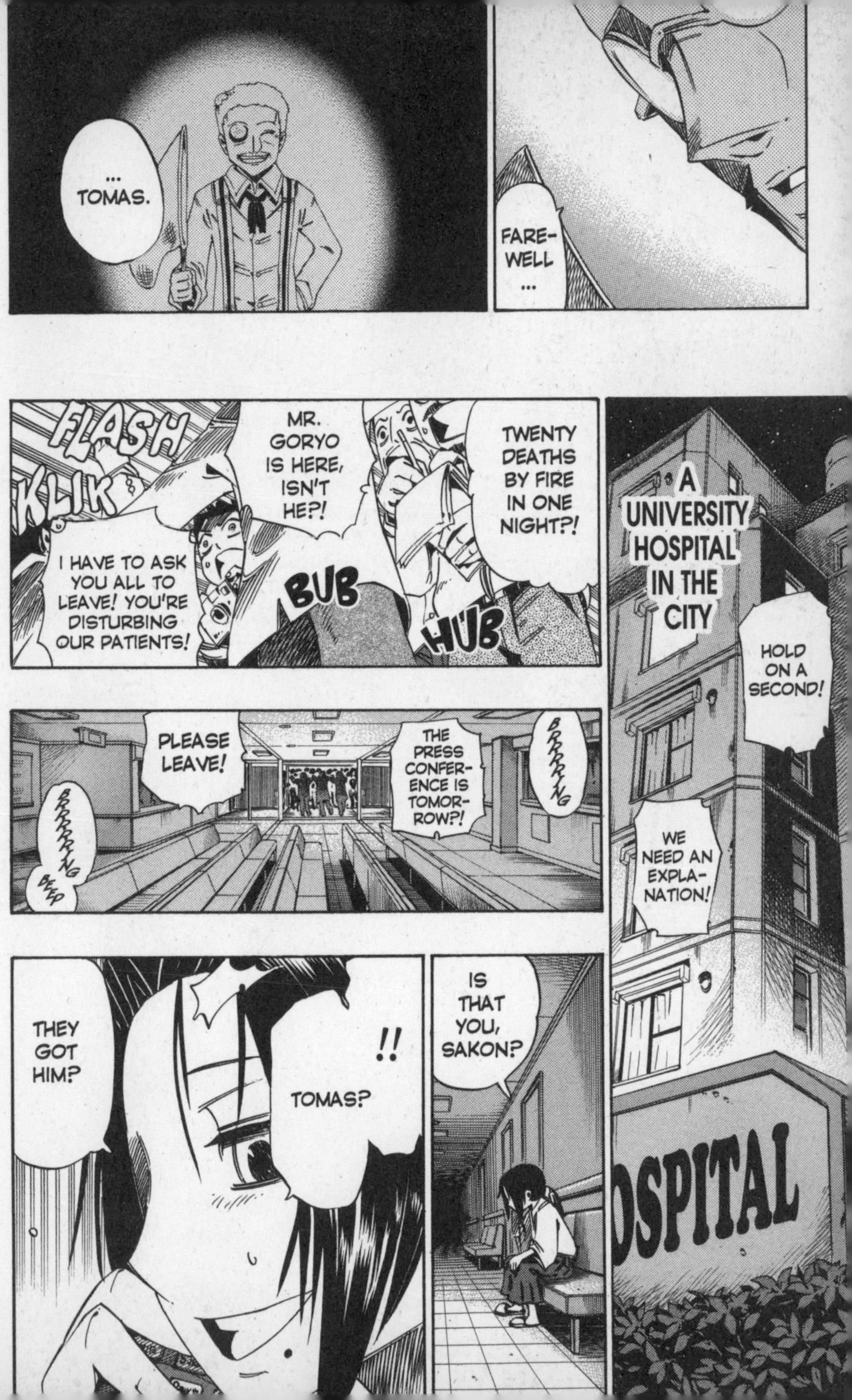
FARE-WELL ...
... TOMAS.
A UNIVERSITY HOSPITAL IN THE CITY
HOLD ON A SECOND!
WE NEED AN EXPLA-NATION!
OSPITAL
TWENTY DEATHS BY FIRE IN ONE NIGHT?!
MR. GORYO IS HERE, ISN'T HE?!
FLASH
KLIK
BUB
HUB
I HAVE TO ASK YOU ALL TO LEAVE! YOU'RE DISTURBING OUR PATIENTS!
BRRRRRING
THE PRESS CONFER-ENCE IS TOMOR-ROW?!
PLEASE LEAVE!
BRRRRRING
BEEP
IS THAT YOU, SAKON?
!!
TOMAS?
THEY GOT HIM?

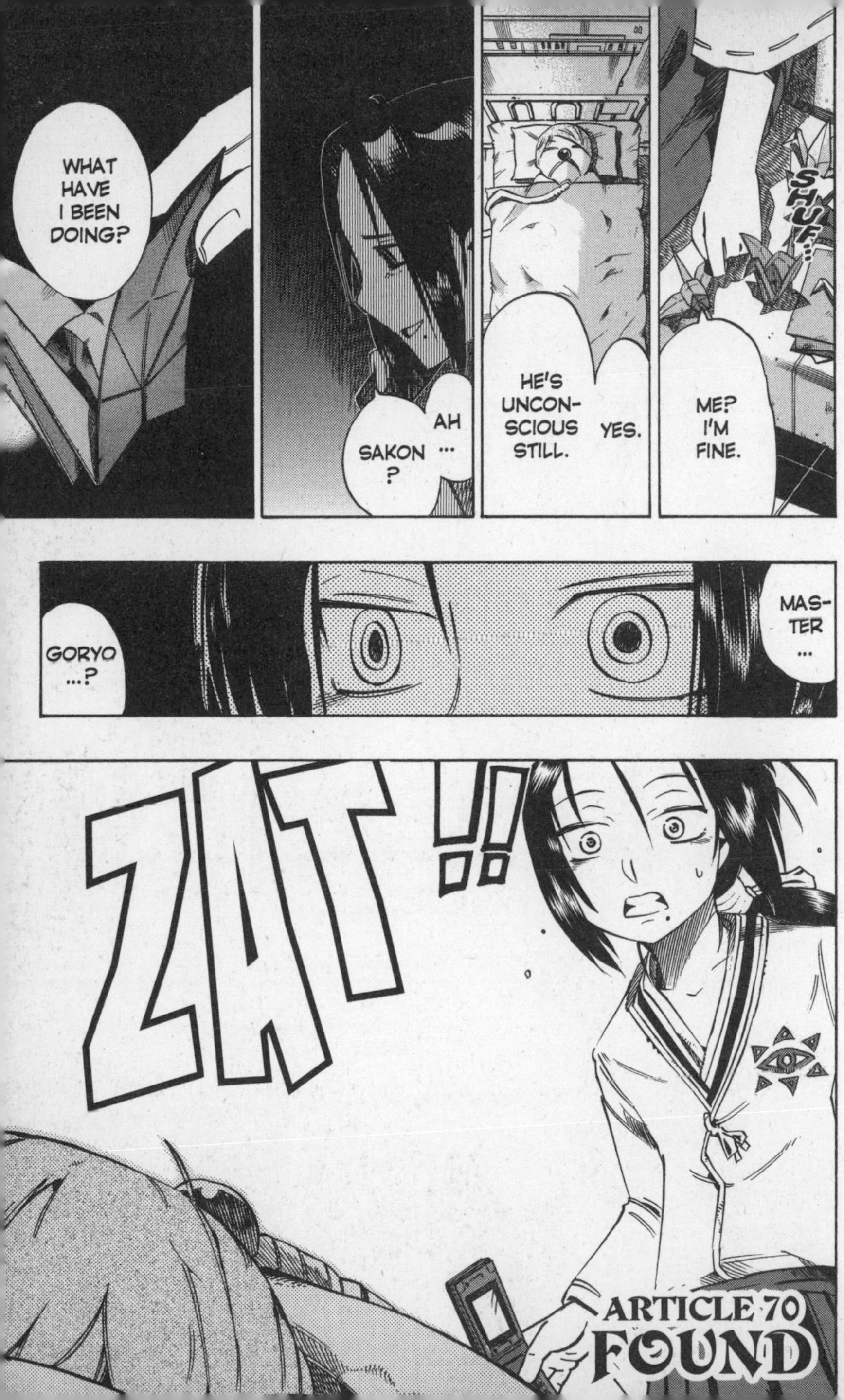
SHUF...
ME? I'M FINE.
YES.
HE'S UNCON- SCIOUS STILL.
AH ...
SAKON ?
WHAT HAVE I BEEN DOING?
MAS- TER ...
GORYO ...?
ZAT!!
ARTICLE 70
FOUND

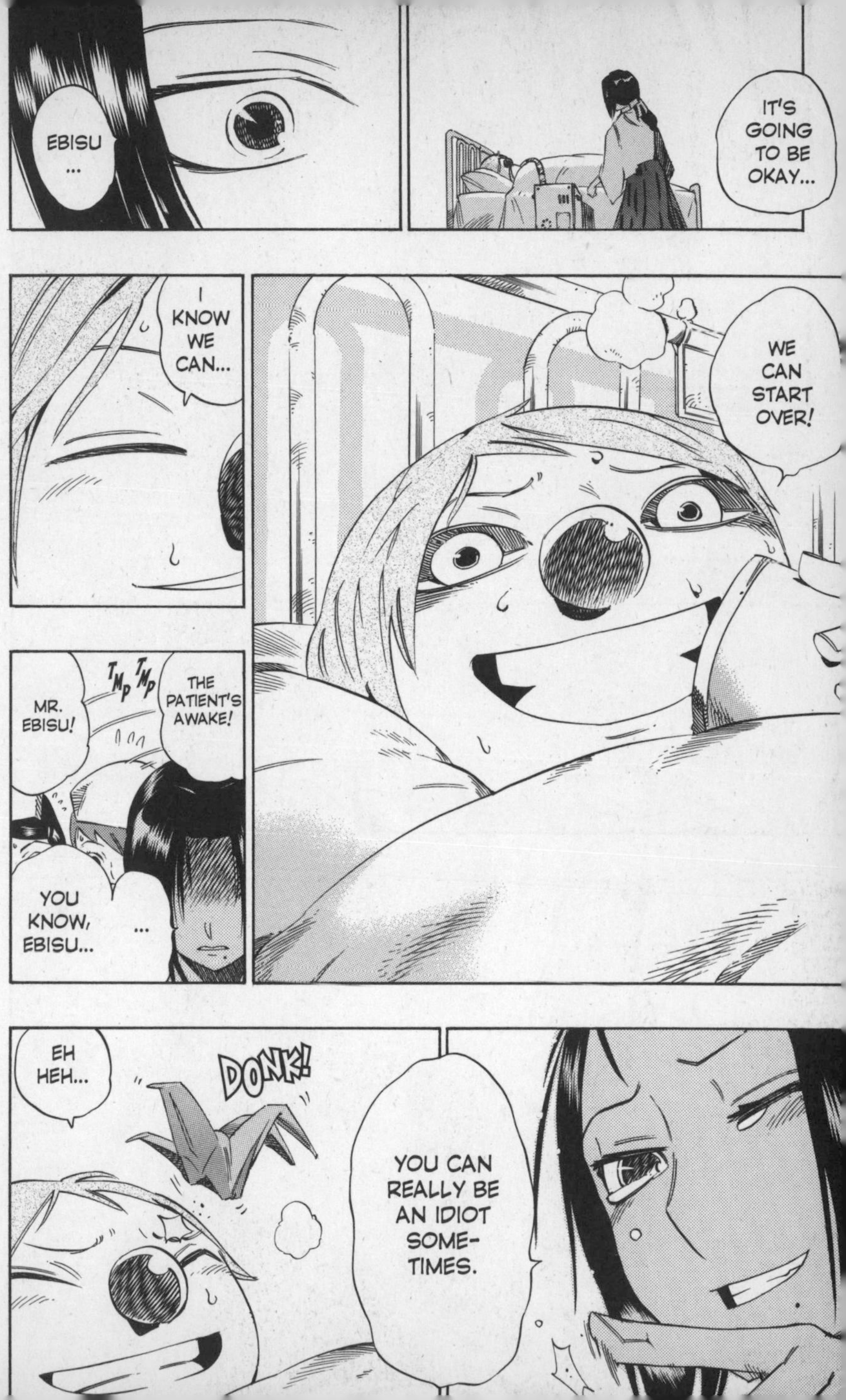
IT'S GOING TO BE OKAY...
EBISU ...
WE CAN START OVER!
I KNOW WE CAN...
THE PATIENT'S AWAKE!
TMP TMP
MR. EBISU!
...
YOU KNOW, EBISU...
YOU CAN REALLY BE AN IDIOT SOME-TIMES.
DONK!
EH HEH...

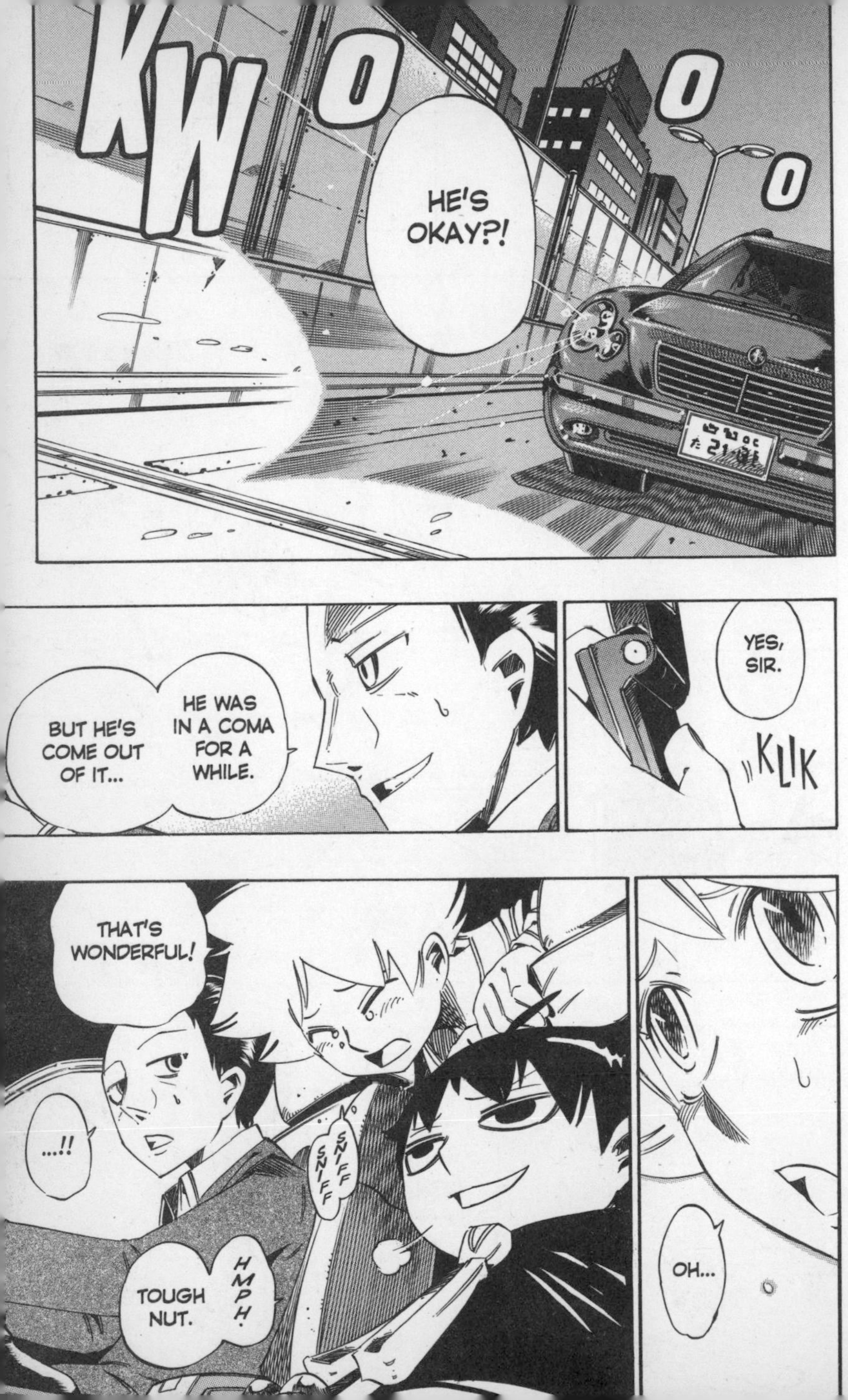
KWOOO
HE'S OKAY?!
YES, SIR.
KLIK
HE WAS IN A COMA FOR A WHILE.
BUT HE'S COME OUT OF IT...
OH...
THAT'S WONDERFUL!
SNIFF SNIFF
...!!
HMPH!
TOUGH NUT.

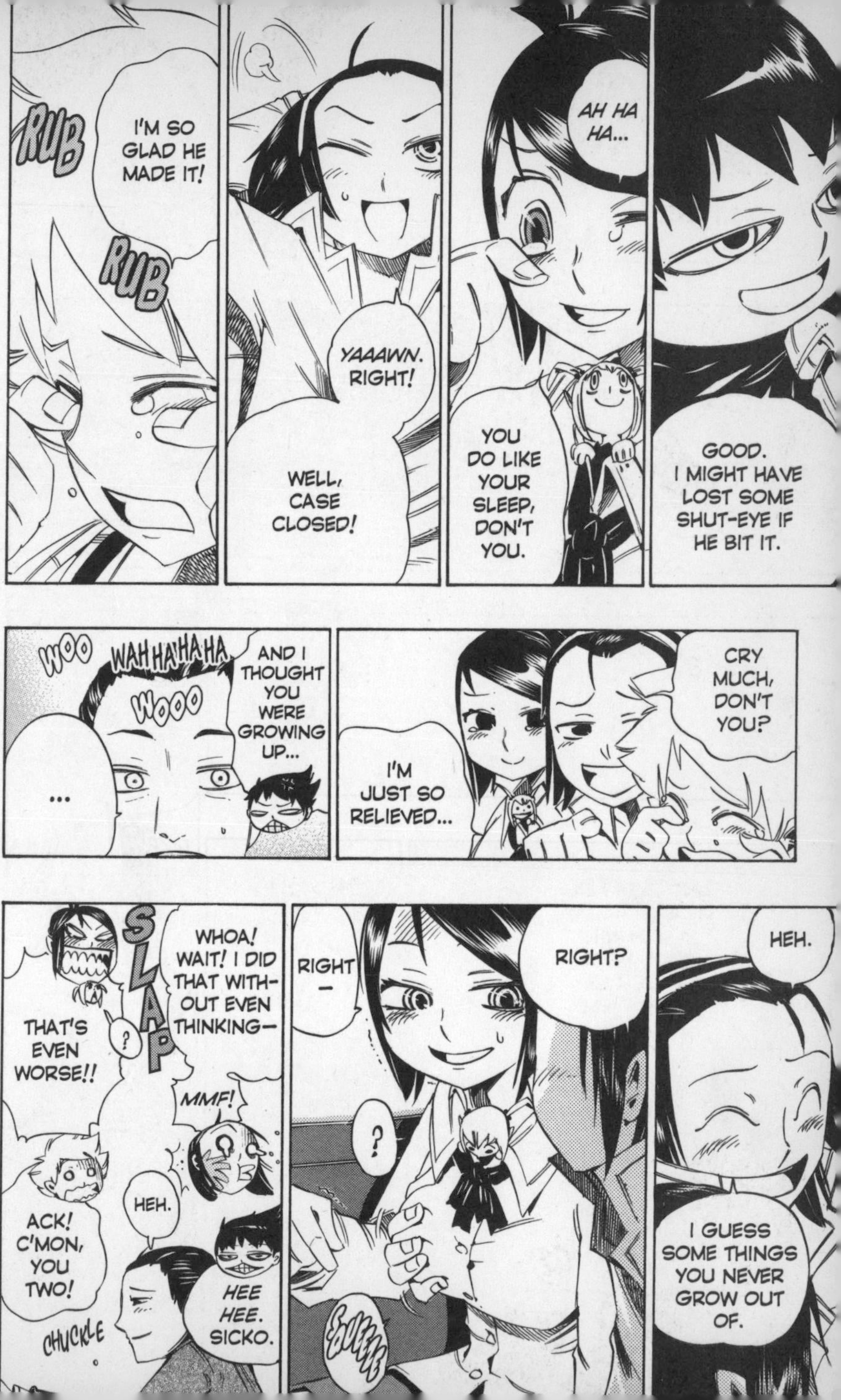
GOOD. I MIGHT HAVE LOST SOME SHUT-EYE IF HE BIT IT.
AH HA HA...
YOU DO LIKE YOUR SLEEP, DON'T YOU.
YAAAWN. RIGHT!
WELL, CASE CLOSED!
RUB
I'M SO GLAD HE MADE IT!
RUB
CRY MUCH, DON'T YOU?
I'M JUST SO RELIEVED...
AND I THOUGHT YOU WERE GROWING UP...
WAH HA HA HA
WOO
WOOO
...
HEH.
I GUESS SOME THINGS YOU NEVER GROW OUT OF.
RIGHT?
RIGHT—
?
WHOA! WAIT! I DID THAT WITH-OUT EVEN THINKING—
SLAP
THAT'S EVEN WORSE!!
?
MMF!
HEH.
ACK! C'MON, YOU TWO!
HEE HEE. SICKO.
CHUCKLE

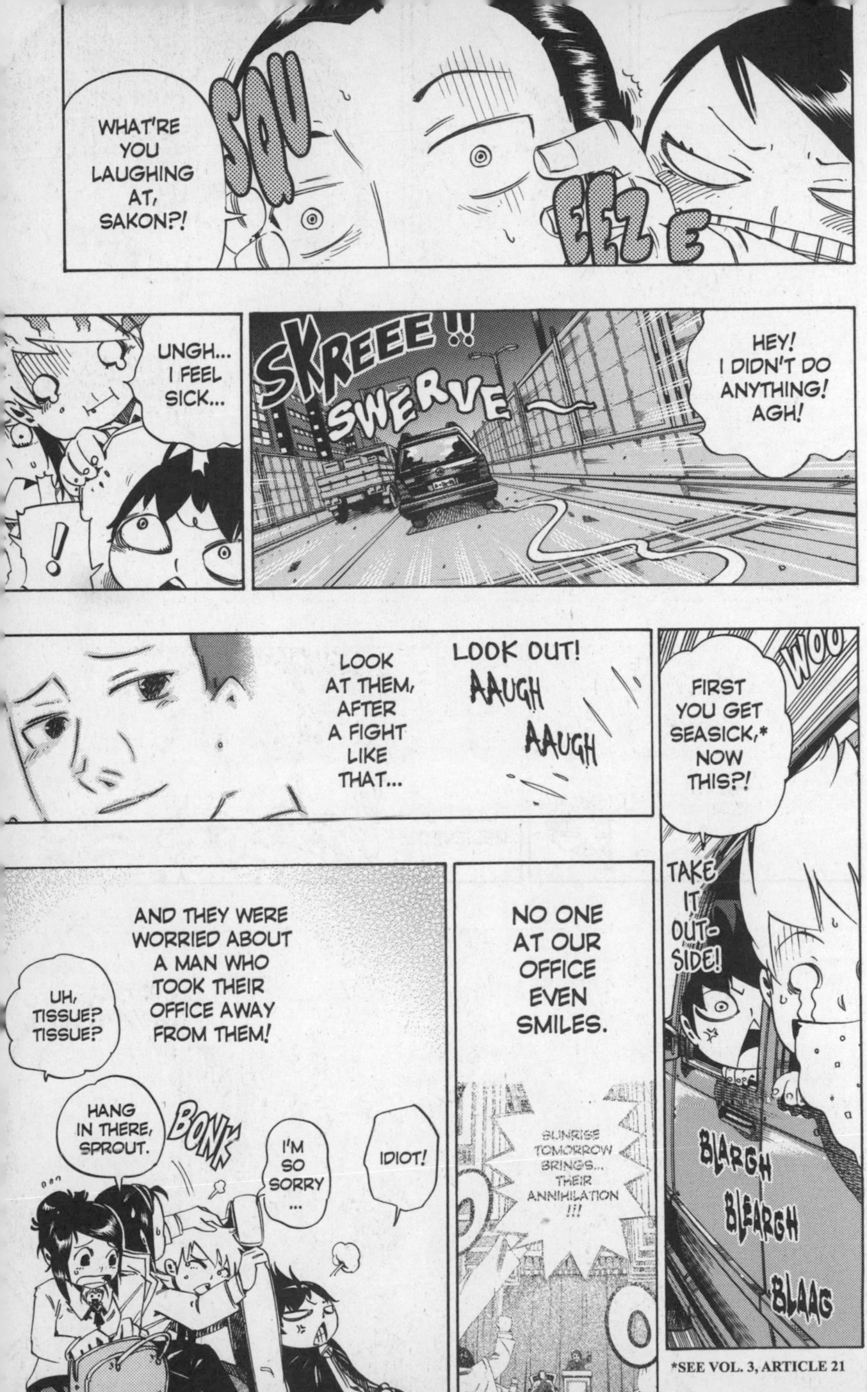
SQU
EEZE
WHAT'RE YOU LAUGHING AT, SAKON?!
HEY! I DIDN'T DO ANYTHING! AGH!
SKREEE!!
SWERVE~
UNGH... I FEEL SICK...
!
WOO
FIRST YOU GET SEASICK,* NOW THIS?!
TAKE IT OUT-SIDE!
BLARGH
BLEARGH
BLAAG
LOOK OUT!
AAUGH
AAUGH
LOOK AT THEM, AFTER A FIGHT LIKE THAT...
NO ONE AT OUR OFFICE EVEN SMILES.
SUNRISE TOMORROW BRINGS... THEIR ANNIHILATION!!!
AND THEY WERE WORRIED ABOUT A MAN WHO TOOK THEIR OFFICE AWAY FROM THEM!
IDIOT!
I'M SO SORRY...
BONK
HANG IN THERE, SPROUT.
UH, TISSUE? TISSUE?

*SEE VOL. 3, ARTICLE 21

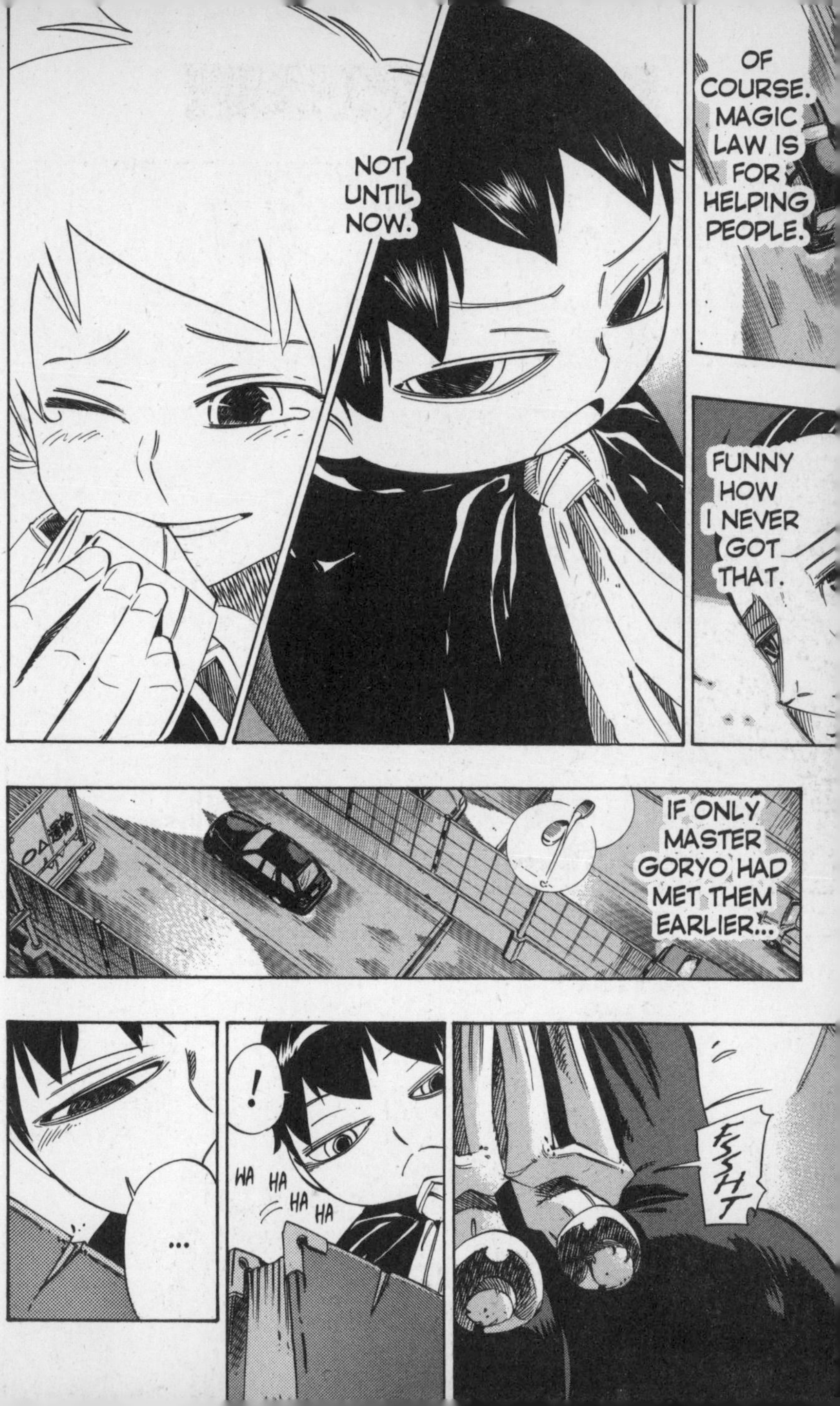
OF COURSE. MAGIC LAW IS FOR HELPING PEOPLE.
FUNNY HOW I NEVER GOT THAT.
NOT UNTIL NOW.
IF ONLY MASTER GORYO HAD MET THEM EARLIER...
FSSHT
!
HA HA HA HA
...

[redacted]

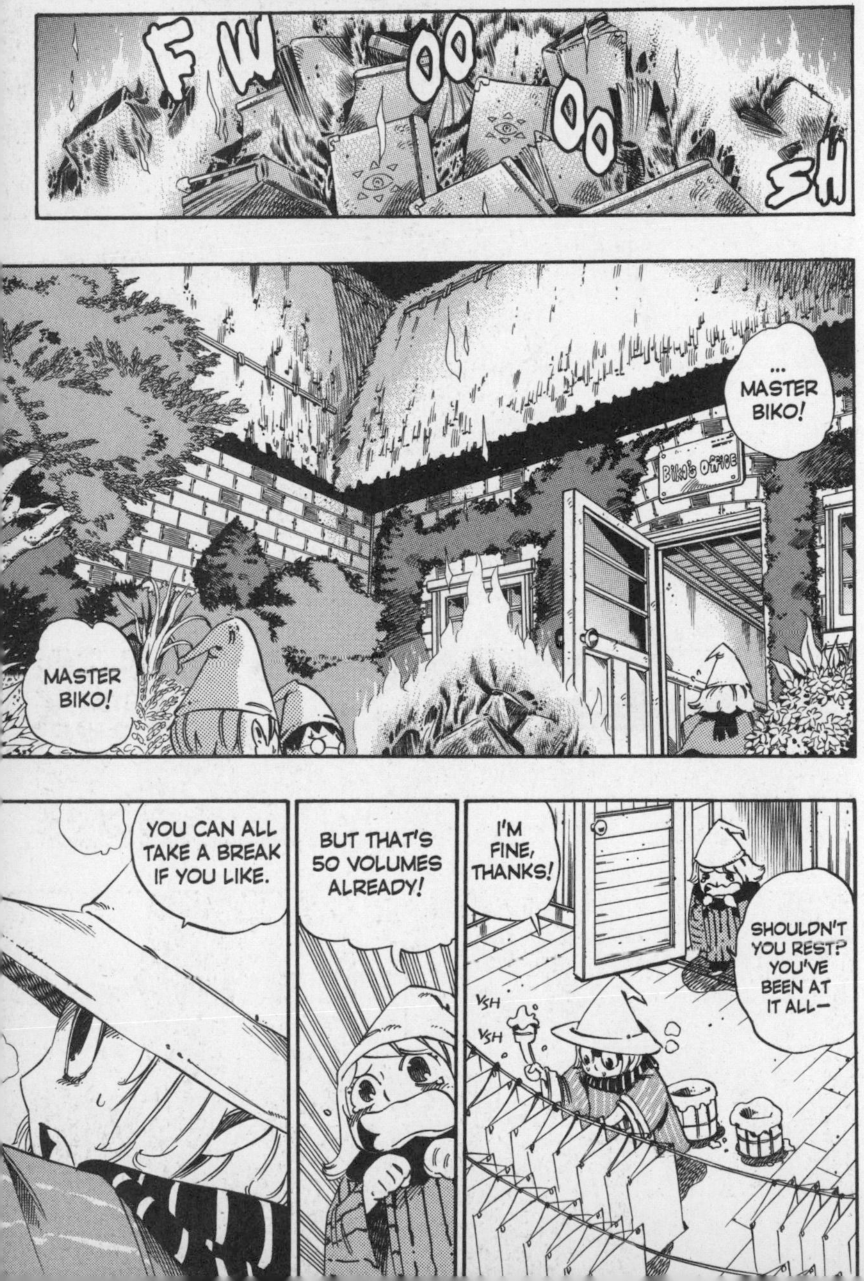
FWOOOOSH
... MASTER BIKO!
MASTER BIKO!
BIKO'S OFFICE
SHOULDN'T YOU REST? YOU'VE BEEN AT IT ALL—
I'M FINE, THANKS!
VSH
VSH
BUT THAT'S 50 VOLUMES ALREADY!
YOU CAN ALL TAKE A BREAK IF YOU LIKE.

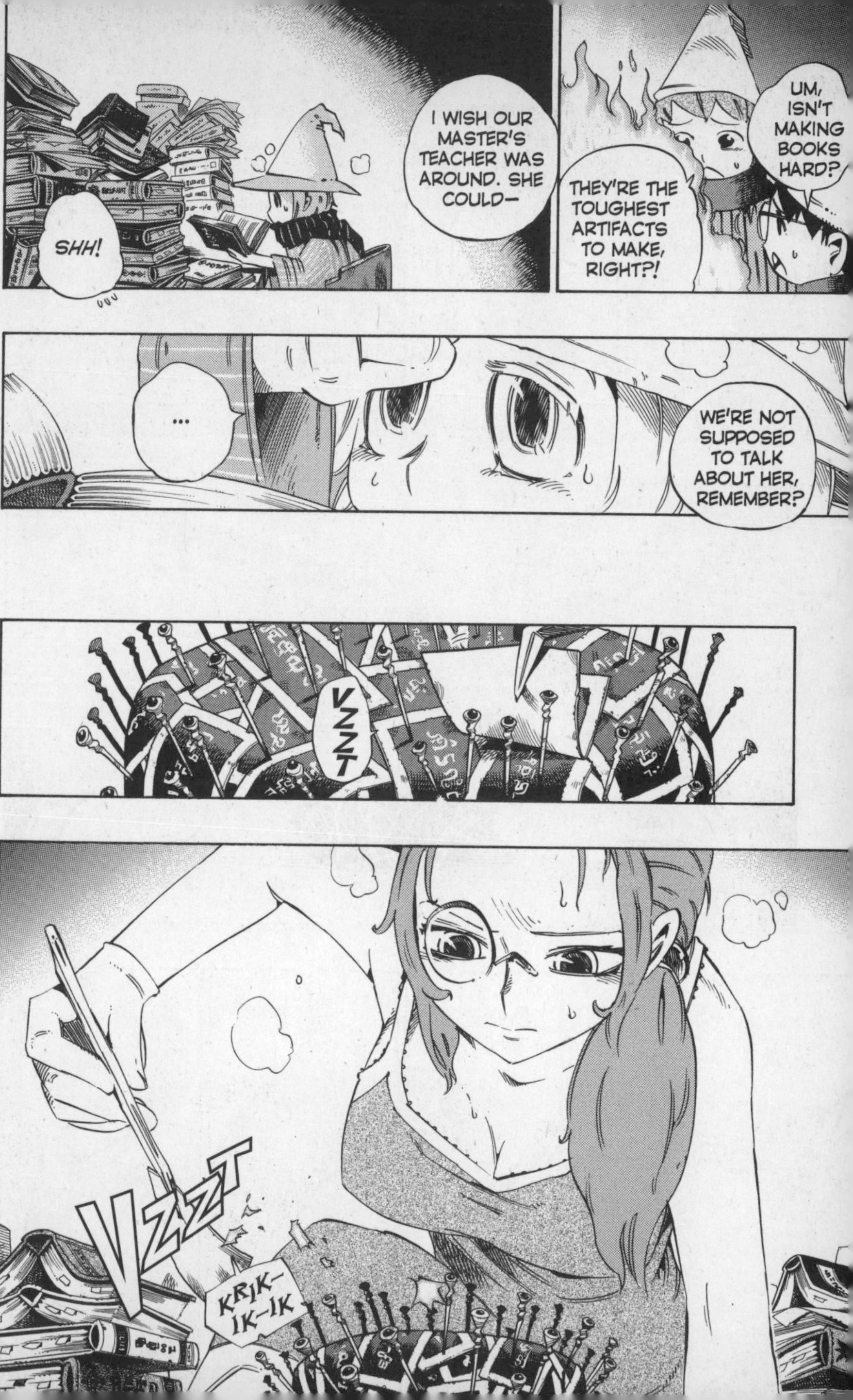
UM, ISN'T MAKING BOOKS HARD?
THEY'RE THE TOUGHEST ARTIFACTS TO MAKE, RIGHT?!
I WISH OUR MASTER'S TEACHER WAS AROUND. SHE COULD—
SHH!
WE'RE NOT SUPPOSED TO TALK ABOUT HER, REMEMBER?
...
VZZT
VZZZT
KRIK-IK-IK

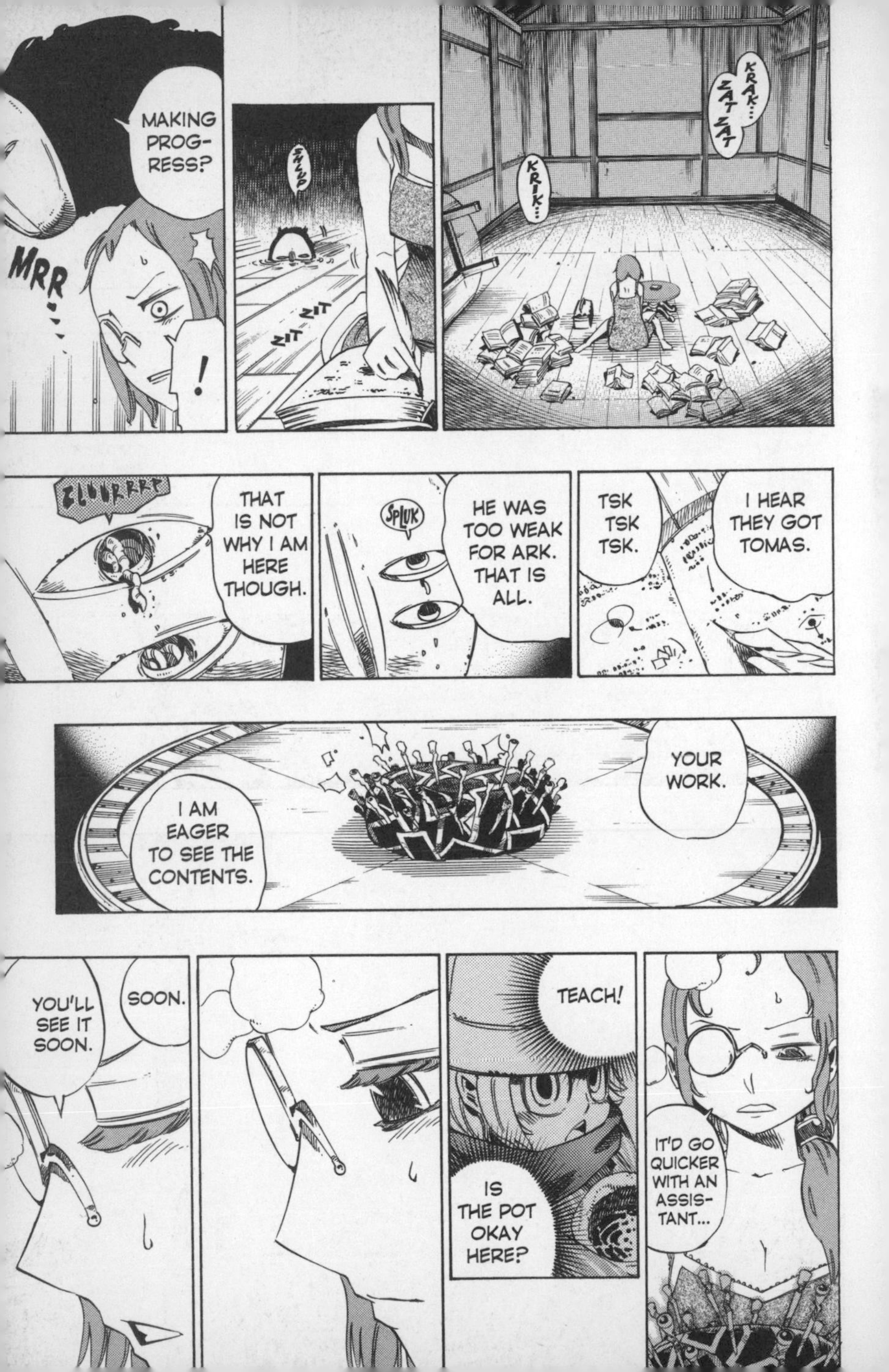
KRAK...
ZAT ZAT
KRIK...
ZIT ZIT
MAKING PROG-RESS?
MRR
!
I HEAR THEY GOT TOMAS.
TSK TSK TSK.
SPLUK
HE WAS TOO WEAK FOR ARK. THAT IS ALL.
THAT IS NOT WHY I AM HERE THOUGH.
YOUR WORK.
I AM EAGER TO SEE THE CONTENTS.
IT'D GO QUICKER WITH AN ASSISTANT...
TEACH!
IS THE POT OKAY HERE?
SOON.
YOU'LL SEE IT SOON.

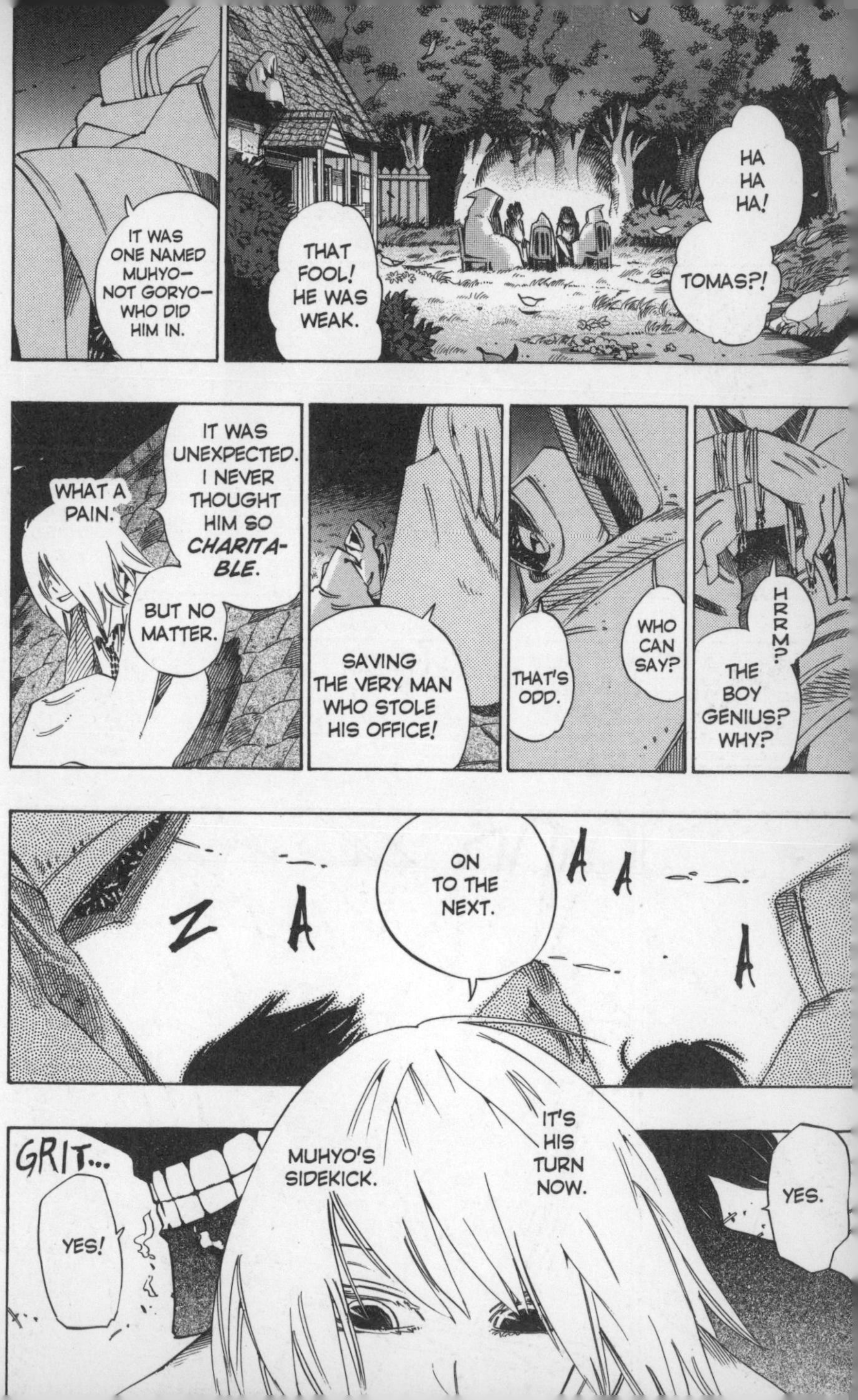
HA HA HA!
TOMAS?!
THAT FOOL! HE WAS WEAK.
IT WAS ONE NAMED MUHYO—NOT GORYO—WHO DID HIM IN.
HRRM?
THE BOY GENIUS? WHY?
WHO CAN SAY?
THAT'S ODD.
SAVING THE VERY MAN WHO STOLE HIS OFFICE!
IT WAS UNEXPECTED. I NEVER THOUGHT HIM SO *CHARITABLE*.
WHAT A PAIN.
BUT NO MATTER.
ON TO THE NEXT.
Z A A A A A
YES.
IT'S HIS TURN NOW.
MUHYO'S SIDEKICK.
GRIT...
YES!

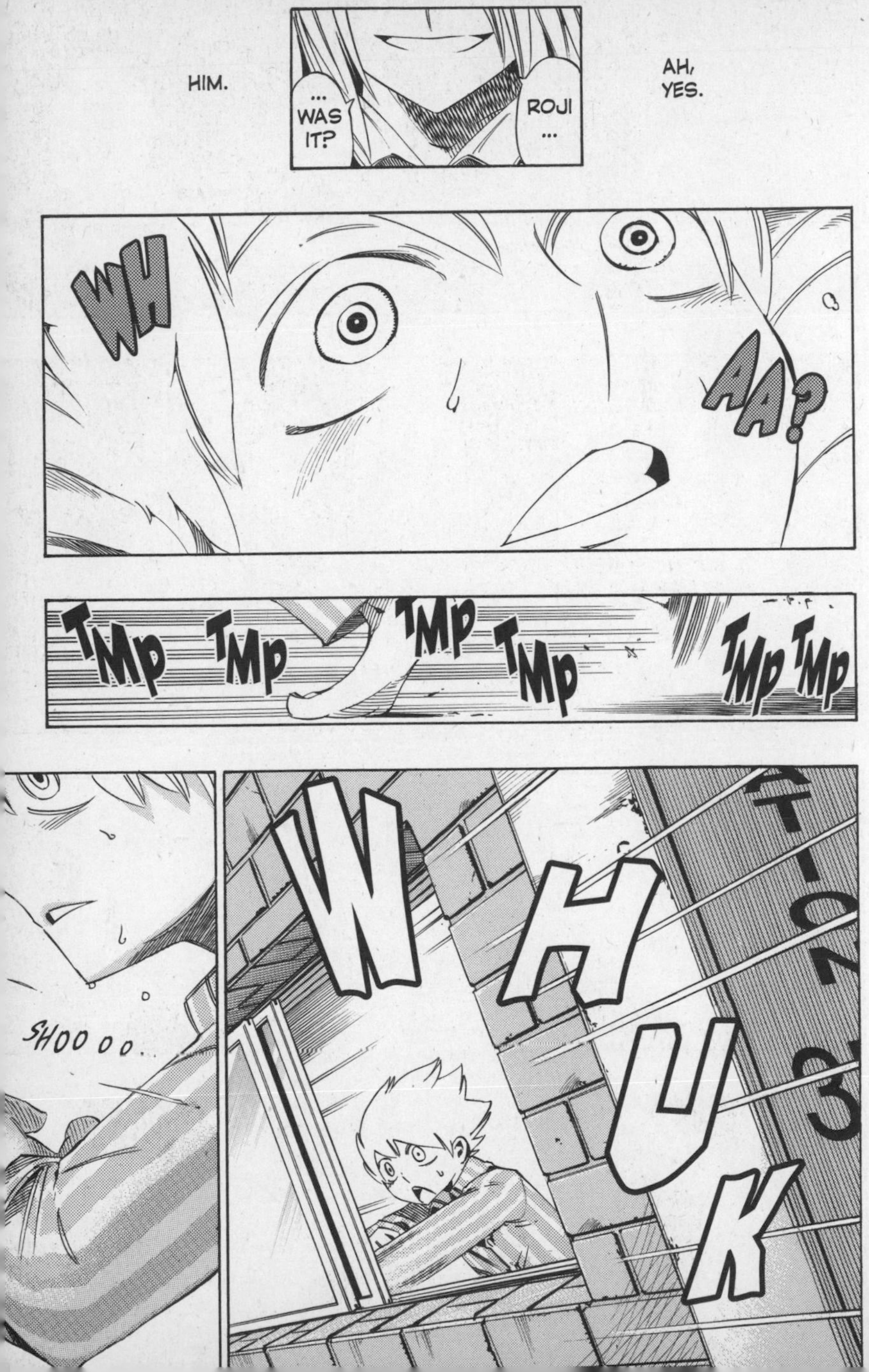
AH, YES.
ROJI ...
... WAS IT?
HIM.
WH
AA?
TMP TMP TMP TMP TMP TMP
WHUK
SHOO O O...

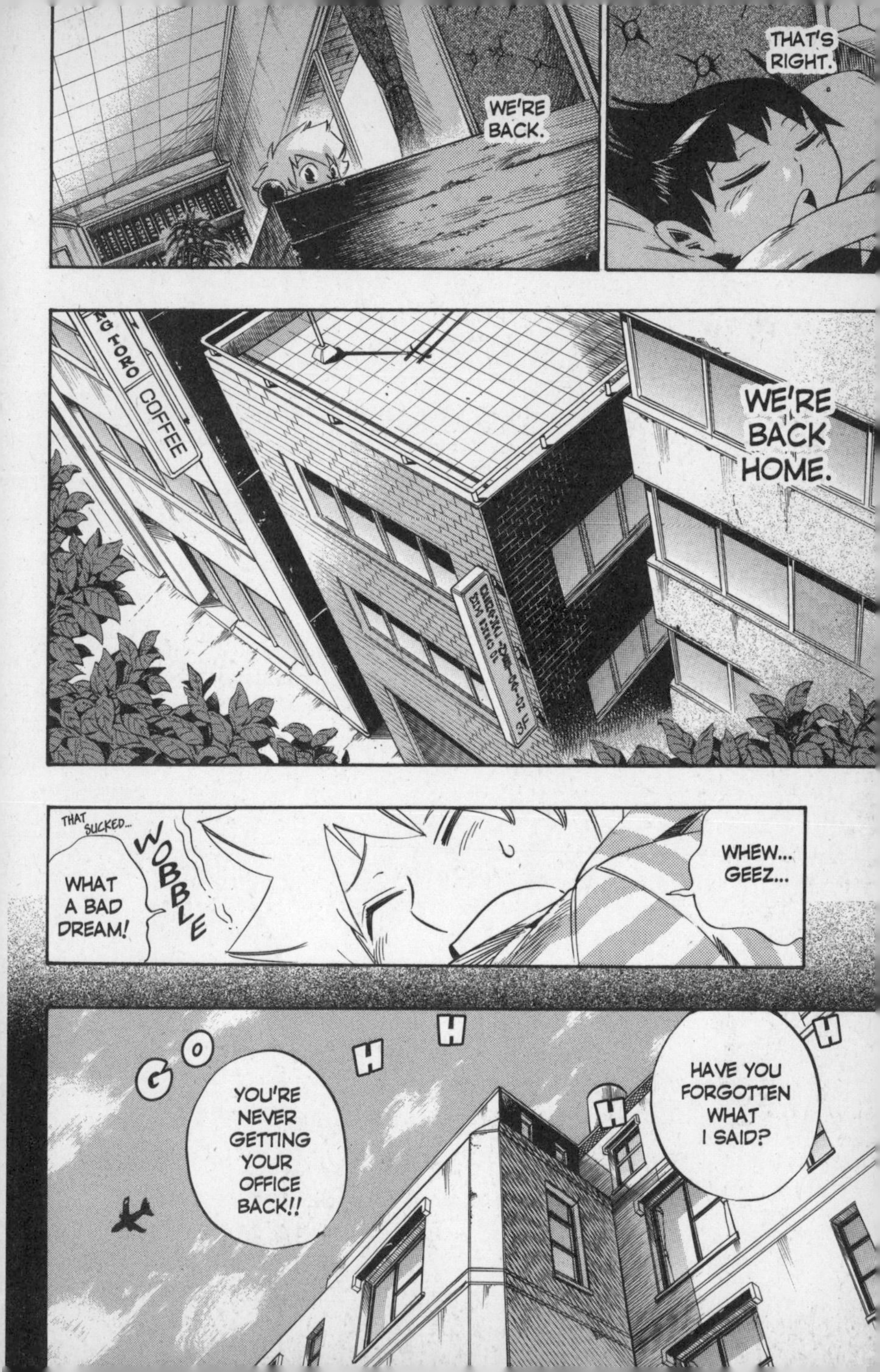
THAT'S RIGHT.
WE'RE BACK.
WE'RE BACK HOME.
NG TORO COFFEE
3F
WHEW... GEEZ...
WOBBLE
WHAT A BAD DREAM!
THAT SUCKED...
GOHHHH
HAVE YOU FORGOTTEN WHAT I SAID?
YOU'RE NEVER GETTING YOUR OFFICE BACK!!

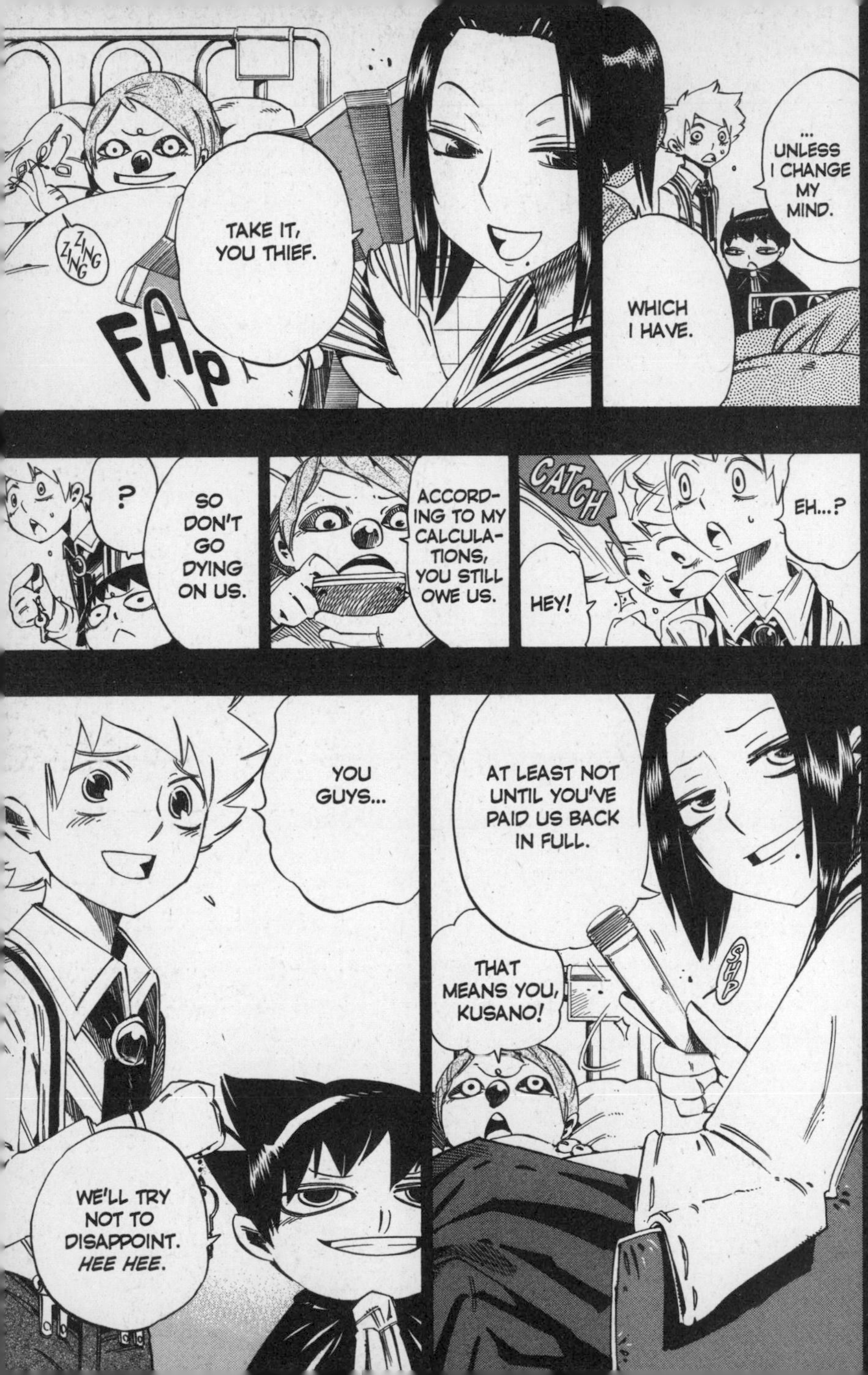

... UNLESS I CHANGE MY MIND.
WHICH I HAVE.
TAKE IT, YOU THIEF.
ZING ZING
FAP
EH...?
CATCH
HEY!
ACCORDING TO MY CALCULATIONS, YOU STILL OWE US.
SO DON'T GO DYING ON US.
?
AT LEAST NOT UNTIL YOU'VE PAID US BACK IN FULL.
SHA
THAT MEANS YOU, KUSANO!
YOU GUYS...
WE'LL TRY NOT TO DISAPPOINT. *HEE HEE.*

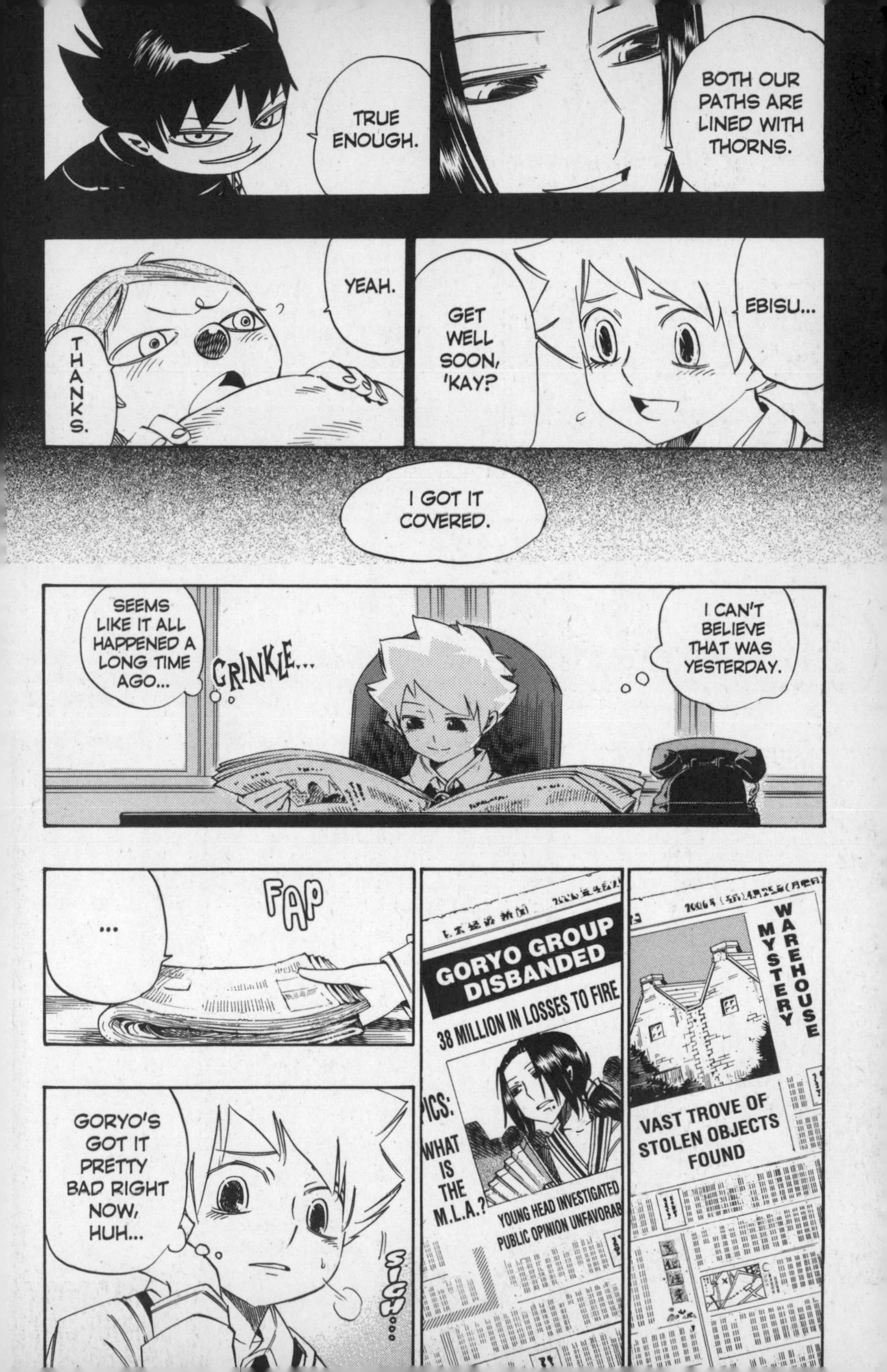
BOTH OUR PATHS ARE LINED WITH THORNS.
TRUE ENOUGH.
EBISU...
GET WELL SOON, 'KAY?
YEAH.
THANKS.
I GOT IT COVERED.
I CAN'T BELIEVE THAT WAS YESTERDAY.
SEEMS LIKE IT ALL HAPPENED A LONG TIME AGO...
CRINKLE...
MYSTERY WAREHOUSE
VAST TROVE OF STOLEN OBJECTS FOUND
GORYO GROUP DISBANDED
38 MILLION IN LOSSES TO FIRE
PICS: WHAT IS THE M.L.A.?
YOUNG HEAD INVESTIGATED
PUBLIC OPINION UNFAVORAB
FAP
...
GORYO'S GOT IT PRETTY BAD RIGHT NOW, HUH...
SIGH...

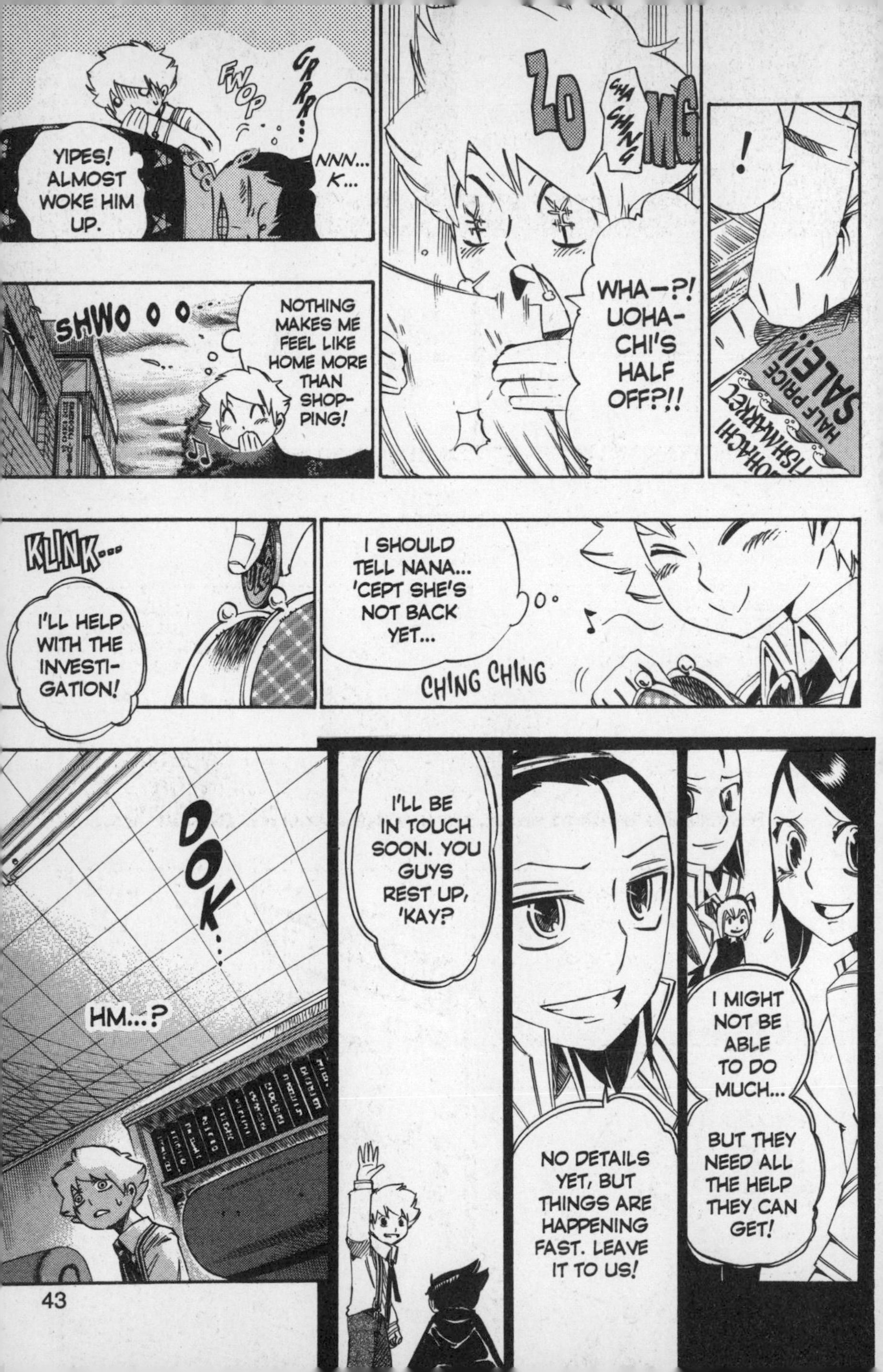
!
UOHACHI FISHMARKET
HALF PRICE
SALE!!
ZO MG
CHA CHING
WHA—?! UOHACHI'S HALF OFF?!!
GRRR...
NNN... K...
FWOP
YIPES! ALMOST WOKE HIM UP.
NOTHING MAKES ME FEEL LIKE HOME MORE THAN SHOPPING!
SHWO O O
I SHOULD TELL NANA... 'CEPT SHE'S NOT BACK YET...
CHING CHING
KLINK...
I'LL HELP WITH THE INVESTIGATION!
I MIGHT NOT BE ABLE TO DO MUCH...
BUT THEY NEED ALL THE HELP THEY CAN GET!
NO DETAILS YET, BUT THINGS ARE HAPPENING FAST. LEAVE IT TO US!
I'LL BE IN TOUCH SOON. YOU GUYS REST UP, 'KAY?
DOK...
HM...?

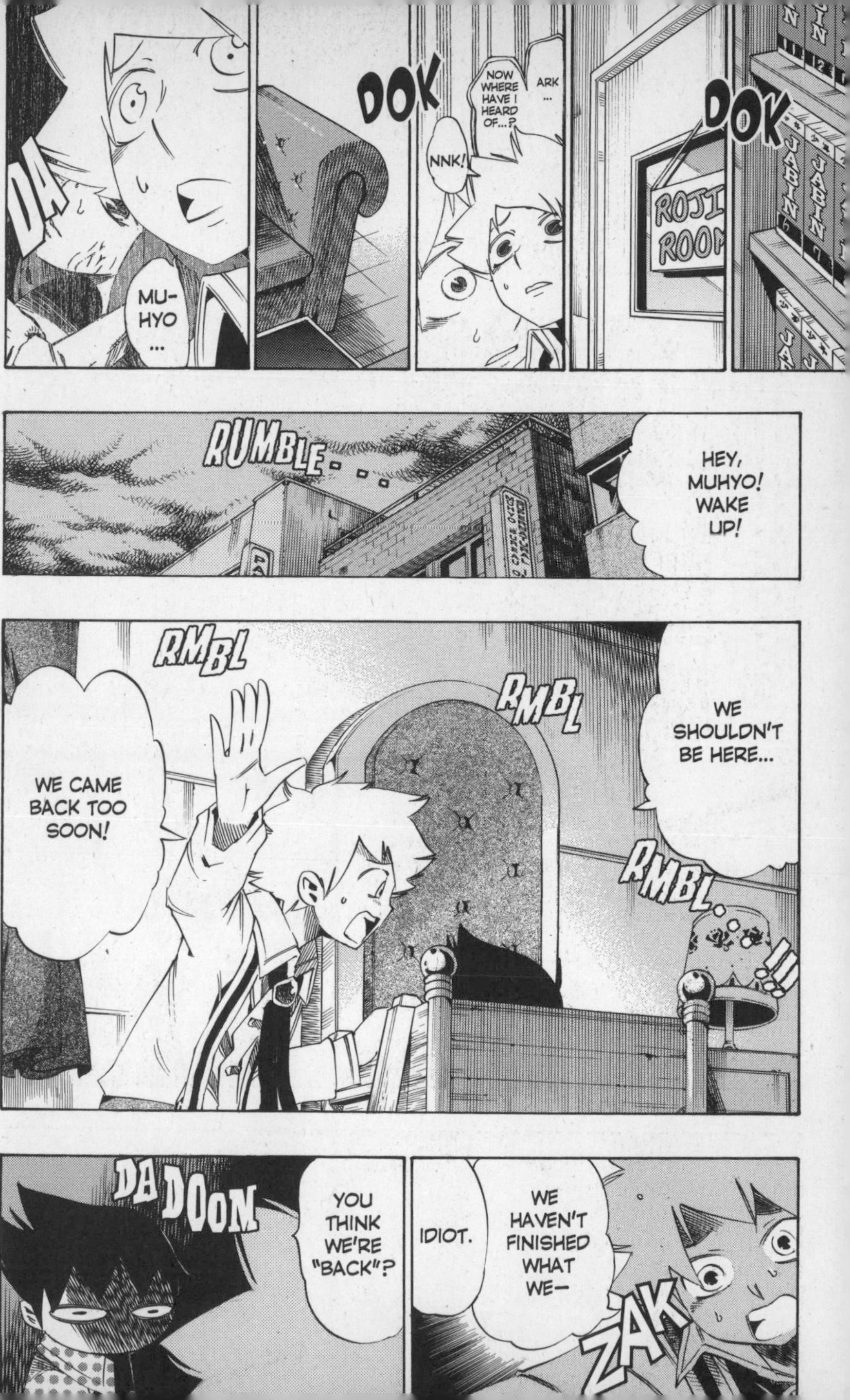
DOK
NOW WHERE HAVE I HEARD OF...?
ARK...
NNK!
DOK
DA
MU-HYO...
RUMBLE...
HEY, MUHYO! WAKE UP!
WE SHOULDN'T BE HERE...
RMBL
RMBL
RMBL
WE CAME BACK TOO SOON!
WE HAVEN'T FINISHED WHAT WE—
ZAK
IDIOT.
YOU THINK WE'RE "BACK"?
DA DOOM

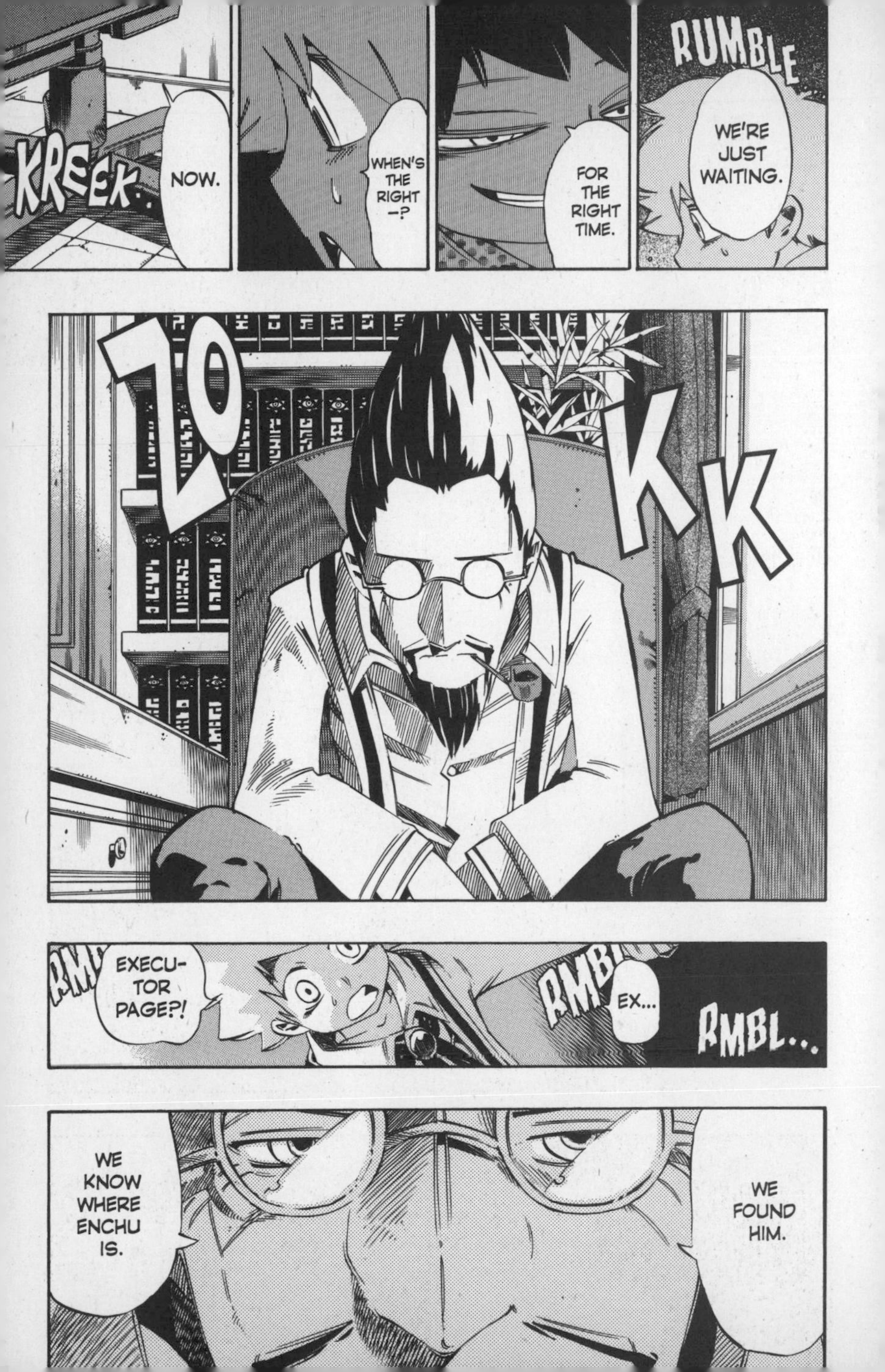
RUMBLE
WE'RE JUST WAITING.
FOR THE RIGHT TIME.
WHEN'S THE RIGHT —?
NOW.
KREEK
ZOKK
RMBL...
EX...
RMBL
EXECUTOR PAGE?!
WE FOUND HIM.
WE KNOW WHERE ENCHU IS.

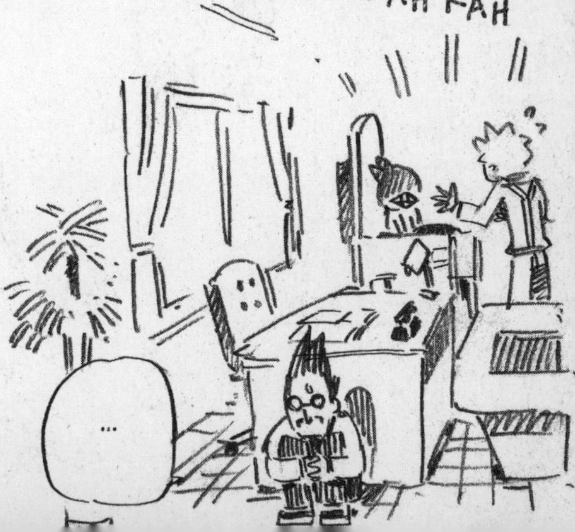
RAH RAH
...

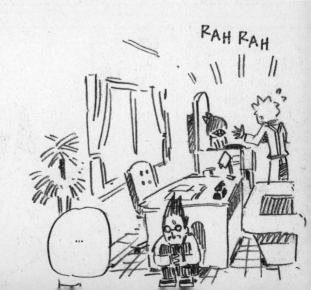

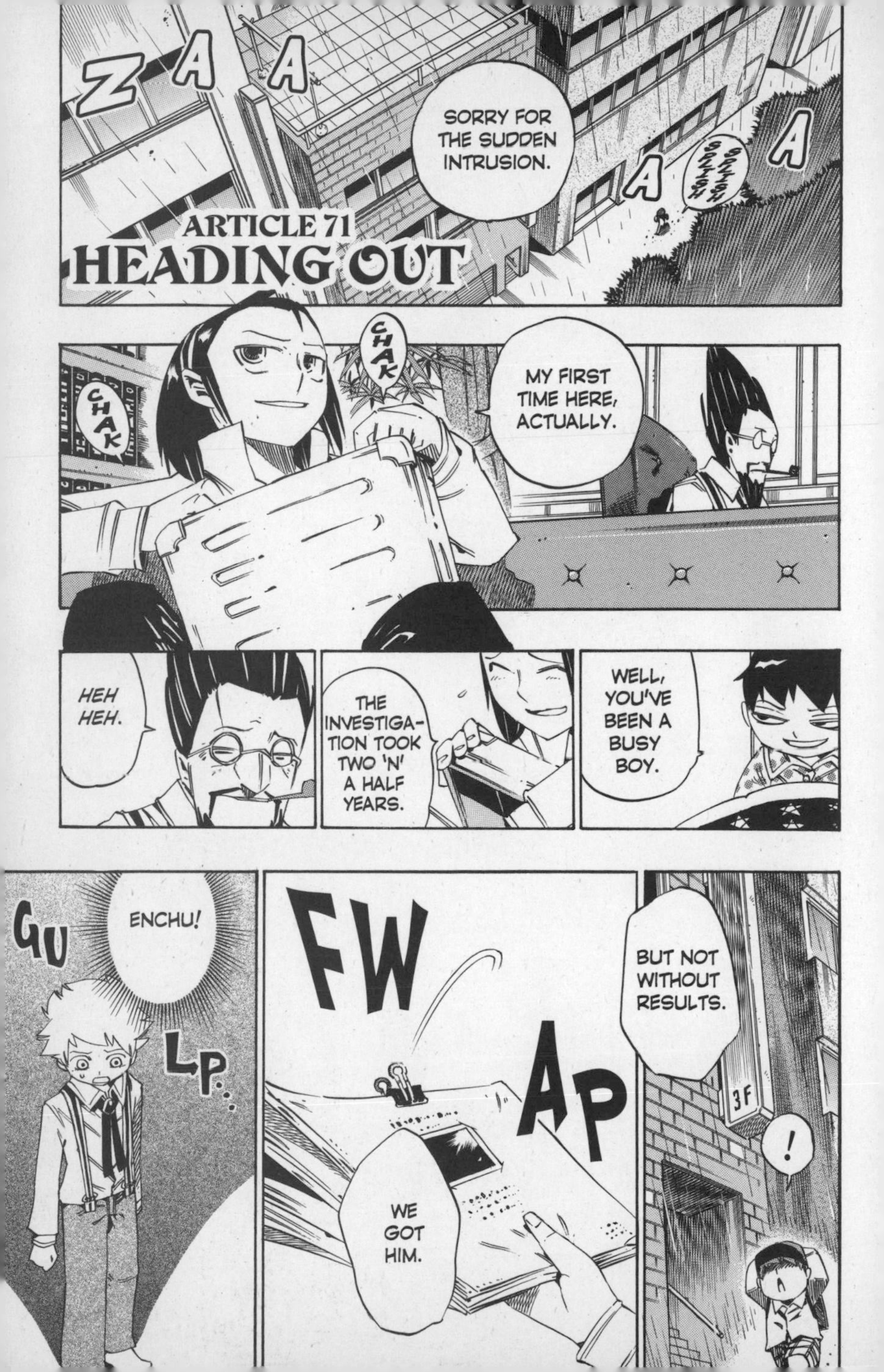
ZAA
AA
SPLITCH SPLITCH
SORRY FOR THE SUDDEN INTRUSION.
ARTICLE 71
HEADING OUT
CHAK
MY FIRST TIME HERE, ACTUALLY.
CHAK
WELL, YOU'VE BEEN A BUSY BOY.
THE INVESTIGATION TOOK TWO 'N' A HALF YEARS.
HEH HEH.
BUT NOT WITHOUT RESULTS.
3F
!
FWAP
WE GOT HIM.
ENCHU!
GULP...

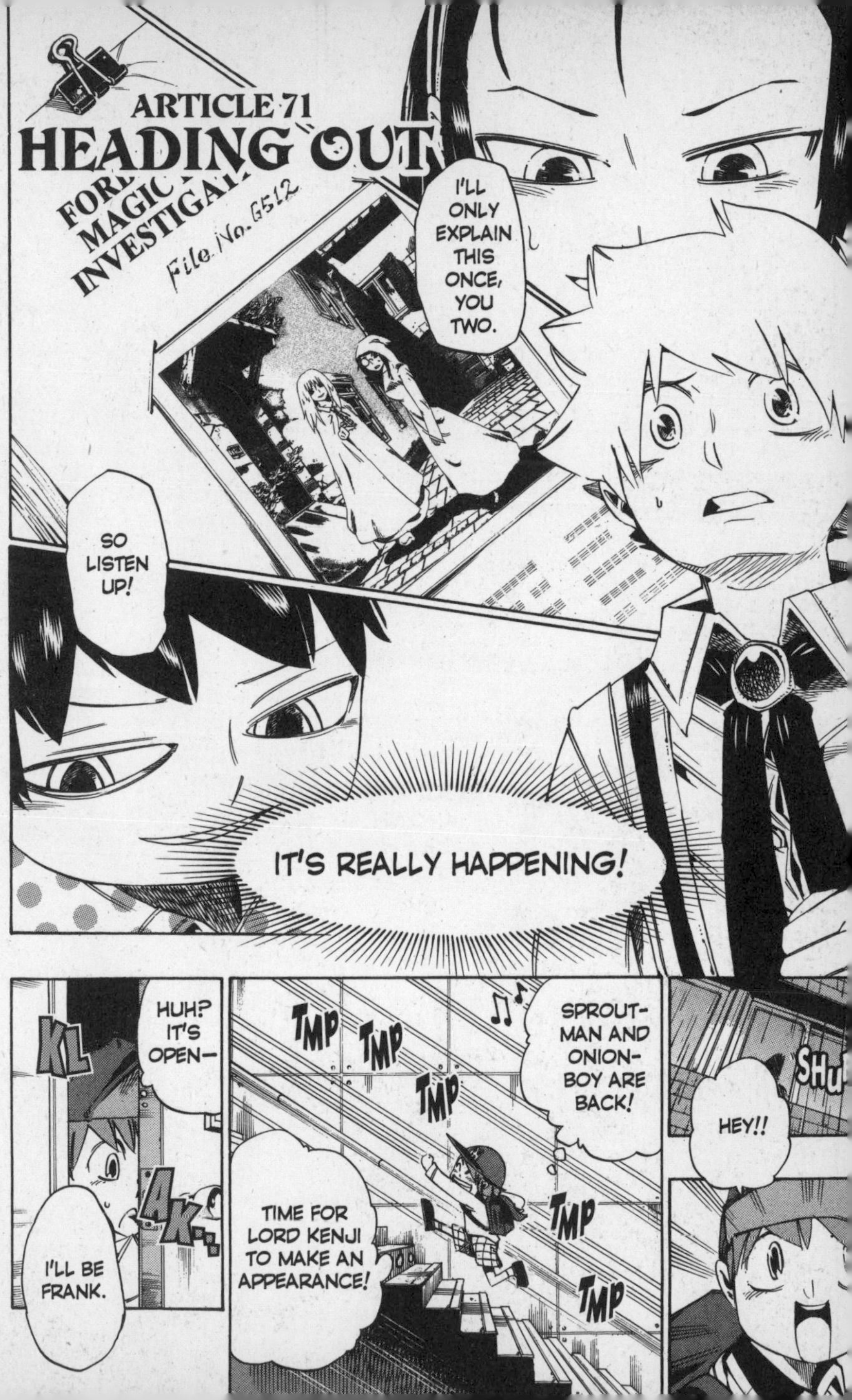
ARTICLE 71
HEADING OUT
File No. G512
I'LL ONLY EXPLAIN THIS ONCE, YOU TWO.
SO LISTEN UP!
IT'S REALLY HAPPENING!
SHU
HEY!!
SPROUT-MAN AND ONION-BOY ARE BACK!
TMP TMP TMP
TIME FOR LORD KENJI TO MAKE AN APPEARANCE!
TMP TMP
HUH? IT'S OPEN—
KL
AK...
I'LL BE FRANK.

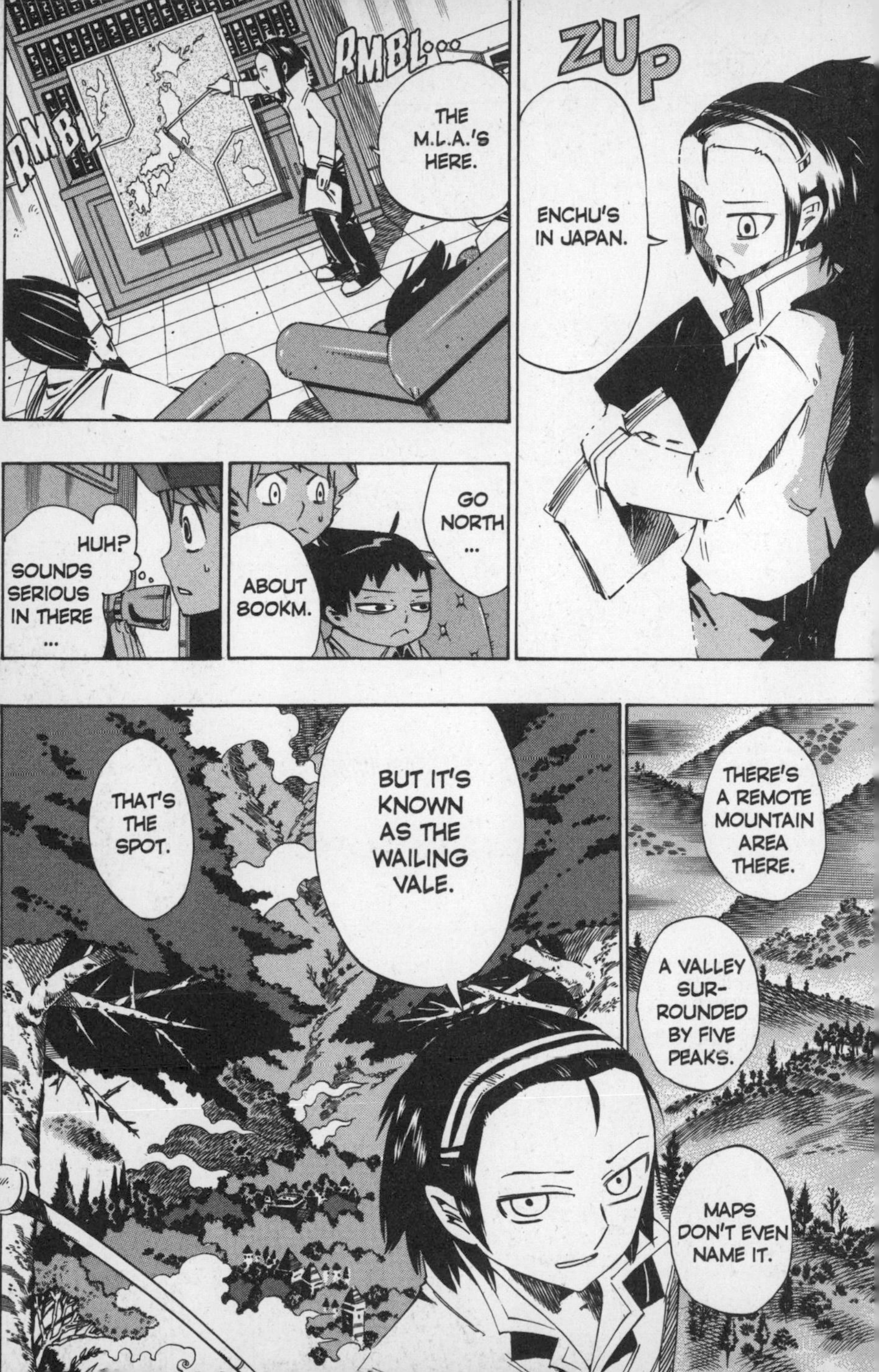
ZUP
ENCHU'S IN JAPAN.
RMBL...
THE M.L.A.'S HERE.
RMBL
GO NORTH ...
ABOUT 800KM.
HUH?
SOUNDS SERIOUS IN THERE ...
THERE'S A REMOTE MOUNTAIN AREA THERE.
A VALLEY SUR-ROUNDED BY FIVE PEAKS.
MAPS DON'T EVEN NAME IT.
BUT IT'S KNOWN AS THE WAILING VALE.
THAT'S THE SPOT.

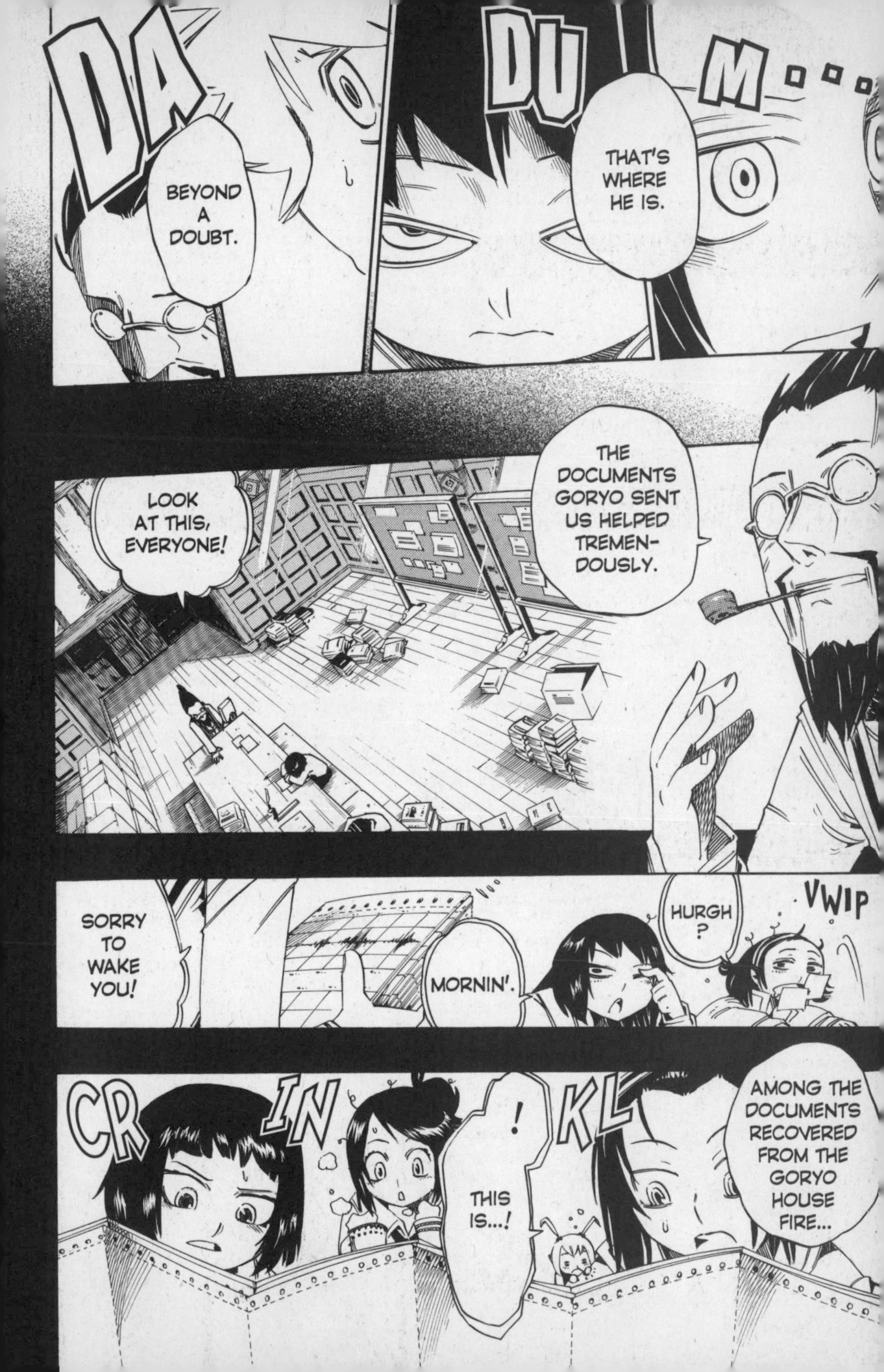
DA DU M...
THAT'S WHERE HE IS.
BEYOND A DOUBT.
THE DOCUMENTS GORYO SENT US HELPED TREMEN-DOUSLY.
LOOK AT THIS, EVERYONE!
VWIP
HURGH?
MORNIN'.
SORRY TO WAKE YOU!
AMONG THE DOCUMENTS RECOVERED FROM THE GORYO HOUSE FIRE...
CR IN KL
!
THIS IS...!

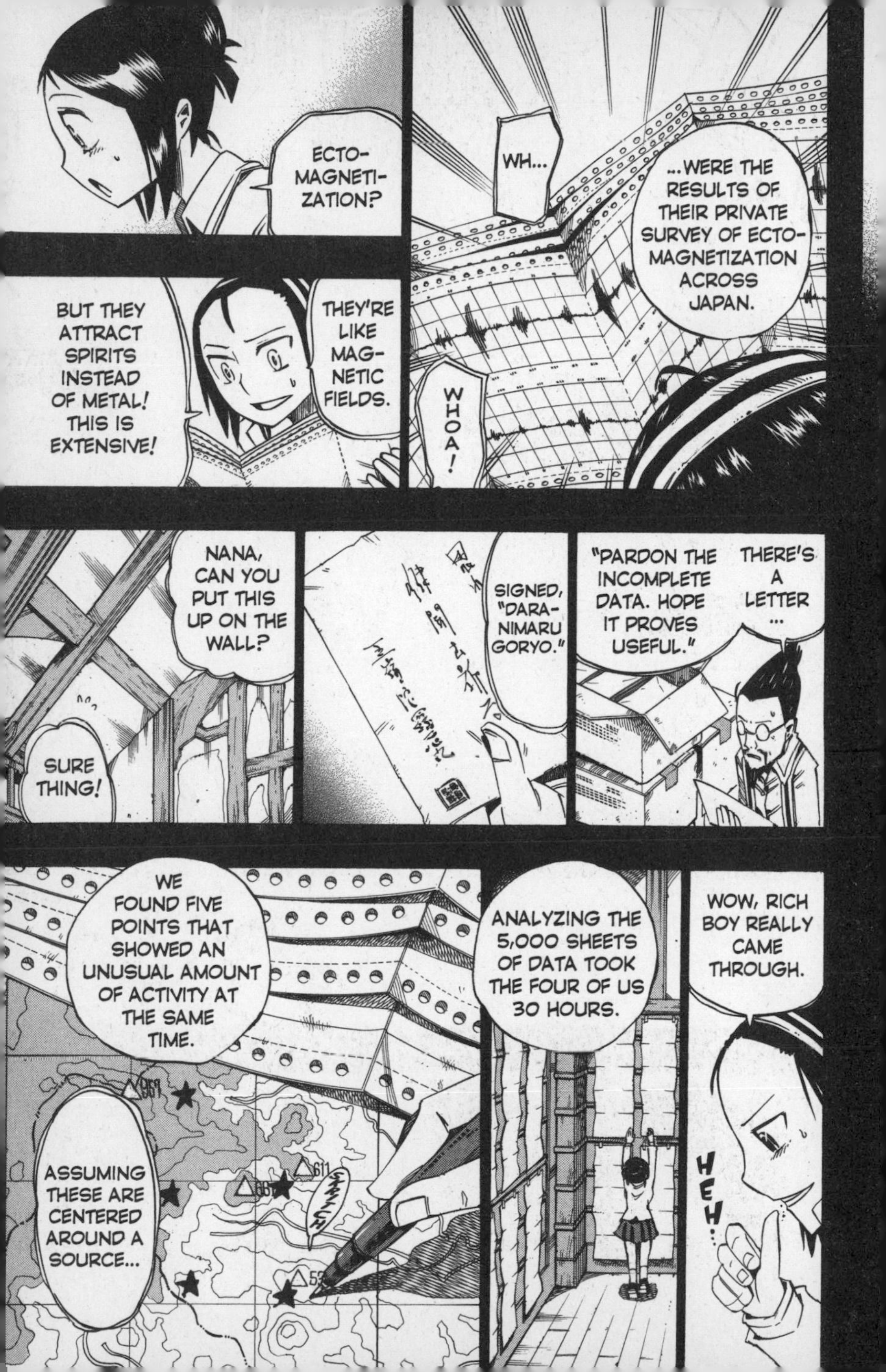
WH...
...WERE THE RESULTS OF THEIR PRIVATE SURVEY OF ECTO-MAGNETIZATION ACROSS JAPAN.
WHOA!
ECTO-MAGNETIZATION?
THEY'RE LIKE MAGNETIC FIELDS.
BUT THEY ATTRACT SPIRITS INSTEAD OF METAL! THIS IS EXTENSIVE!
THERE'S A LETTER...
"PARDON THE INCOMPLETE DATA. HOPE IT PROVES USEFUL."
SIGNED, "DARANIMARU GORYO."
NANA, CAN YOU PUT THIS UP ON THE WALL?
SURE THING!
WOW, RICH BOY REALLY CAME THROUGH.
HEH...
ANALYZING THE 5,000 SHEETS OF DATA TOOK THE FOUR OF US 30 HOURS.
WE FOUND FIVE POINTS THAT SHOWED AN UNUSUAL AMOUNT OF ACTIVITY AT THE SAME TIME.
ASSUMING THESE ARE CENTERED AROUND A SOURCE...

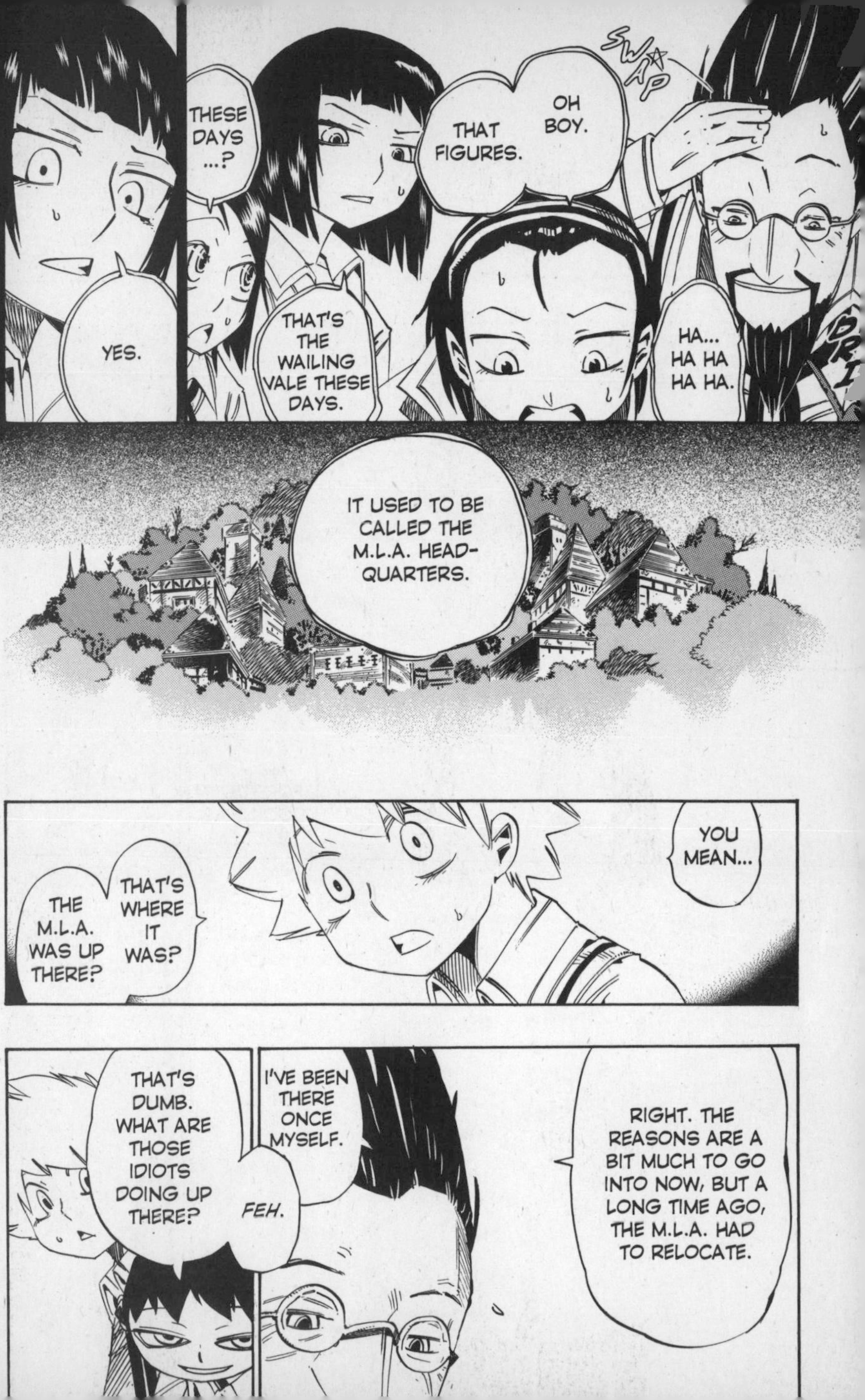
SWAP
OH BOY. THAT FIGURES.
THESE DAYS ...?
HA... HA HA HA HA.
THAT'S THE WAILING VALE THESE DAYS.
YES.
IT USED TO BE CALLED THE M.L.A. HEAD-QUARTERS.
YOU MEAN...
THAT'S WHERE IT WAS? THE M.L.A. WAS UP THERE?
RIGHT. THE REASONS ARE A BIT MUCH TO GO INTO NOW, BUT A LONG TIME AGO, THE M.L.A. HAD TO RELOCATE.
I'VE BEEN THERE ONCE MYSELF.
FEH.
THAT'S DUMB. WHAT ARE THOSE IDIOTS DOING UP THERE?

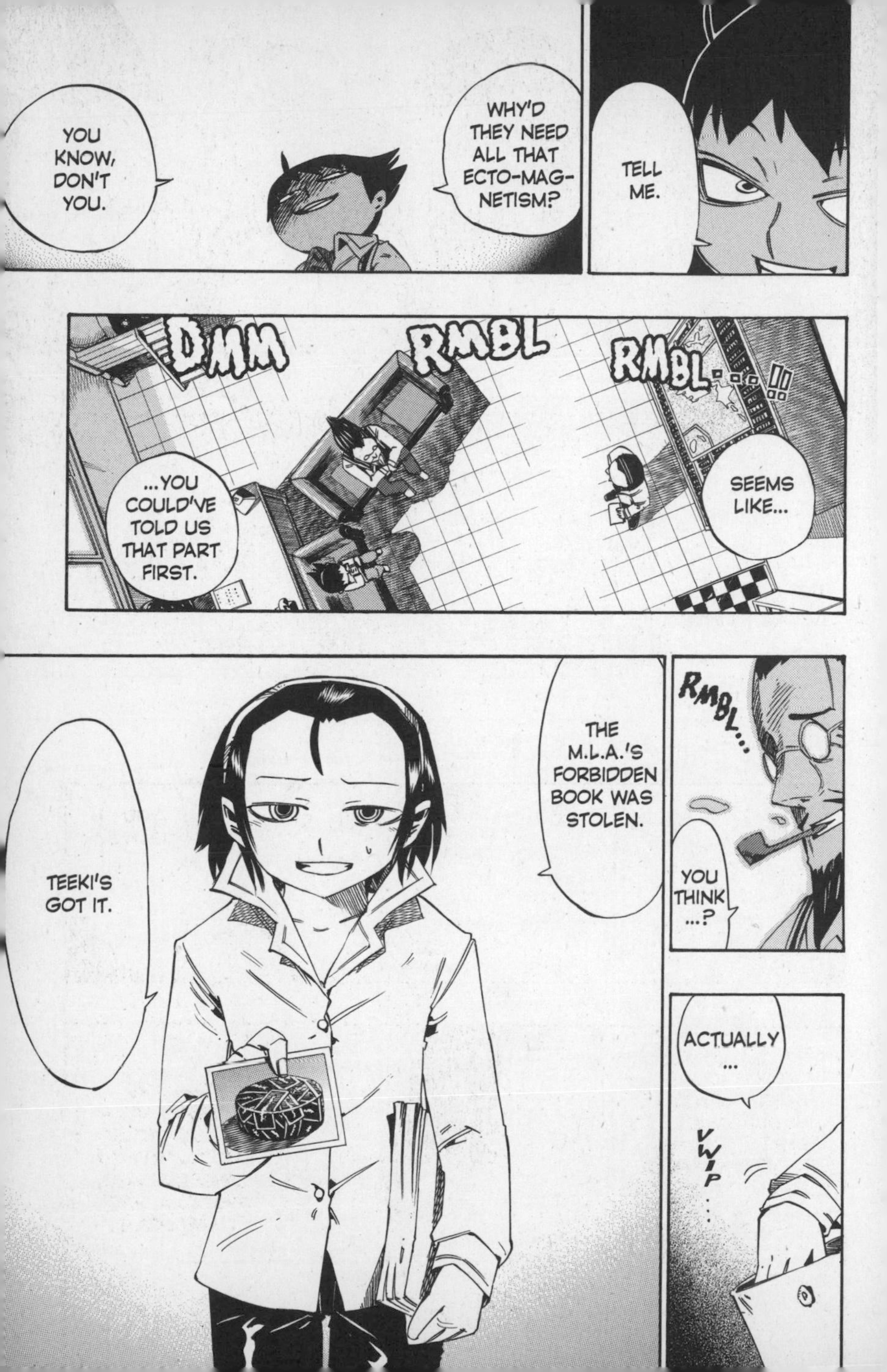
TELL ME.
WHY'D THEY NEED ALL THAT ECTO-MAGNETISM?
YOU KNOW, DON'T YOU.
RMBL... !!
RMBL
DMM
SEEMS LIKE...
...YOU COULD'VE TOLD US THAT PART FIRST.
RMBL...
YOU THINK ...?
ACTUALLY ...
VWIP...
THE M.L.A.'S FORBIDDEN BOOK WAS STOLEN.
TEEKI'S GOT IT.

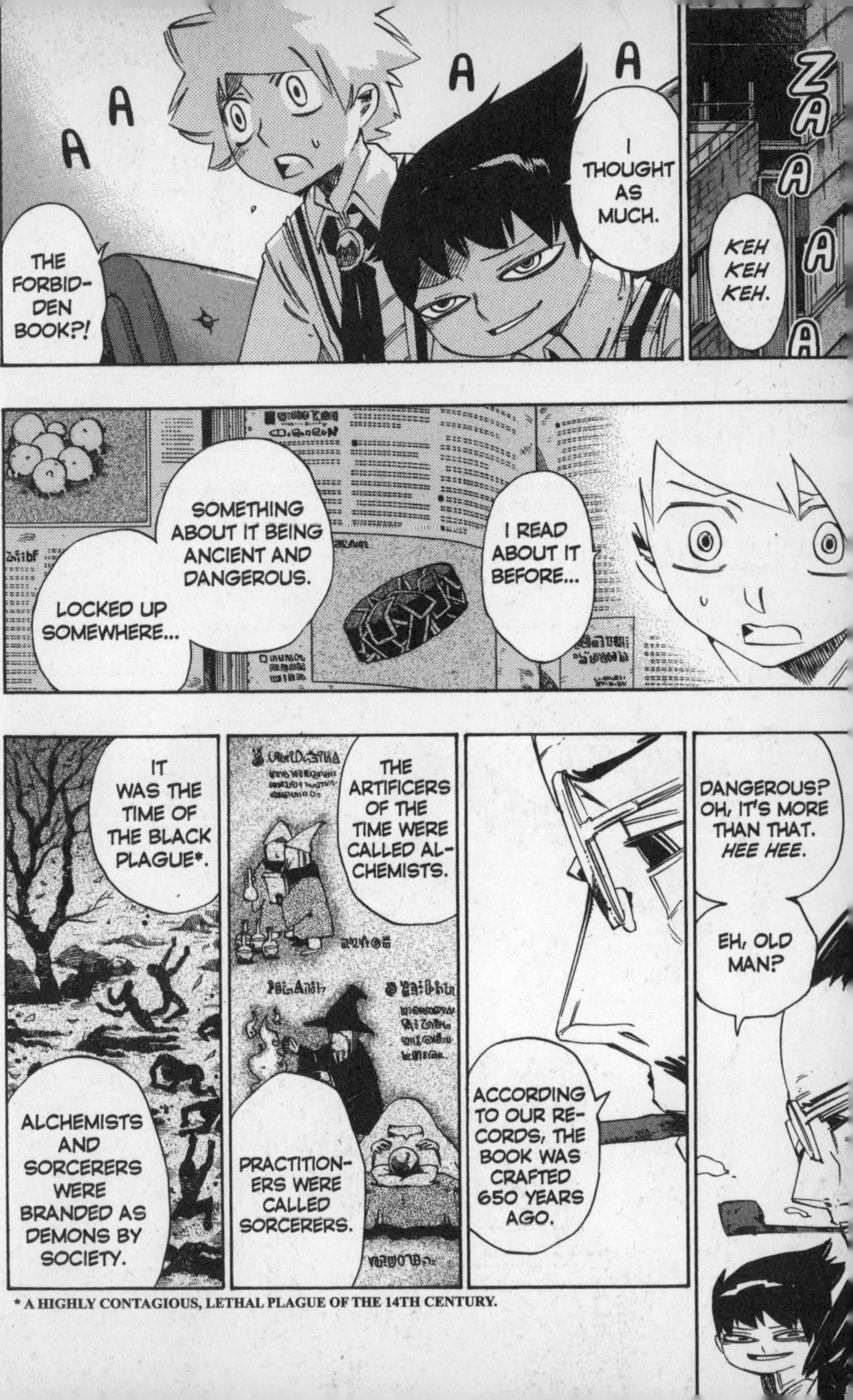
ZAAAAA
KEH KEH KEH.
A A A A A
I THOUGHT AS MUCH.
THE FORBIDDEN BOOK?!
I READ ABOUT IT BEFORE...
SOMETHING ABOUT IT BEING ANCIENT AND DANGEROUS.
LOCKED UP SOMEWHERE...
DANGEROUS? OH, IT'S MORE THAN THAT. *HEE HEE.*
EH, OLD MAN?
ACCORDING TO OUR RECORDS, THE BOOK WAS CRAFTED 650 YEARS AGO.
THE ARTIFICERS OF THE TIME WERE CALLED ALCHEMISTS.
PRACTITIONERS WERE CALLED SORCERERS.
IT WAS THE TIME OF THE BLACK PLAGUE*.
ALCHEMISTS AND SORCERERS WERE BRANDED AS DEMONS BY SOCIETY.

*** A HIGHLY CONTAGIOUS, LETHAL PLAGUE OF THE 14TH CENTURY.**

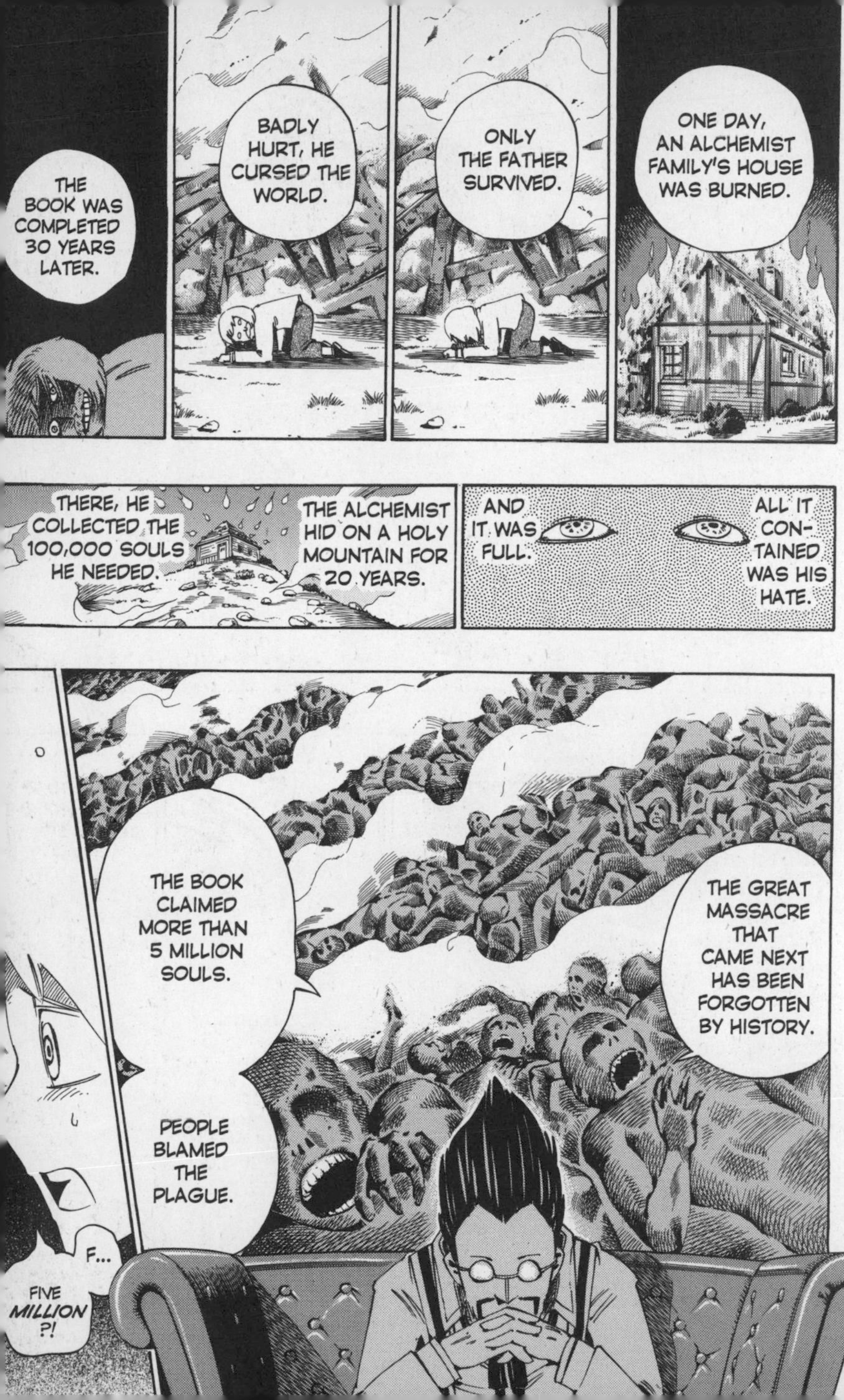
ONE DAY, AN ALCHEMIST FAMILY'S HOUSE WAS BURNED.
ONLY THE FATHER SURVIVED.
BADLY HURT, HE CURSED THE WORLD.
THE BOOK WAS COMPLETED 30 YEARS LATER.
ALL IT CONTAINED WAS HIS HATE.
AND IT WAS FULL.
THE ALCHEMIST HID ON A HOLY MOUNTAIN FOR 20 YEARS.
THERE, HE COLLECTED THE 100,000 SOULS HE NEEDED.
THE GREAT MASSACRE THAT CAME NEXT HAS BEEN FORGOTTEN BY HISTORY.
THE BOOK CLAIMED MORE THAN 5 MILLION SOULS.
PEOPLE BLAMED THE PLAGUE.
F...
FIVE *MILLION* ?!

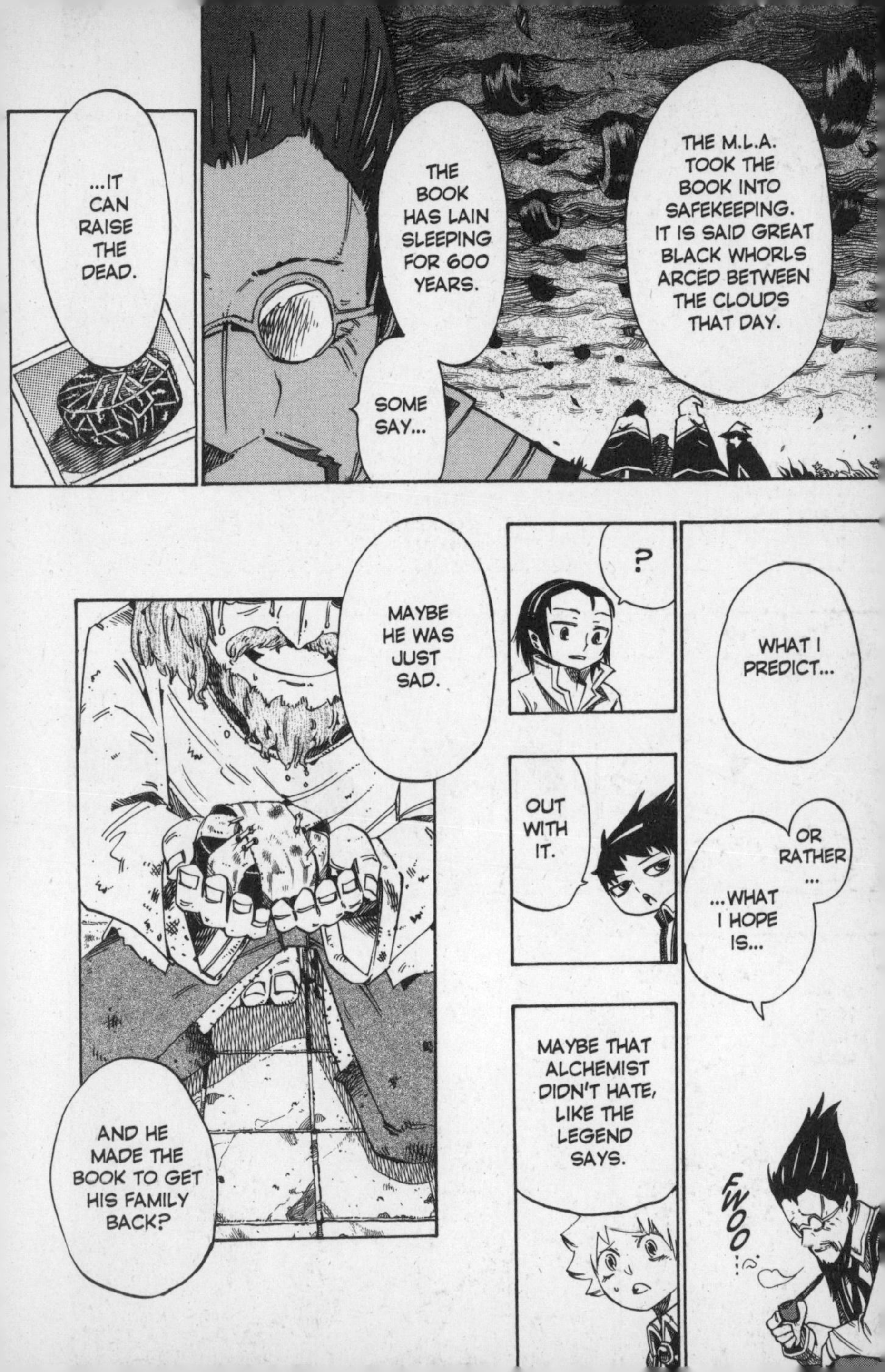
THE M.L.A. TOOK THE BOOK INTO SAFEKEEPING. IT IS SAID GREAT BLACK WHORLS ARCED BETWEEN THE CLOUDS THAT DAY.
THE BOOK HAS LAIN SLEEPING FOR 600 YEARS.
SOME SAY...
...IT CAN RAISE THE DEAD.
WHAT I PREDICT...
?
OUT WITH IT.
OR RATHER ...
...WHAT I HOPE IS...
MAYBE THAT ALCHEMIST DIDN'T HATE, LIKE THE LEGEND SAYS.
FWOO...
MAYBE HE WAS JUST SAD.
AND HE MADE THE BOOK TO GET HIS FAMILY BACK?

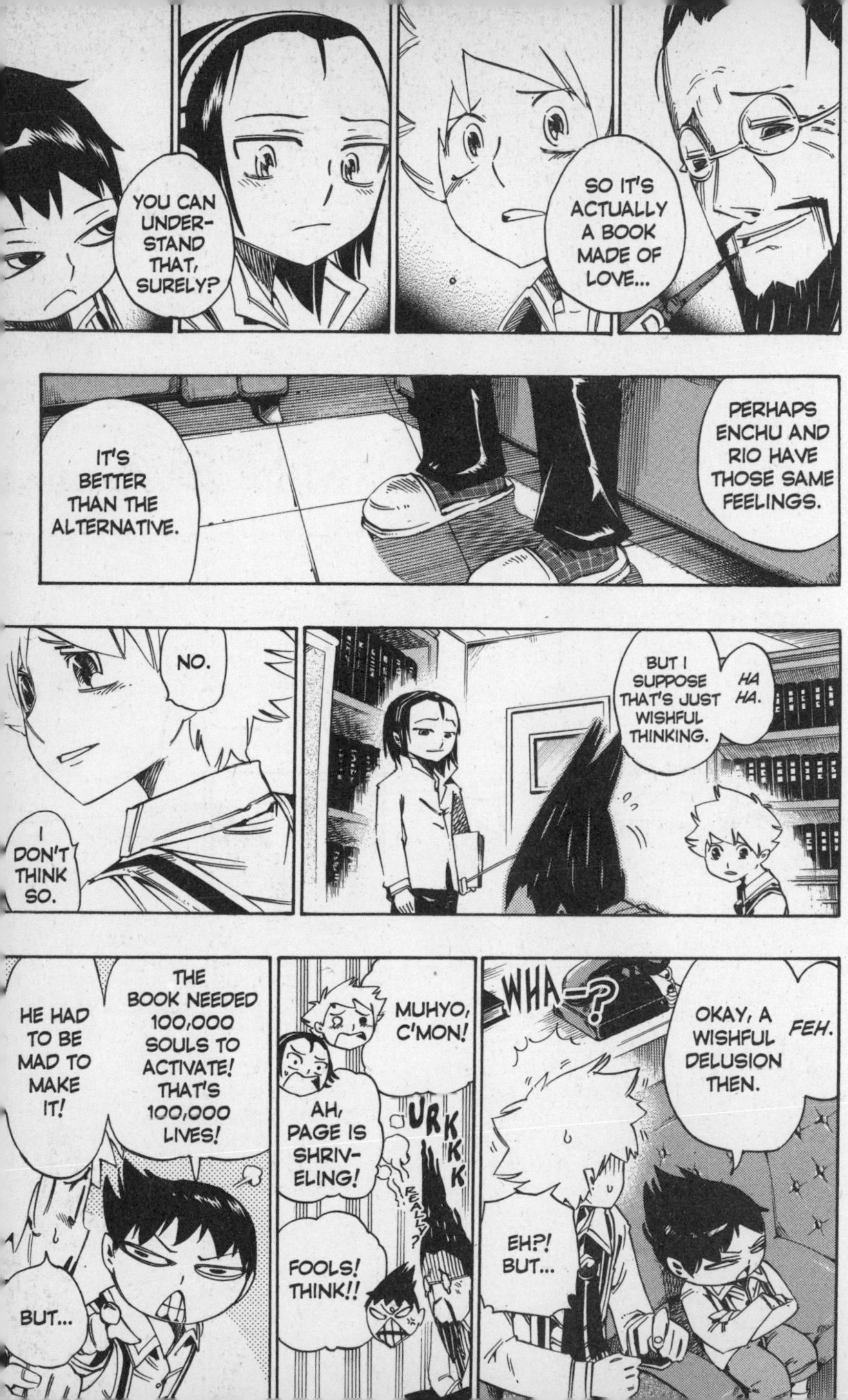
SO IT'S ACTUALLY A BOOK MADE OF LOVE...
YOU CAN UNDER-STAND THAT, SURELY?
PERHAPS ENCHU AND RIO HAVE THOSE SAME FEELINGS.
IT'S BETTER THAN THE ALTERNATIVE.
BUT I SUPPOSE THAT'S JUST WISHFUL THINKING.
HA HA.
NO.
I DON'T THINK SO.
WHA-?
FEH.
OKAY, A WISHFUL DELUSION THEN.
EH?! BUT...
MUHYO, C'MON!
AH, PAGE IS SHRIV-ELING!
URKKK
REALLY?
FOOLS! THINK!!
THE BOOK NEEDED 100,000 SOULS TO ACTIVATE! THAT'S 100,000 LIVES!
HE HAD TO BE MAD TO MAKE IT!
BUT...

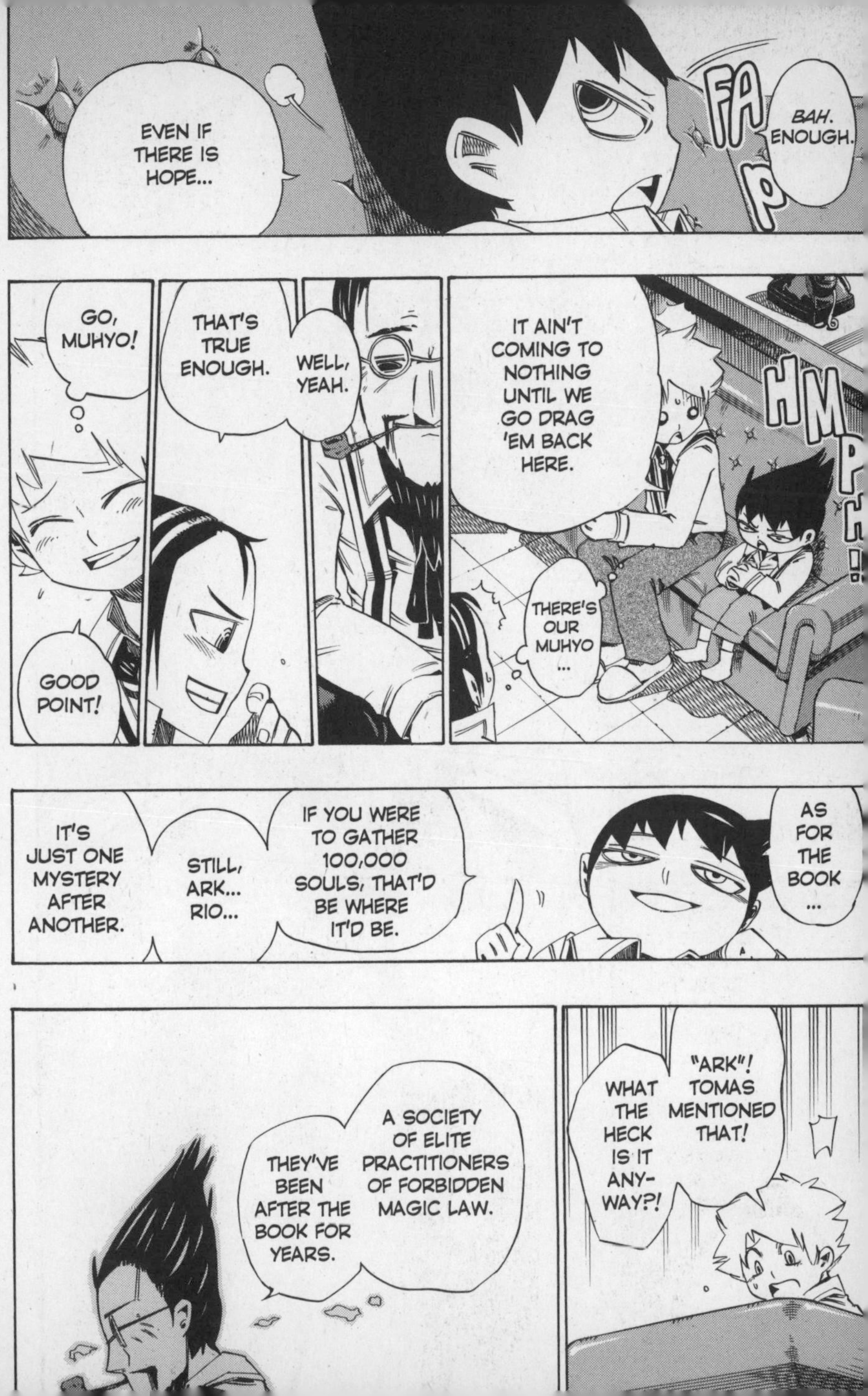
BAH. ENOUGH.
FAP
EVEN IF THERE IS HOPE...
HMPH!!
IT AIN'T COMING TO NOTHING UNTIL WE GO DRAG 'EM BACK HERE.
THERE'S OUR MUHYO...
WELL, YEAH.
THAT'S TRUE ENOUGH.
GO, MUHYO!
GOOD POINT!
AS FOR THE BOOK...
IF YOU WERE TO GATHER 100,000 SOULS, THAT'D BE WHERE IT'D BE.
STILL, ARK... RIO...
IT'S JUST ONE MYSTERY AFTER ANOTHER.
"ARK"! TOMAS MENTIONED THAT!
WHAT THE HECK IS IT ANY-WAY?!
A SOCIETY OF ELITE PRACTITIONERS OF FORBIDDEN MAGIC LAW.
THEY'VE BEEN AFTER THE BOOK FOR YEARS.

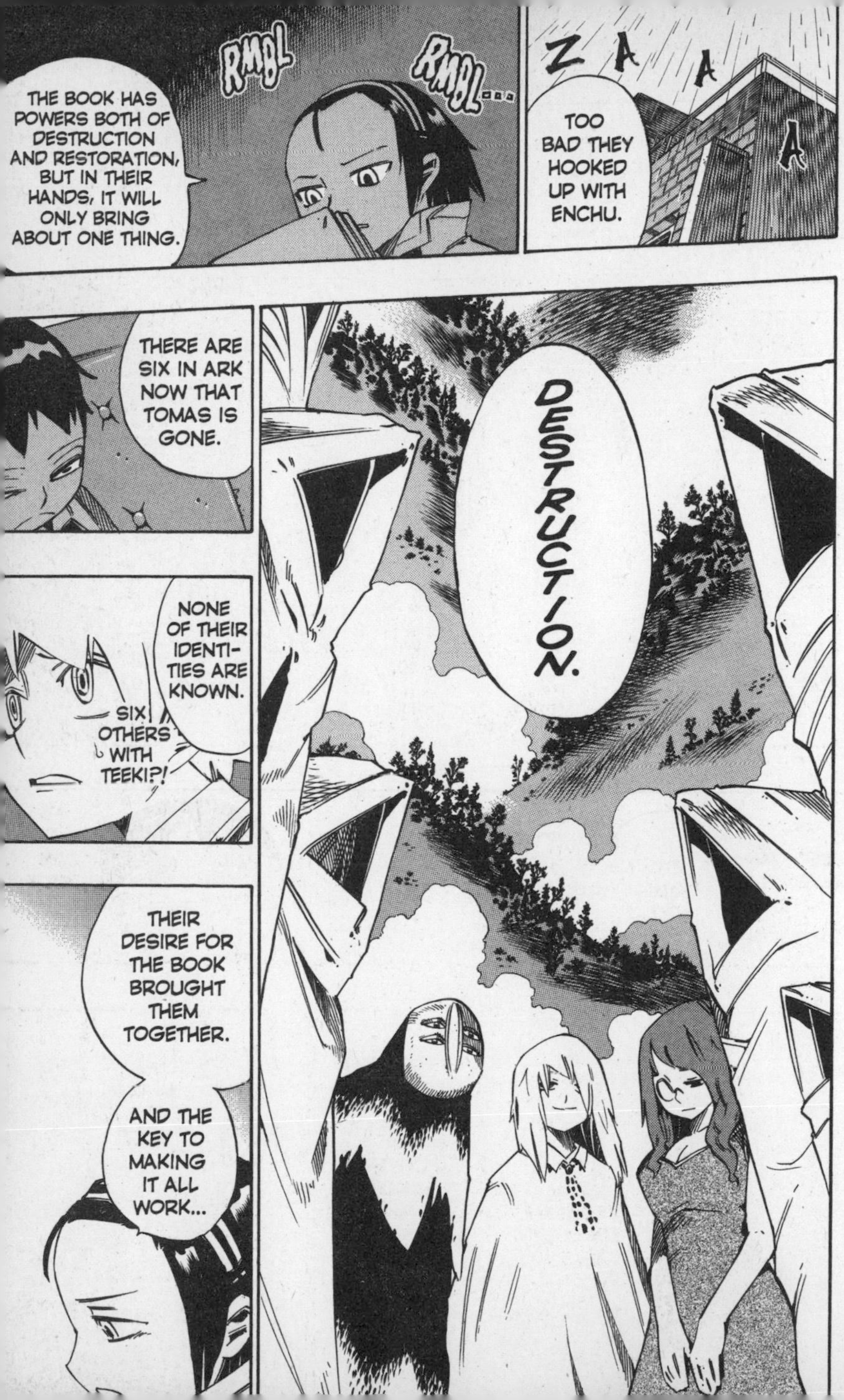
ZAAA
TOO BAD THEY HOOKED UP WITH ENCHU.
RMBL RMBL...
THE BOOK HAS POWERS BOTH OF DESTRUCTION AND RESTORATION, BUT IN THEIR HANDS, IT WILL ONLY BRING ABOUT ONE THING.
DESTRUCTION.
THERE ARE SIX IN ARK NOW THAT TOMAS IS GONE.
NONE OF THEIR IDENTITIES ARE KNOWN.
SIX OTHERS WITH TEEKI?!
THEIR DESIRE FOR THE BOOK BROUGHT THEM TOGETHER.
AND THE KEY TO MAKING IT ALL WORK...

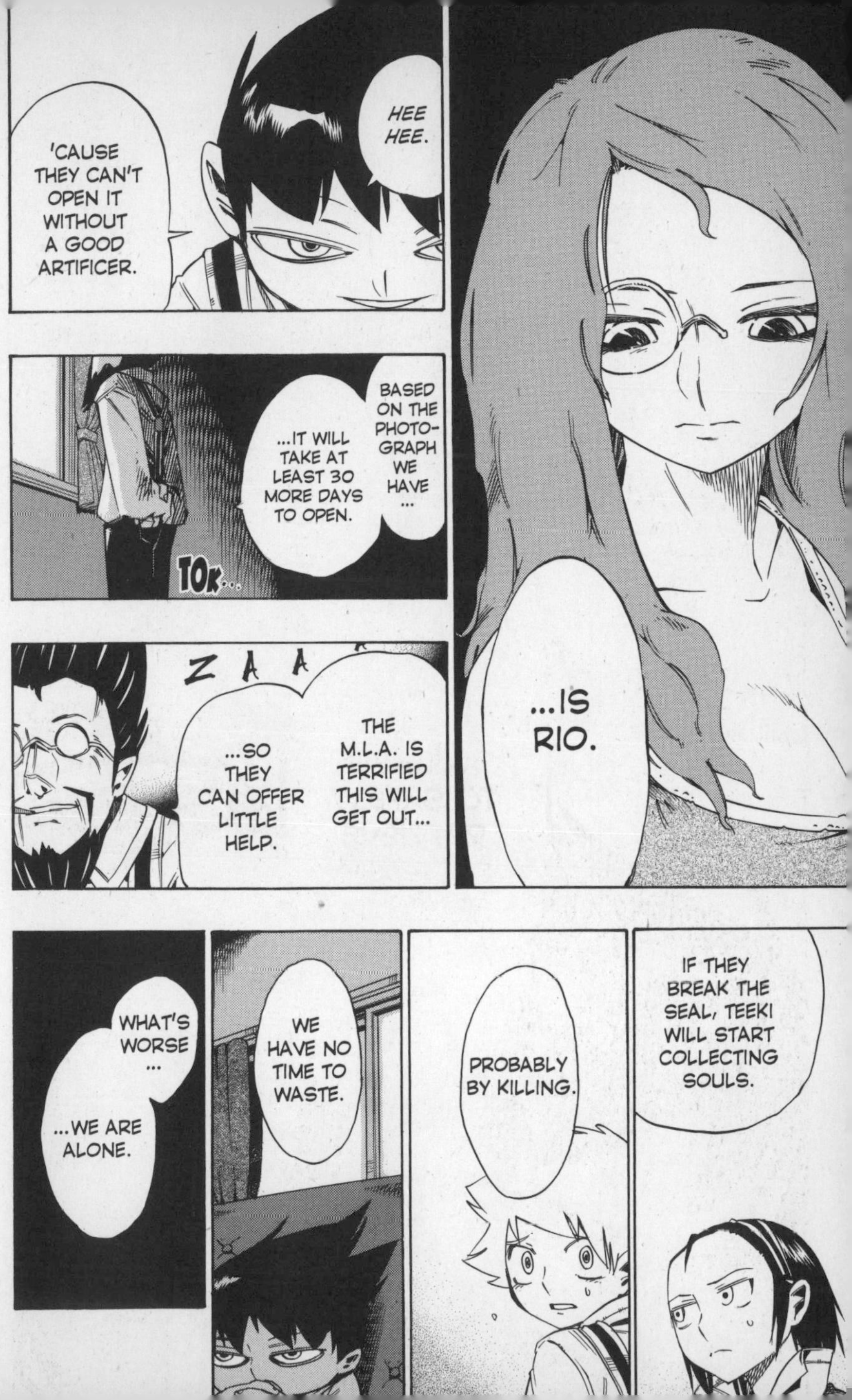
...IS RIO.
HEE HEE.
'CAUSE THEY CAN'T OPEN IT WITHOUT A GOOD ARTIFICER.
BASED ON THE PHOTOGRAPH WE HAVE...
...IT WILL TAKE AT LEAST 30 MORE DAYS TO OPEN.
TOK...
ZAA
THE M.L.A. IS TERRIFIED THIS WILL GET OUT...
...SO THEY CAN OFFER LITTLE HELP.
IF THEY BREAK THE SEAL, TEEKI WILL START COLLECTING SOULS.
PROBABLY BY KILLING.
WE HAVE NO TIME TO WASTE.
WHAT'S WORSE...
...WE ARE ALONE.

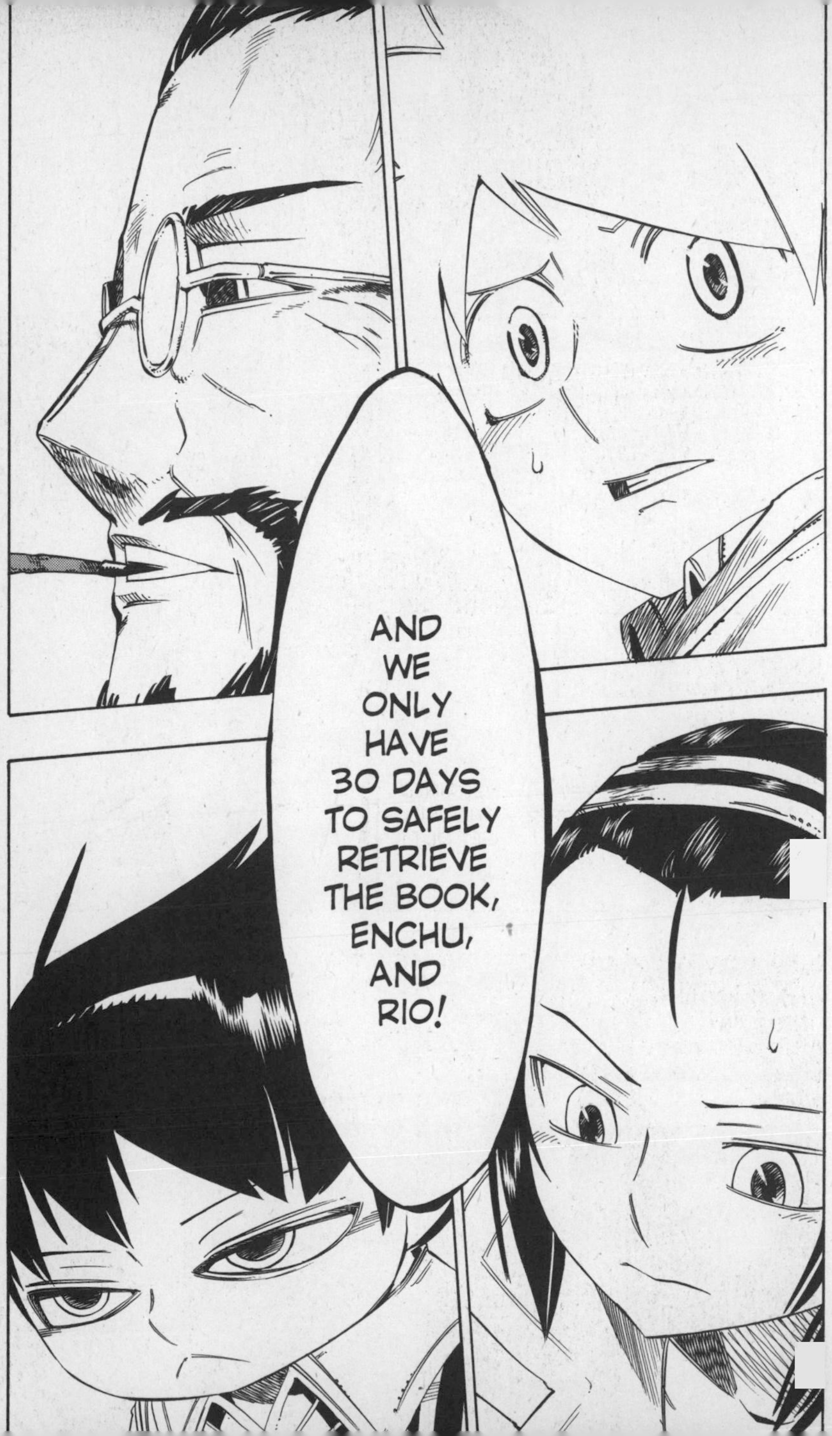
AND WE ONLY HAVE 30 DAYS TO SAFELY RETRIEVE THE BOOK, ENCHU, AND RIO!

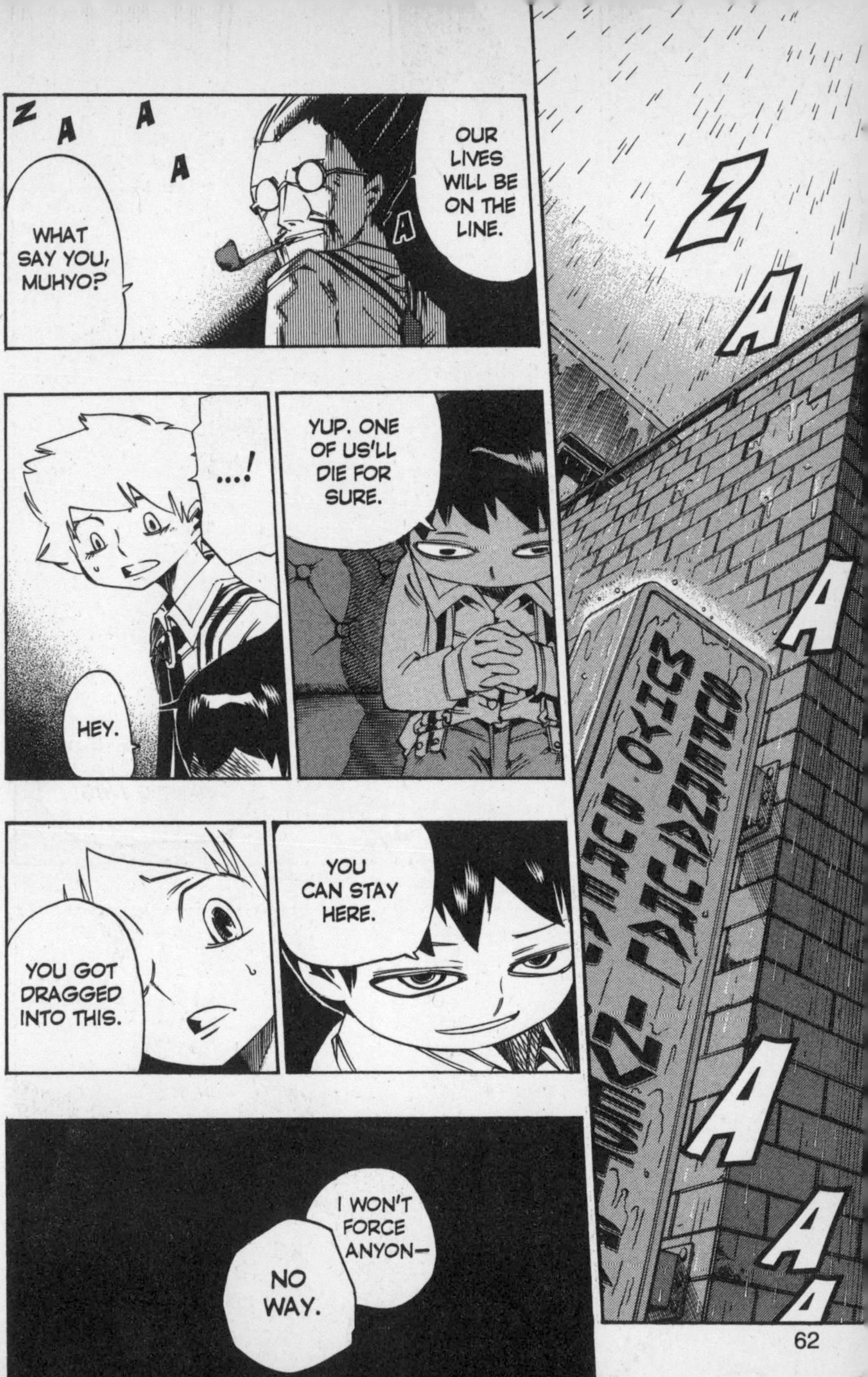
ZAAAAAA
ZAAAA
OUR LIVES WILL BE ON THE LINE.
WHAT SAY YOU, MUHYO?
YUP. ONE OF US'LL DIE FOR SURE.
...!
HEY.
YOU CAN STAY HERE.
YOU GOT DRAGGED INTO THIS.
I WON'T FORCE ANYON—
NO WAY.

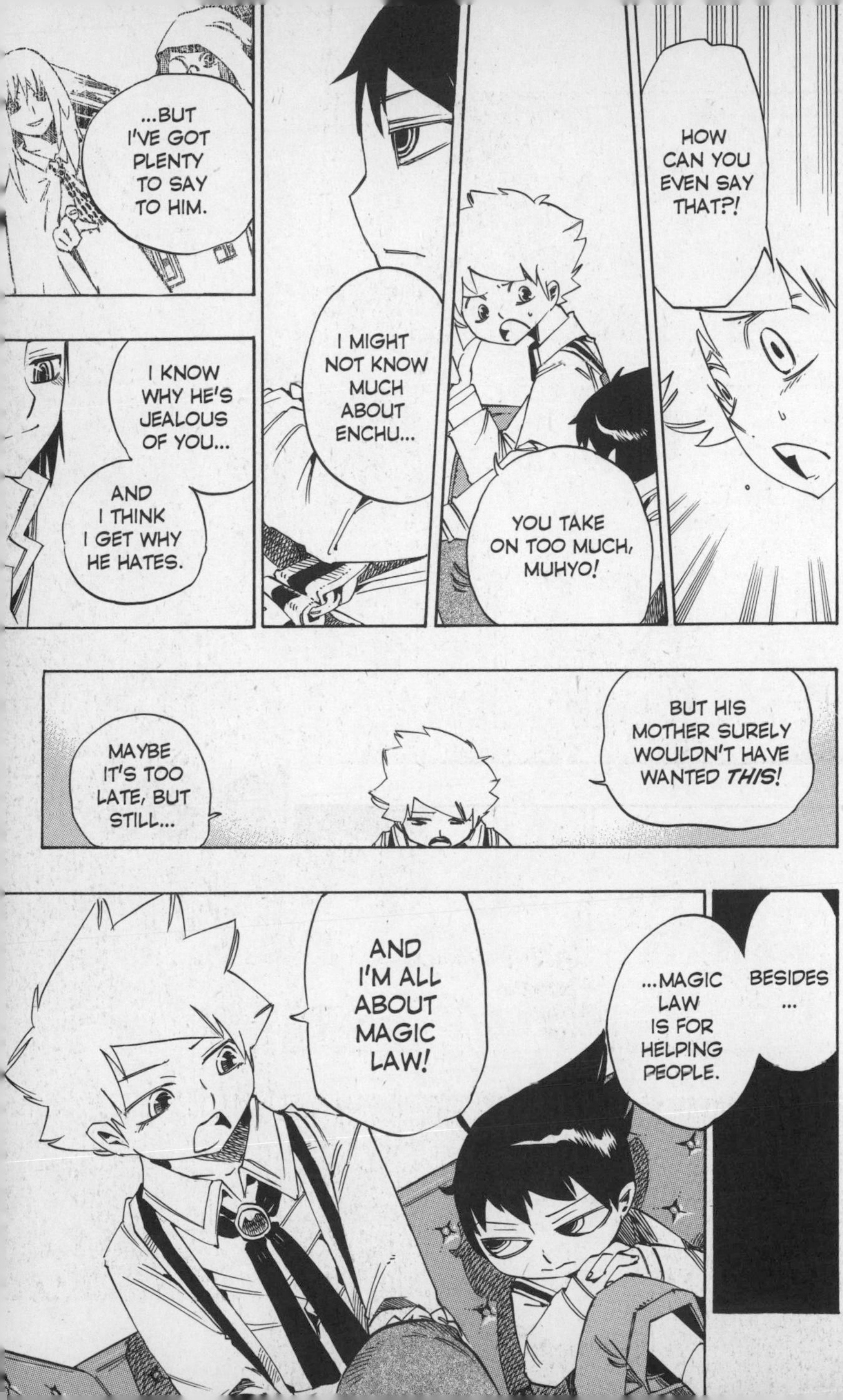
HOW CAN YOU EVEN SAY THAT?!
YOU TAKE ON TOO MUCH, MUHYO!
I MIGHT NOT KNOW MUCH ABOUT ENCHU...
...BUT I'VE GOT PLENTY TO SAY TO HIM.
I KNOW WHY HE'S JEALOUS OF YOU...
AND I THINK I GET WHY HE HATES.
BUT HIS MOTHER SURELY WOULDN'T HAVE WANTED *THIS*!
MAYBE IT'S TOO LATE, BUT STILL...
BESIDES...
...MAGIC LAW IS FOR HELPING PEOPLE.
AND I'M ALL ABOUT MAGIC LAW!

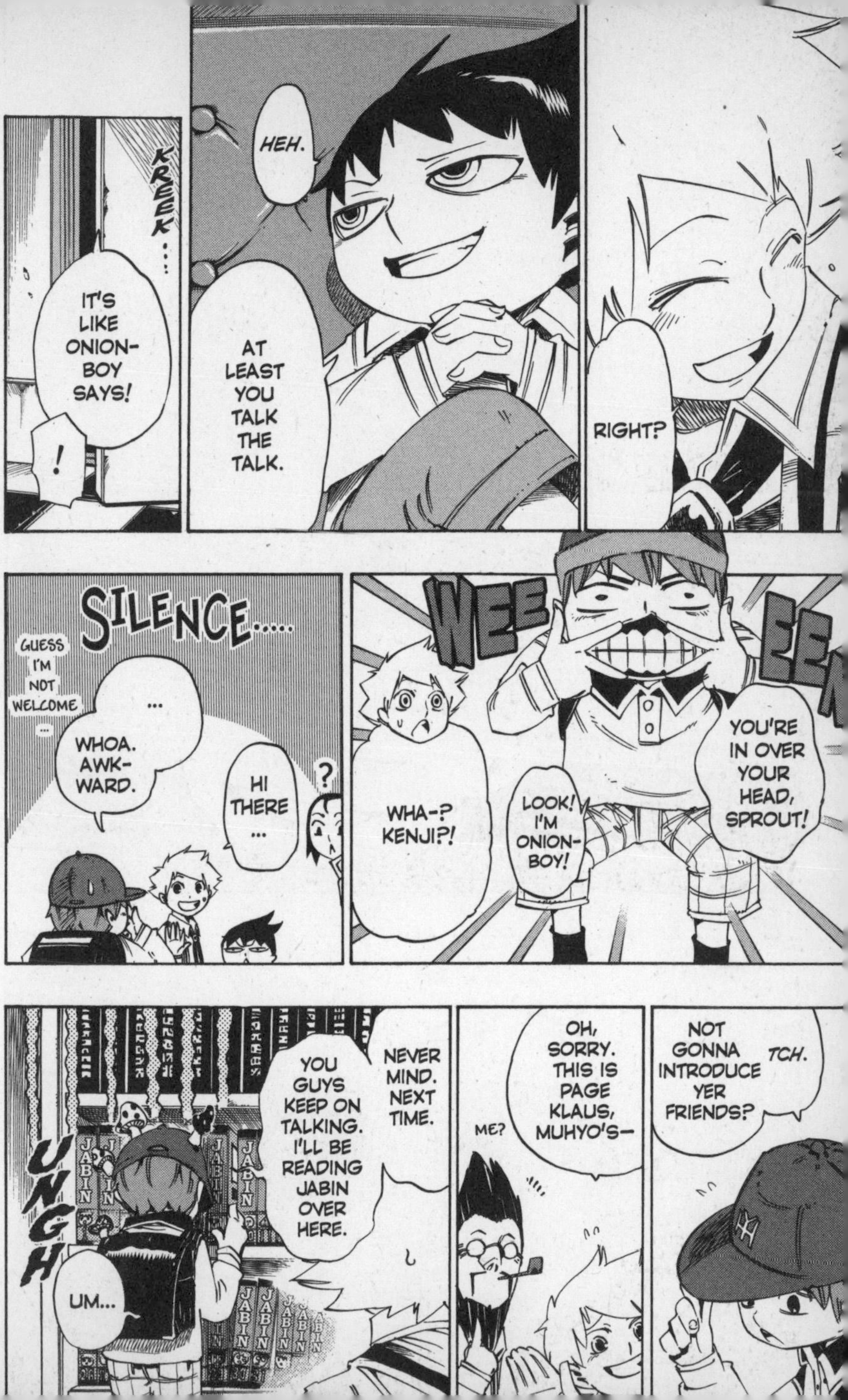
RIGHT?
HEH.
AT LEAST YOU TALK THE TALK.
KREEK...
IT'S LIKE ONION-BOY SAYS!
!
WEE
EEN
YOU'RE IN OVER YOUR HEAD, SPROUT!
LOOK! I'M ONION-BOY!
WHA-? KENJI?!
SILENCE.....
GUESS I'M NOT WELCOME ...
... WHOA. AWK-WARD.
?
HI THERE ...
TCH.
NOT GONNA INTRODUCE YER FRIENDS?
OH, SORRY. THIS IS PAGE KLAUS, MUHYO'S—
ME?
NEVER MIND. NEXT TIME.
YOU GUYS KEEP ON TALKING. I'LL BE READING JABIN OVER HERE.
UNGH
UM...

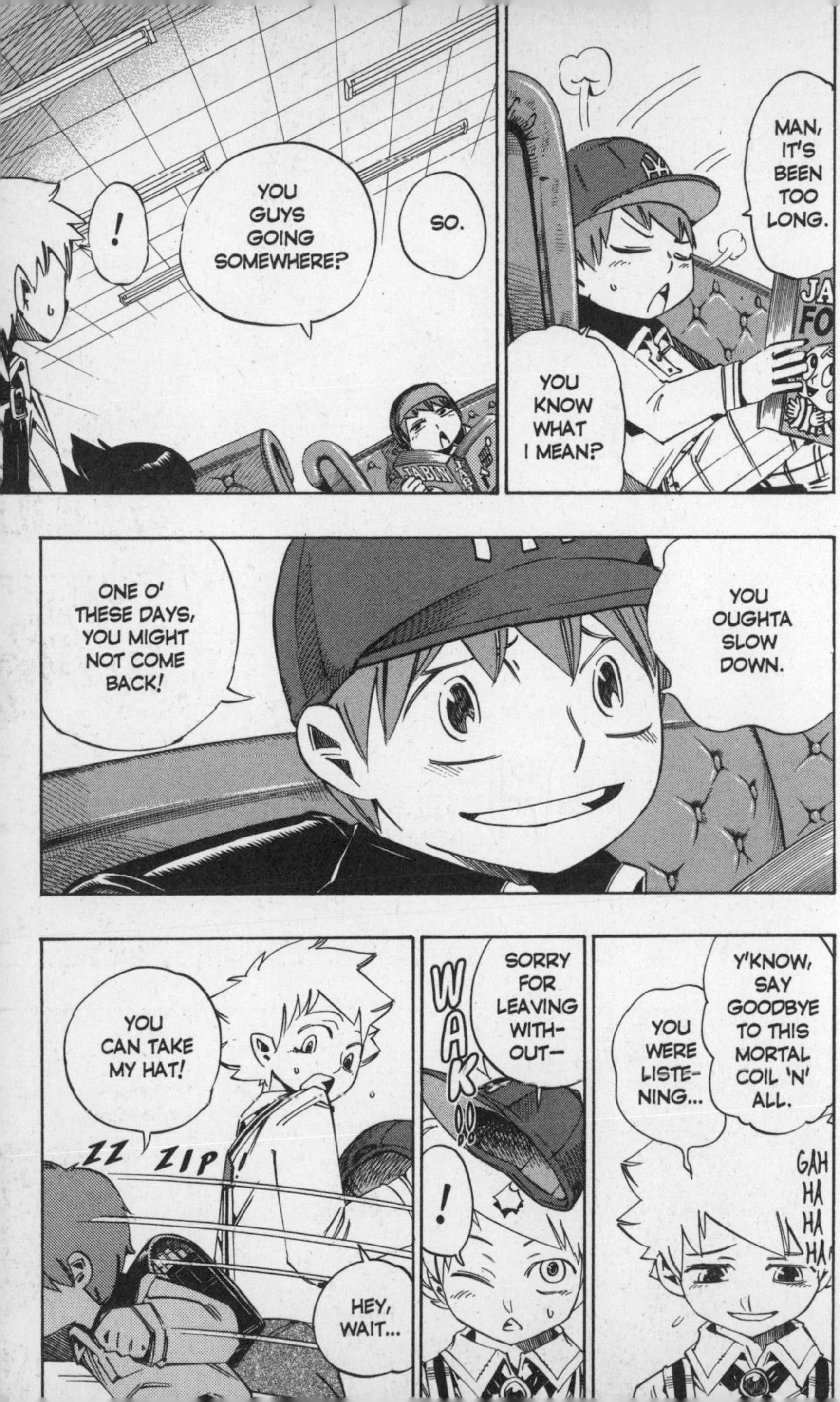
MAN, IT'S BEEN TOO LONG.
YOU KNOW WHAT I MEAN?
SO.
YOU GUYS GOING SOMEWHERE?
!
YOU OUGHTA SLOW DOWN.
ONE O' THESE DAYS, YOU MIGHT NOT COME BACK!
Y'KNOW, SAY GOODBYE TO THIS MORTAL COIL 'N' ALL.
YOU WERE LISTE-NING...
GAH HA HA HA HA
SORRY FOR LEAVING WITH-OUT—
WAK!!
!
YOU CAN TAKE MY HAT!
ZZ ZIP
HEY, WAIT...

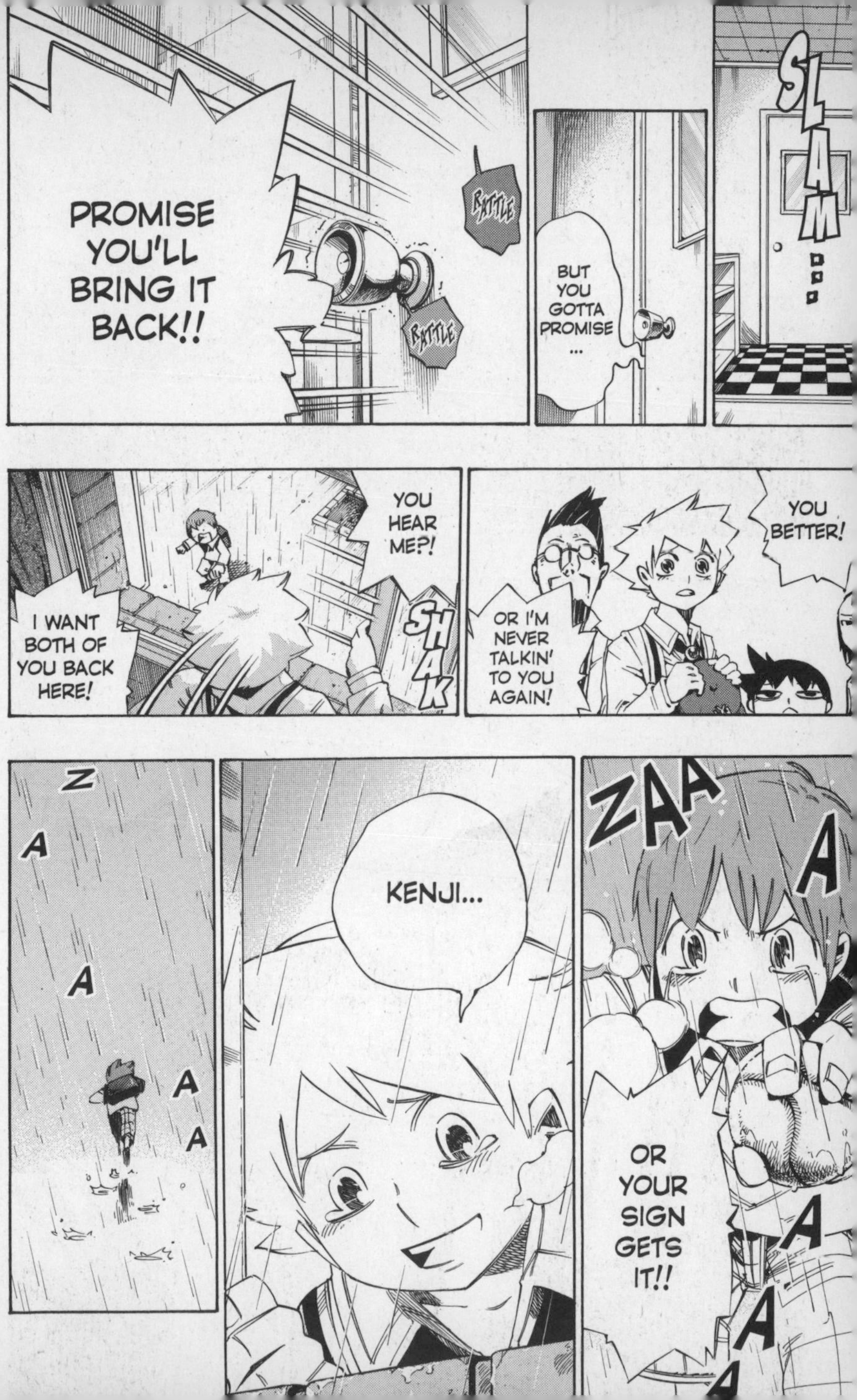
SLAM...
BUT YOU GOTTA PROMISE ...
RATTLE
RATTLE
PROMISE YOU'LL BRING IT BACK!!
YOU BETTER!
OR I'M NEVER TALKIN' TO YOU AGAIN!
YOU HEAR ME?!
SHAK
I WANT BOTH OF YOU BACK HERE!
ZAAAAAA
OR YOUR SIGN GETS IT!!
KENJI...
ZAAAA

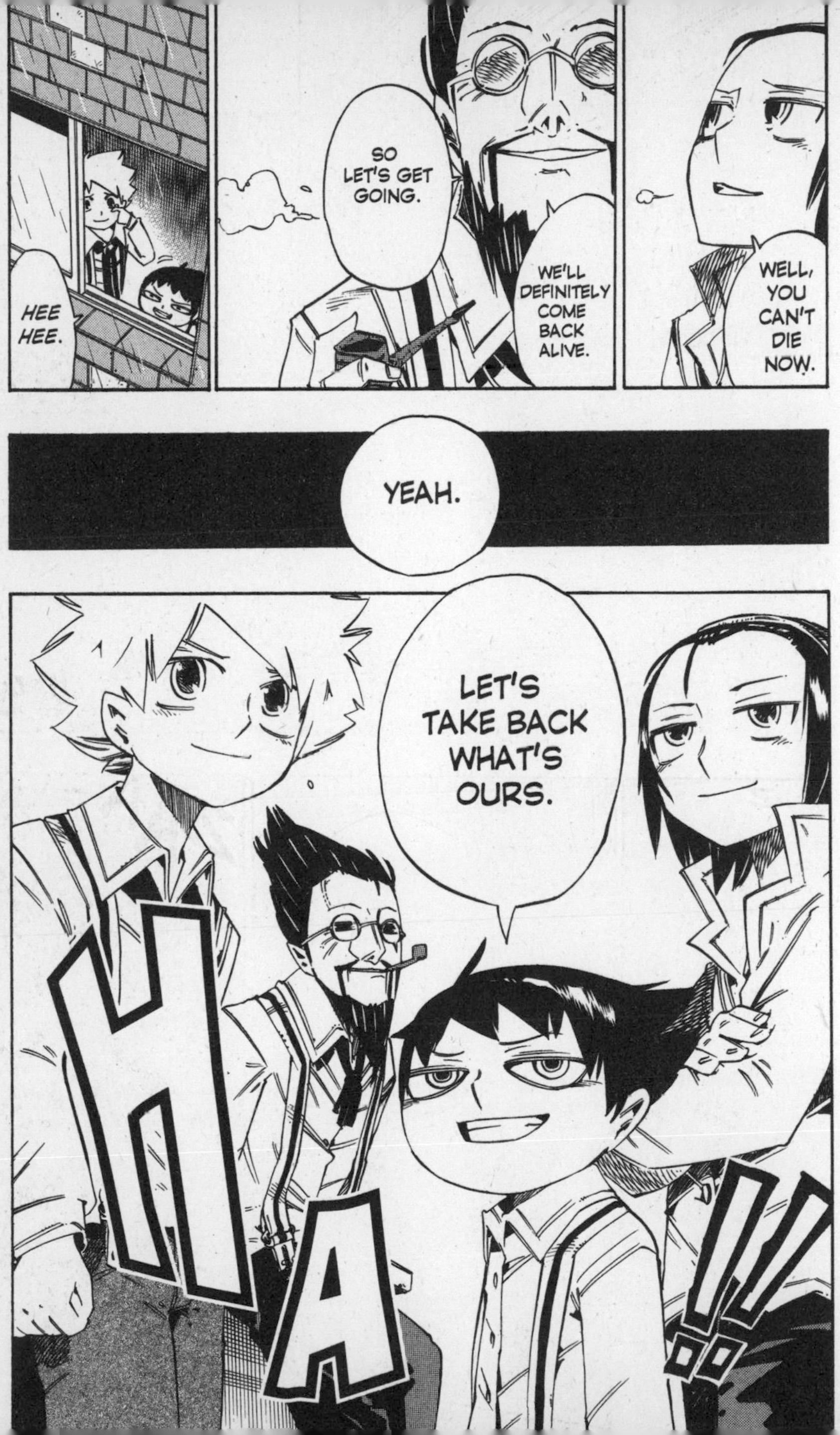
WELL, YOU CAN'T DIE NOW.
WE'LL DEFINITELY COME BACK ALIVE.
SO LET'S GET GOING.
HEE HEE.
YEAH.
LET'S TAKE BACK WHAT'S OURS.
HA!!

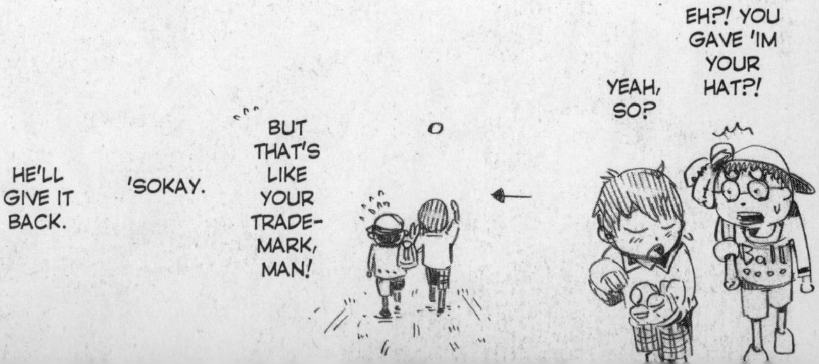

EH?! YOU GAVE 'IM YOUR HAT?!
YEAH, SO?
BUT THAT'S LIKE YOUR TRADE-MARK, MAN!
'SOKAY.
HE'LL GIVE IT BACK.

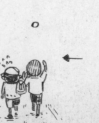

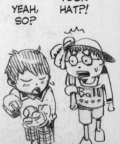

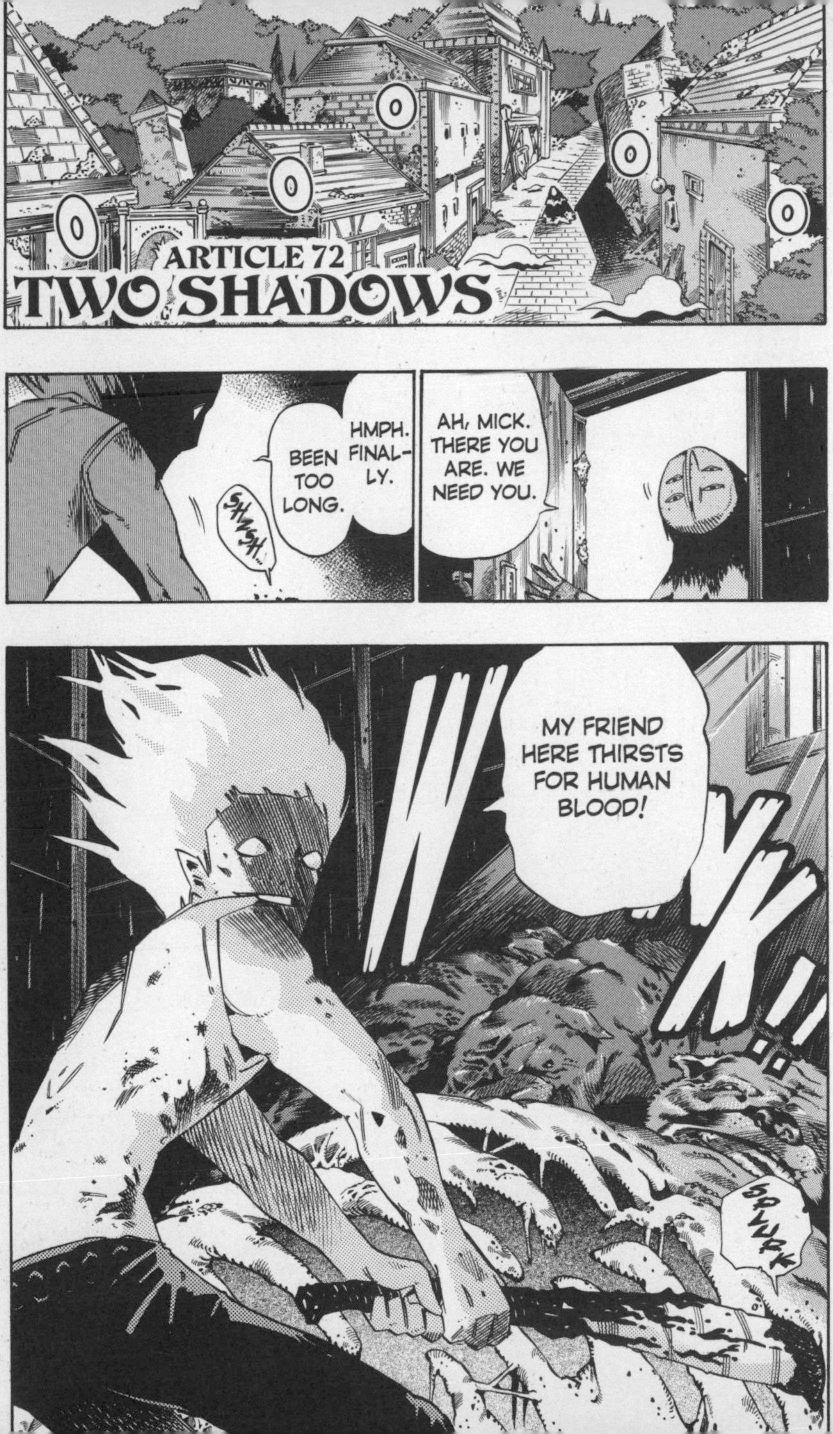
ARTICLE 72
TWO SHADOWS
AH, MICK. THERE YOU ARE. WE NEED YOU.
HMPH. FINAL-LY.
BEEN TOO LONG.
SHASH...
MY FRIEND HERE THIRSTS FOR HUMAN BLOOD!
NX!!
SPLURK

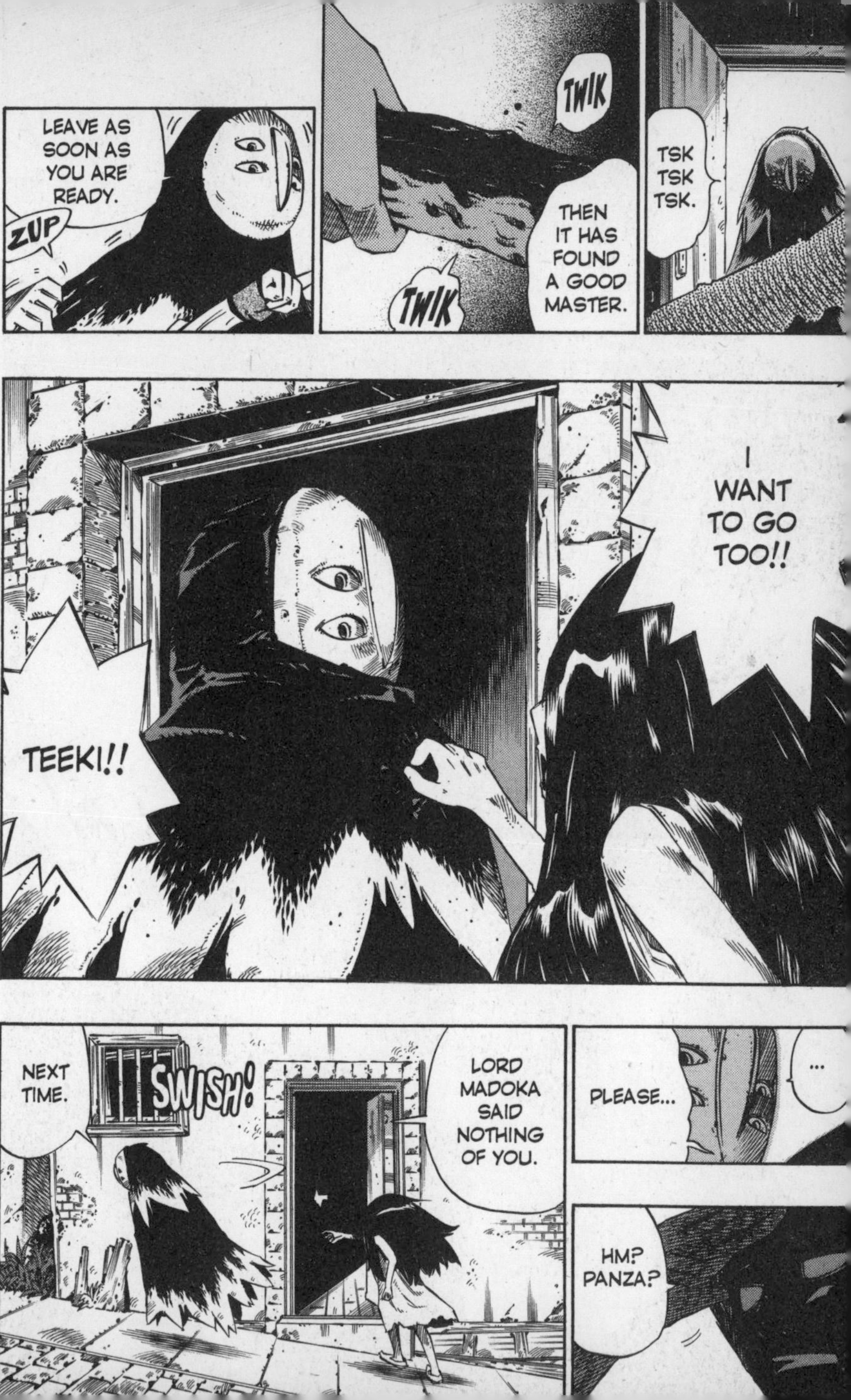
TSK TSK TSK.
TWIK
THEN IT HAS FOUND A GOOD MASTER.
TWIK
LEAVE AS SOON AS YOU ARE READY.
ZUP
I WANT TO GO TOO!!
TEEKI!!
...
PLEASE...
HM? PANZA?
LORD MADOKA SAID NOTHING OF YOU.
SWISH
NEXT TIME.

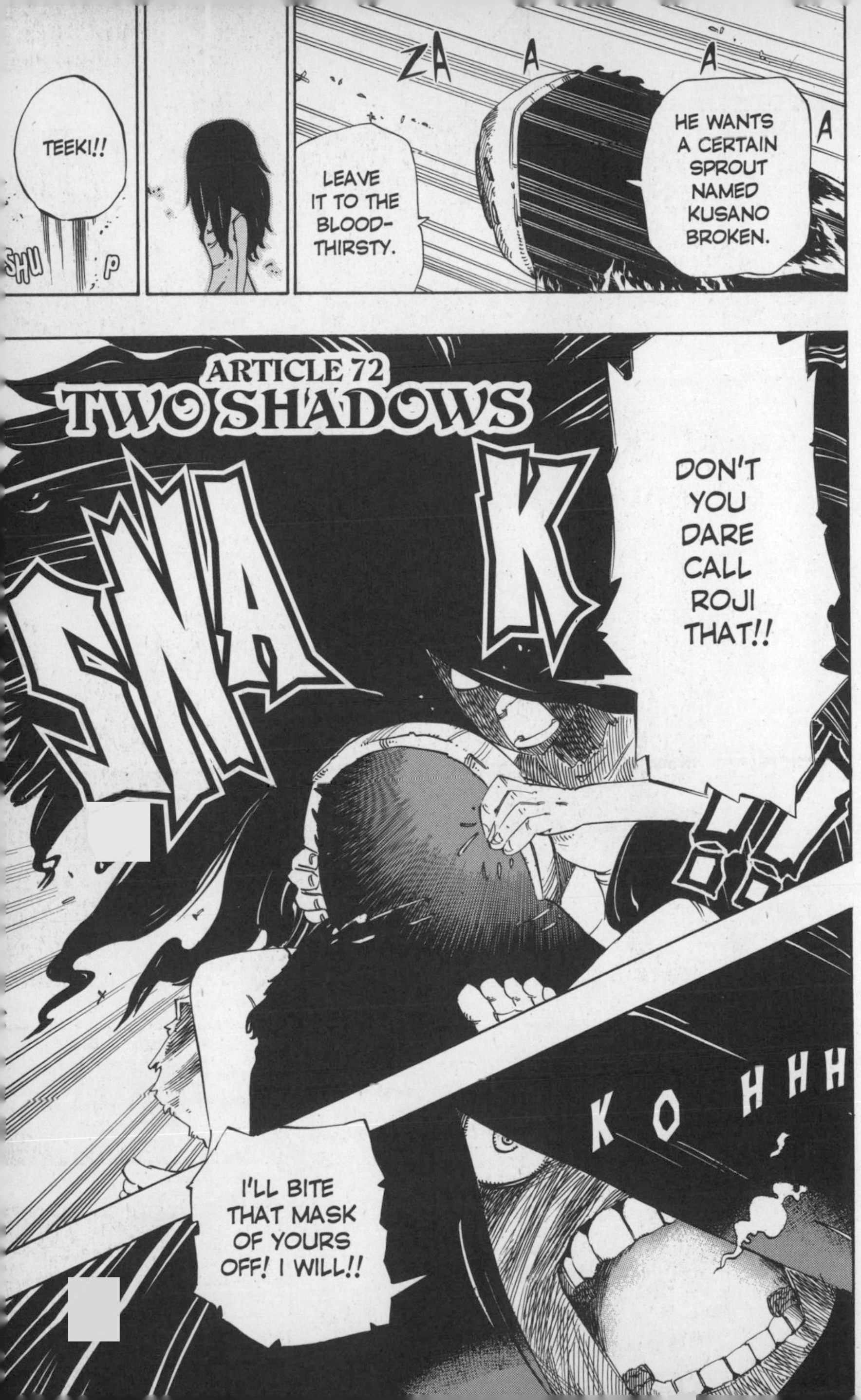
ZA A A A
HE WANTS A CERTAIN SPROUT NAMED KUSANO BROKEN.
LEAVE IT TO THE BLOOD-THIRSTY.
TEEKI!!
SHU P
ARTICLE 72
TWO SHADOWS
DON'T YOU DARE CALL ROJI THAT!!
K O H H H
I'LL BITE THAT MASK OF YOURS OFF! I WILL!!

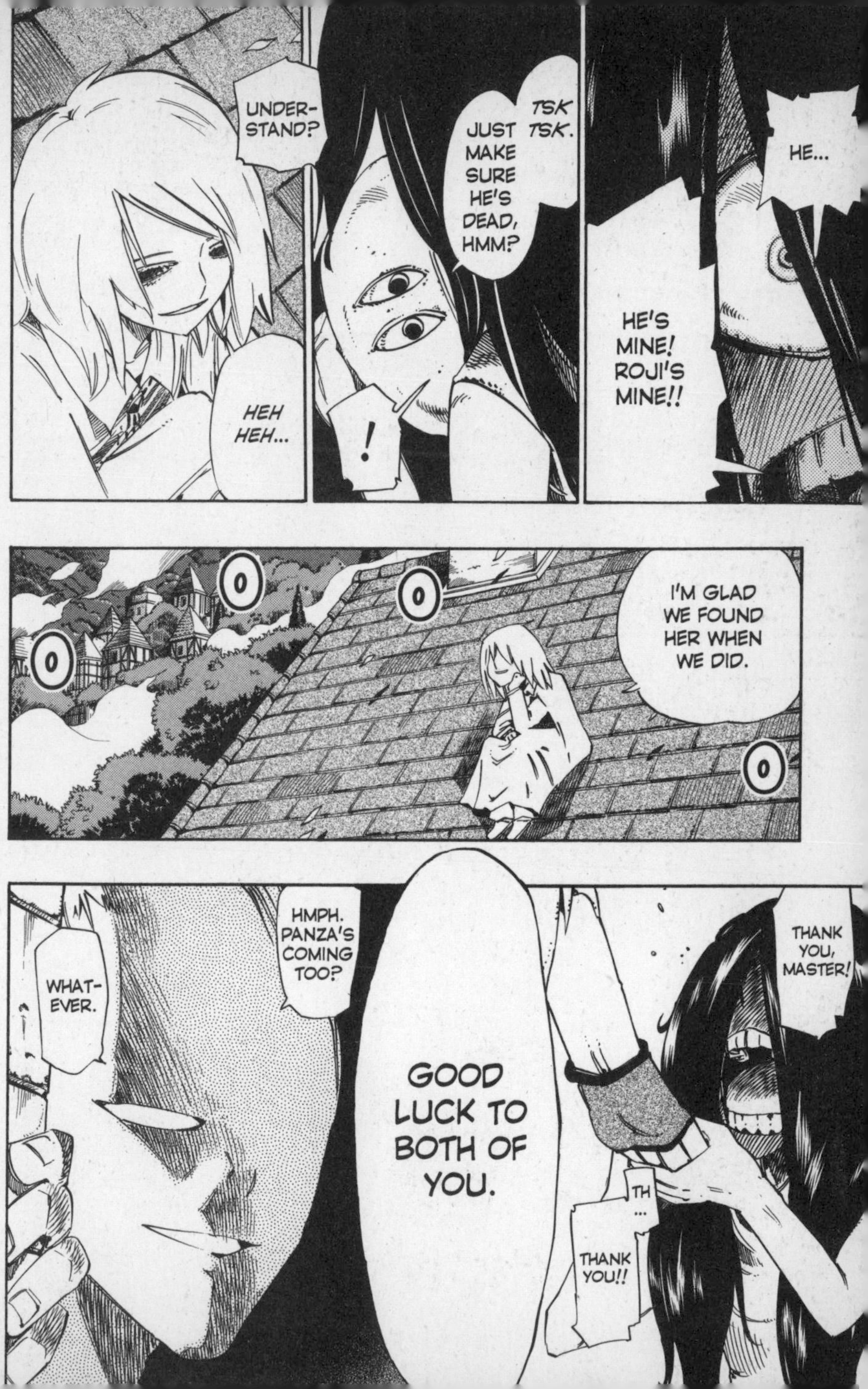
HE...
HE'S MINE! ROJI'S MINE!!
TSK TSK.
JUST MAKE SURE HE'S DEAD, HMM?
!
UNDER-STAND?
HEH HEH...
I'M GLAD WE FOUND HER WHEN WE DID.
THANK YOU, MASTER!
GOOD LUCK TO BOTH OF YOU.
TH...
THANK YOU!!
HMPH. PANZA'S COMING TOO?
WHAT-EVER.

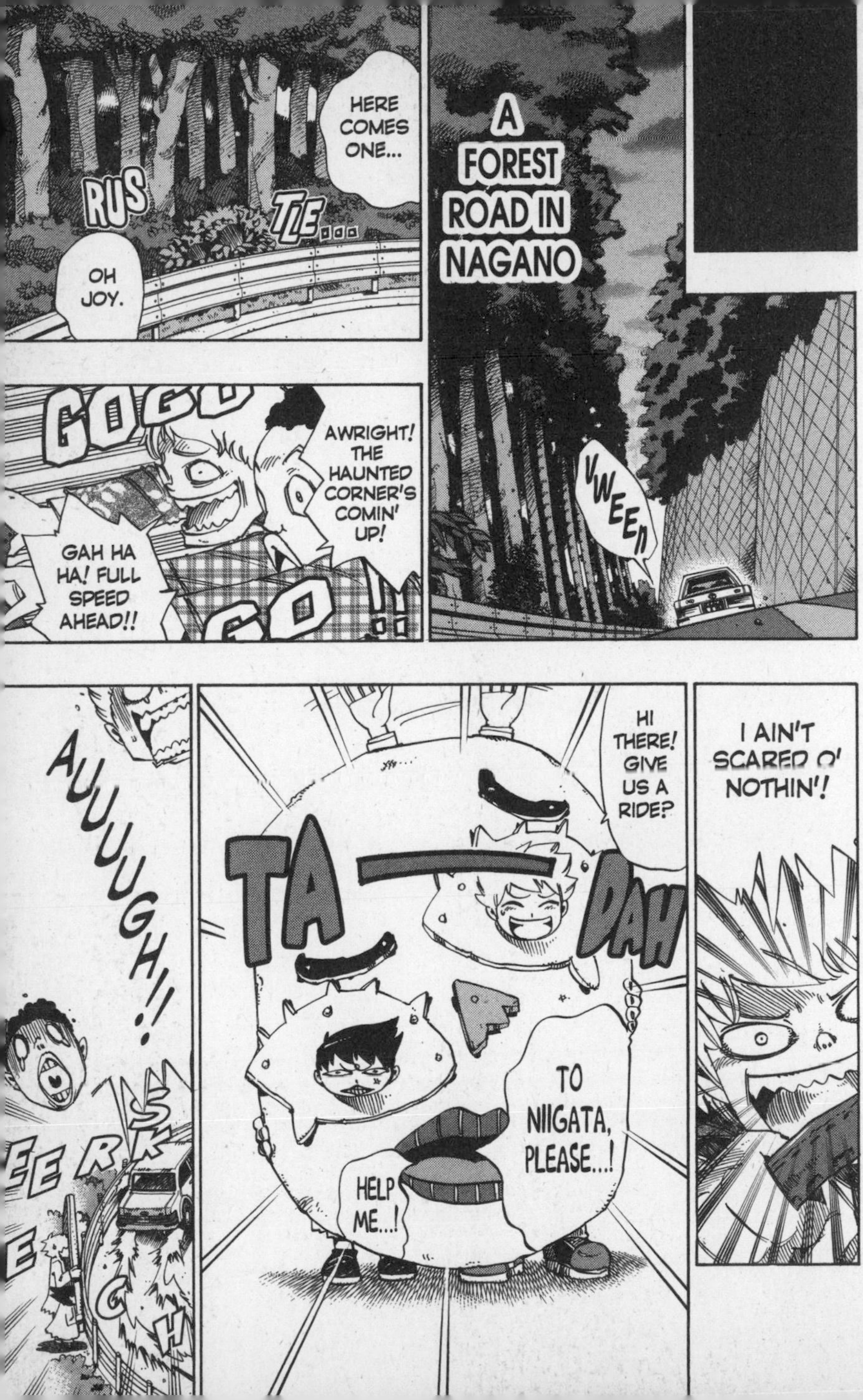
A FOREST ROAD IN NAGANO
VWEE!!
HERE COMES ONE...
RUS
TLE...
OH JOY.
GOGO
AWRIGHT! THE HAUNTED CORNER'S COMIN' UP!
GAH HA HA! FULL SPEED AHEAD!!
GO!!
I AIN'T SCARED O' NOTHIN'!
HI THERE! GIVE US A RIDE?
TA—DAH
TO NIIGATA, PLEASE...!
HELP ME...!
AUUUUGH!!

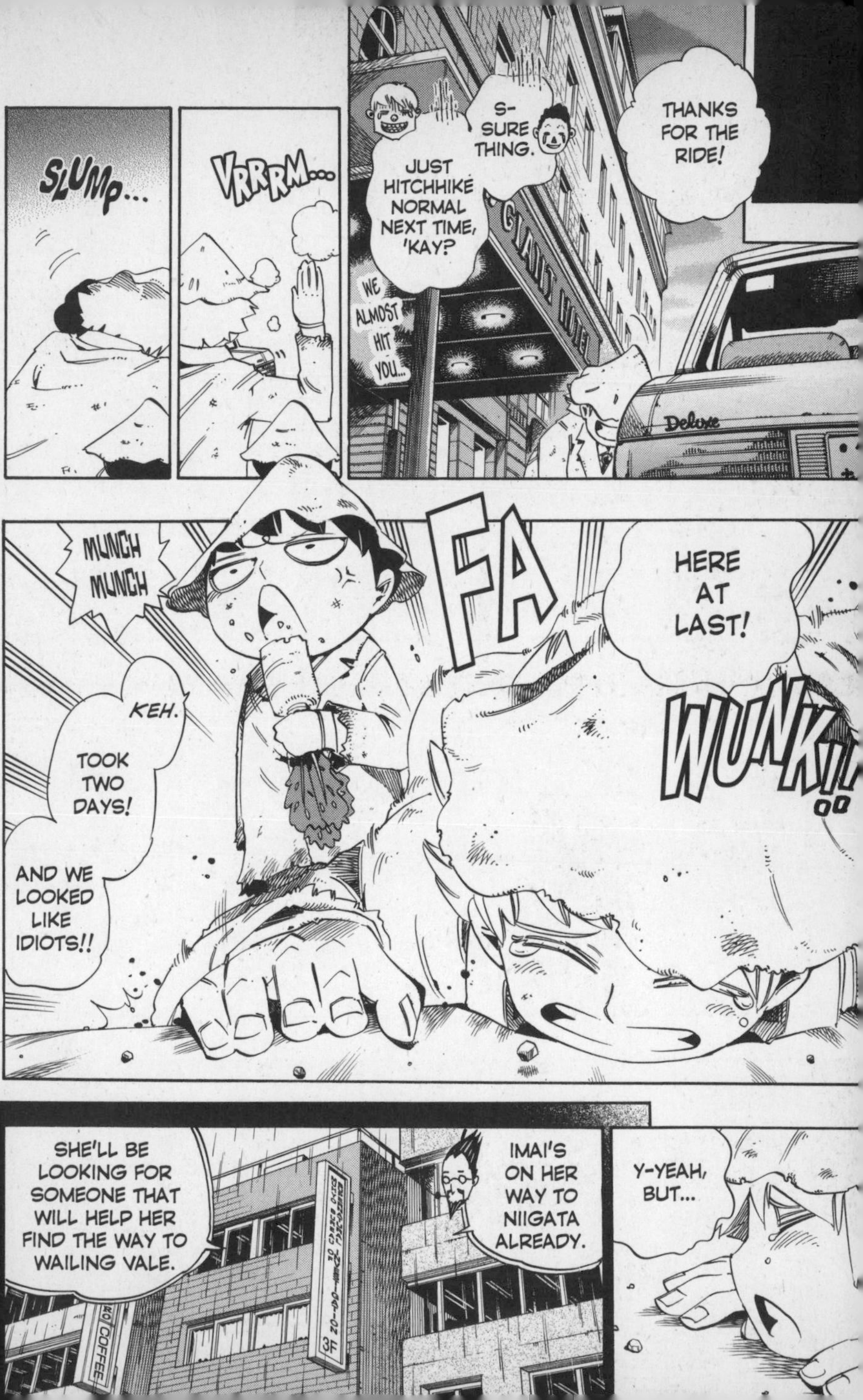
THANKS FOR THE RIDE!
S- SURE THING.
JUST HITCHHIKE NORMAL NEXT TIME, 'KAY?
WE ALMOST HIT YOU...
Deluxe
VRRRM...
SLUMP...
HERE AT LAST!
FA
WUNK!!
MUNCH MUNCH
KEH.
TOOK TWO DAYS!
AND WE LOOKED LIKE IDIOTS!!
Y-YEAH, BUT...
IMAI'S ON HER WAY TO NIIGATA ALREADY.
SHE'LL BE LOOKING FOR SOMEONE THAT WILL HELP HER FIND THE WAY TO WAILING VALE.
3F
COFFEE

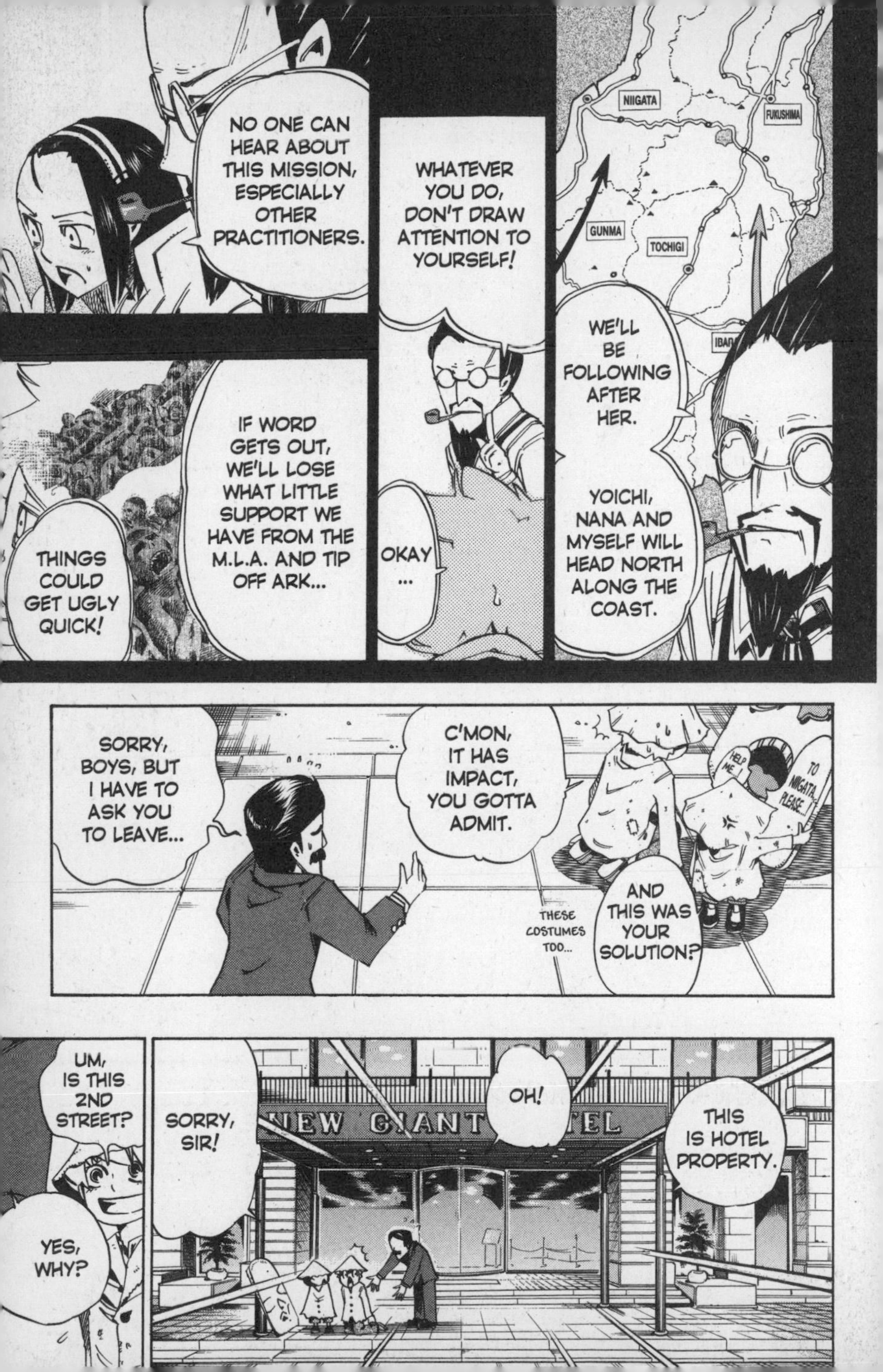
NIIGATA
FUKUSHIMA
GUNMA
TOCHIGI
WE'LL BE FOLLOWING AFTER HER.
YOICHI, NANA AND MYSELF WILL HEAD NORTH ALONG THE COAST.
WHATEVER YOU DO, DON'T DRAW ATTENTION TO YOURSELF!
OKAY...
NO ONE CAN HEAR ABOUT THIS MISSION, ESPECIALLY OTHER PRACTITIONERS.
IF WORD GETS OUT, WE'LL LOSE WHAT LITTLE SUPPORT WE HAVE FROM THE M.L.A. AND TIP OFF ARK...
THINGS COULD GET UGLY QUICK!
TO NIIGATA PLEASE...!
HELP ME...!
AND THIS WAS YOUR SOLUTION?
THESE COSTUMES TOO...
C'MON, IT HAS IMPACT, YOU GOTTA ADMIT.
SORRY, BOYS, BUT I HAVE TO ASK YOU TO LEAVE...
THIS IS HOTEL PROPERTY.
OH!
SORRY, SIR!
NEW GIANT
UM, IS THIS 2ND STREET?
YES, WHY?

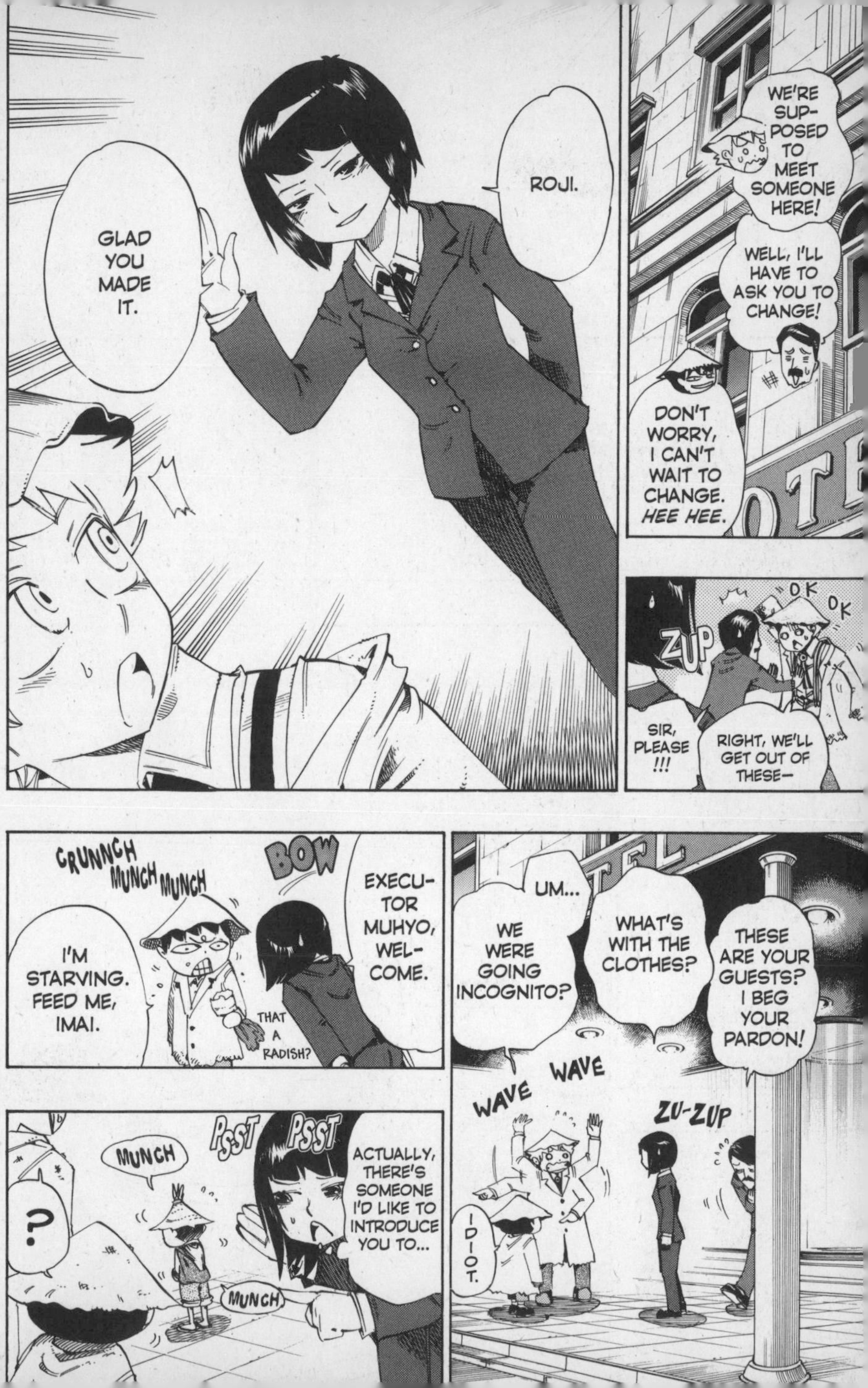
WE'RE SUP-POSED TO MEET SOMEONE HERE!
WELL, I'LL HAVE TO ASK YOU TO CHANGE!
DON'T WORRY, I CAN'T WAIT TO CHANGE. *HEE HEE.*
OK OK
ZUP
RIGHT, WE'LL GET OUT OF THESE—
SIR, PLEASE!!!
ROJI.
GLAD YOU MADE IT.
THESE ARE YOUR GUESTS? I BEG YOUR PARDON!
WHAT'S WITH THE CLOTHES?
UM... WE WERE GOING INCOGNITO?
ZU-ZUP
WAVE WAVE
I-DI-OT.
BOW
EXECU-TOR MUHYO, WEL-COME.
CRUNNCH MUNCH MUNCH
THAT A RADISH?
I'M STARVING. FEED ME, IMAI.
PSST PSST
ACTUALLY, THERE'S SOMEONE I'D LIKE TO INTRODUCE YOU TO...
MUNCH
MUNCH
?

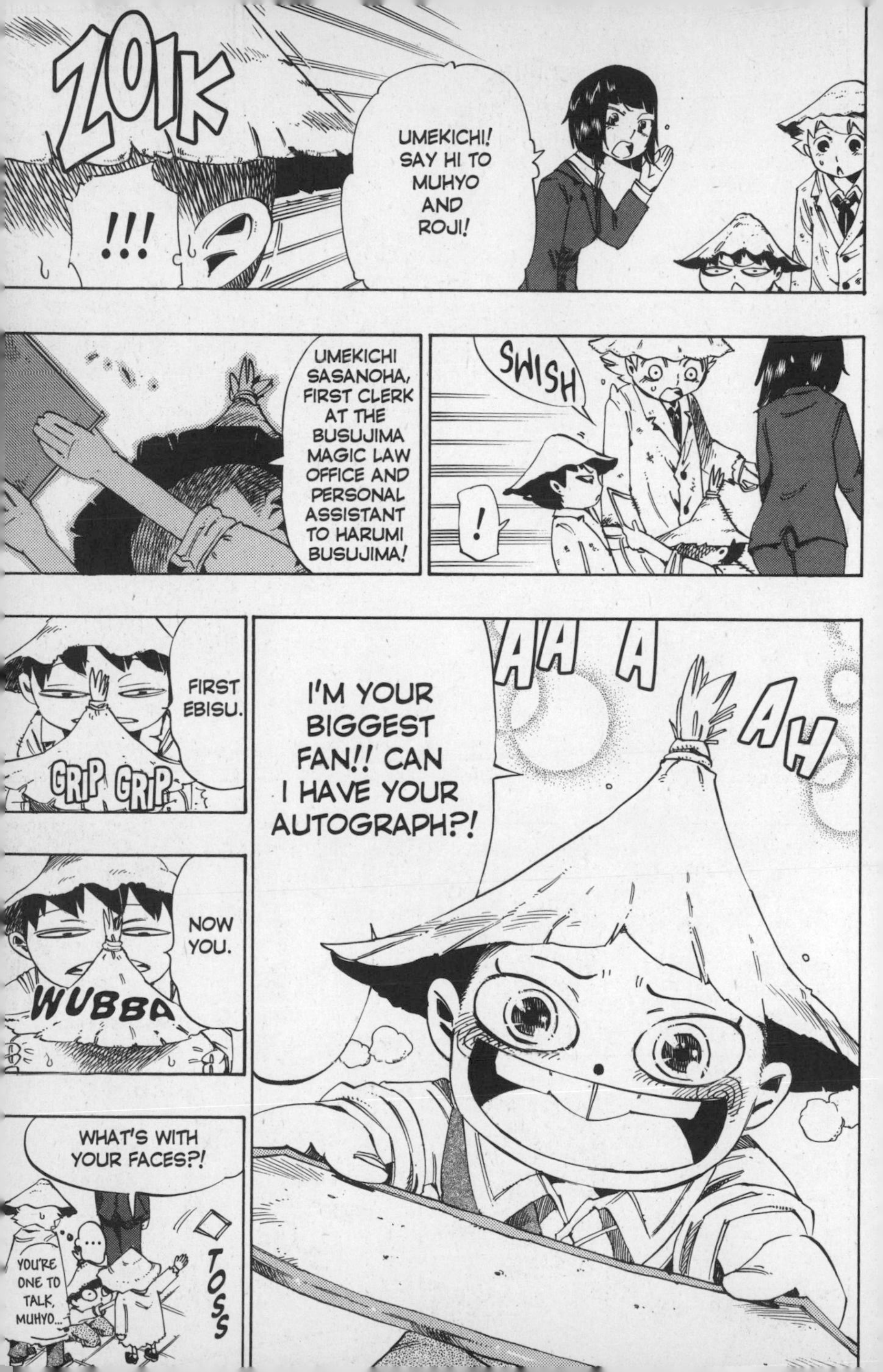
UMEKICHI! SAY HI TO MUHYO AND ROJI!
ZOIK
!!!
SWISH
!
UMEKICHI SASANOHA, FIRST CLERK AT THE BUSUJIMA MAGIC LAW OFFICE AND PERSONAL ASSISTANT TO HARUMI BUSUJIMA!
AAAAH
I'M YOUR BIGGEST FAN!! CAN I HAVE YOUR AUTOGRAPH?!
FIRST EBISU.
GRIP GRIP
NOW YOU.
WUBBA
WHAT'S WITH YOUR FACES?!
...
TOSS
YOU'RE ONE TO TALK, MUHYO...

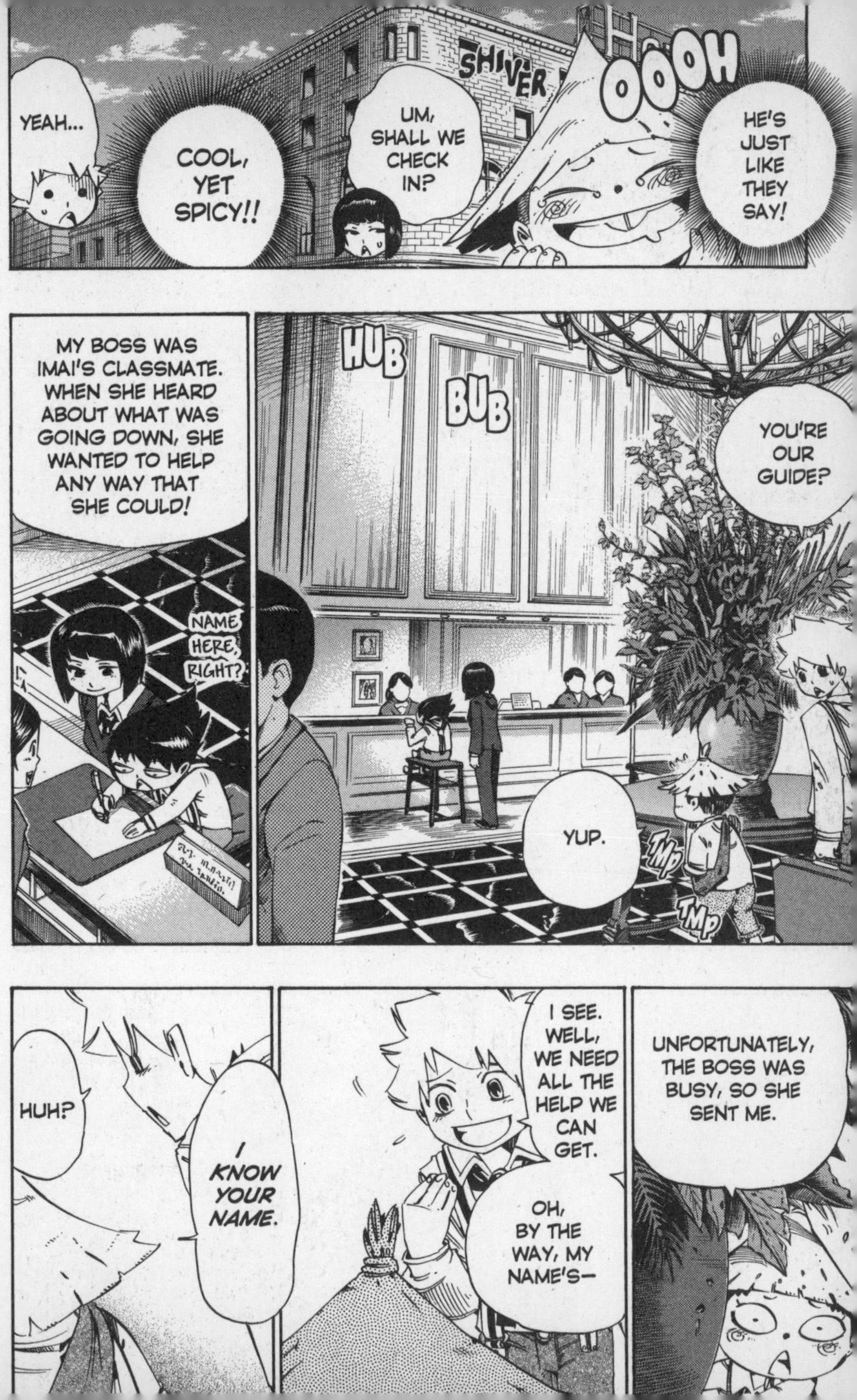
OOOH
HE'S JUST LIKE THEY SAY!
SHIVER
UM, SHALL WE CHECK IN?
COOL, YET SPICY!!
YEAH...
HUB BUB
YOU'RE OUR GUIDE?
YUP.
TMP TMP
MY BOSS WAS IMAI'S CLASSMATE. WHEN SHE HEARD ABOUT WHAT WAS GOING DOWN, SHE WANTED TO HELP ANY WAY THAT SHE COULD!
NAME HERE, RIGHT?
UNFORTUNATELY, THE BOSS WAS BUSY, SO SHE SENT ME.
I SEE. WELL, WE NEED ALL THE HELP WE CAN GET.
OH, BY THE WAY, MY NAME'S—
I KNOW YOUR NAME.
HUH?

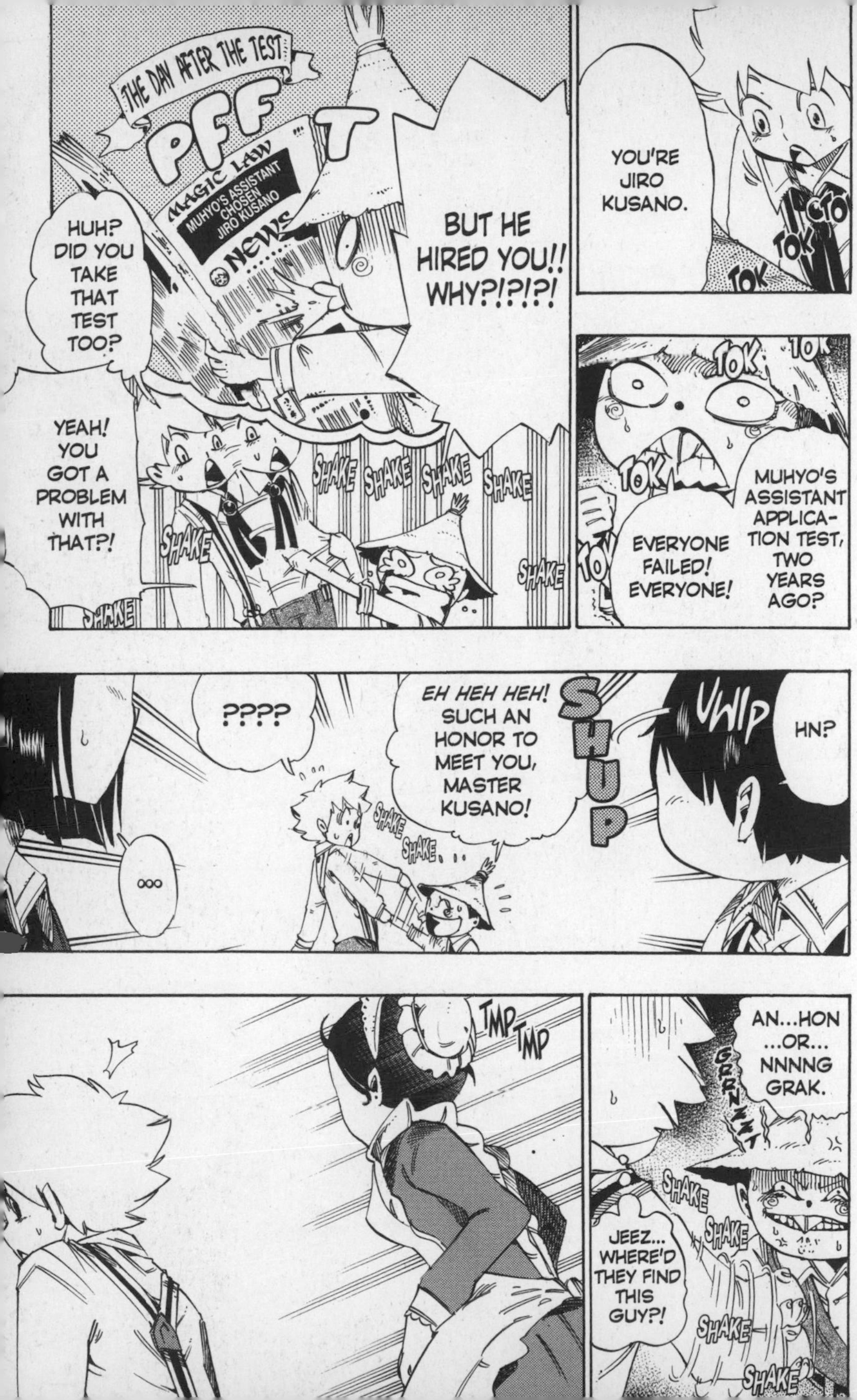
YOU'RE JIRO KUSANO.
TOK
TOK
TOK
TOK
TOK
MUHYO'S ASSISTANT APPLICATION TEST, TWO YEARS AGO?
EVERYONE FAILED! EVERYONE!
TOK
TOK
THE DAY AFTER THE TEST
PFFFT
MAGIC LAW NEWS
MUHYO'S ASSISTANT CHOSEN JIRO KUSANO
BUT HE HIRED YOU!! WHY?!?!?!
HUH? DID YOU TAKE THAT TEST TOO?
YEAH! YOU GOT A PROBLEM WITH THAT?!
SHAKE SHAKE SHAKE SHAKE
SHAKE
SHAKE
SHAKE
HN?
UWIP
SHUP
EH HEH HEH! SUCH AN HONOR TO MEET YOU, MASTER KUSANO!
SHAKE SHAKE...
????
...
AN...HON ...OR... NNNNG GRAK.
GRRNZZT
JEEZ... WHERE'D THEY FIND THIS GUY?!
SHAKE
SHAKE
SHAKE
SHAKE
TMP TMP

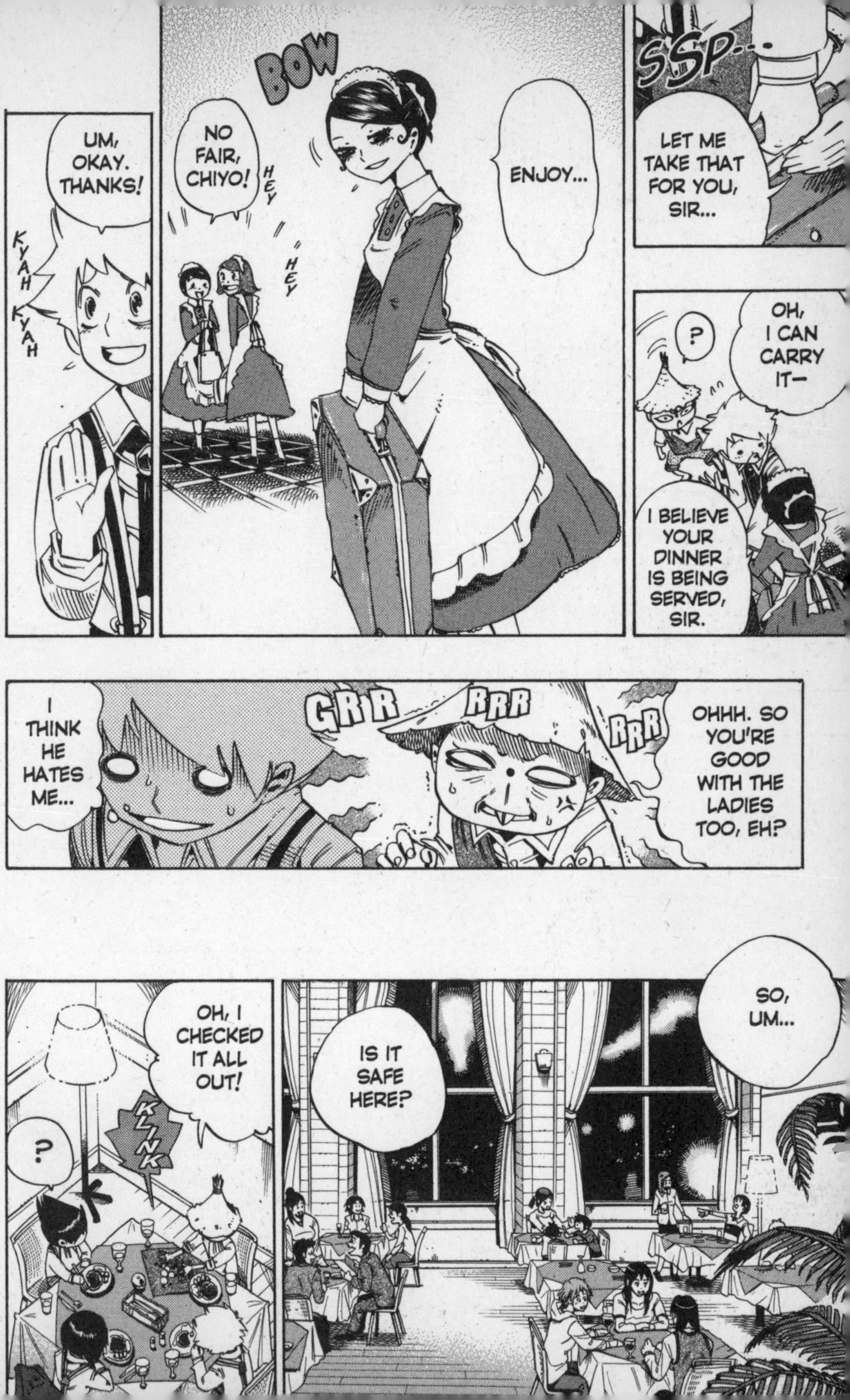
SSP...
LET ME TAKE THAT FOR YOU, SIR...
OH, I CAN CARRY IT—
?
I BELIEVE YOUR DINNER IS BEING SERVED, SIR.
BOW
ENJOY...
NO FAIR, CHIYO!
HEY
HEY
UM, OKAY. THANKS!
KYAH KYAH
OHHH. SO YOU'RE GOOD WITH THE LADIES TOO, EH?
RRR
RRR
GRR
I THINK HE HATES ME...
SO, UM...
IS IT SAFE HERE?
OH, I CHECKED IT ALL OUT!
KLINK
?

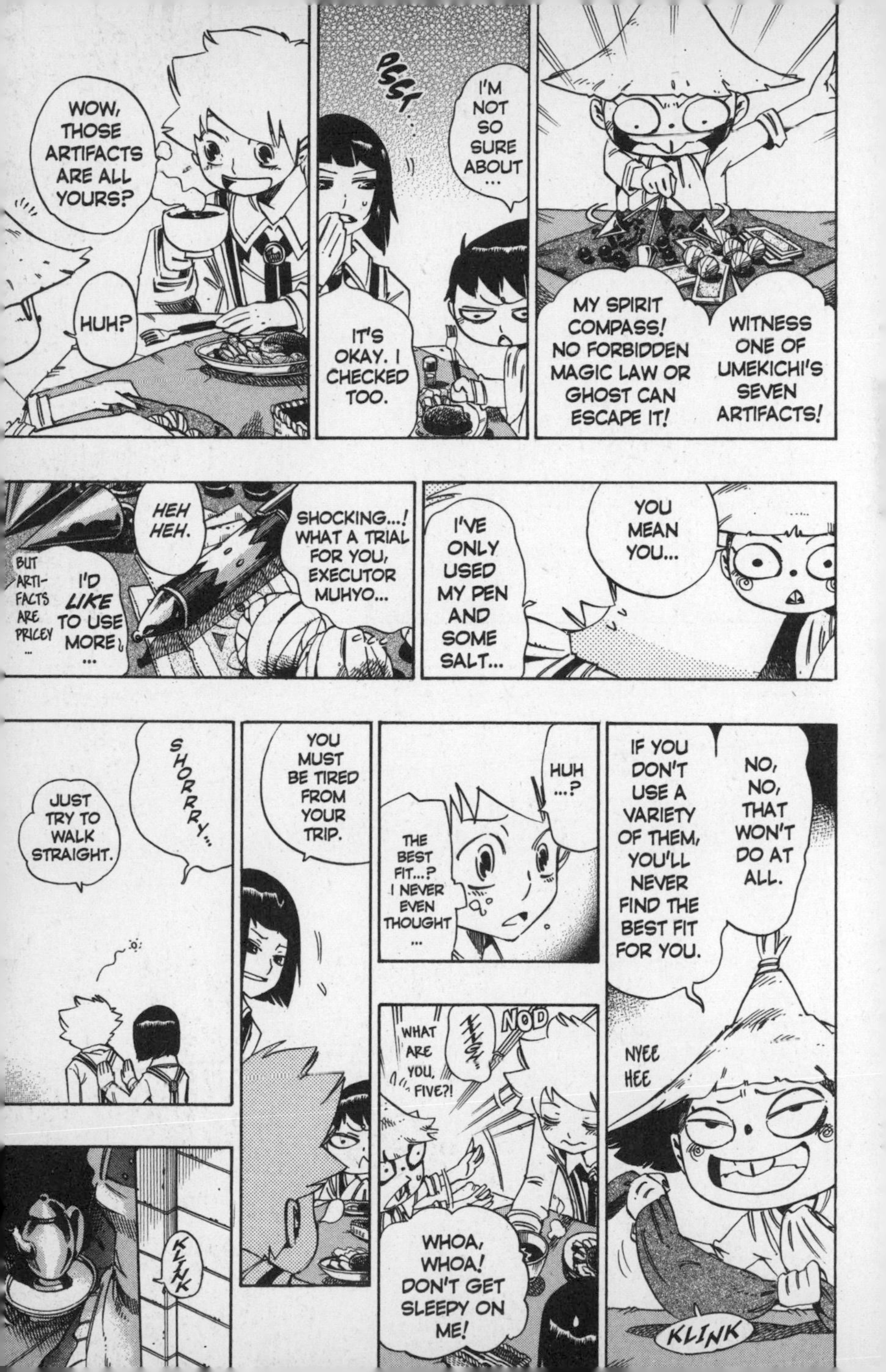
WITNESS ONE OF UMEKICHI'S SEVEN ARTIFACTS!
MY SPIRIT COMPASS! NO FORBIDDEN MAGIC LAW OR GHOST CAN ESCAPE IT!
PSSST...
I'M NOT SO SURE ABOUT...
IT'S OKAY. I CHECKED TOO.
WOW, THOSE ARTIFACTS ARE ALL YOURS?
HUH?
YOU MEAN YOU...
......
I'VE ONLY USED MY PEN AND SOME SALT...
SHOCKING...! WHAT A TRIAL FOR YOU, EXECUTOR MUHYO...
HEH HEH.
I'D LIKE TO USE MORE...
BUT ARTIFACTS ARE PRICEY...
NO, NO, THAT WON'T DO AT ALL.
IF YOU DON'T USE A VARIETY OF THEM, YOU'LL NEVER FIND THE BEST FIT FOR YOU.
NYEE HEE
KLINK
HUH...?
THE BEST FIT...? I NEVER EVEN THOUGHT...
NOD
NNG
WHAT ARE YOU, FIVE?!
WHOA, WHOA! DON'T GET SLEEPY ON ME!
YOU MUST BE TIRED FROM YOUR TRIP.
SHORRRY...
JUST TRY TO WALK STRAIGHT.
KLINK

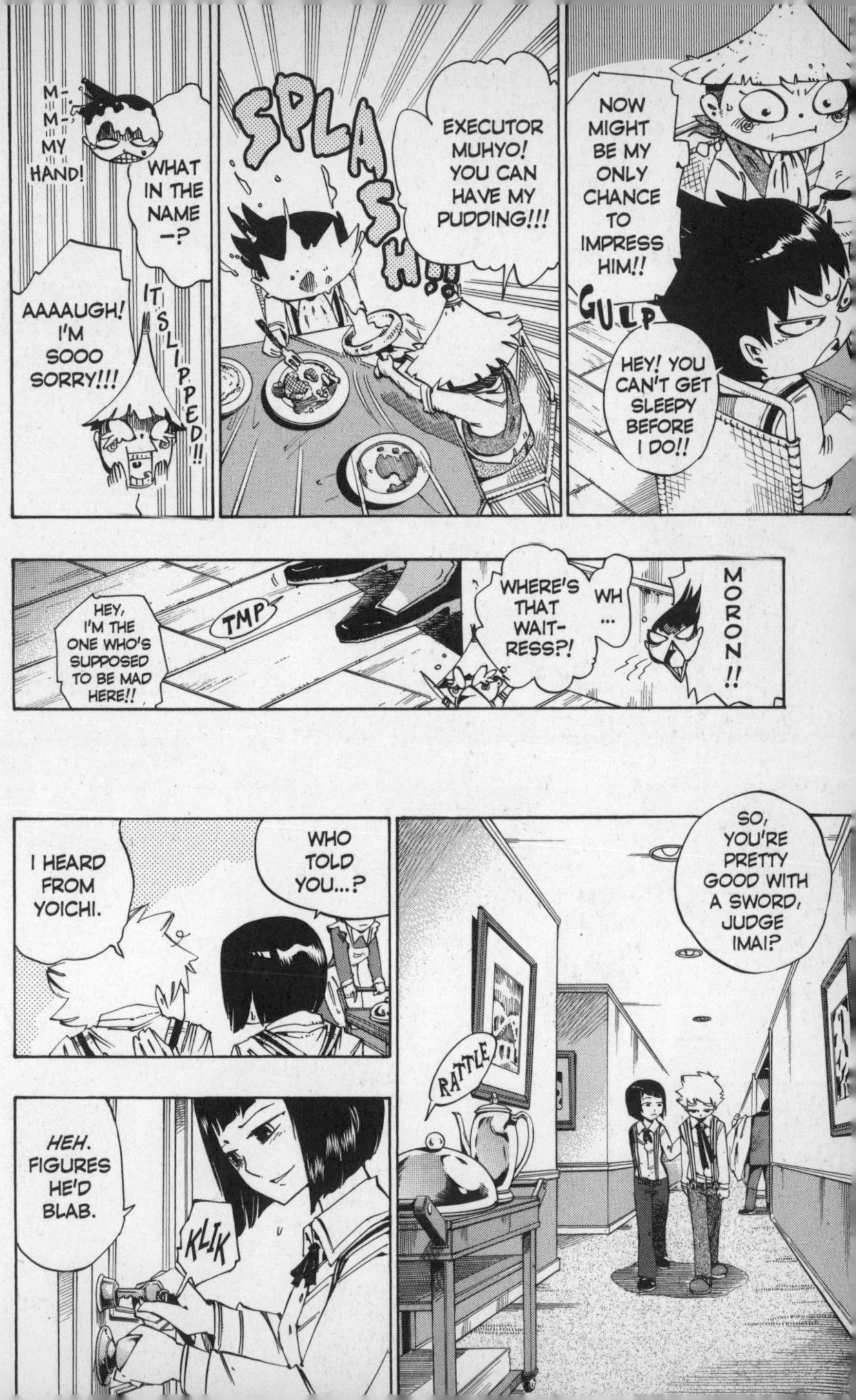
NOW MIGHT BE MY ONLY CHANCE TO IMPRESS HIM!!
GULP
HEY! YOU CAN'T GET SLEEPY BEFORE I DO!!
SPLASH!!
EXECUTOR MUHYO! YOU CAN HAVE MY PUDDING!!!
WHAT IN THE NAME—?
M-M-MY HAND!
IT SLIPPED!!
AAAAUGH! I'M SOOO SORRY!!!
MORON!!
WH...
WHERE'S THAT WAITRESS?!
TMP
HEY, I'M THE ONE WHO'S SUPPOSED TO BE MAD HERE!!
SO, YOU'RE PRETTY GOOD WITH A SWORD, JUDGE IMAI?
RATTLE
WHO TOLD YOU...?
I HEARD FROM YOICHI.
HEH. FIGURES HE'D BLAB.
KLIK

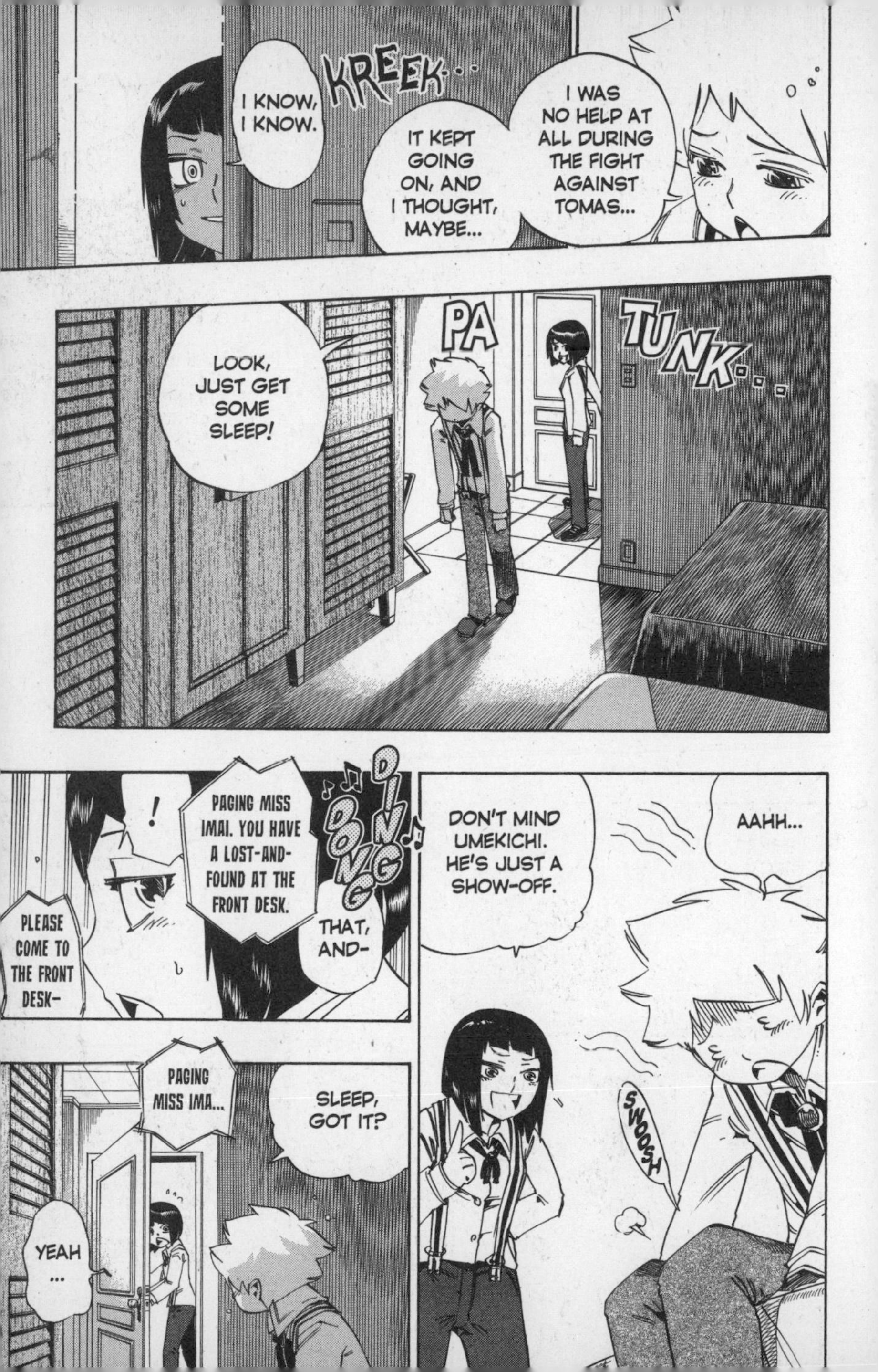
I WAS NO HELP AT ALL DURING THE FIGHT AGAINST TOMAS...
IT KEPT GOING ON, AND I THOUGHT, MAYBE...
KREEK...
I KNOW, I KNOW.
TUNK...
PA
LOOK, JUST GET SOME SLEEP!
AAHH...
DON'T MIND UMEKICHI. HE'S JUST A SHOW-OFF.
SWOOSH
DING DONG
PAGING MISS IMAI. YOU HAVE A LOST-AND-FOUND AT THE FRONT DESK.
!
THAT, AND-
PLEASE COME TO THE FRONT DESK-
SLEEP, GOT IT?
PAGING MISS IMA...
YEAH ...

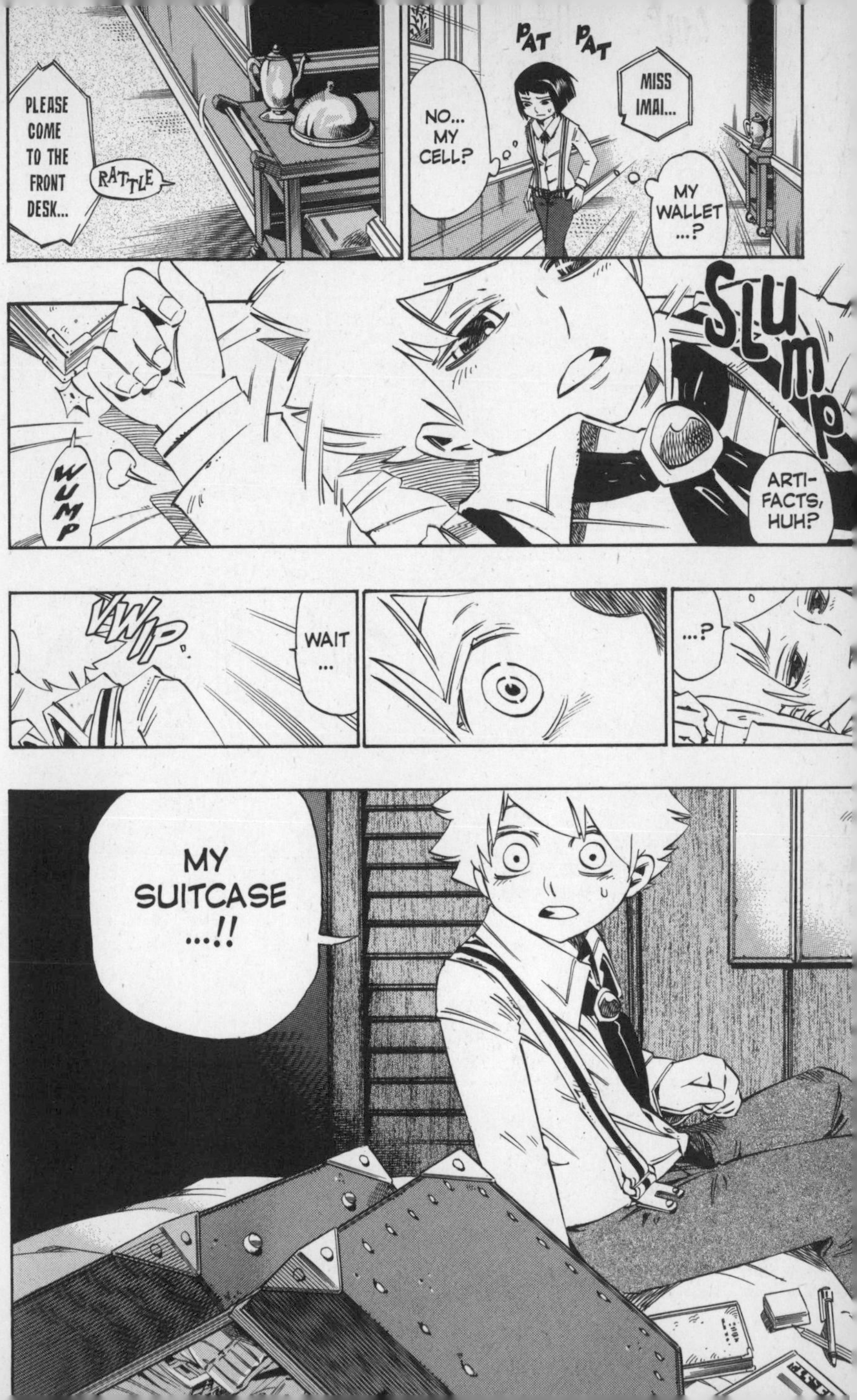
PAT PAT
MISS IMAI...
NO... MY CELL?
MY WALLET ...?
PLEASE COME TO THE FRONT DESK...
RATTLE
SLUMP
ARTI-FACTS, HUH?
WUMP
...?
WAIT ...
VWIP
MY SUITCASE ...!!

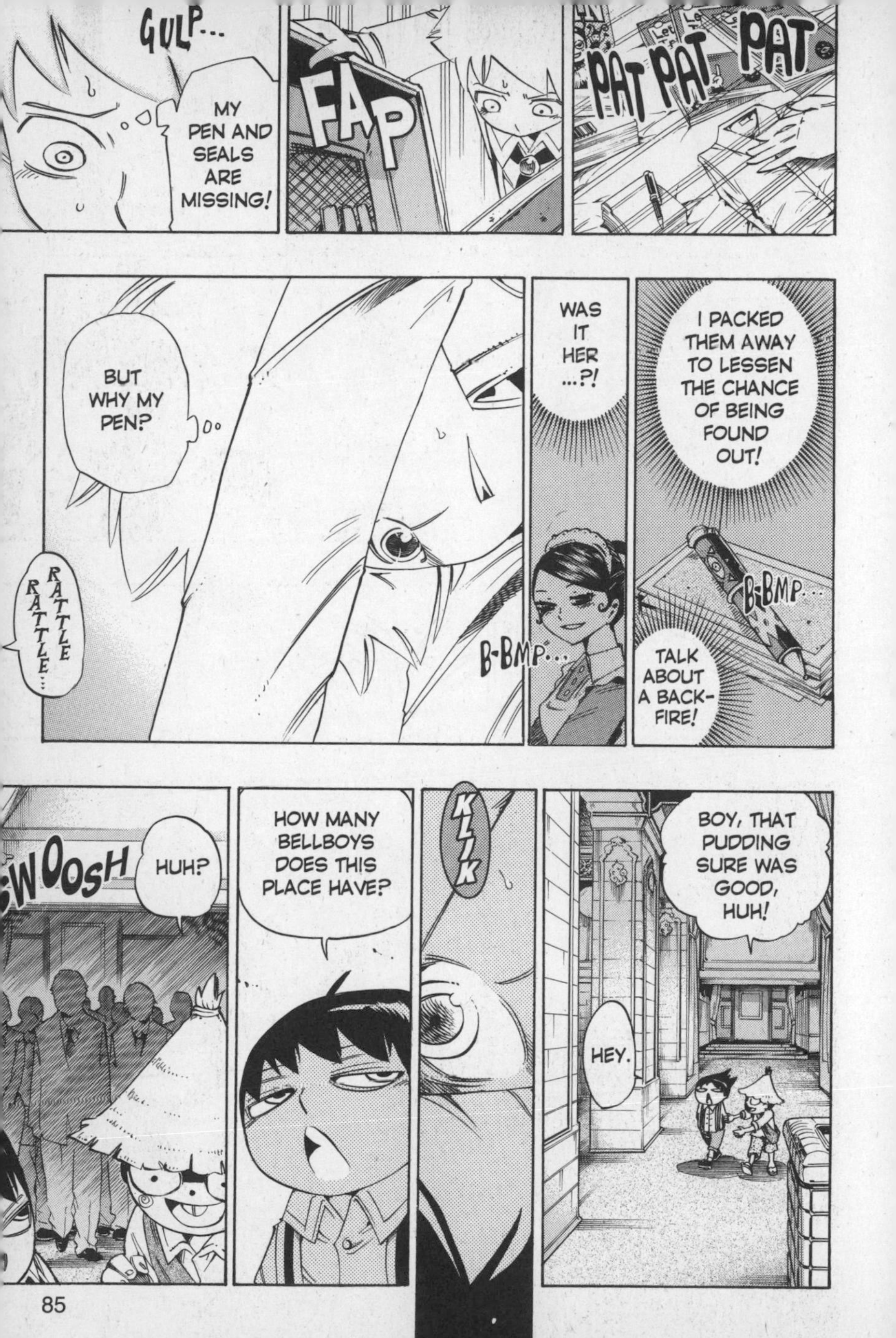
PAT PAT PAT
FAP
GULP...
MY PEN AND SEALS ARE MISSING!
I PACKED THEM AWAY TO LESSEN THE CHANCE OF BEING FOUND OUT!
B-BMP...
TALK ABOUT A BACK-FIRE!
WAS IT HER ...?!
B-BMP...
BUT WHY MY PEN?
RATTLE RATTLE...
BOY, THAT PUDDING SURE WAS GOOD, HUH!
HEY.
KLIK
HOW MANY BELLBOYS DOES THIS PLACE HAVE?
HUH?
WOOSH

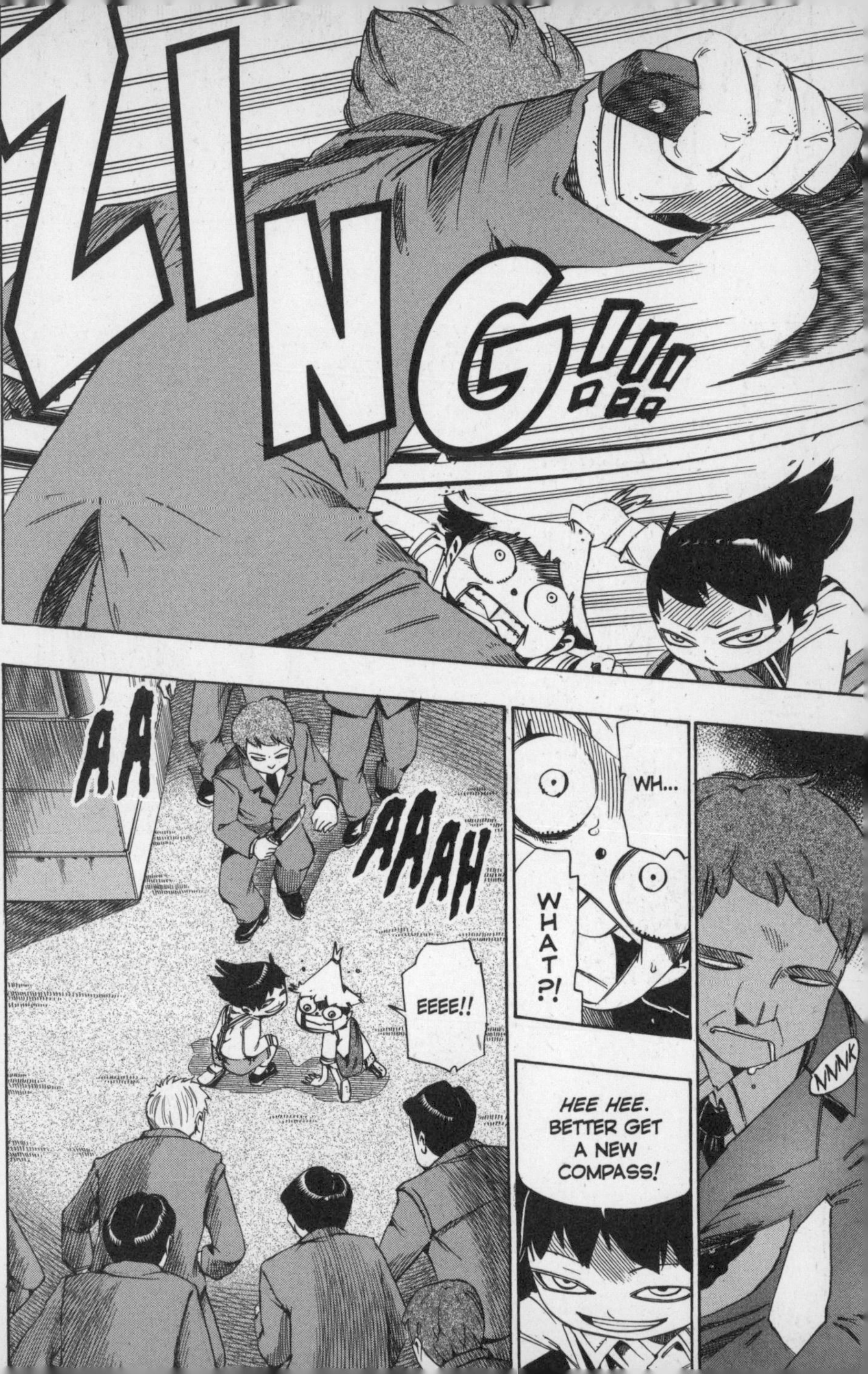

ZING!!!
NNNK
WH...
WHAT?!
HEE HEE. BETTER GET A NEW COMPASS!
AA AAAAH
EEEE!!

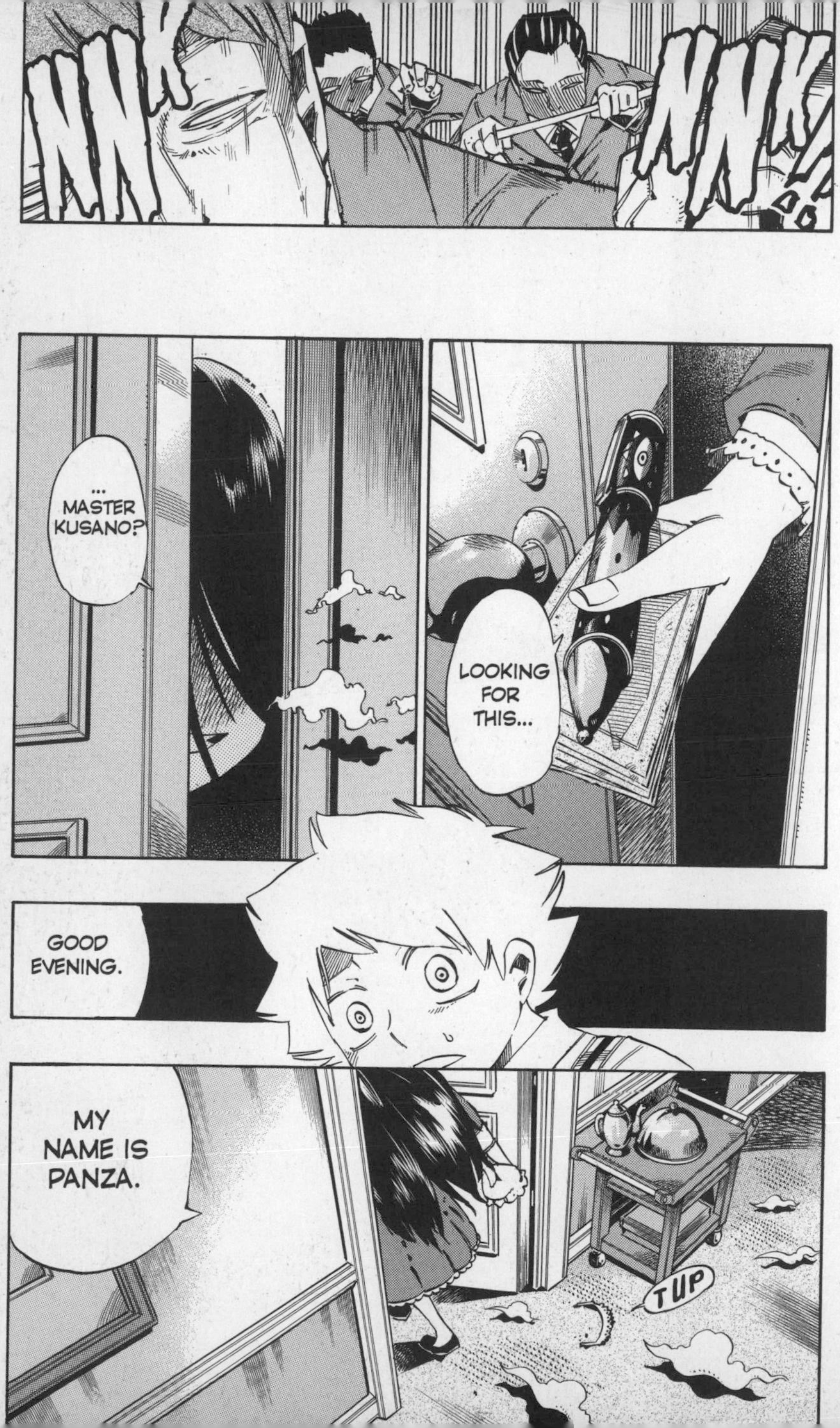
NNK!
NNK
LOOKING FOR THIS...
... MASTER KUSANO?
GOOD EVENING.
MY NAME IS PANZA.
TUP

THE STAFFERS LIKE DRAWING KOOKY PICTURES, SO HERE'RE A FEW!
(THERE'RE LOTS MORE!)

CHECK IT OUT!

SOME FUN ART

BY TSUYOPON

BY FUKUDA

BY ENDO

BY KIMURA

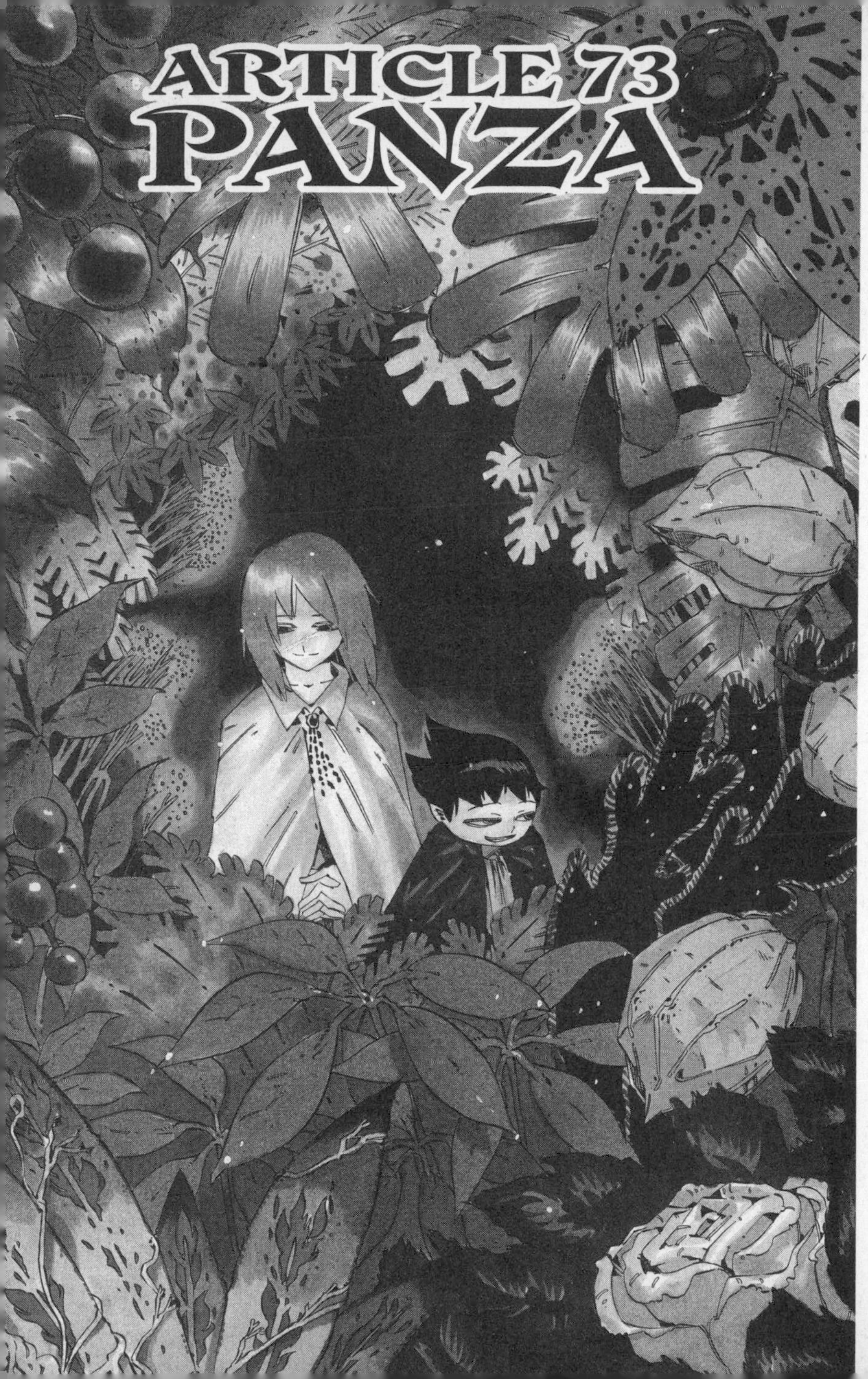
ARTICLE 73
PANZA

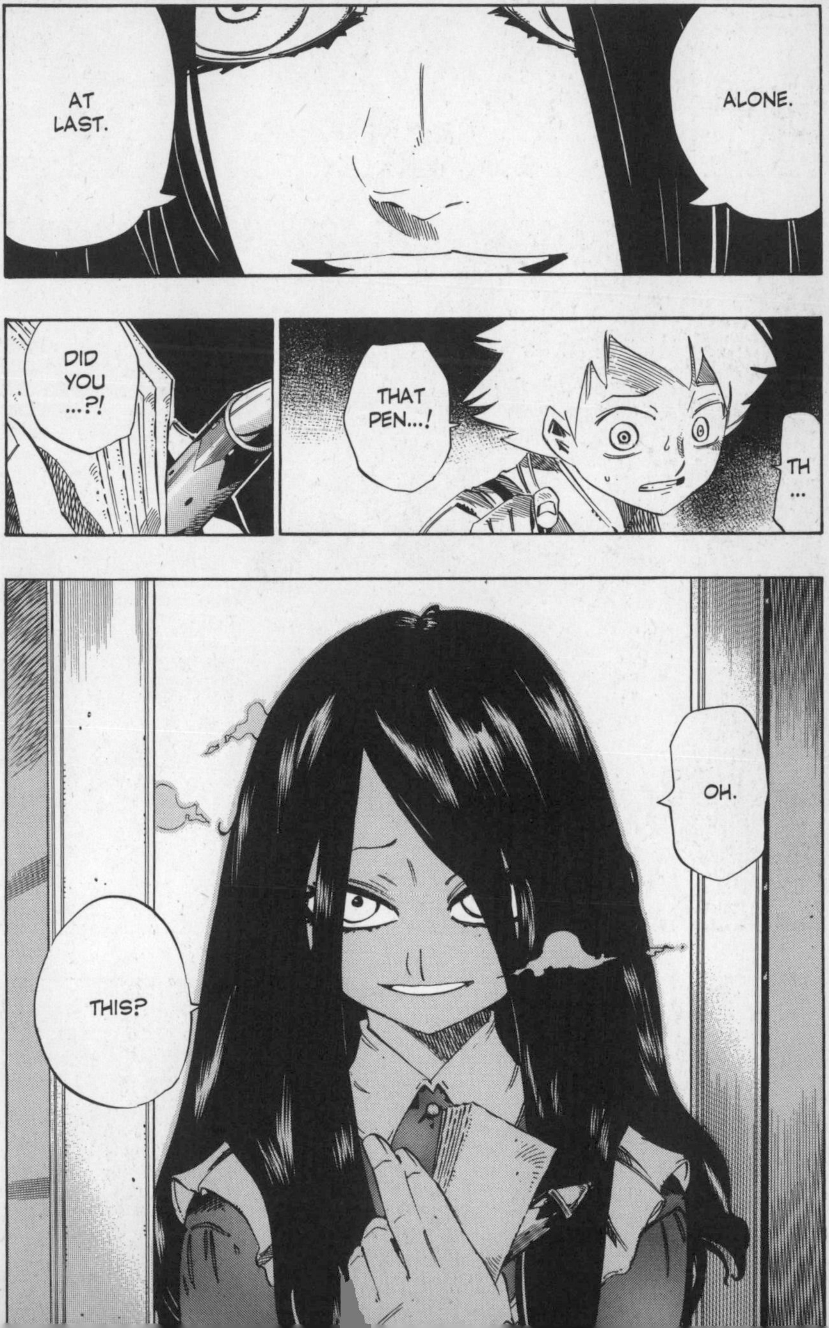
ALONE.
AT LAST.
TH ...
THAT PEN...!
DID YOU ...?!
OH.
THIS?

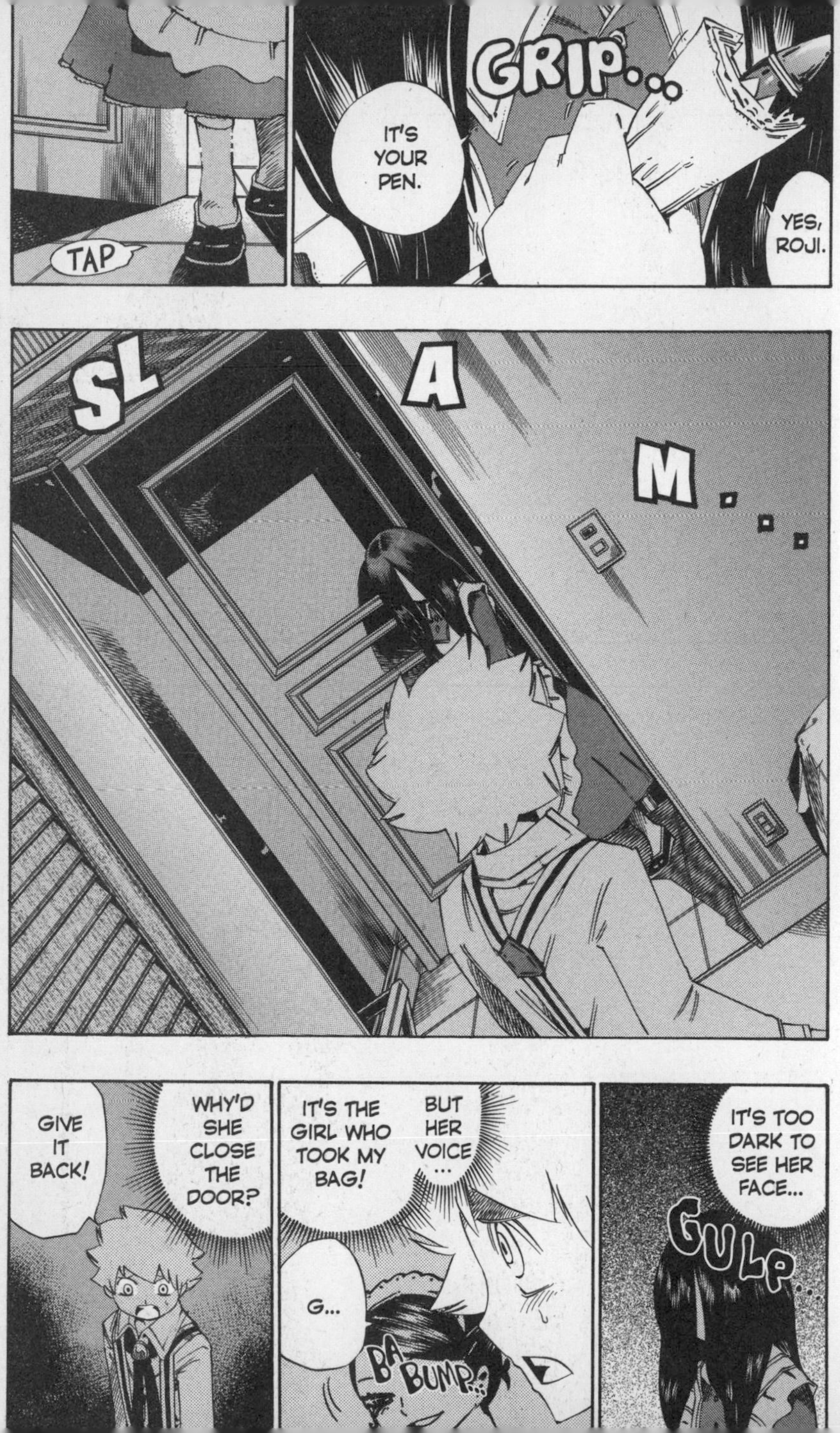
GRIP...
IT'S YOUR PEN.
YES, ROJI.
TAP
SLAM...
IT'S TOO DARK TO SEE HER FACE...
GULP...
BUT HER VOICE...
IT'S THE GIRL WHO TOOK MY BAG!
G...
BA BUMP...
WHY'D SHE CLOSE THE DOOR?
GIVE IT BACK!

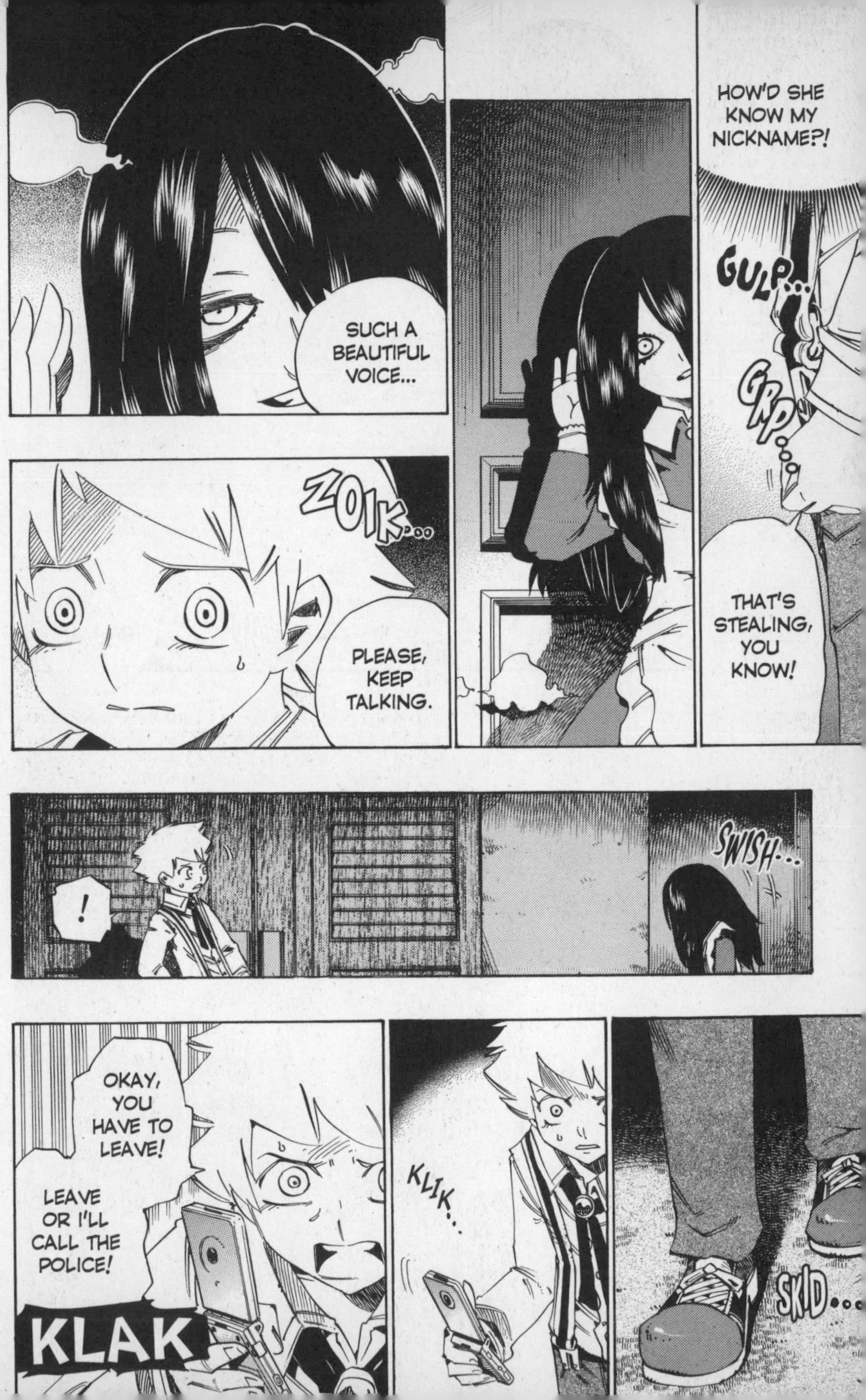
HOW'D SHE KNOW MY NICKNAME?!
GULP...
GRP...
THAT'S STEALING, YOU KNOW!
SUCH A BEAUTIFUL VOICE...
ZOIK...
PLEASE, KEEP TALKING.
SWISH...
!
SKID...
KLIK...
OKAY, YOU HAVE TO LEAVE!
LEAVE OR I'LL CALL THE POLICE!
KLAK

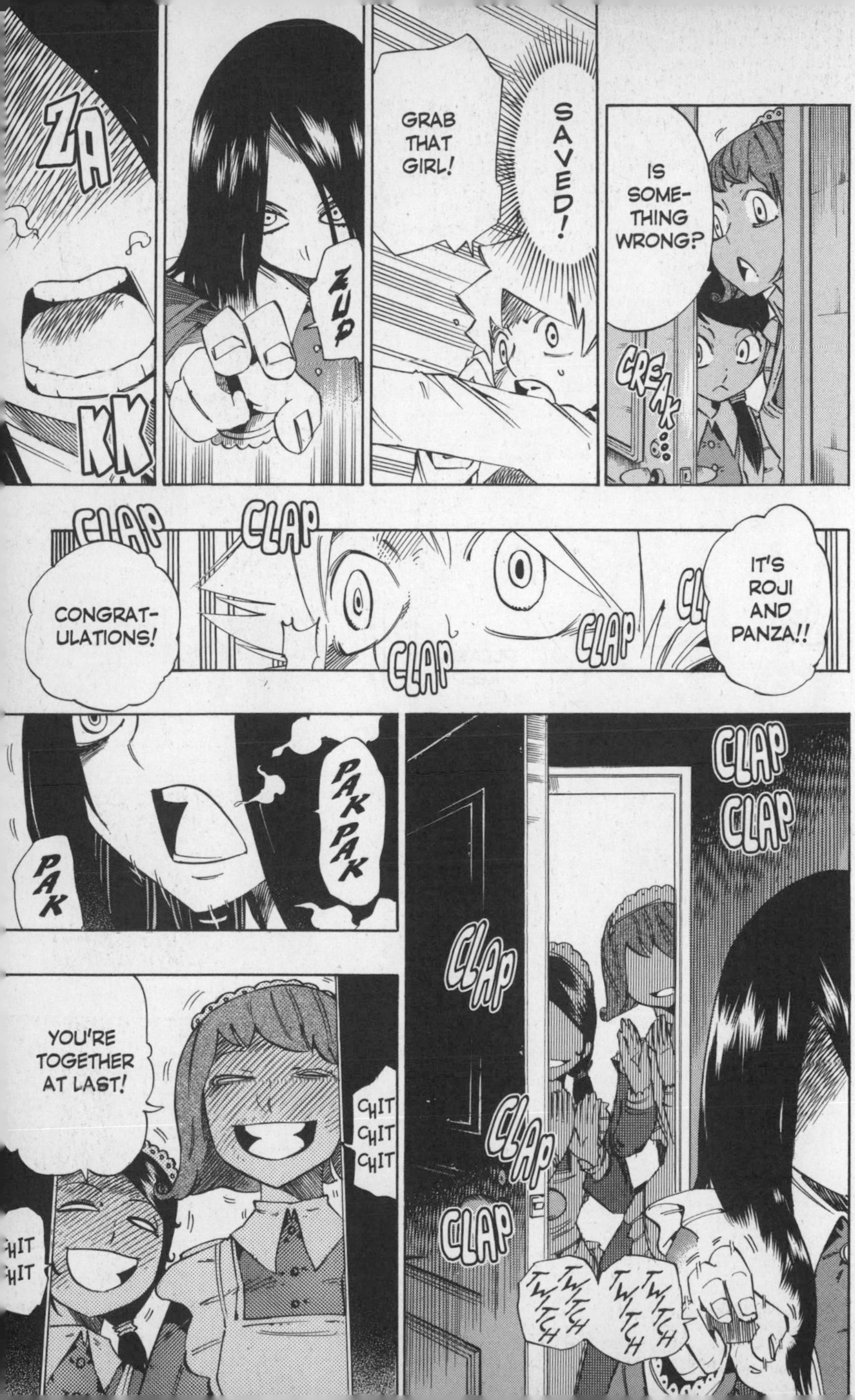
IS SOME-THING WRONG?
CREAK...
SAVED!
GRAB THAT GIRL!
ZUP
ZA
KK
IT'S ROJI AND PANZA!!
CLAP
CLAP
CLAP
CLAP
CLAP
CONGRATULATIONS!
CLAP
CLAP
CLAP
CLAP
CLAP
CLAP
TWITCH TWITCH
TWITCH TWITCH
PAK PAK
PAK
YOU'RE TOGETHER AT LAST!
CHIT CHIT CHIT
HIT HIT

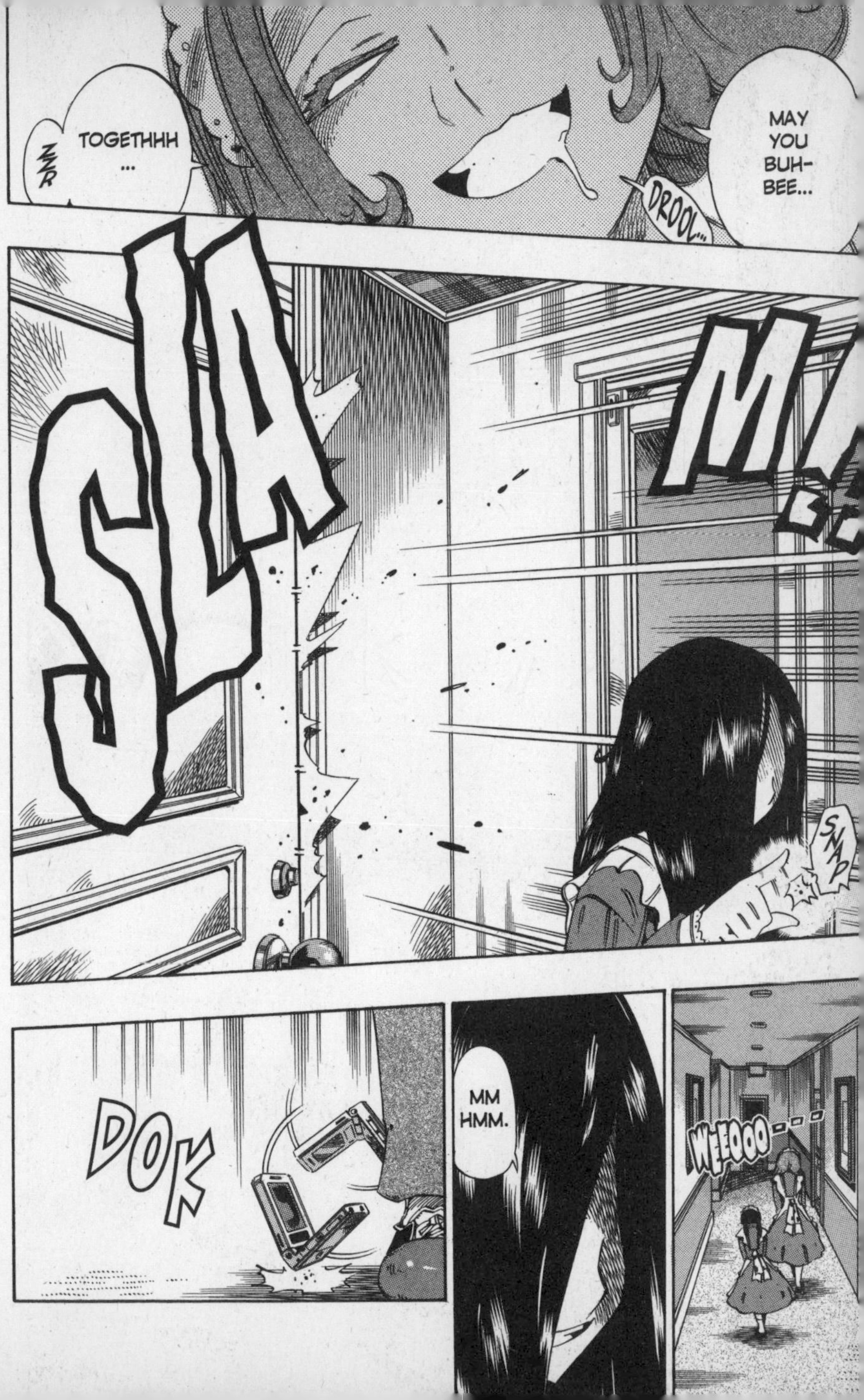

MAY YOU BUH-BEE...
DROOL...
TOGETHHH ...
ZZZR
M
SLA
SNAP
WEEOOO - - -
MM HMM.
DOK

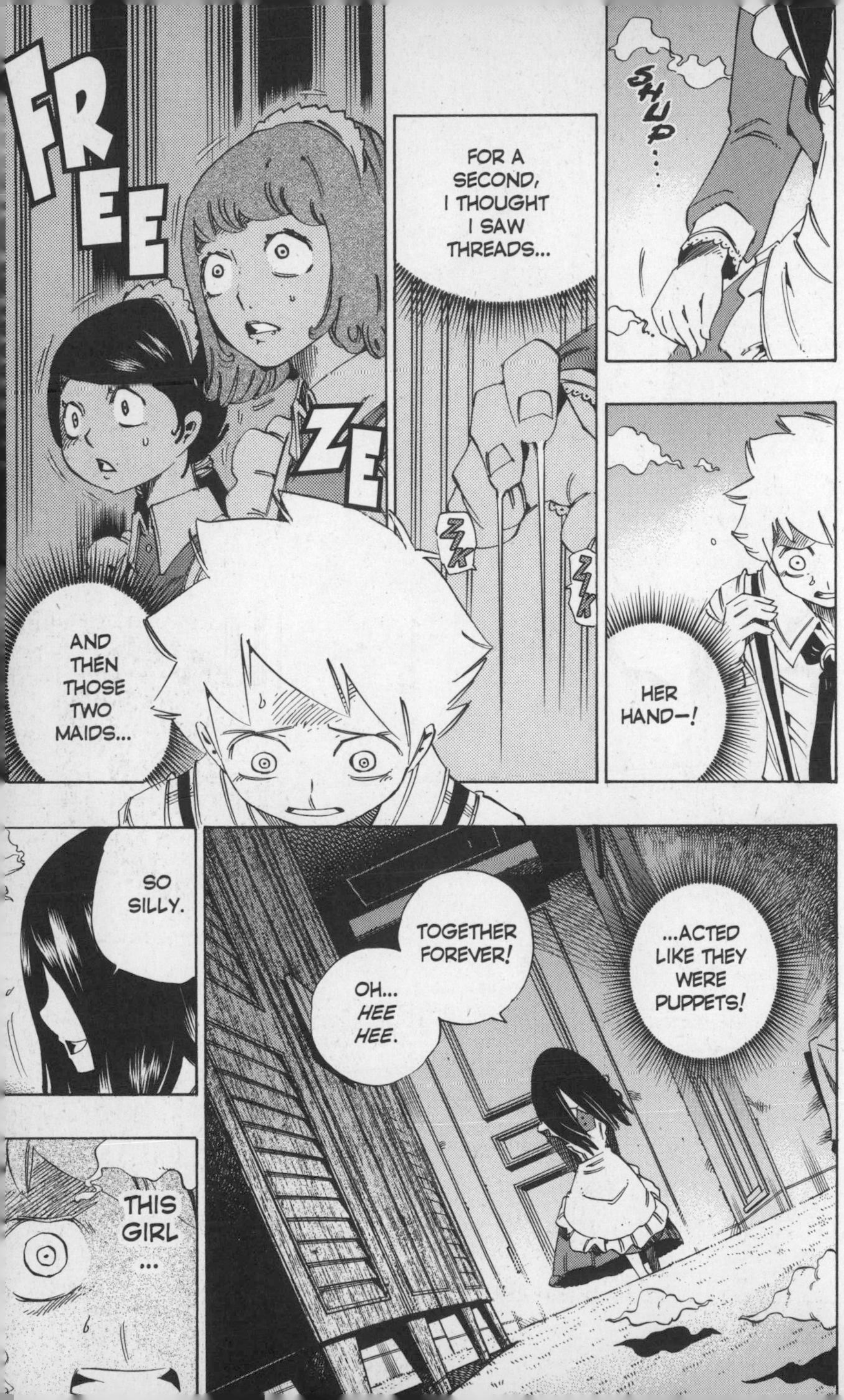
SHUP...
HER HAND—!
FOR A SECOND, I THOUGHT I SAW THREADS...
ZZK
ZZK
FREE
ZE
AND THEN THOSE TWO MAIDS...
...ACTED LIKE THEY WERE PUPPETS!
TOGETHER FOREVER!
OH... HEE HEE.
SO SILLY.
THIS GIRL ...

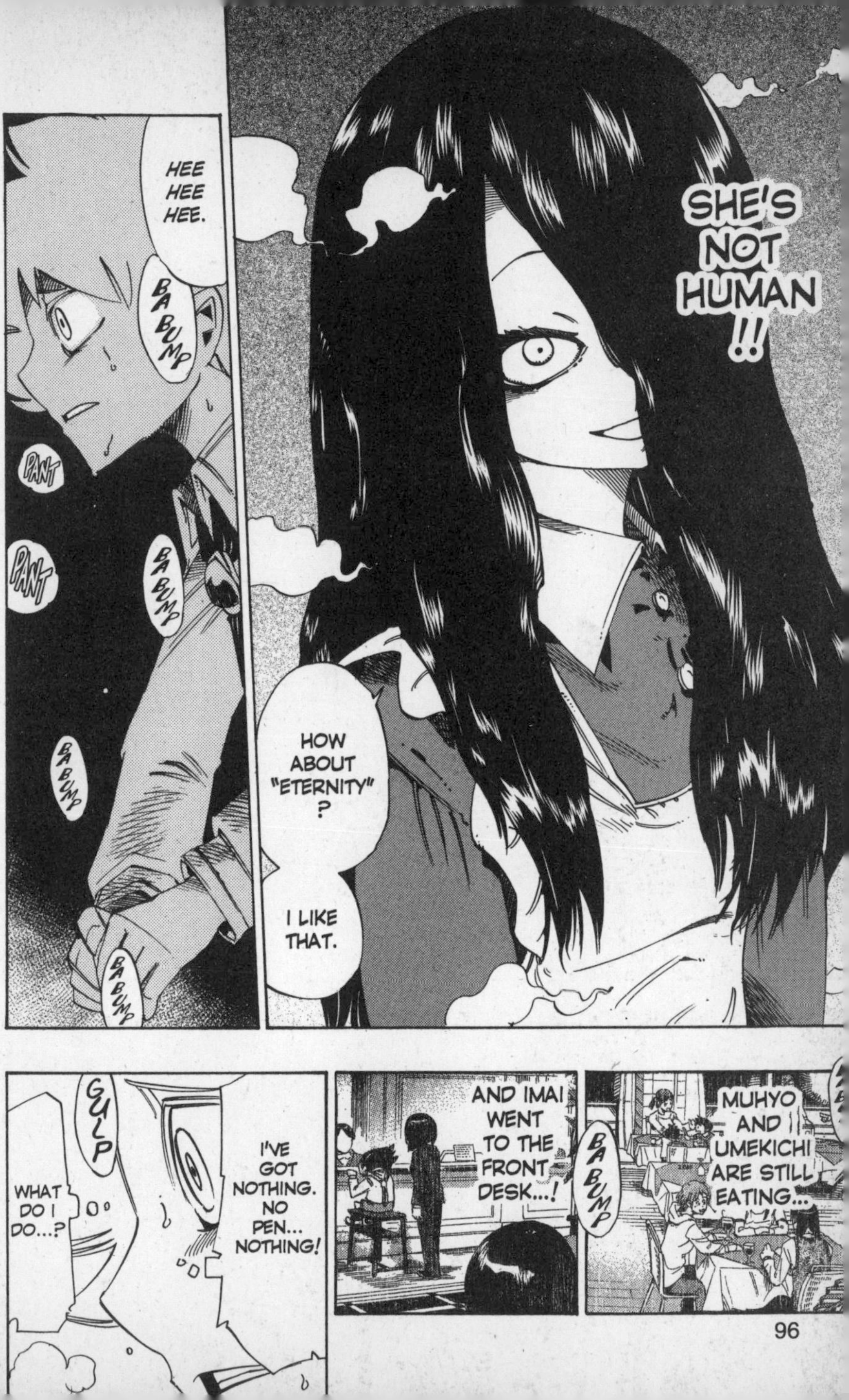
SHE'S NOT HUMAN!!
HOW ABOUT "ETERNITY"?
I LIKE THAT.
HEE HEE HEE.
BA BUMP
PANT
BA BUMP
PANT
BA BUMP
BA BUMP
MUHYO AND UMEKICHI ARE STILL EATING...
BA BUMP
AND IMAI WENT TO THE FRONT DESK...!
GULP
I'VE GOT NOTHING. NO PEN... NOTHING!
WHAT DO I DO...?

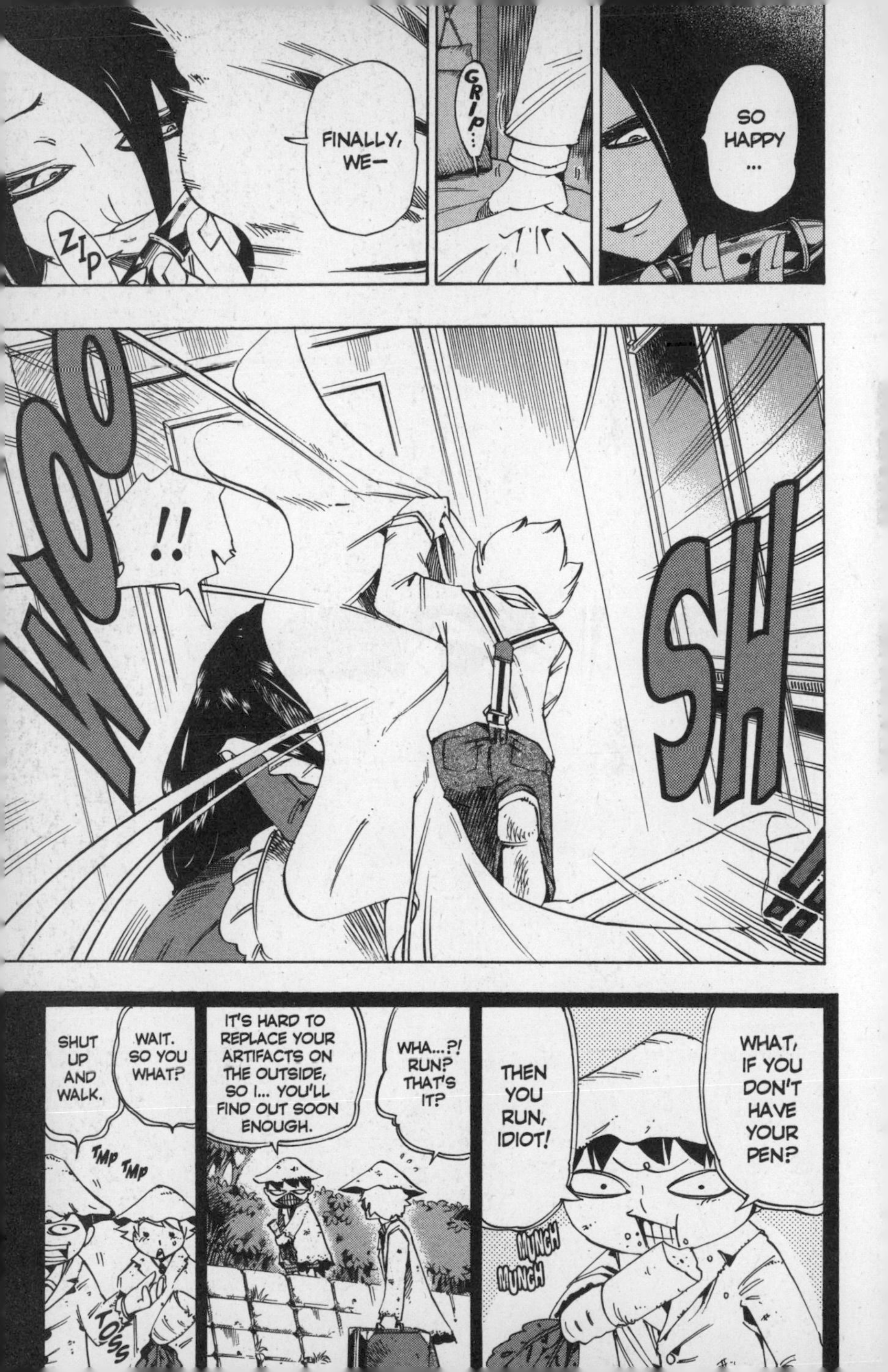
SO HAPPY ...
GRIP...
FINALLY, WE—
ZIP
SH
!!
WOOO
WHAT, IF YOU DON'T HAVE YOUR PEN?
THEN YOU RUN, IDIOT!
MUNCH
MUNCH
WHA...?! RUN? THAT'S IT?
IT'S HARD TO REPLACE YOUR ARTIFACTS ON THE OUTSIDE, SO I... YOU'LL FIND OUT SOON ENOUGH.
WAIT. SO YOU WHAT?
SHUT UP AND WALK.
TMP TMP
TOSS

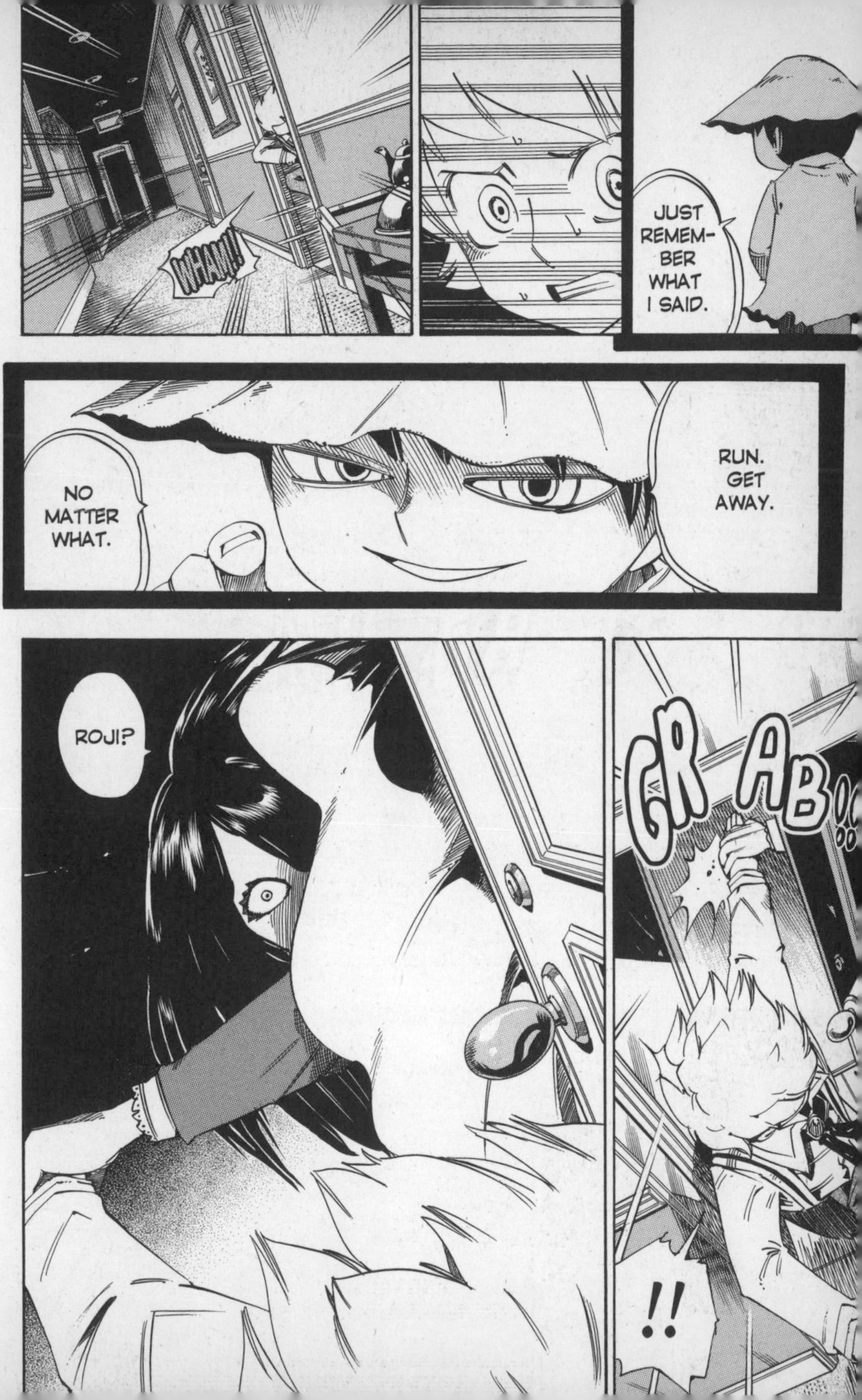
JUST REMEMBER WHAT I SAID.
WHAM!!
RUN. GET AWAY.
NO MATTER WHAT.
GRAB!!
!!
ROJI?

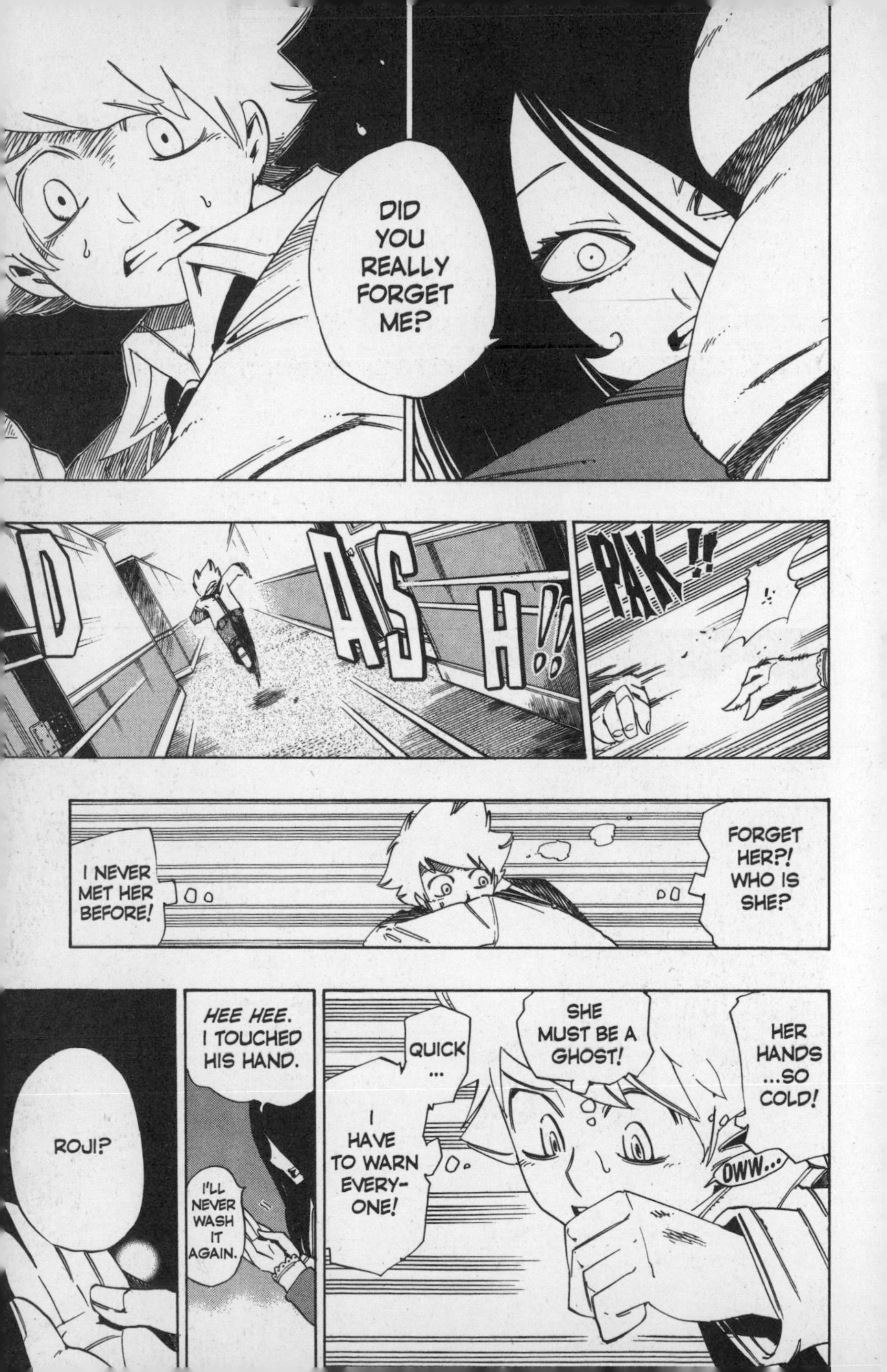
DID YOU REALLY FORGET ME?
PAK!!
DASH!!
FORGET HER?! WHO IS SHE?
I NEVER MET HER BEFORE!
HER HANDS ...SO COLD!
OWW...
SHE MUST BE A GHOST!
QUICK...
I HAVE TO WARN EVERY-ONE!
HEE HEE. I TOUCHED HIS HAND.
I'LL NEVER WASH IT AGAIN.
ROJI?

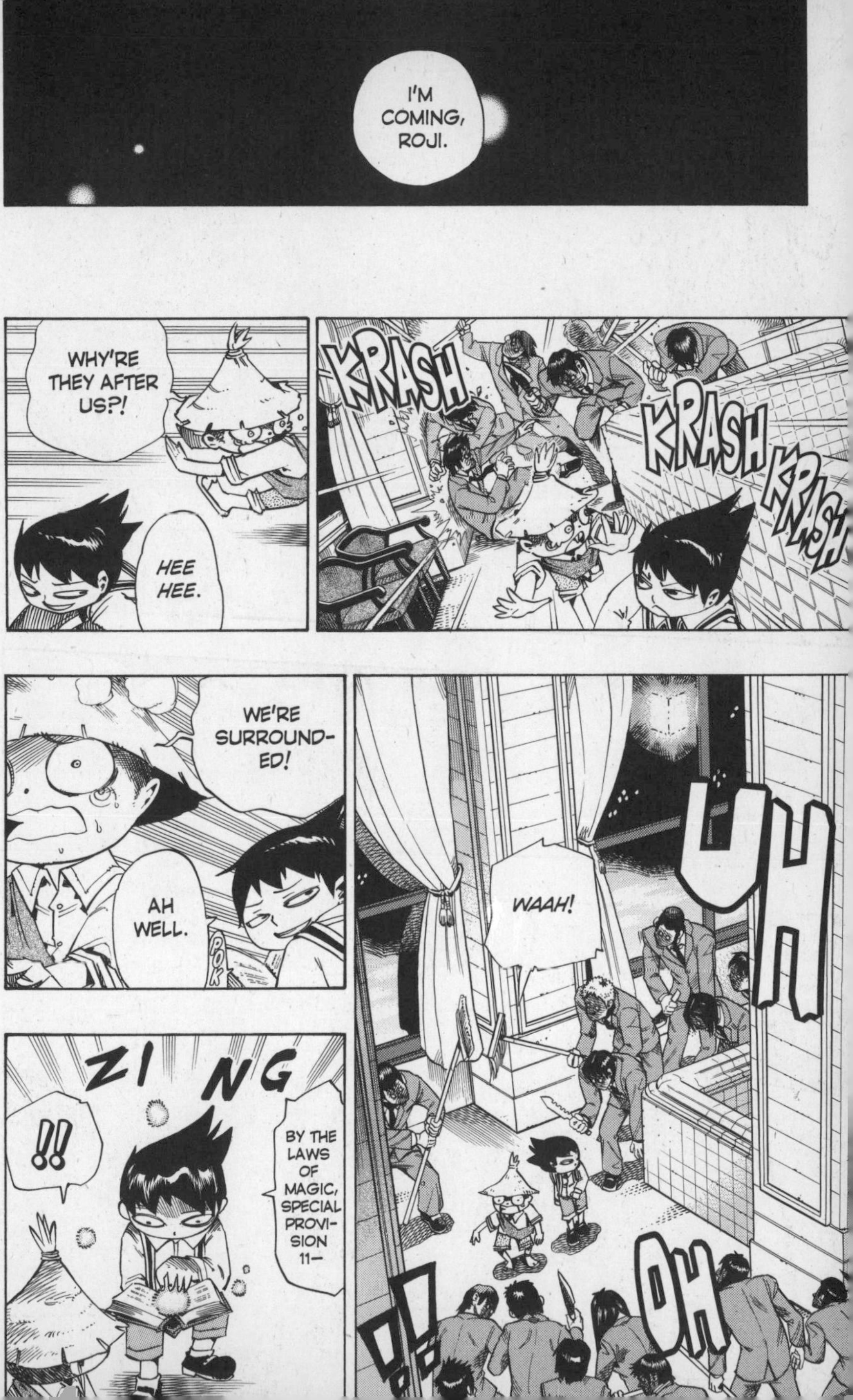
I'M COMING, ROJI.
KRASH
KRASH
KRASH
WHY'RE THEY AFTER US?!
HEE HEE.
UHH
WAAH!
OH
!!
WE'RE SURROUND-ED!
AH WELL.
POK
ZING
!!
BY THE LAWS OF MAGIC, SPECIAL PROVISION 11—

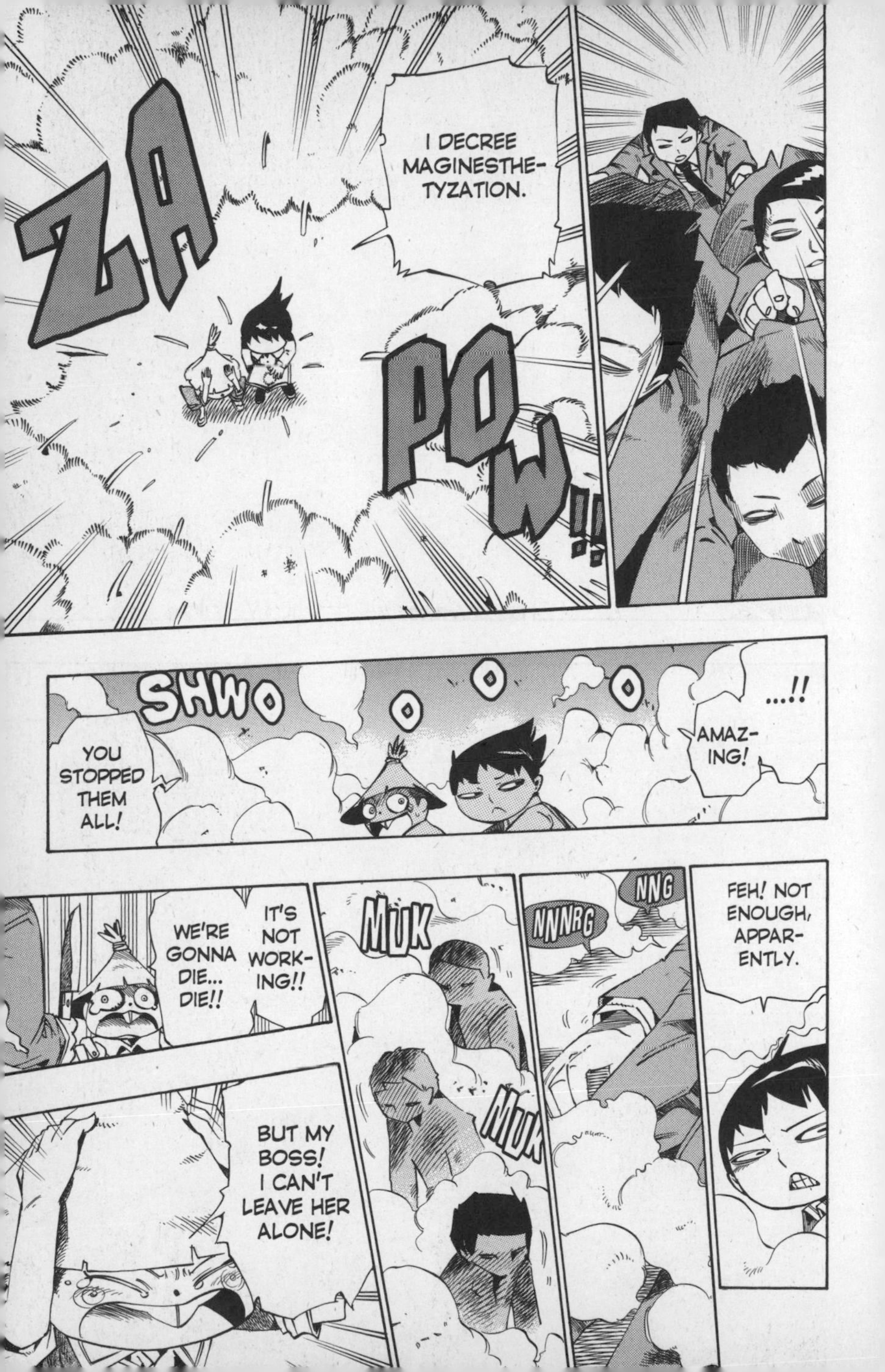
I DECREE MAGINESTHE-TYZATION.
POW!!
ZA
SHWOOOO
...!!
AMAZ-ING!
YOU STOPPED THEM ALL!
FEH! NOT ENOUGH, APPAR-ENTLY.
NNG
NNNRG
MUK
MUK
IT'S NOT WORK-ING!!
WE'RE GONNA DIE... DIE!!
BUT MY BOSS! I CAN'T LEAVE HER ALONE!

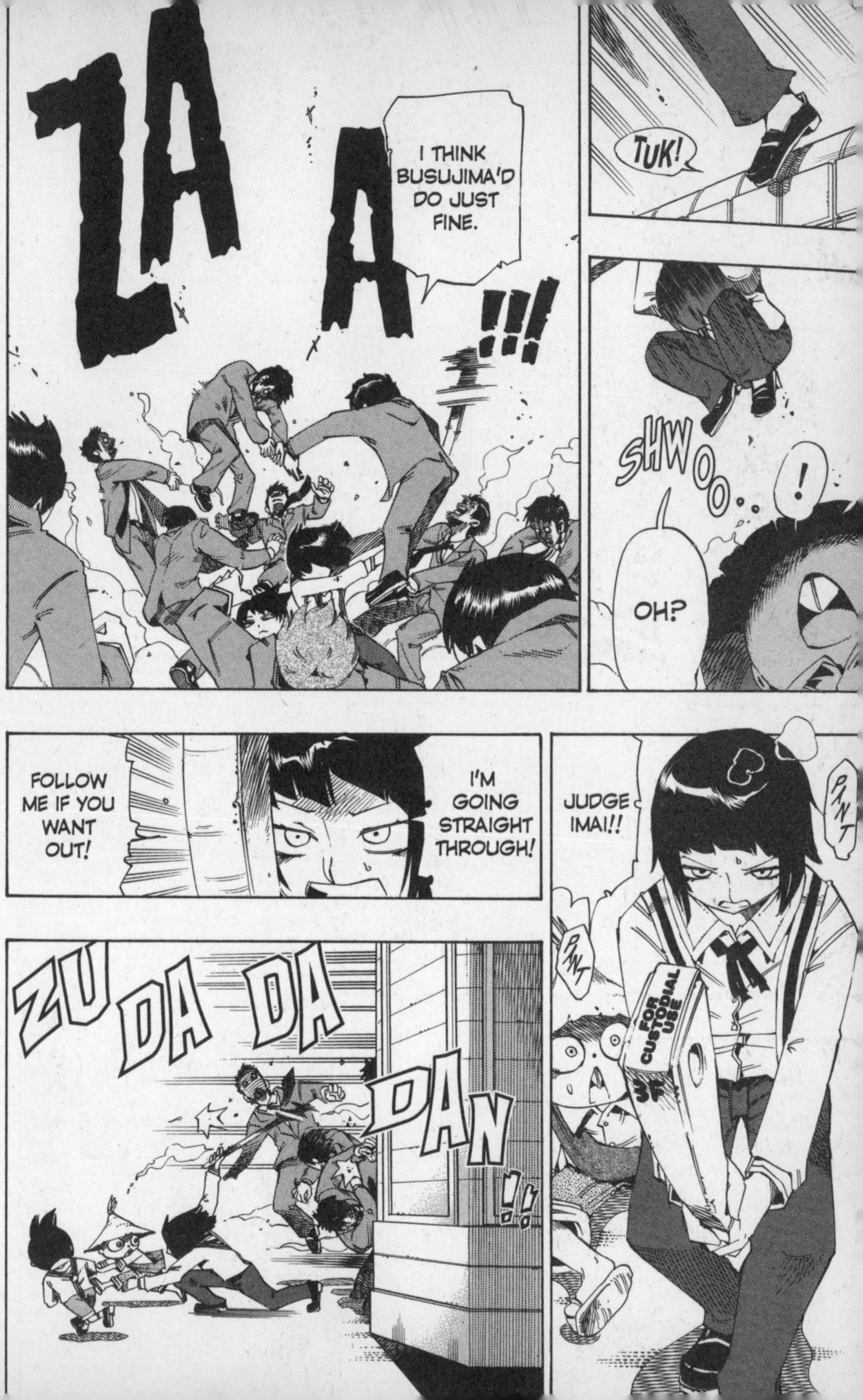
TUK!
SHWOO..!
OH?
I THINK BUSUJIMA'D DO JUST FINE.
ZA A!!!
PANT
JUDGE IMAI!!
PANT
FOR CUSTODIAL USE
3F
I'M GOING STRAIGHT THROUGH!
FOLLOW ME IF YOU WANT OUT!
ZU DA DA DA
DAN!!

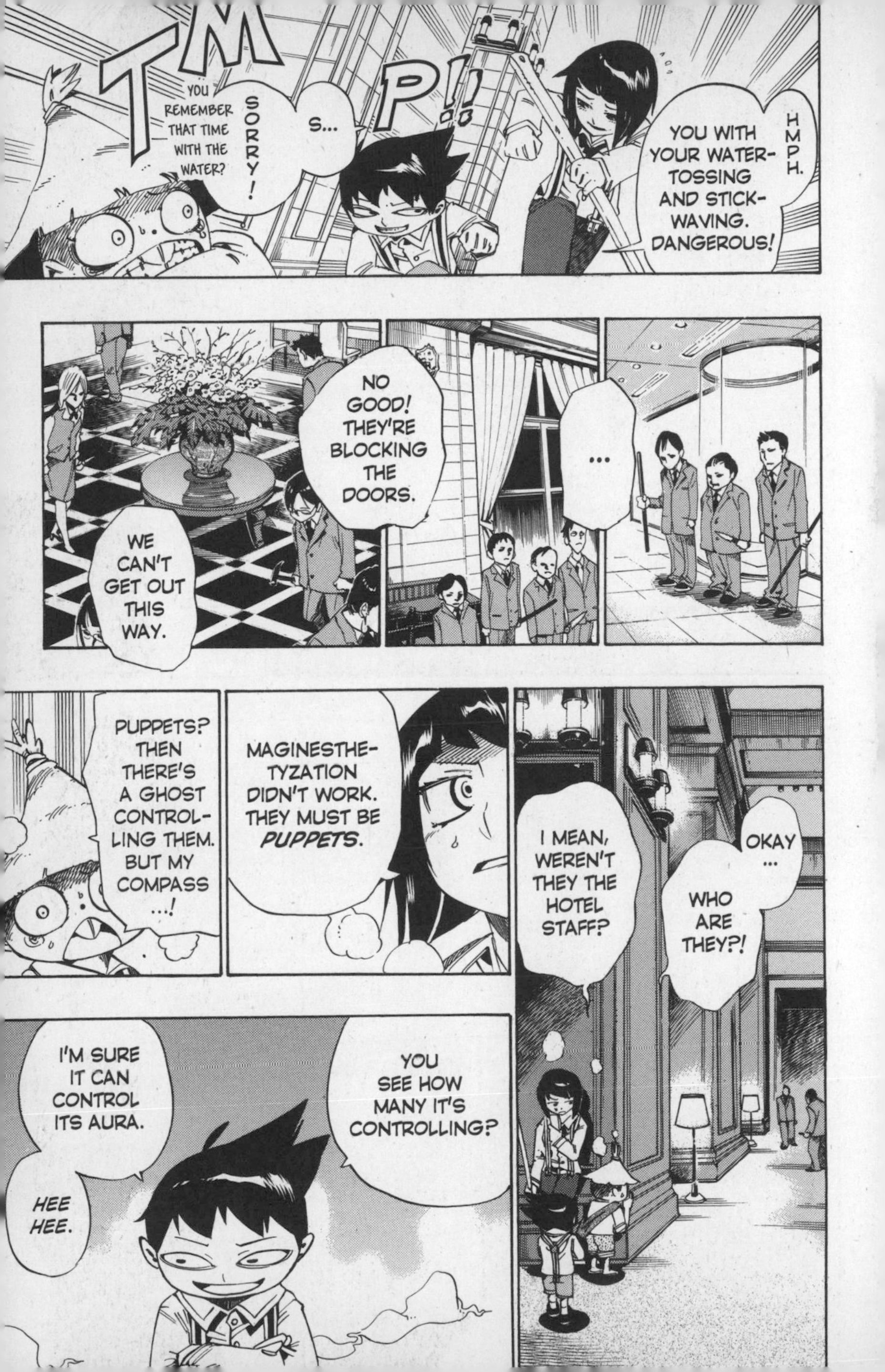
HMPH.
YOU WITH YOUR WATER-TOSSING AND STICK-WAVING. DANGEROUS!
TMP!!
S...
SORRY!
YOU REMEMBER THAT TIME WITH THE WATER?
...
NO GOOD! THEY'RE BLOCKING THE DOORS.
WE CAN'T GET OUT THIS WAY.
OKAY...
WHO ARE THEY?!
I MEAN, WEREN'T THEY THE HOTEL STAFF?
MAGINESTHETYZATION DIDN'T WORK. THEY MUST BE *PUPPETS*.
PUPPETS? THEN THERE'S A GHOST CONTROLLING THEM. BUT MY COMPASS ...!
YOU SEE HOW MANY IT'S CONTROLLING?
I'M SURE IT CAN CONTROL ITS AURA.
HEE HEE.

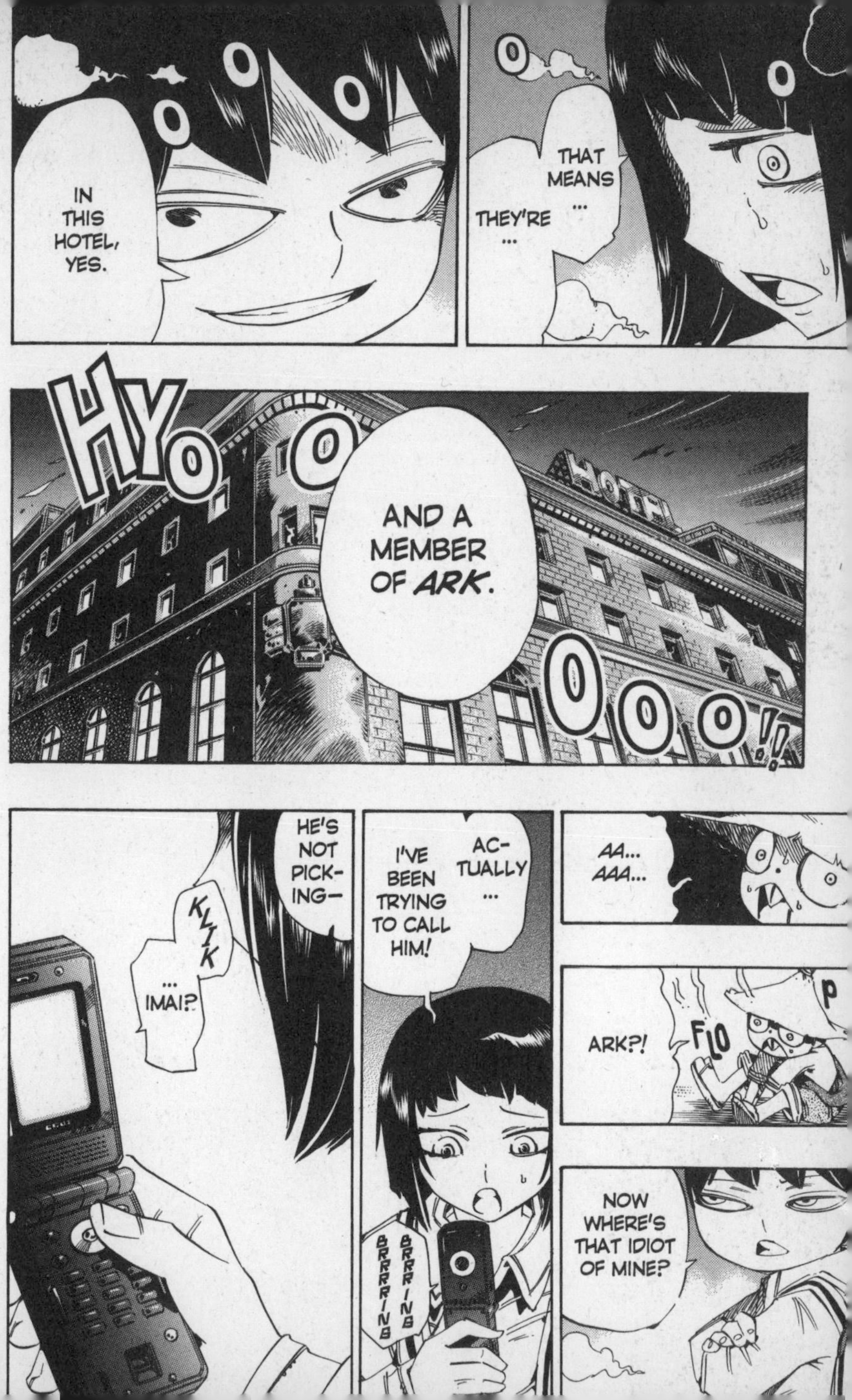
THAT MEANS ... THEY'RE ...
IN THIS HOTEL, YES.
AND A MEMBER OF ARK.
HYOOOOO!!
AA... AAA...
ARK?!
FLOP
NOW WHERE'S THAT IDIOT OF MINE?
ACTUALLY ...
I'VE BEEN TRYING TO CALL HIM!
BRRRING BRRRING
HE'S NOT PICKING-
KLIK
... IMAI?

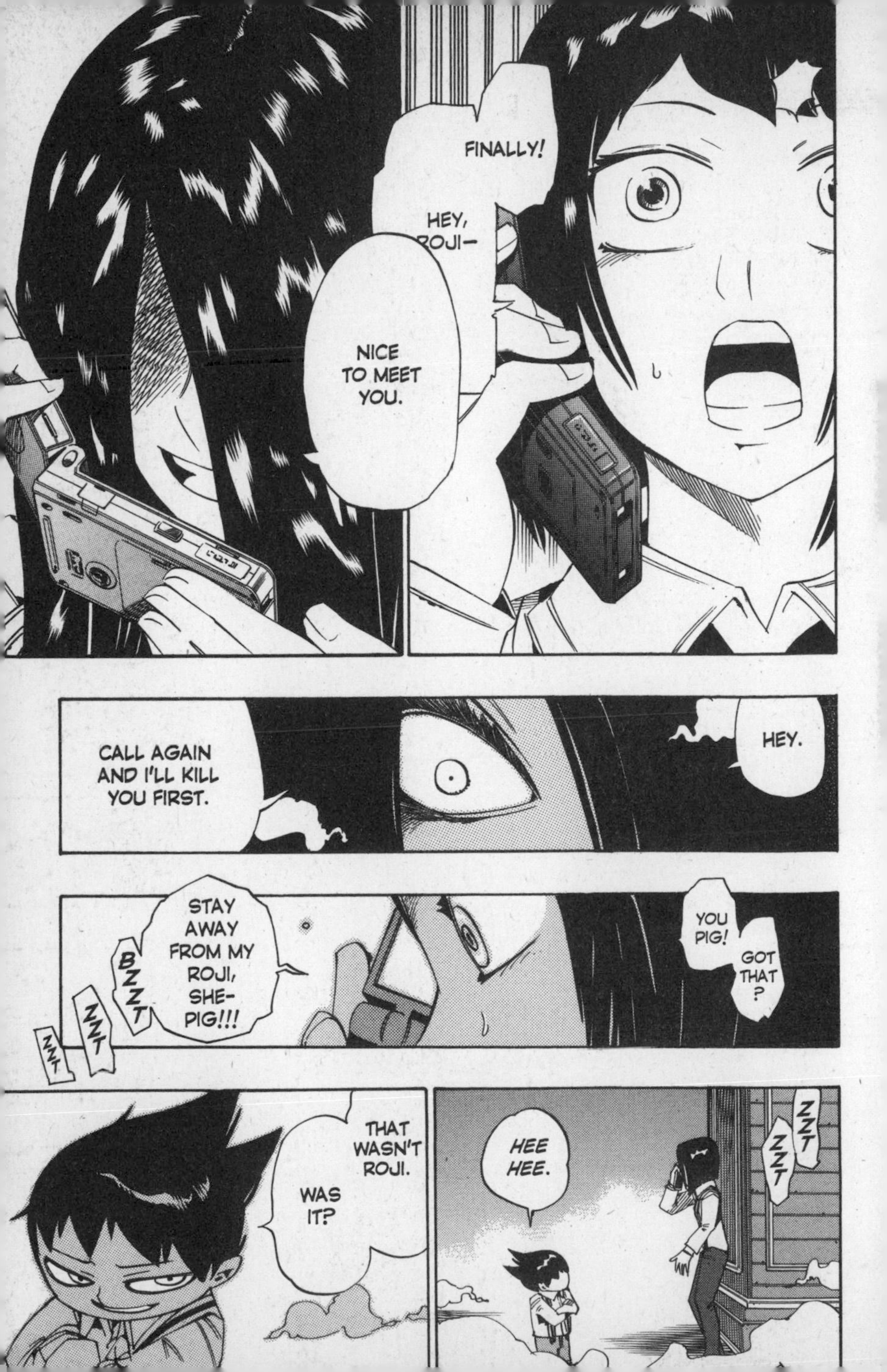
FINALLY!
HEY, ROJI—
NICE TO MEET YOU.
HEY.
CALL AGAIN AND I'LL KILL YOU FIRST.
YOU PIG!
GOT THAT?
STAY AWAY FROM MY ROJI, SHE-PIG!!!
BZZT
ZZT
ZZT
ZZT
ZZT
HEE HEE.
THAT WASN'T ROJI.
WAS IT?

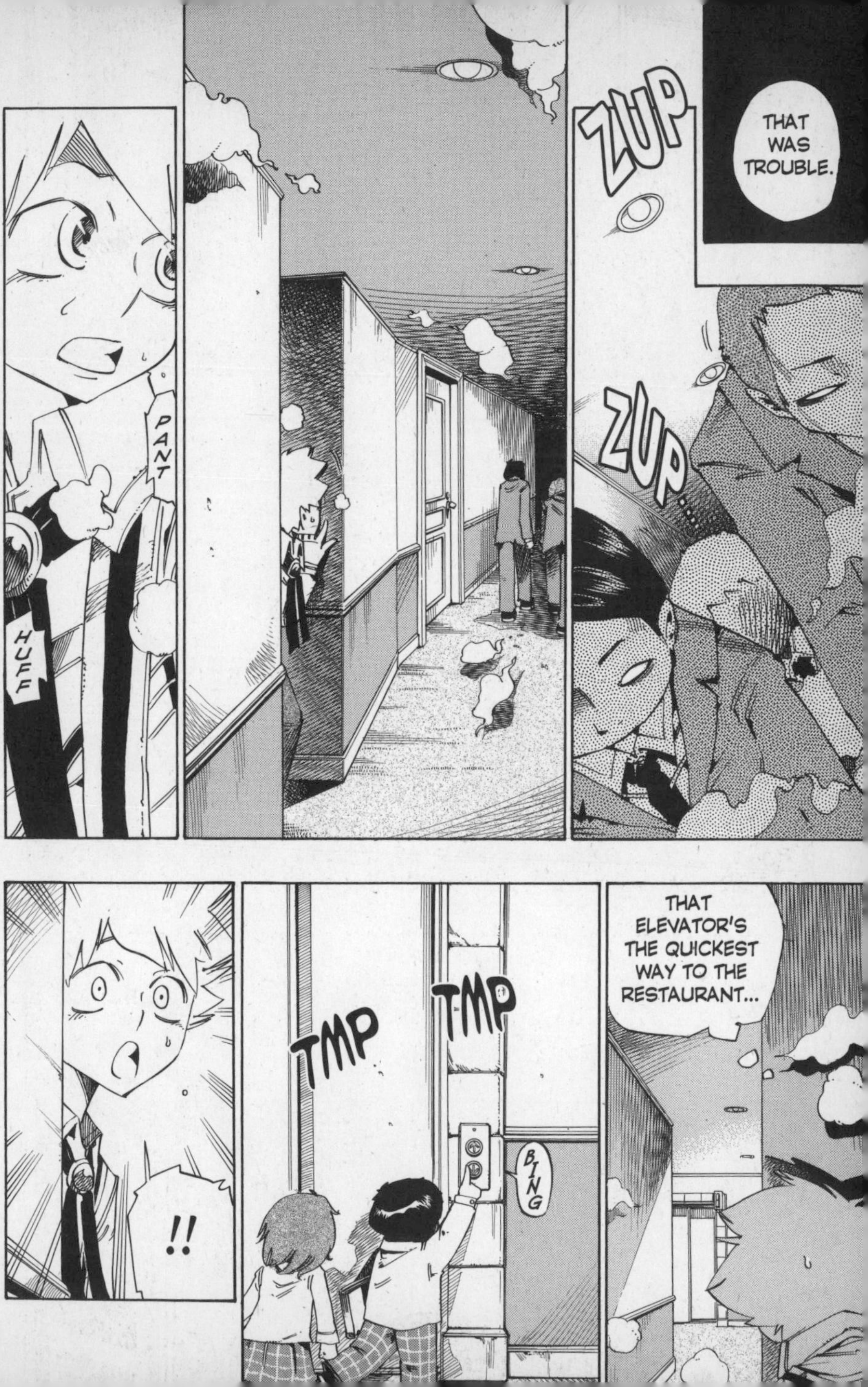
THAT WAS TROUBLE.
ZUP
ZUP...
PANT
HUFF
THAT ELEVATOR'S THE QUICKEST WAY TO THE RESTAURANT...
TMP
TMP
BING
!!

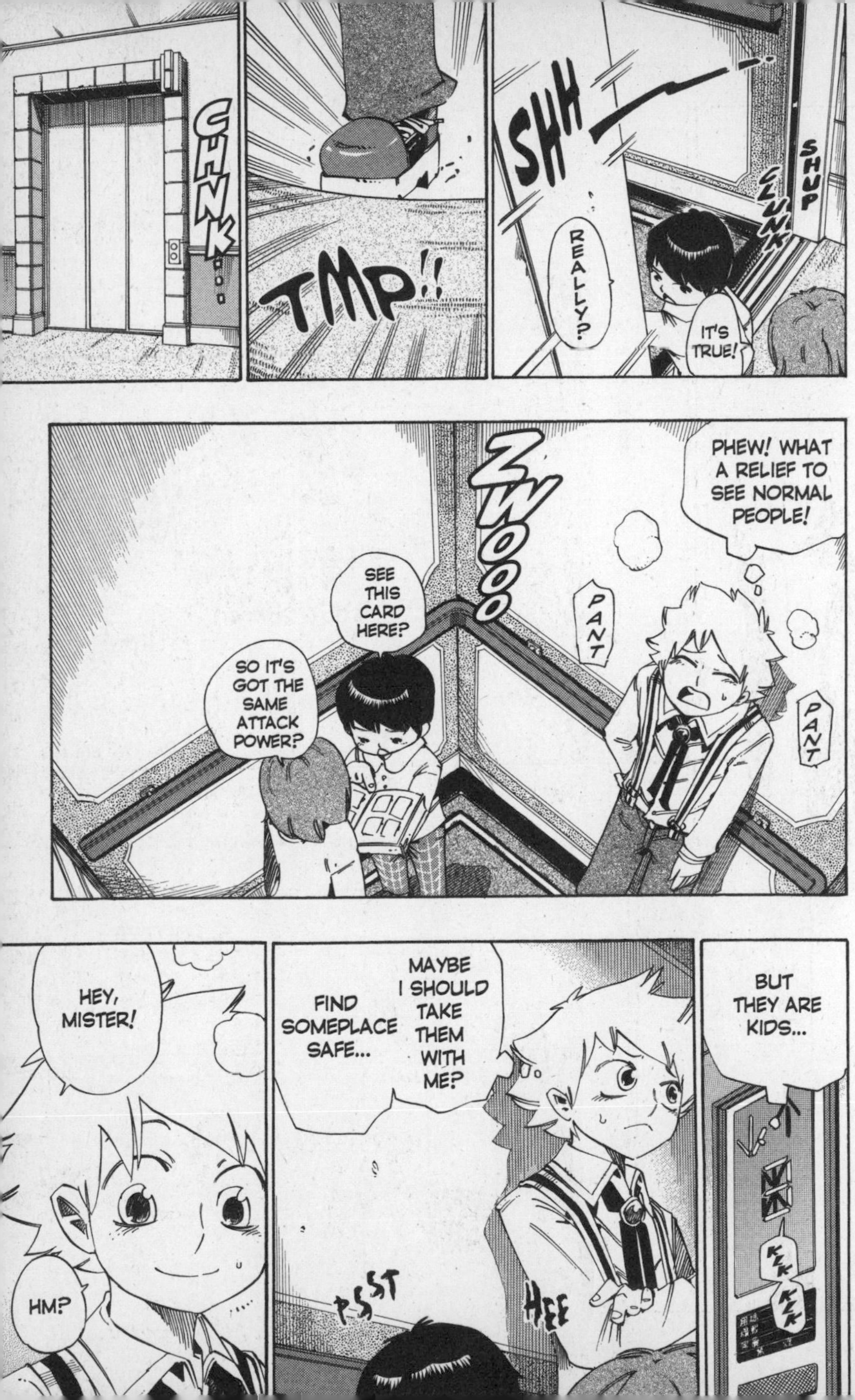
SHUP
CLUNK
SHH
REALLY?
IT'S TRUE!
TMP!!
CHNK...
PHEW! WHAT A RELIEF TO SEE NORMAL PEOPLE!
ZWOOOO
PANT
PANT
SEE THIS CARD HERE?
SO IT'S GOT THE SAME ATTACK POWER?
BUT THEY ARE KIDS...
KEK KEK
MAYBE I SHOULD TAKE THEM WITH ME?
FIND SOMEPLACE SAFE...
HEE
PSST
HEY, MISTER!
HM?

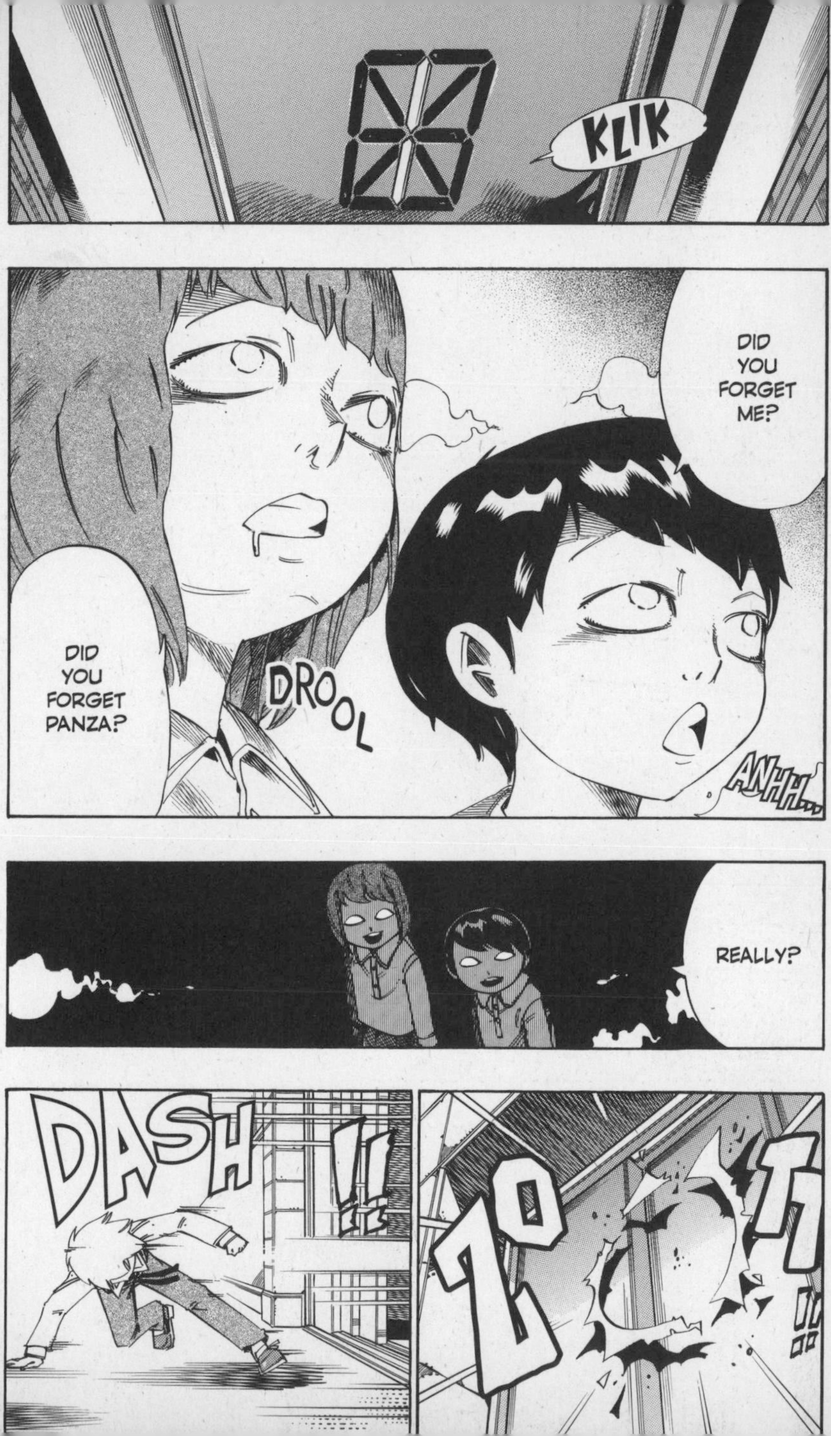
KLIK
DID YOU FORGET ME?
DID YOU FORGET PANZA?
DROOL
ANHH...
REALLY?
ZOT!!
DASH!!

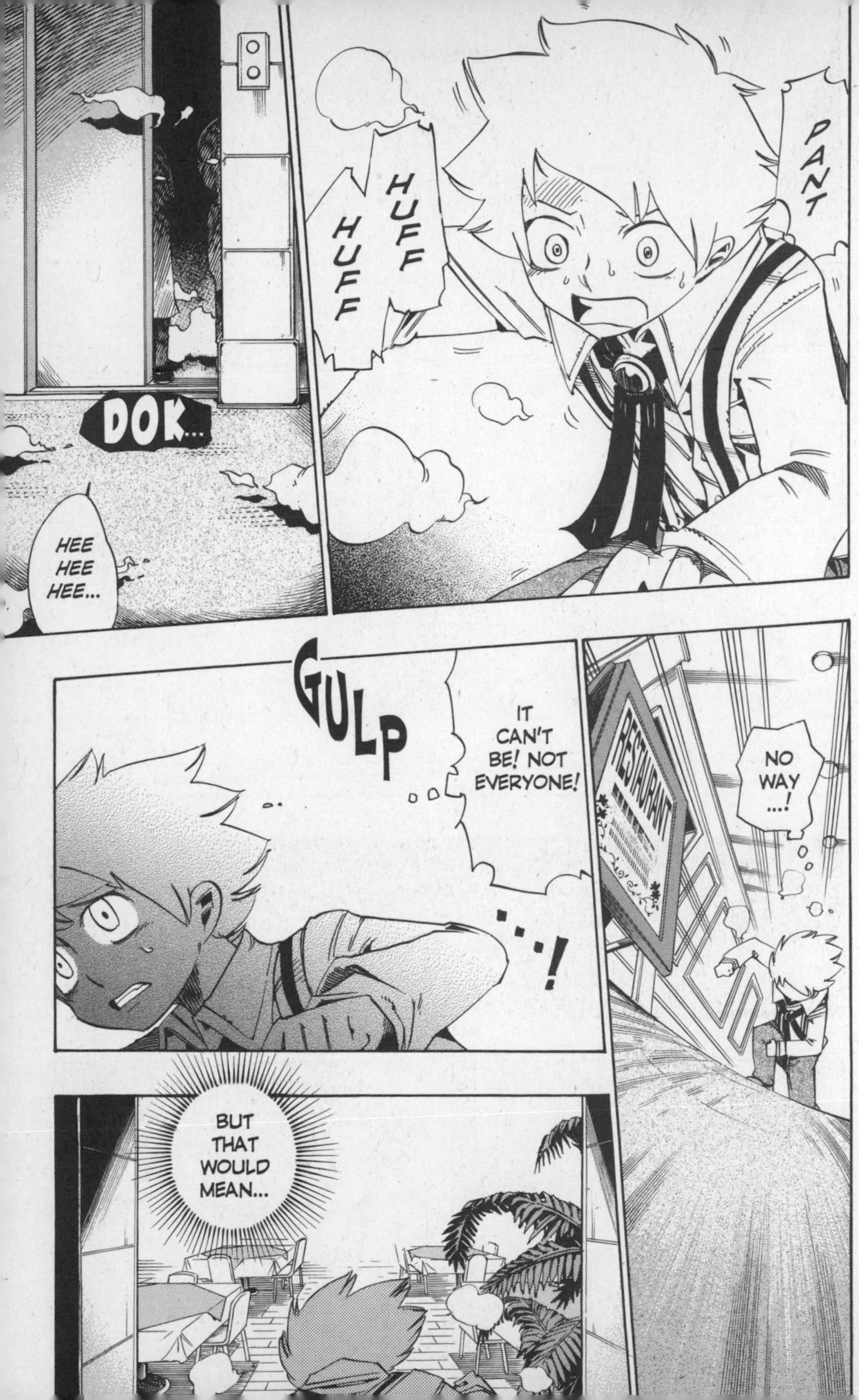
PANT
HUFF
HUFF
HUFF
DOK...
HEE HEE HEE...
NO WAY ...!
RESTAURANT
GULP
IT CAN'T BE! NOT EVERYONE!
...!
BUT THAT WOULD MEAN...

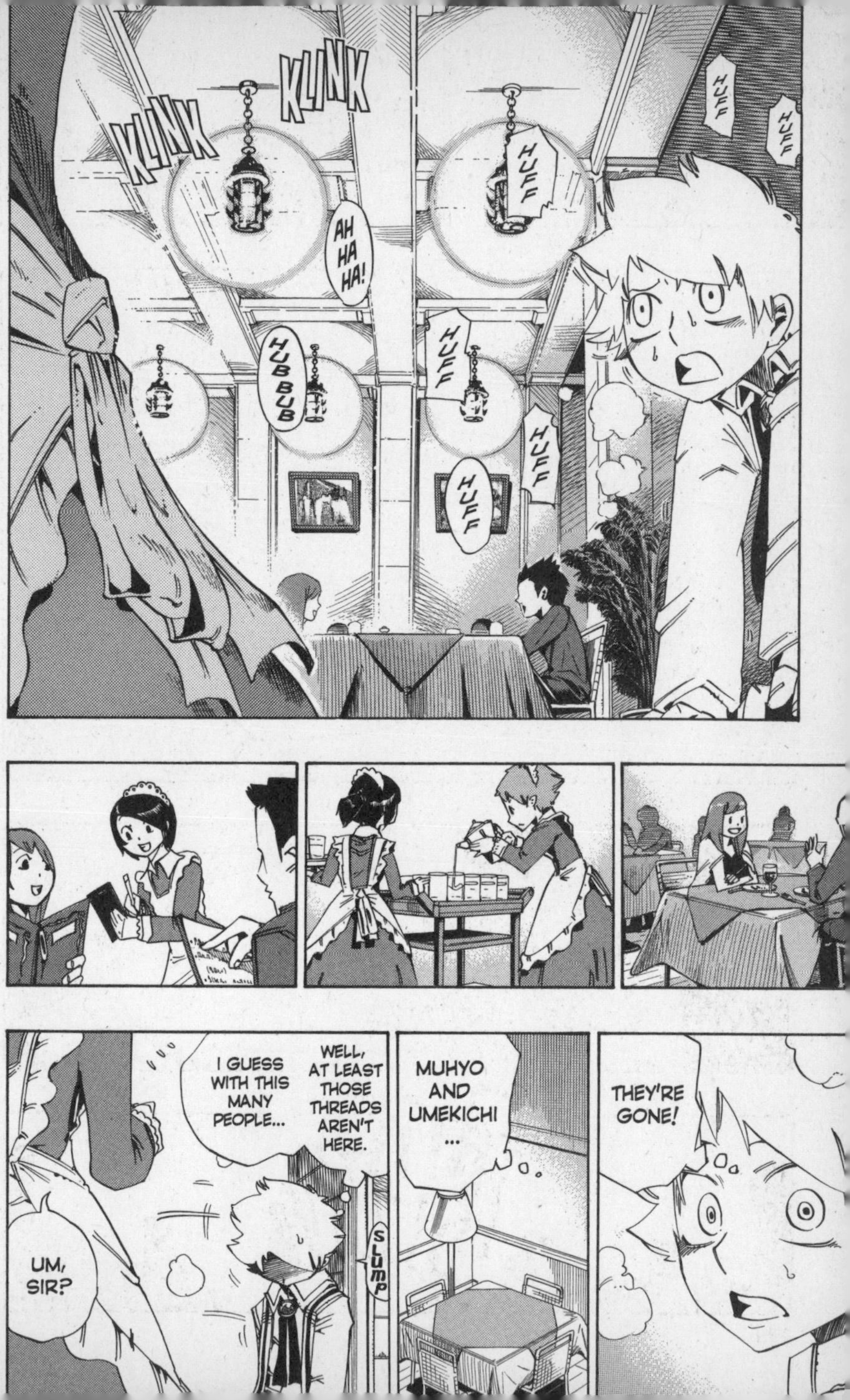
HUFF
HUFF
KLINK
KLINK
HUFF
AH HA HA!
HUFF
HUBBUB
HUFF
HUFF
THEY'RE GONE!
MUHYO AND UMEKICHI ...
WELL, AT LEAST THOSE THREADS AREN'T HERE.
I GUESS WITH THIS MANY PEOPLE...
SLUMP
UM, SIR?

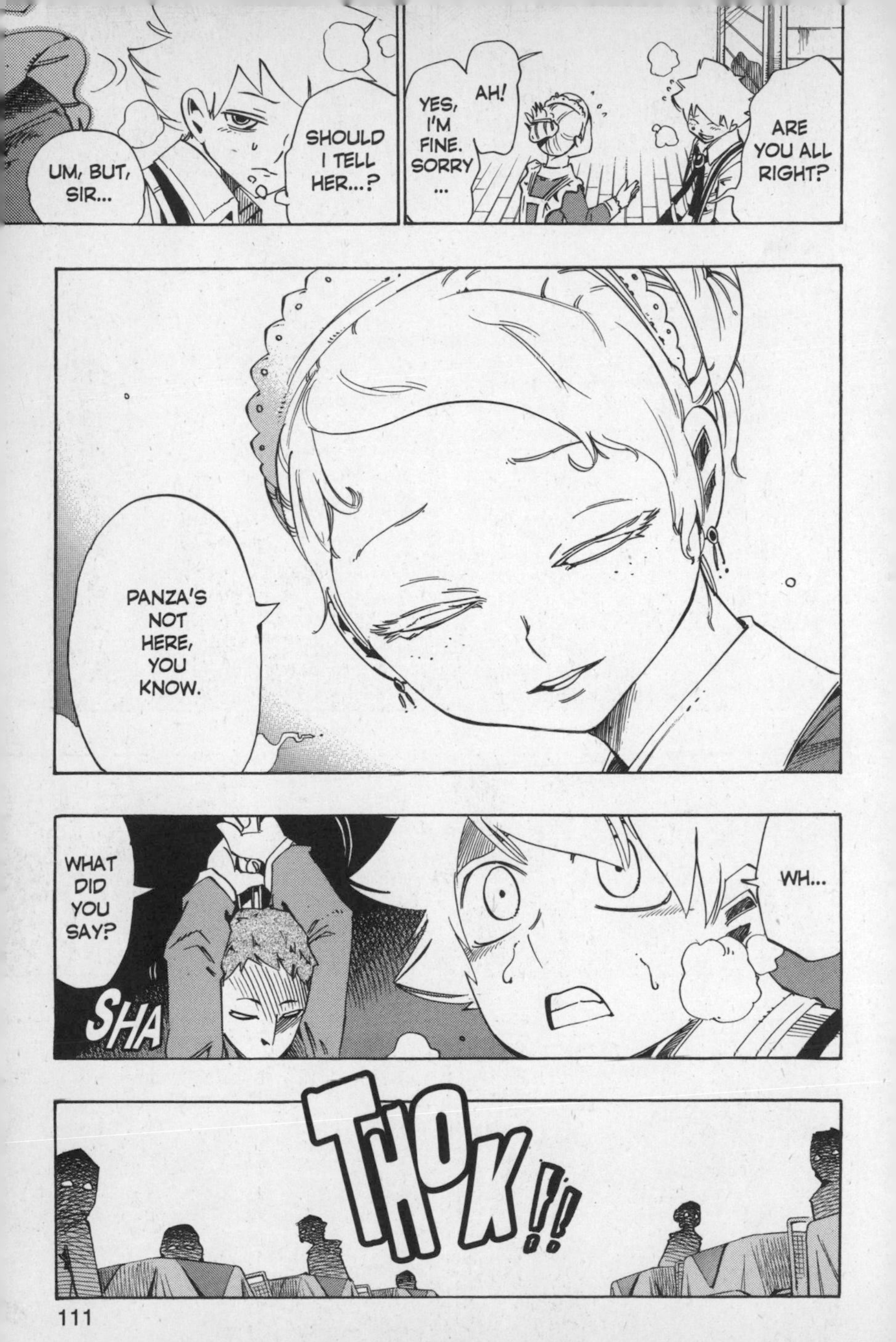
ARE YOU ALL RIGHT?
AH!
YES, I'M FINE. SORRY ...
SHOULD I TELL HER...?
UM, BUT, SIR...
PANZA'S NOT HERE, YOU KNOW.
WH...
WHAT DID YOU SAY?
SHA
THOK!!

Q: ARE ALL THE ENVOYS MUHYO SUMMONS SCARY? OR ARE THERE NICE ONES LIKE YUURI AND THE SEVEN-FACED DOG?

-ANONYMOUS, MIYAGI PREFECTURE

A: THEY'RE MOSTLY THE SCARY "SOULS! I WANT TO DEVOUR MORE SOULS!" TYPE. OUTSIDE OF A CONTRACT, EXECUTORS ARE JUST PEOPLE AND ENVOYS ARE JUST MONSTERS. THE SEVEN-FACED DOG AND YUURI ARE EXCEPTIONS THOUGH. IF THEY SPEND ENOUGH TIME TOGETHER, A FRIENDSHIP CAN DEVELOP BETWEEN EXECUTOR AND ENVOY. THE SEVEN-FACED DOG IS REALLY MORE OF A PET THAN A FRIEND THOUGH. MUHYO'S A GOOD TRAINER...

Q: THOSE ENVOYS FROM THE UNDERWORLD ARE PRETTY TOUGH, BUT I WAS WONDERING, ARE THERE GIRL ENVOYS AND BOY ENVOYS? DO THEY EVER FALL IN LOVE?

-N.A., KAGOSHIMA PREFECTURE

A: UM... LET'S ASK YUURI, SHALL WE?

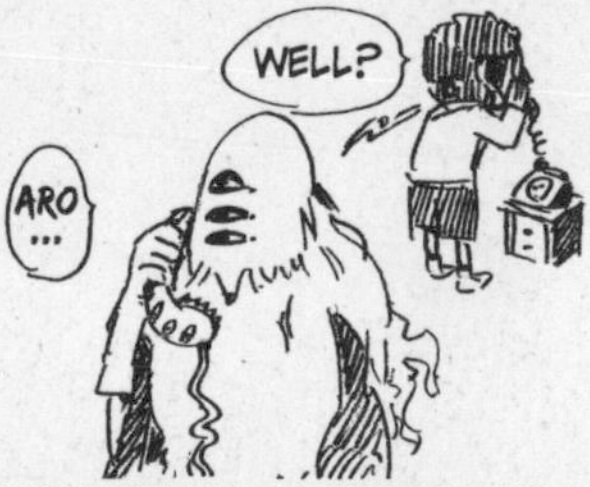
WELL?
ARO...

HE LOOKED OFF INTO THE DISTANCE AND SAID NOTHING FOR TEN MINUTES... SO I'M GUESSING THE ANSWER'S "YEAH."

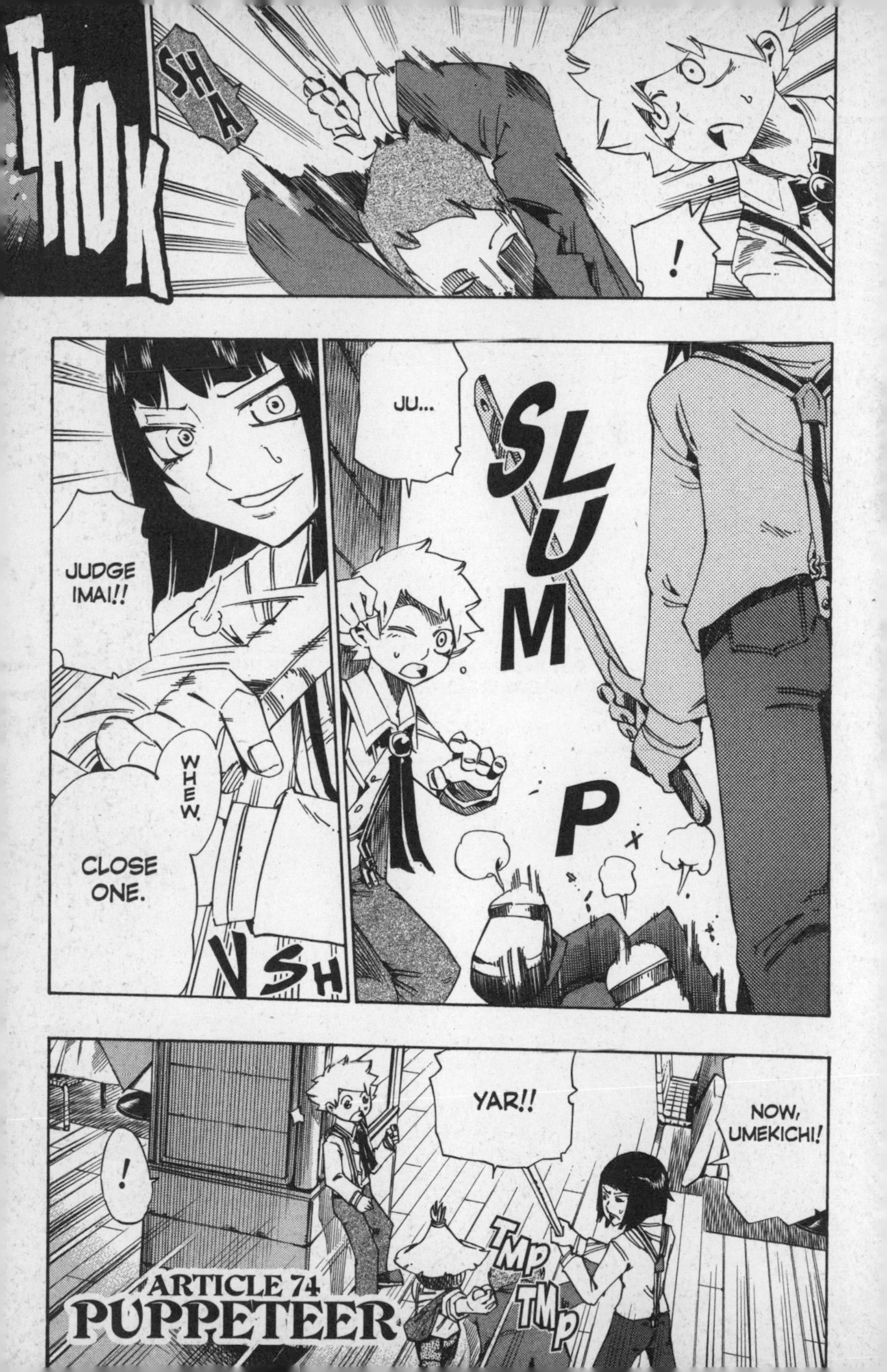
SHA
!
THOK
JU...
SLUMP
JUDGE IMAI!!
WHEW.
CLOSE ONE.
VSH
NOW, UMEKICHI!
YAR!!
!
TMP
TMP
ARTICLE 74
PUPPETEER

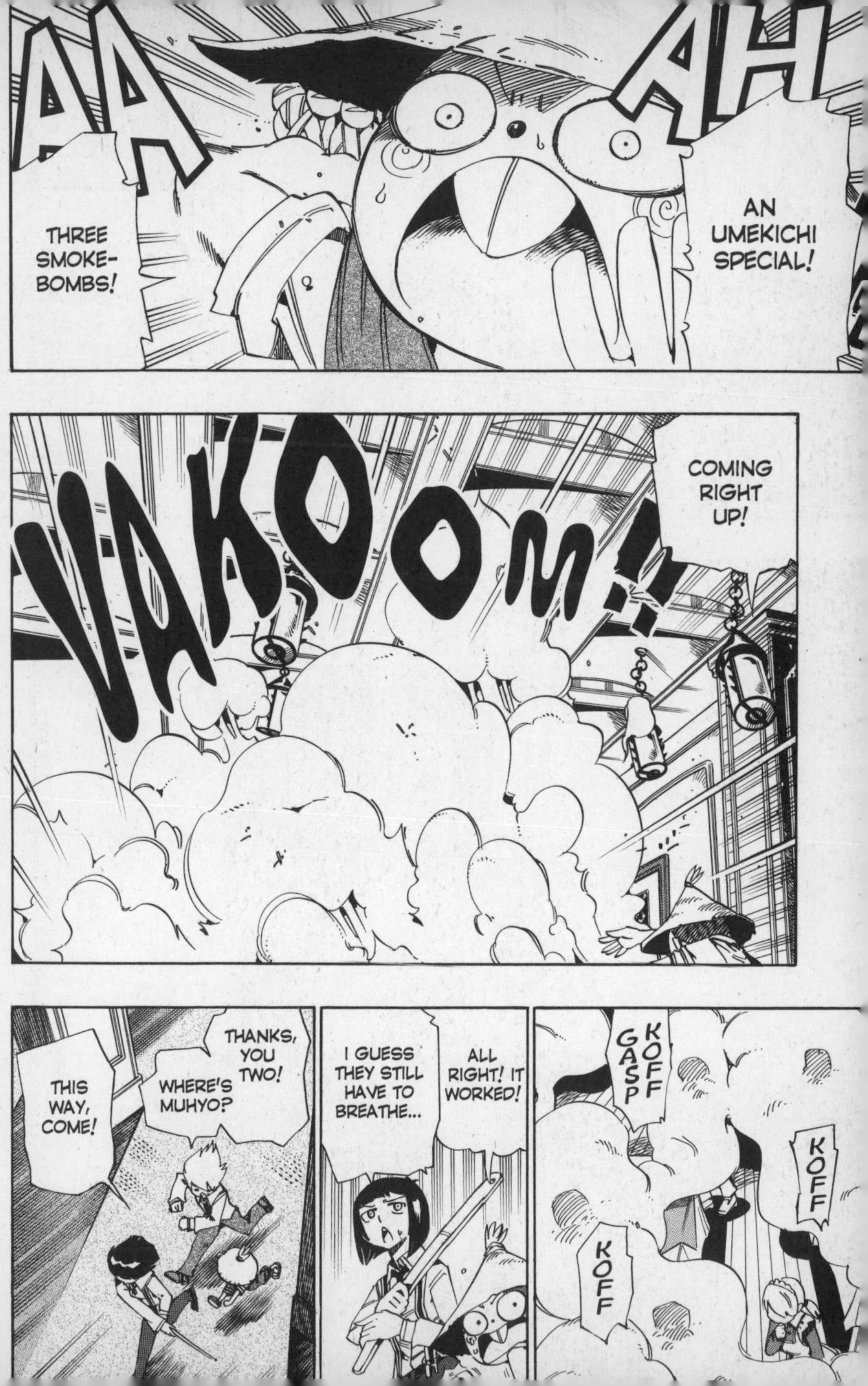

AAAH
AN UMEKICHI SPECIAL!
THREE SMOKE-BOMBS!
COMING RIGHT UP!
VAKOOM!!
KOFF
GASP
KOFF
KOFF
ALL RIGHT! IT WORKED!
I GUESS THEY STILL HAVE TO BREATHE...
THANKS, YOU TWO!
WHERE'S MUHYO?
THIS WAY, COME!

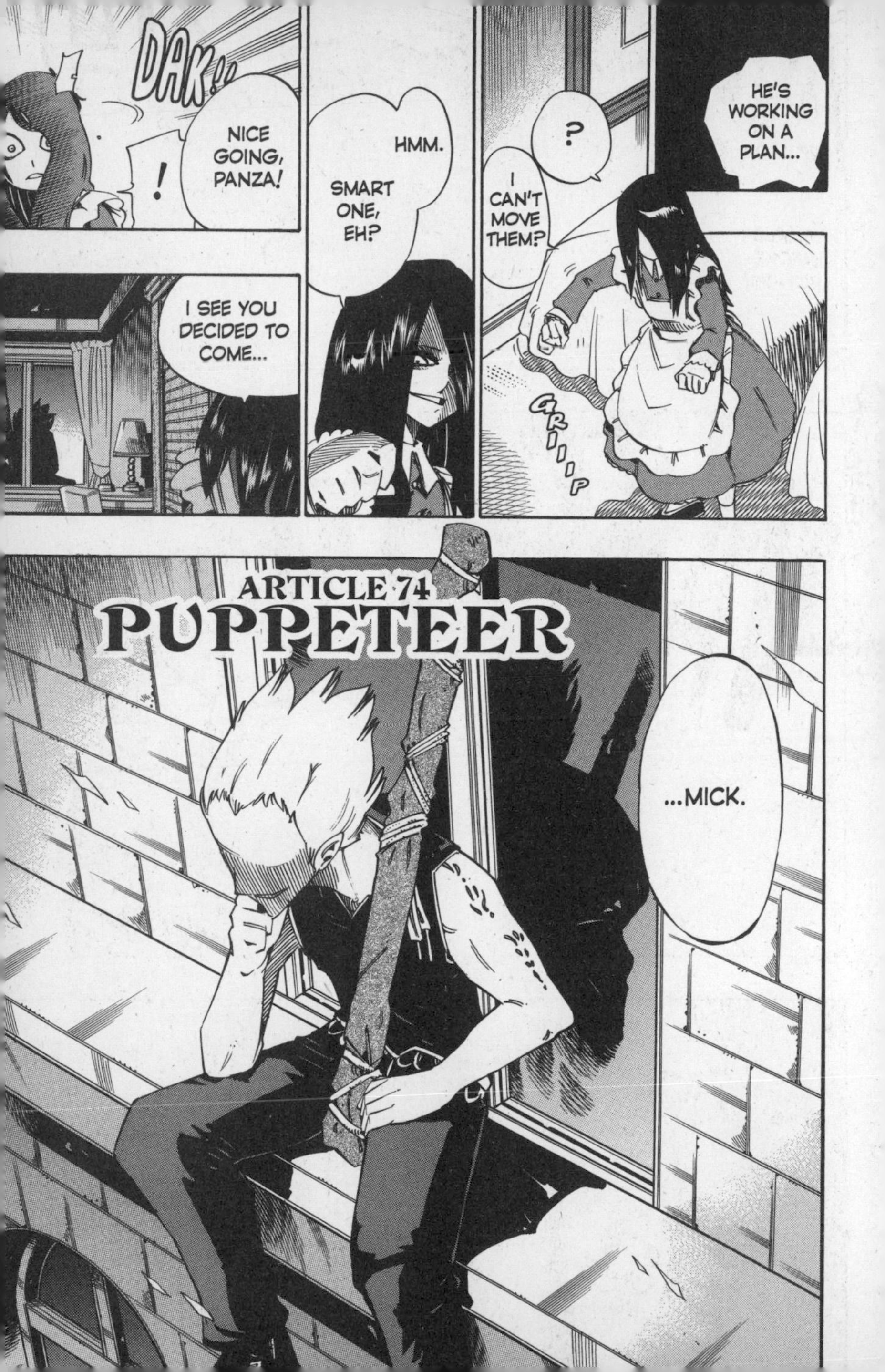
HE'S WORKING ON A PLAN...
?
I CAN'T MOVE THEM?
GRIIIP
HMM.
SMART ONE, EH?
DAK!!
NICE GOING, PANZA!
!
I SEE YOU DECIDED TO COME...
ARTICLE 74
PUPPETEER
...MICK.

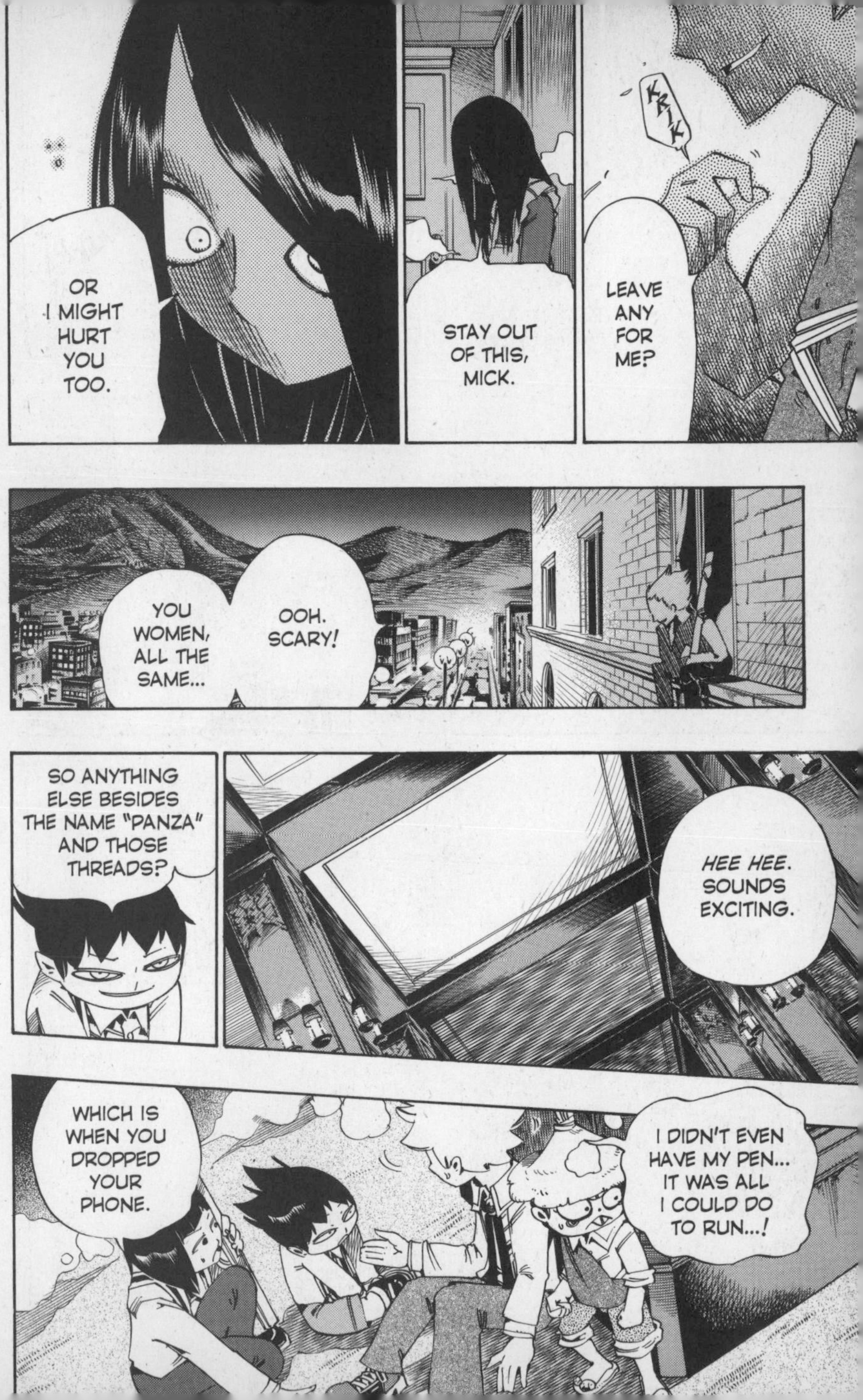
KRIK
LEAVE ANY FOR ME?
STAY OUT OF THIS, MICK.
OR I MIGHT HURT YOU TOO.
OOH. SCARY!
YOU WOMEN, ALL THE SAME...
HEE HEE. SOUNDS EXCITING.
SO ANYTHING ELSE BESIDES THE NAME "PANZA" AND THOSE THREADS?
I DIDN'T EVEN HAVE MY PEN... IT WAS ALL I COULD DO TO RUN...!
WHICH IS WHEN YOU DROPPED YOUR PHONE.

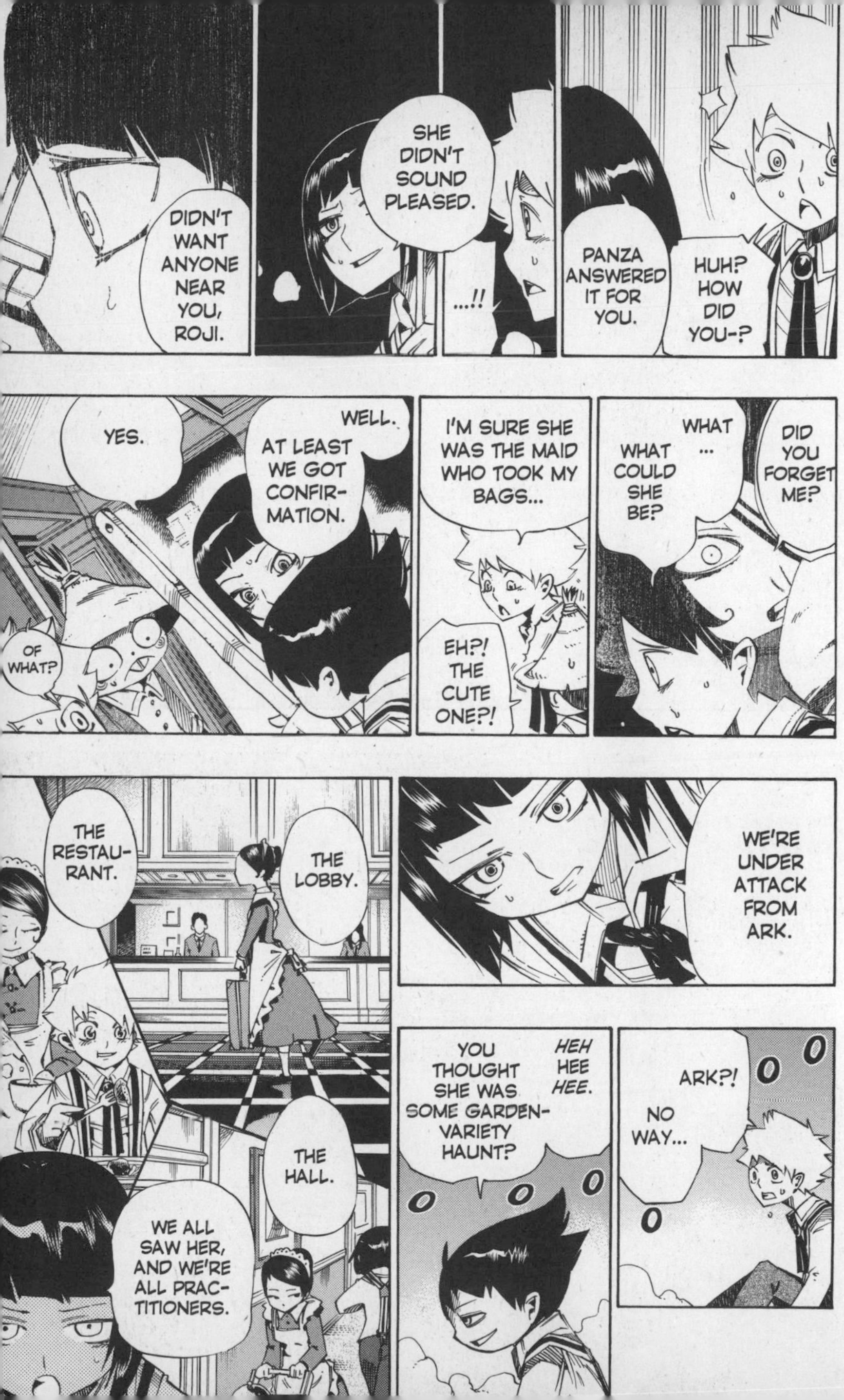
HUH? HOW DID YOU-?
PANZA ANSWERED IT FOR YOU.
...!!
SHE DIDN'T SOUND PLEASED.
DIDN'T WANT ANYONE NEAR YOU, ROJI.
DID YOU FORGET ME?
WHAT ...
WHAT COULD SHE BE?
I'M SURE SHE WAS THE MAID WHO TOOK MY BAGS...
EH?! THE CUTE ONE?!
WELL. AT LEAST WE GOT CONFIRMATION.
YES.
OF WHAT?
WE'RE UNDER ATTACK FROM ARK.
ARK?!
NO WAY...
HEH HEE HEE.
YOU THOUGHT SHE WAS SOME GARDEN-VARIETY HAUNT?
THE LOBBY.
THE RESTAURANT.
THE HALL.
WE ALL SAW HER, AND WE'RE ALL PRACTITIONERS.

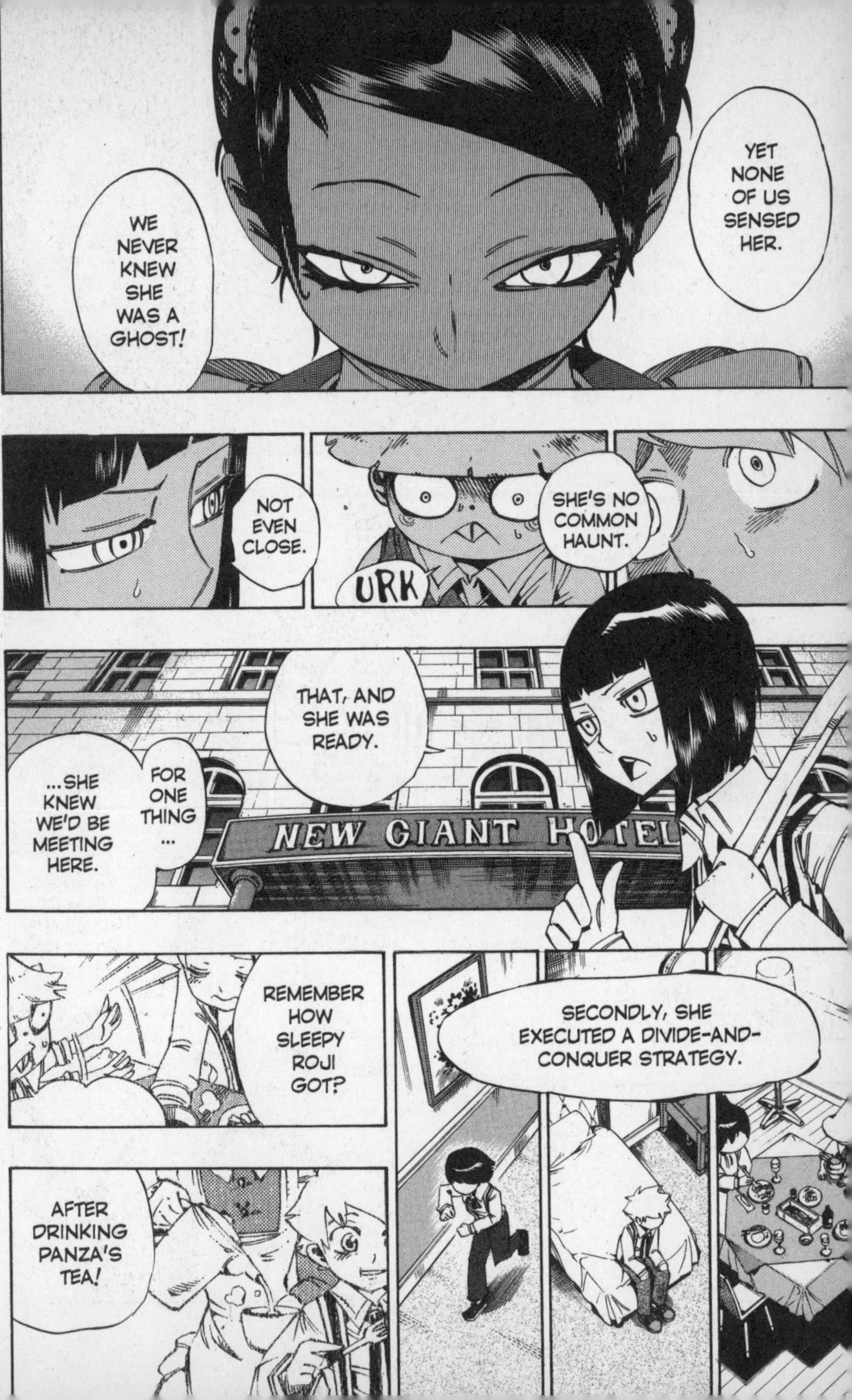

YET NONE OF US SENSED HER.
WE NEVER KNEW SHE WAS A GHOST!
SHE'S NO COMMON HAUNT.
URK
NOT EVEN CLOSE.
THAT, AND SHE WAS READY.
NEW GIANT HOTEL
FOR ONE THING ...
...SHE KNEW WE'D BE MEETING HERE.
SECONDLY, SHE EXECUTED A DIVIDE-AND-CONQUER STRATEGY.
REMEMBER HOW SLEEPY ROJI GOT?
AFTER DRINKING PANZA'S TEA!

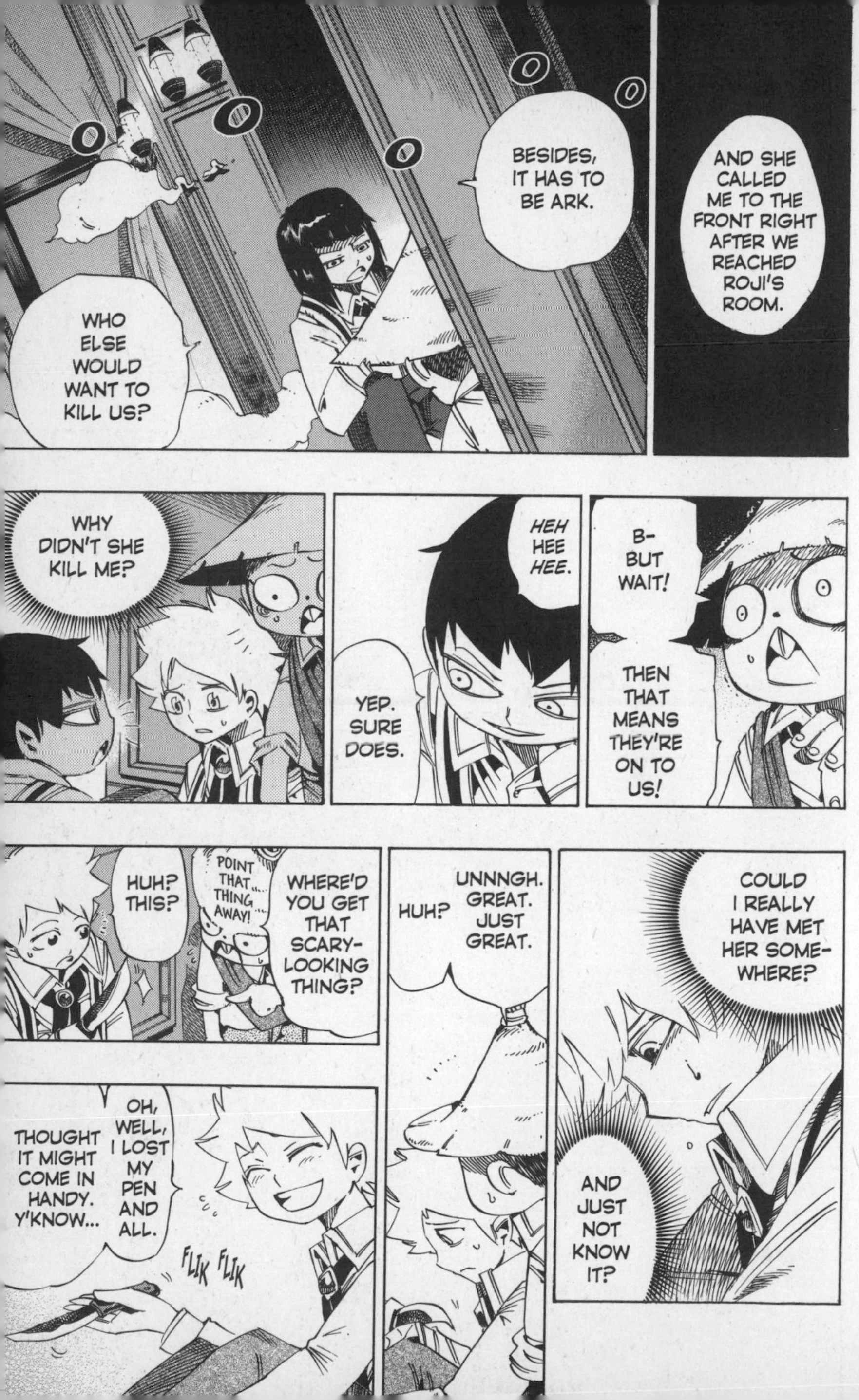
AND SHE CALLED ME TO THE FRONT RIGHT AFTER WE REACHED ROJI'S ROOM.
BESIDES, IT HAS TO BE ARK.
WHO ELSE WOULD WANT TO KILL US?
B-BUT WAIT!
THEN THAT MEANS THEY'RE ON TO US!
HEH HEE HEE.
YEP. SURE DOES.
WHY DIDN'T SHE KILL ME?
COULD I REALLY HAVE MET HER SOME-WHERE?
AND JUST NOT KNOW IT?
UNNNGH. GREAT. JUST GREAT.
HUH?
WHERE'D YOU GET THAT SCARY-LOOKING THING?
POINT THAT THING AWAY!
HUH? THIS?
OH, WELL, I LOST MY PEN AND ALL.
THOUGHT IT MIGHT COME IN HANDY. Y'KNOW...
FLIK FLIK

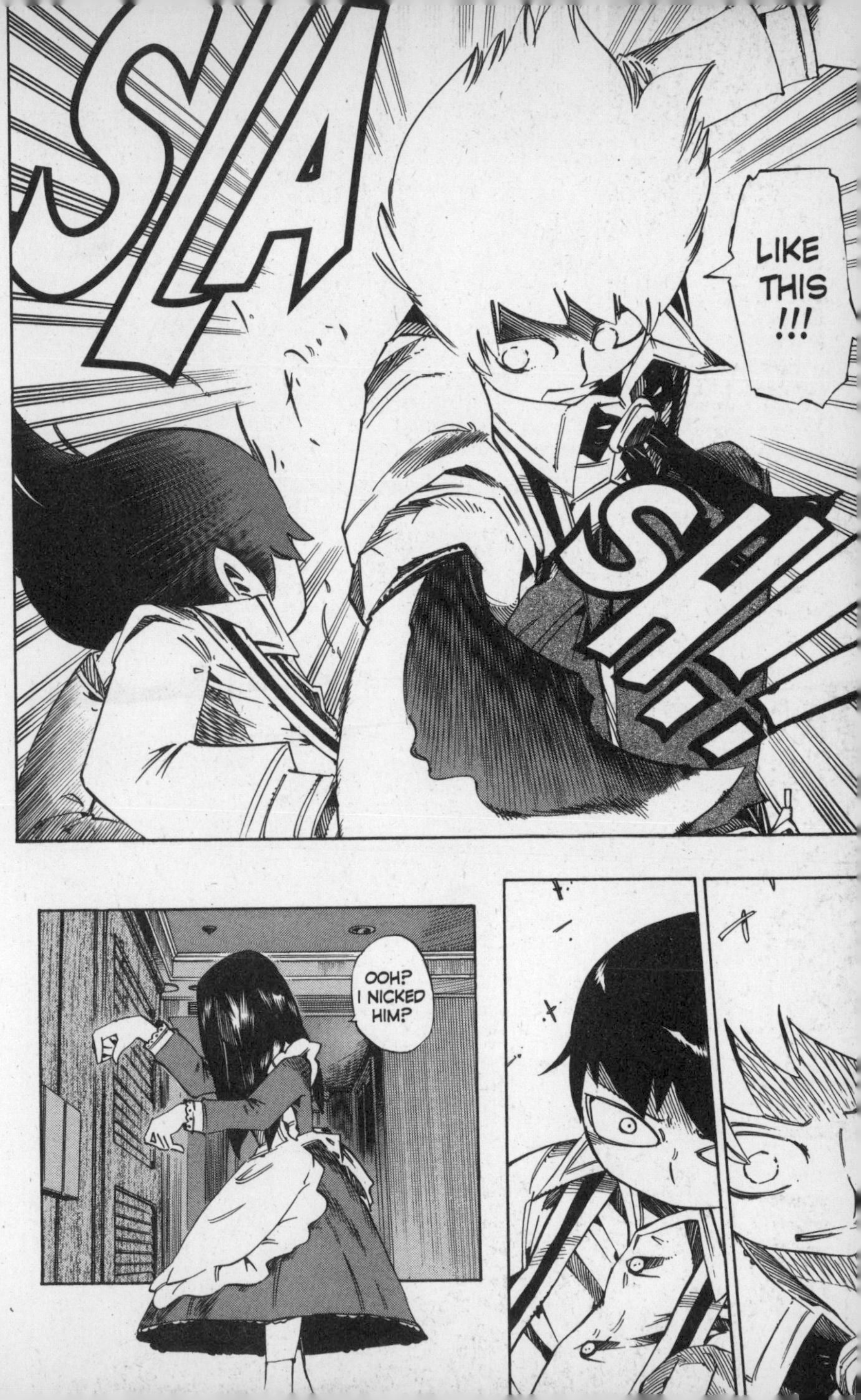
LIKE THIS !!!
SIA
SH
OOH? I NICKED HIM?

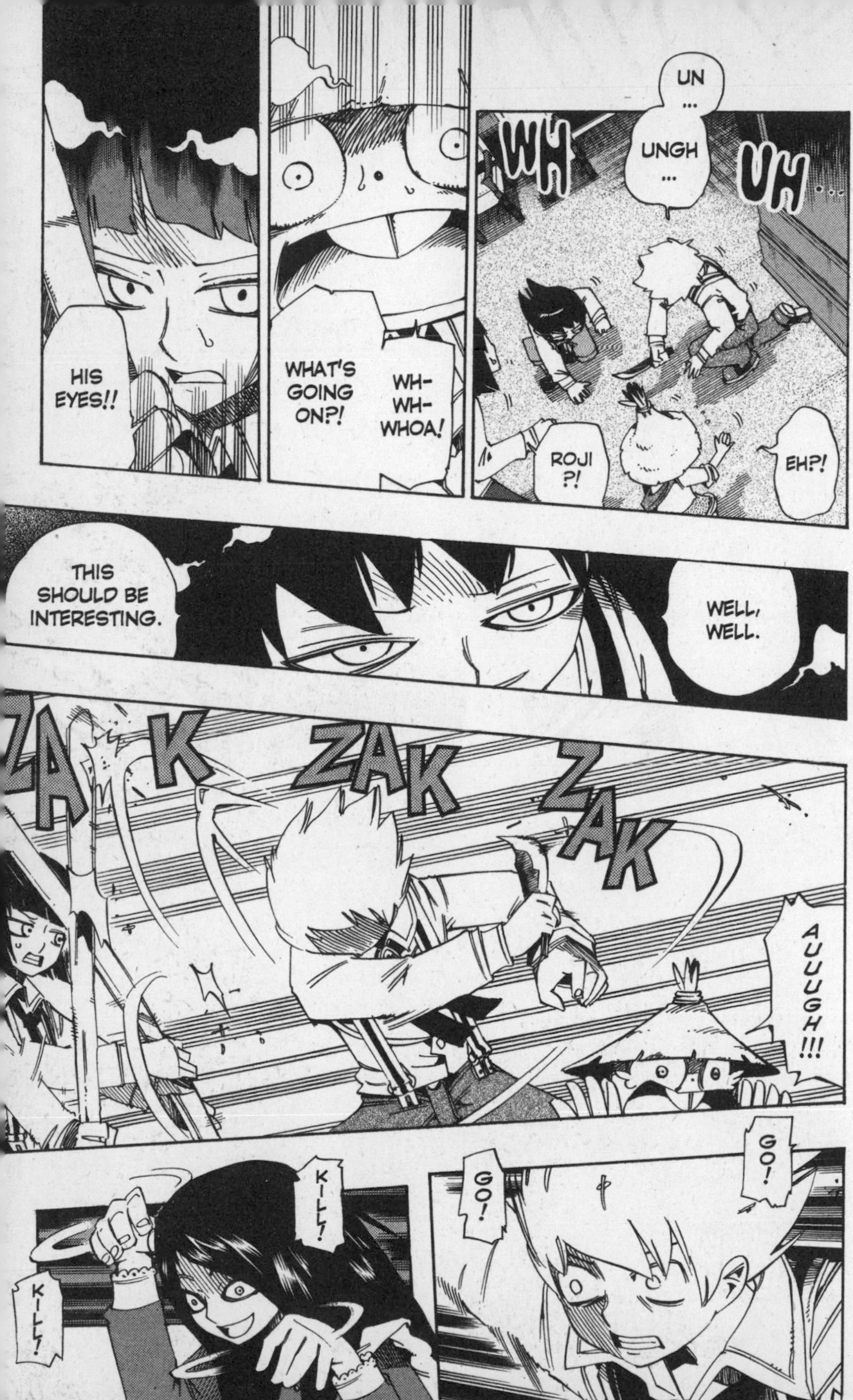
UH...
UN ... UNGH ...
AWH
EH?!
ROJI ?!
WH- WH- WHOA!
WHAT'S GOING ON?!
HIS EYES!!
WELL, WELL.
THIS SHOULD BE INTERESTING.
AUUUGH!!!
ZAK
ZAK
ZA K
GO!
GO!
KILL!
KILL!

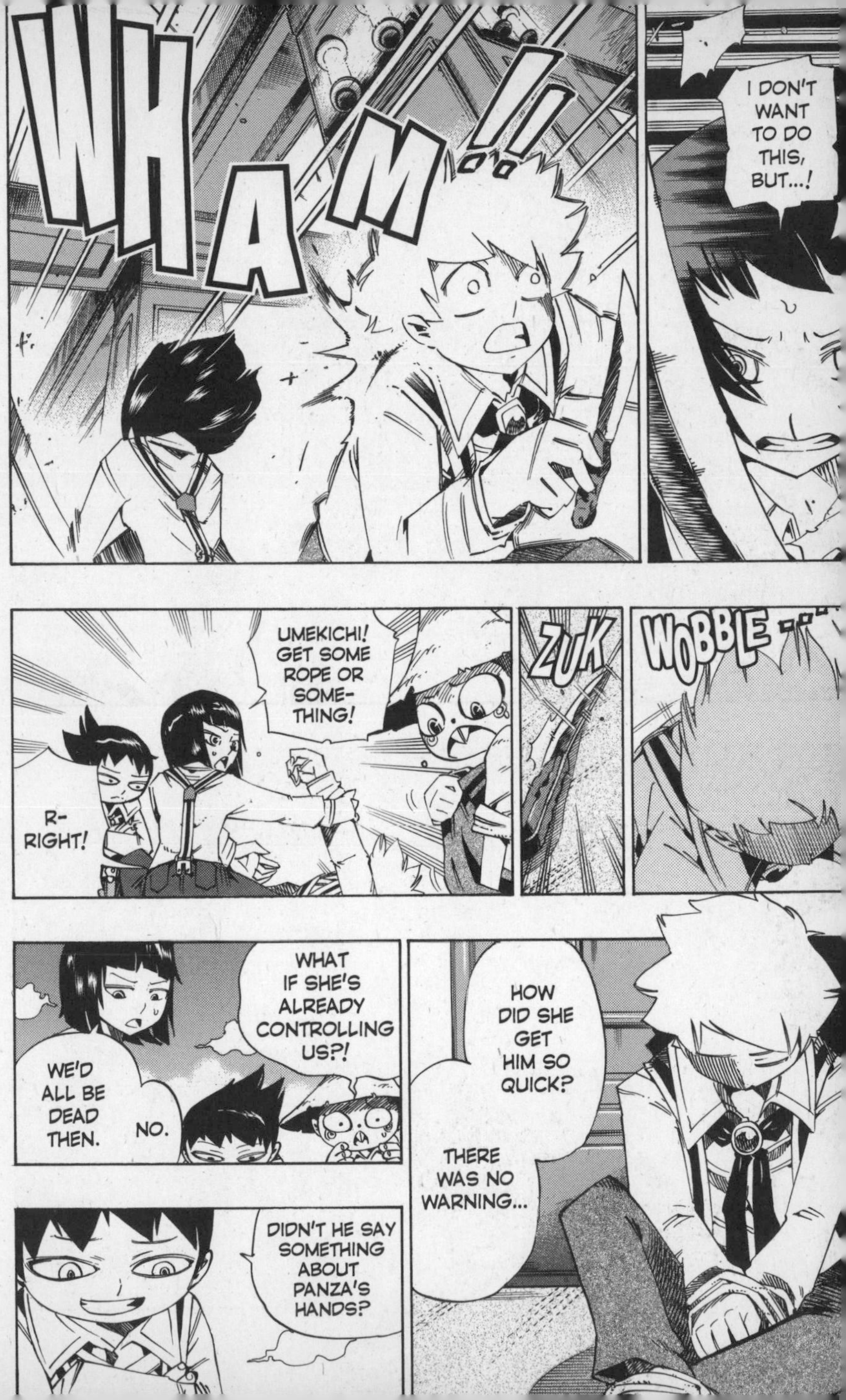
I DON'T WANT TO DO THIS, BUT...!
WHAM!!
WOBBLE
ZUK
UMEKICHI! GET SOME ROPE OR SOME-THING!
R-RIGHT!
HOW DID SHE GET HIM SO QUICK?
THERE WAS NO WARNING...
WHAT IF SHE'S ALREADY CONTROLLING US?!
NO.
WE'D ALL BE DEAD THEN.
DIDN'T HE SAY SOMETHING ABOUT PANZA'S HANDS?

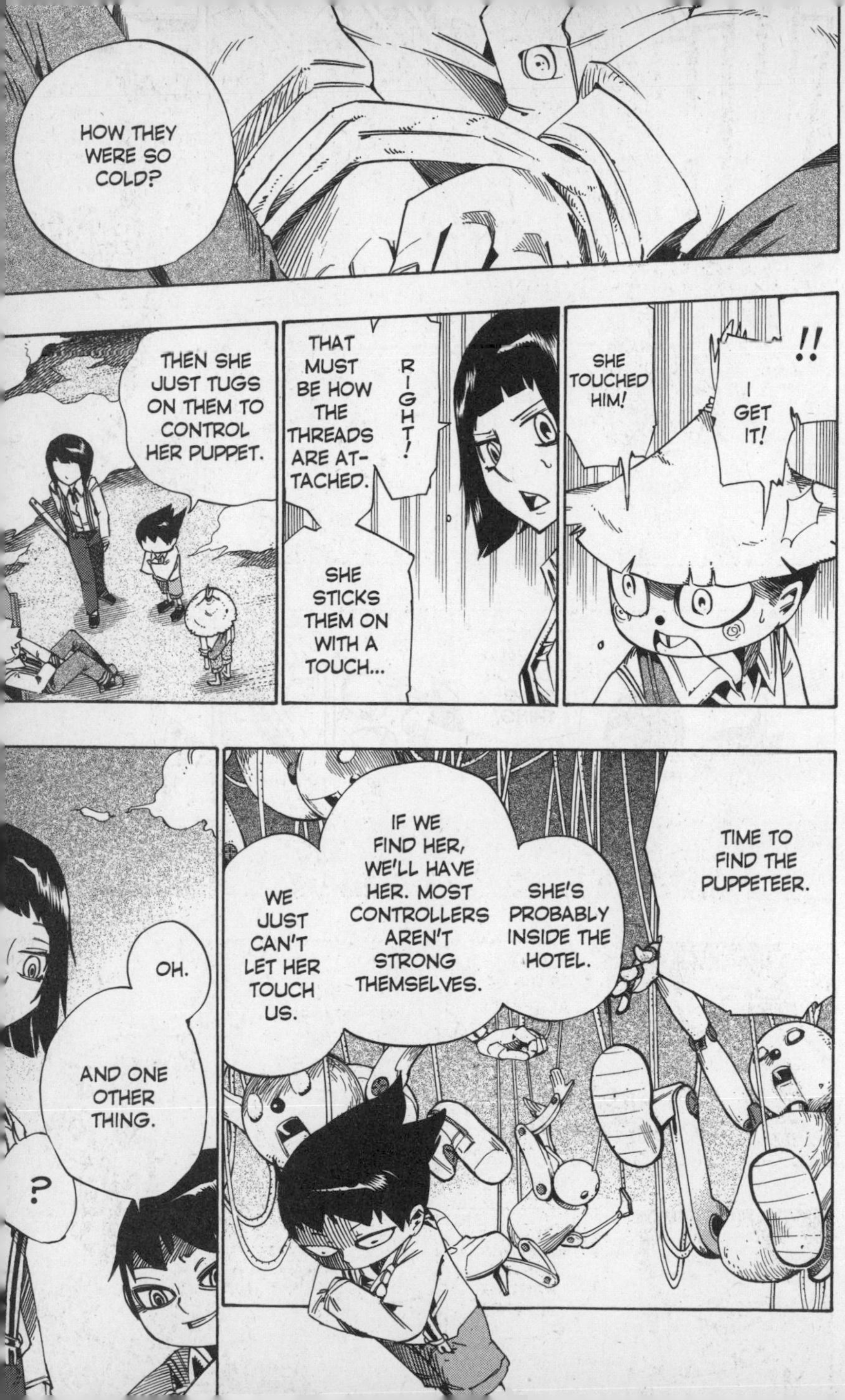
HOW THEY WERE SO COLD?
!!
I GET IT!
SHE TOUCHED HIM!
RIGHT!
THAT MUST BE HOW THE THREADS ARE AT-TACHED.
SHE STICKS THEM ON WITH A TOUCH...
THEN SHE JUST TUGS ON THEM TO CONTROL HER PUPPET.
TIME TO FIND THE PUPPETEER.
SHE'S PROBABLY INSIDE THE HOTEL.
IF WE FIND HER, WE'LL HAVE HER. MOST CONTROLLERS AREN'T STRONG THEMSELVES.
WE JUST CAN'T LET HER TOUCH US.
OH.
AND ONE OTHER THING.
?

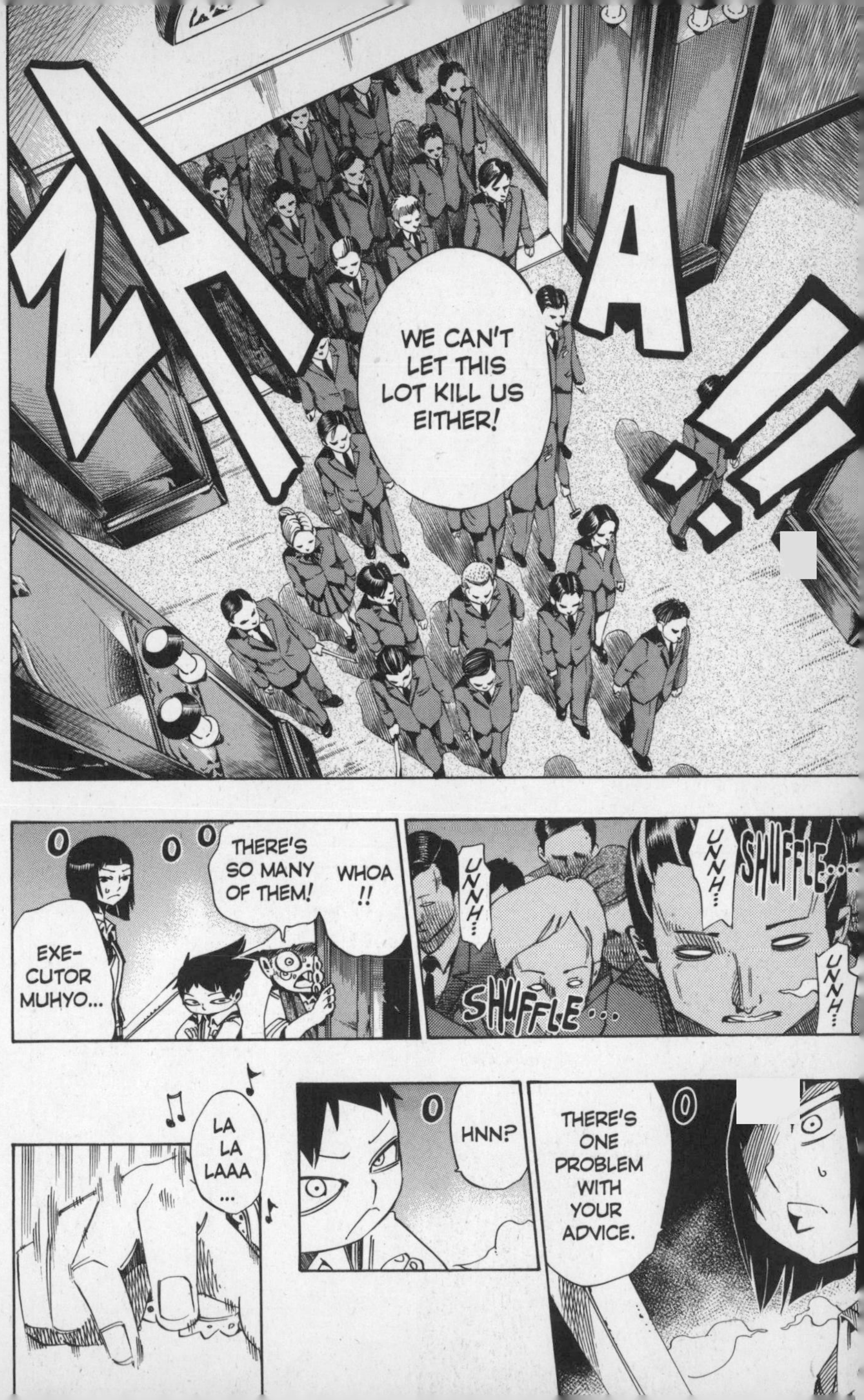
WE CAN'T LET THIS LOT KILL US EITHER!
UNNH...
SHUFFLE...
UNNH...
UNNH...
SHUFFLE...
WHOA !!
THERE'S SO MANY OF THEM!
EXE-CUTOR MUHYO...
THERE'S ONE PROBLEM WITH YOUR ADVICE.
HNN?
LA LA LAAA ...

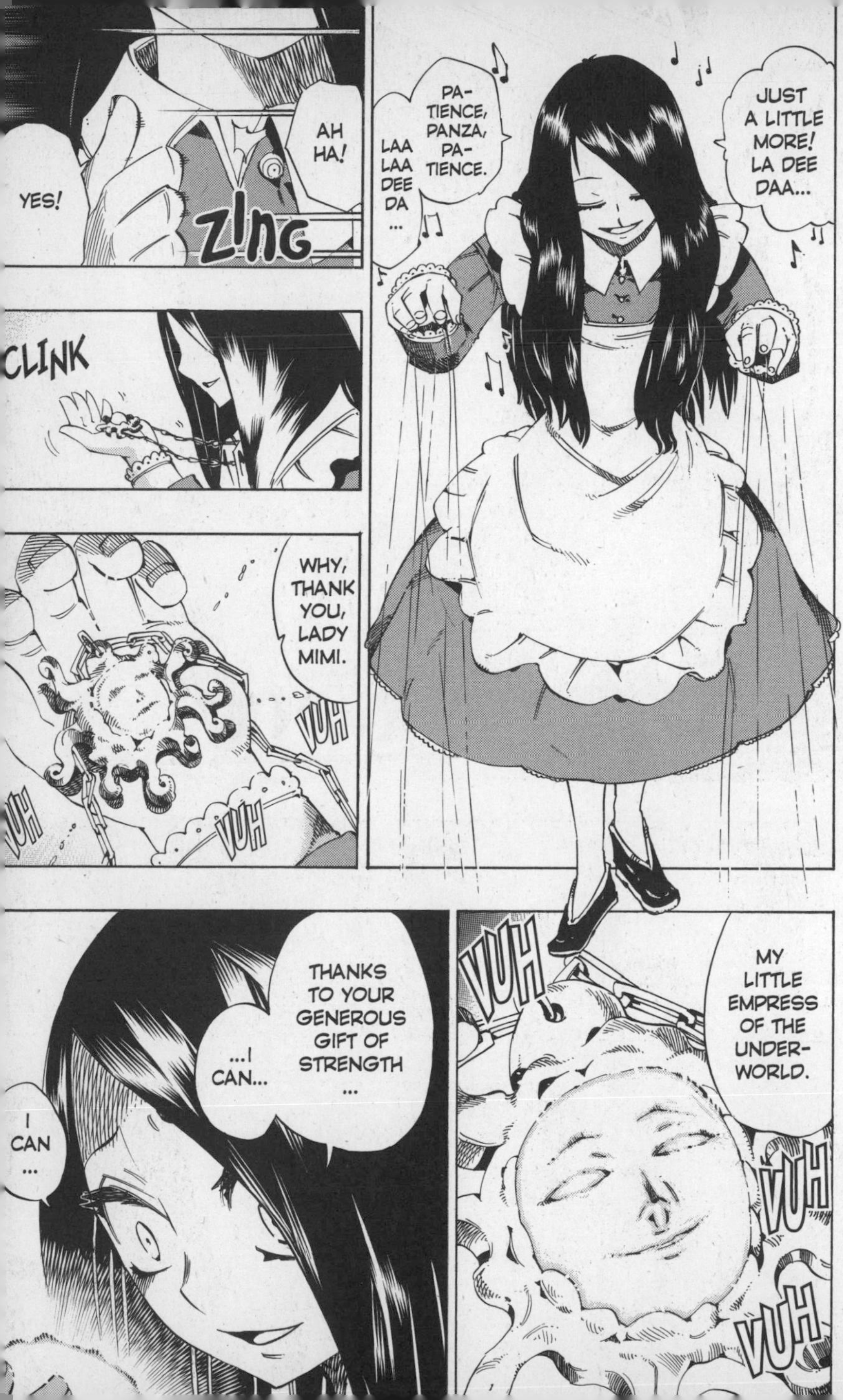
JUST A LITTLE MORE! LA DEE DAA...
PA-TIENCE, PANZA, PA-TIENCE.
LAA LAA DEE DA ...
AH HA!
YES!
ZING
CLINK
WHY, THANK YOU, LADY MIMI.
VUH
VUH
VUH
MY LITTLE EMPRESS OF THE UNDER-WORLD.
VUH
VUH
VUH
THANKS TO YOUR GENEROUS GIFT OF STRENGTH ...
...I CAN...
I CAN ...

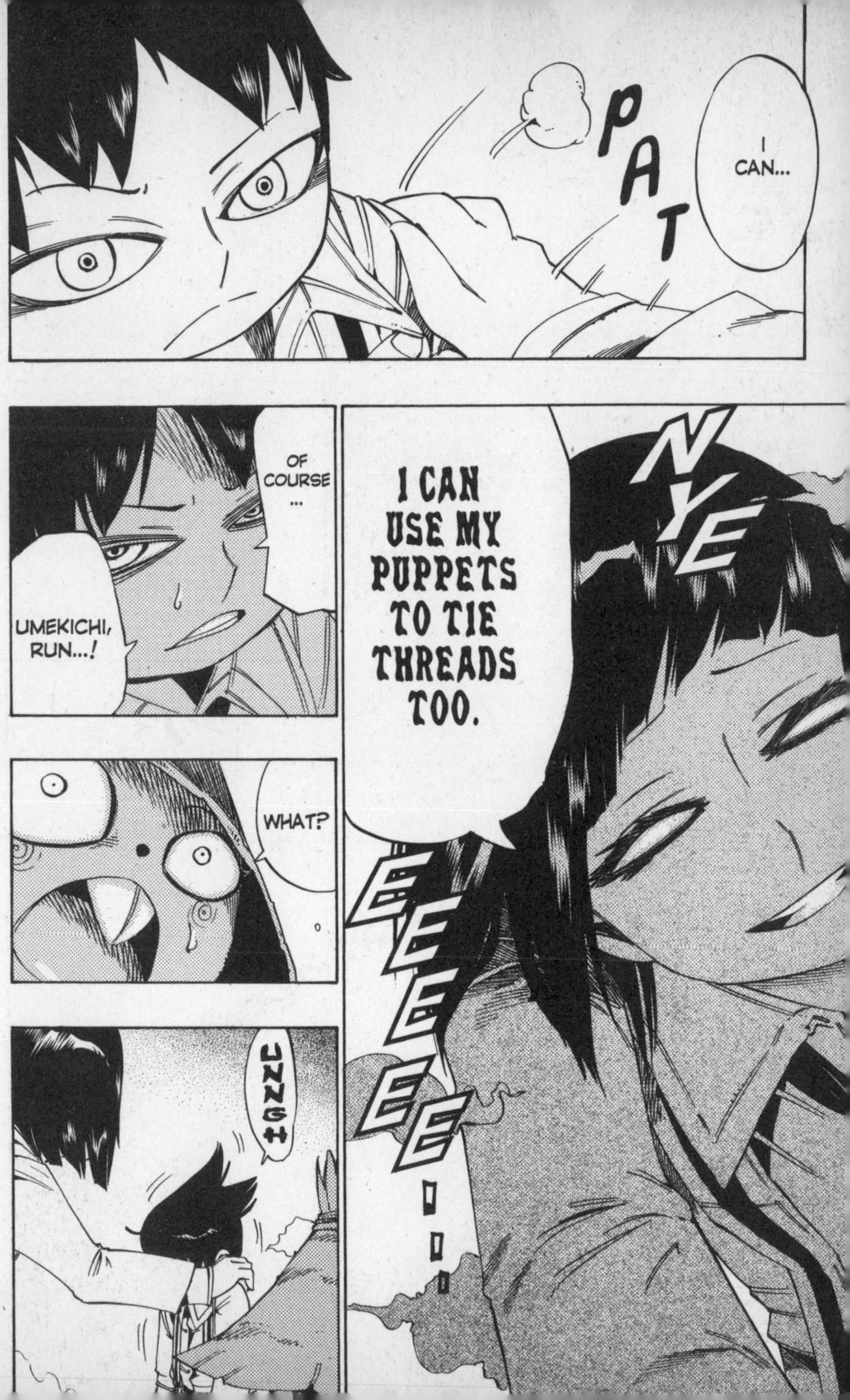
I CAN...
PAT
I CAN USE MY PUPPETS TO TIE THREADS TOO.
NYEEEEEEEE!!!
OF COURSE ...
UMEKICHI, RUN...!
WHAT?
UNNGH

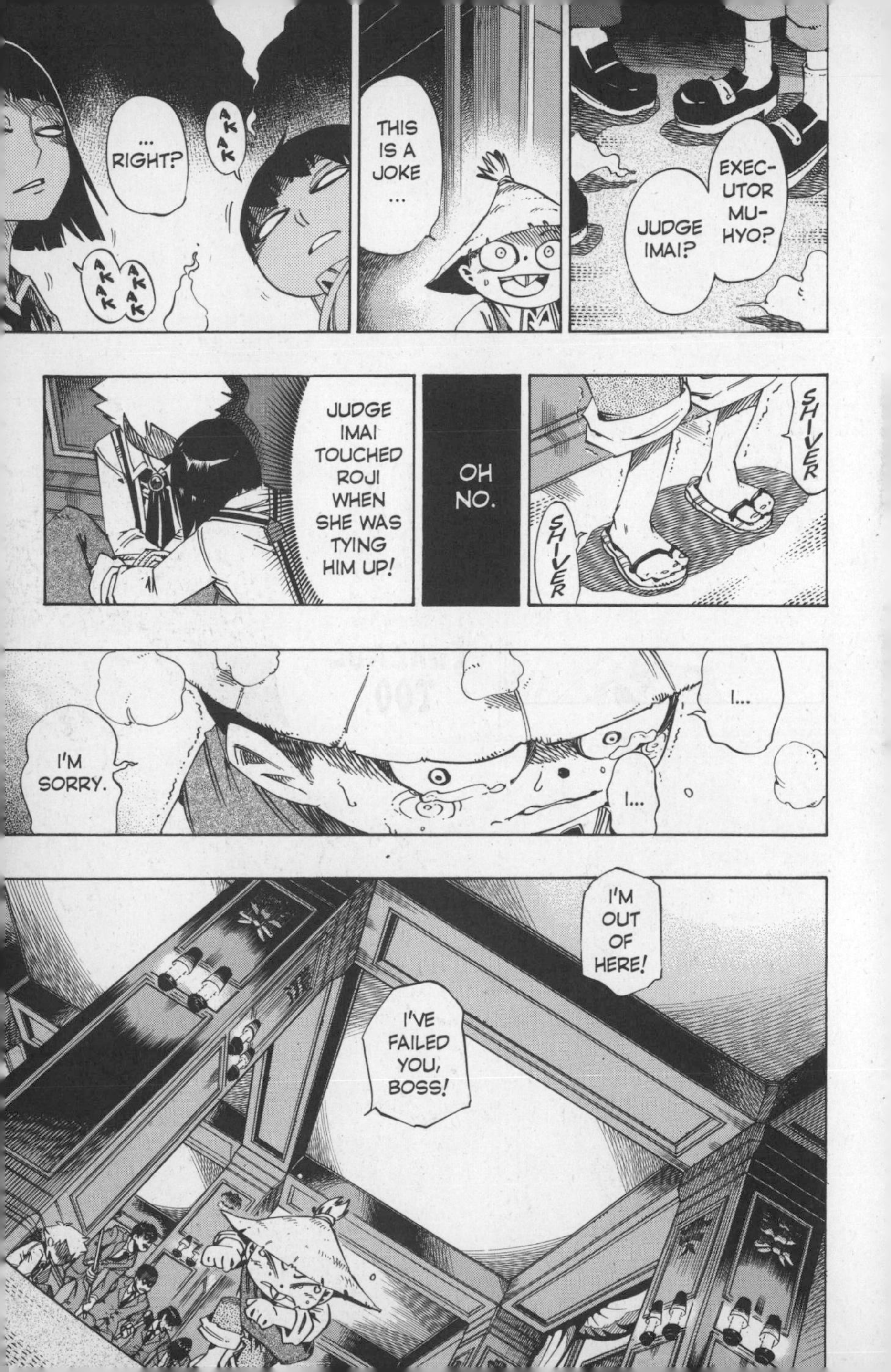
EXECUTOR MUHYO?
JUDGE IMAI?
THIS IS A JOKE ...
AKAKAK
... RIGHT?
AKAKAK
AKAKAK
SHIVER
SHIVER
OH NO.
JUDGE IMAI TOUCHED ROJI WHEN SHE WAS TYING HIM UP!
I...
I...
I'M SORRY.
I'M OUT OF HERE!
I'VE FAILED YOU, BOSS!

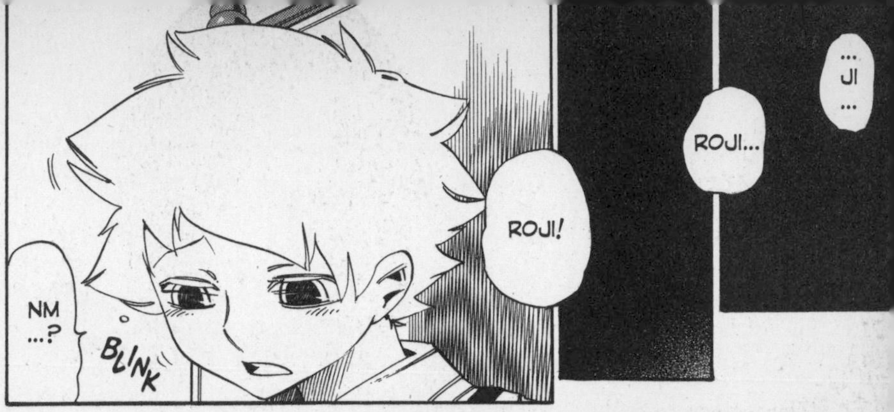
...JI...
ROJI...
ROJI!
NM...?
BLINK
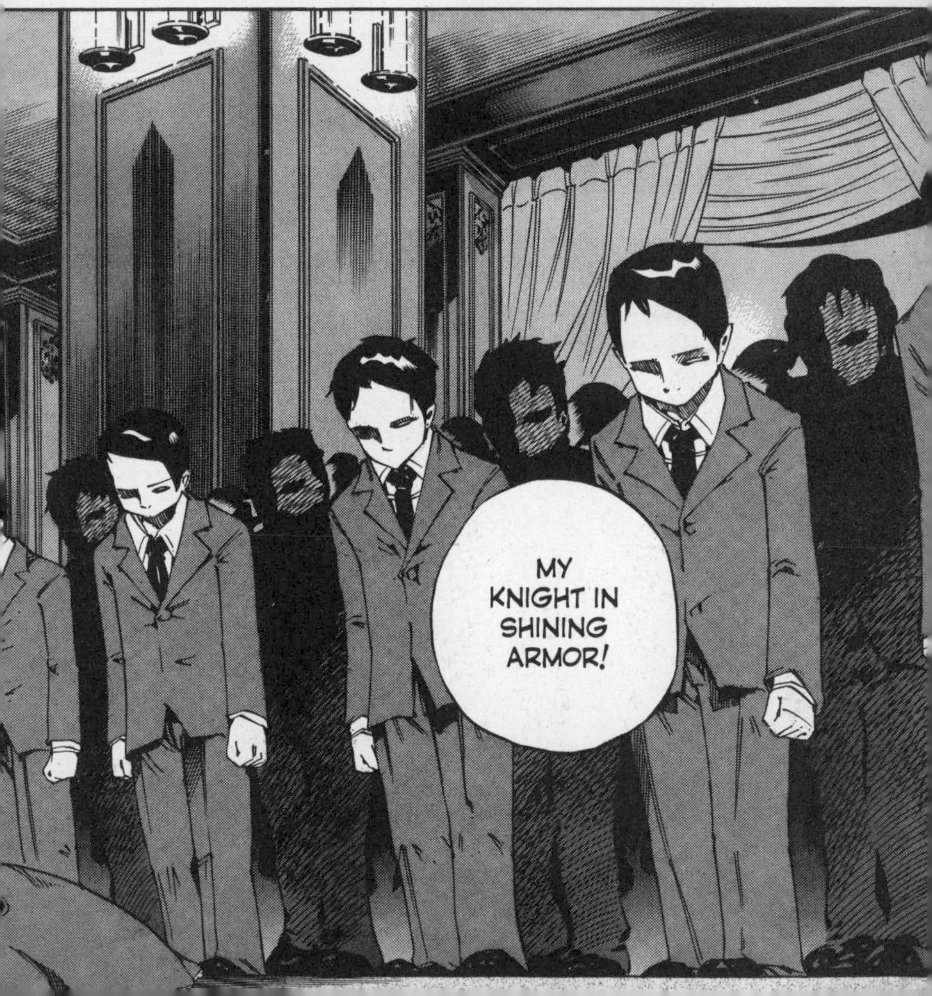
MY KNIGHT IN SHINING ARMOR!

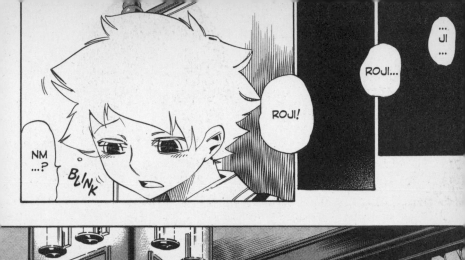

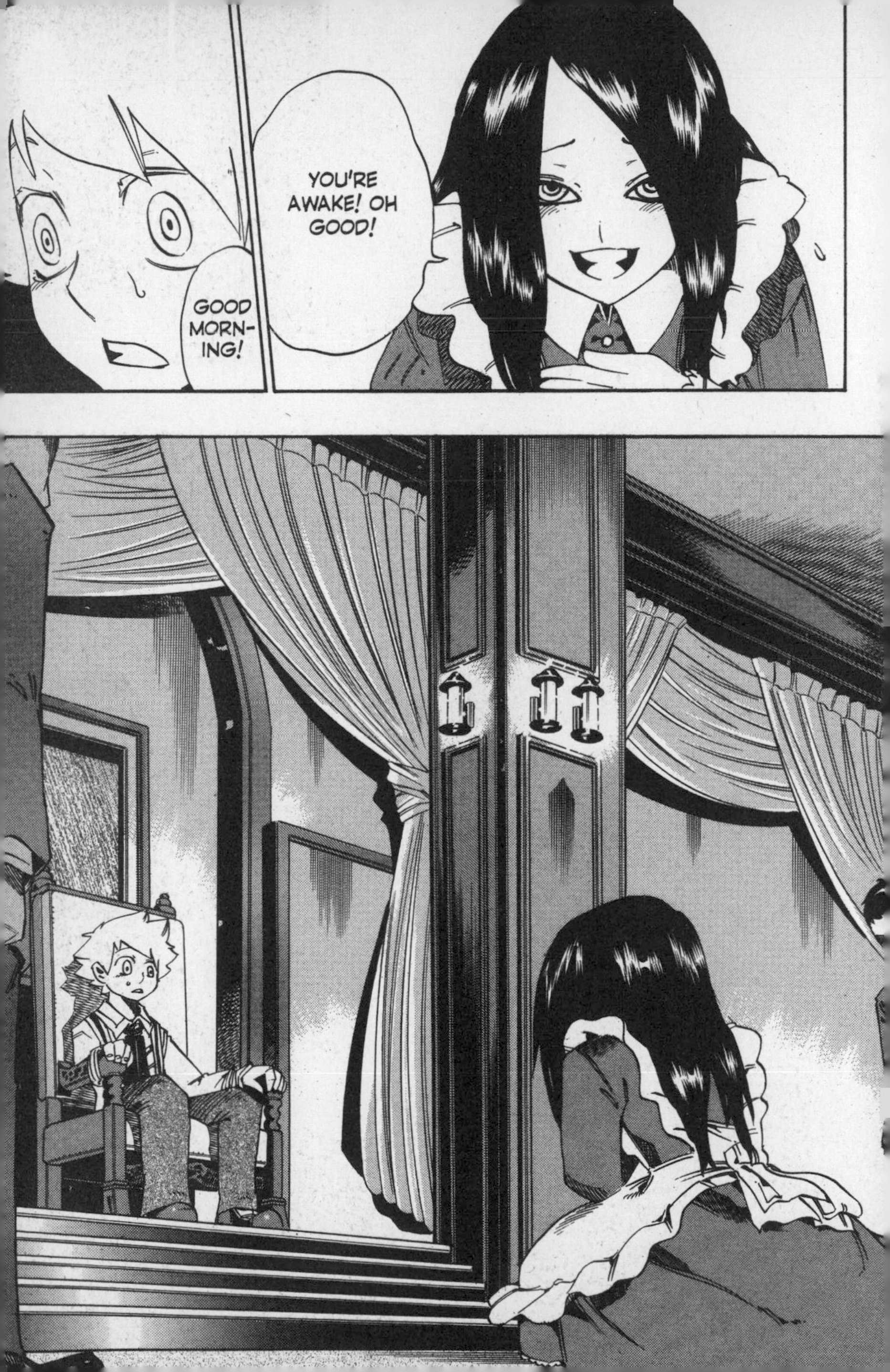
YOU'RE AWAKE! OH GOOD!
GOOD MORNING!

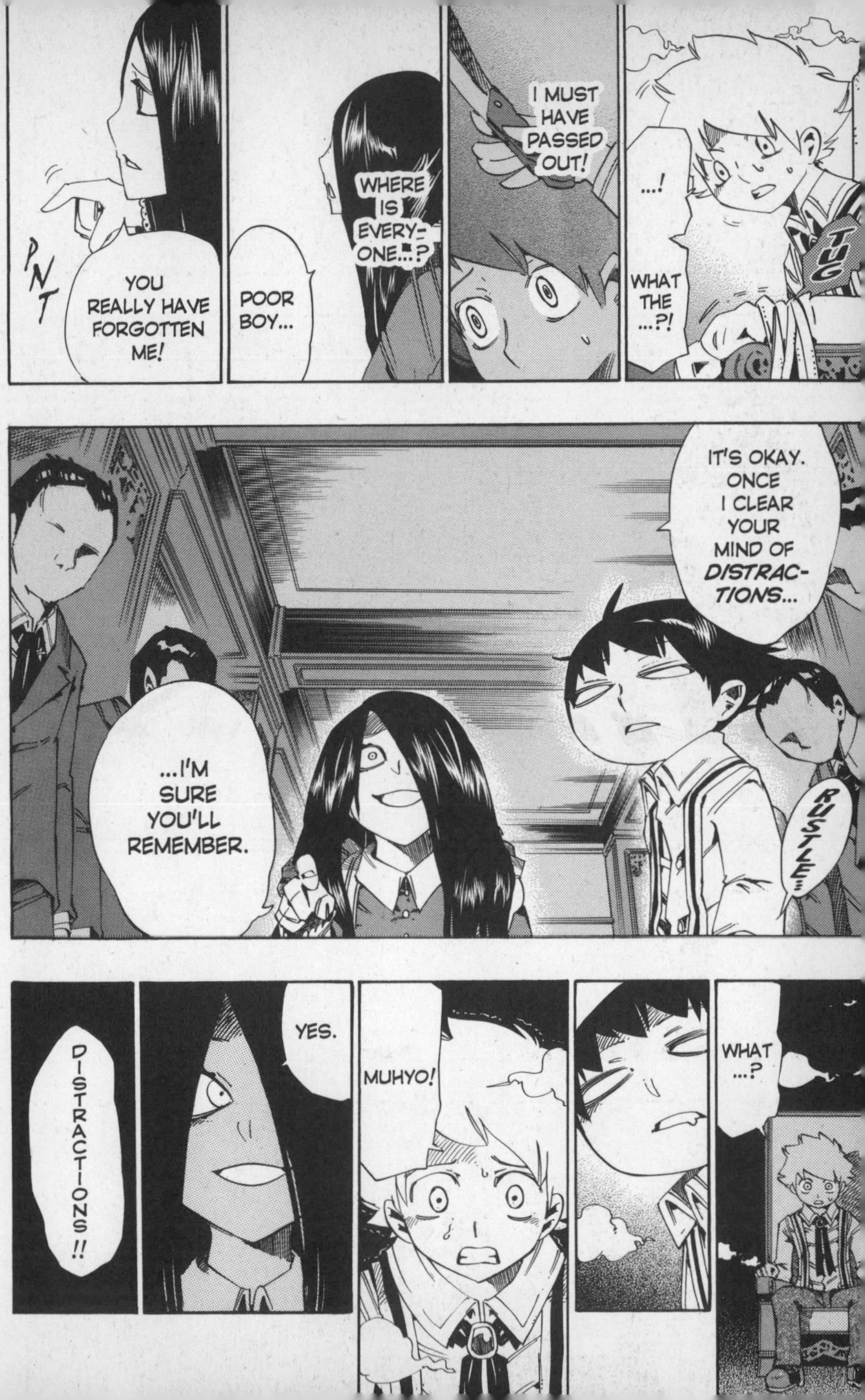

...!
WHAT THE ...?!
TUG
I MUST HAVE PASSED OUT!
WHERE IS EVERYONE...?
POOR BOY...
PNT
YOU REALLY HAVE FORGOTTEN ME!
IT'S OKAY. ONCE I CLEAR YOUR MIND OF DISTRACTIONS...
RUSTLE...
...I'M SURE YOU'LL REMEMBER.
WHAT ...?
MUHYO!
YES.
DISTRACTIONS!!

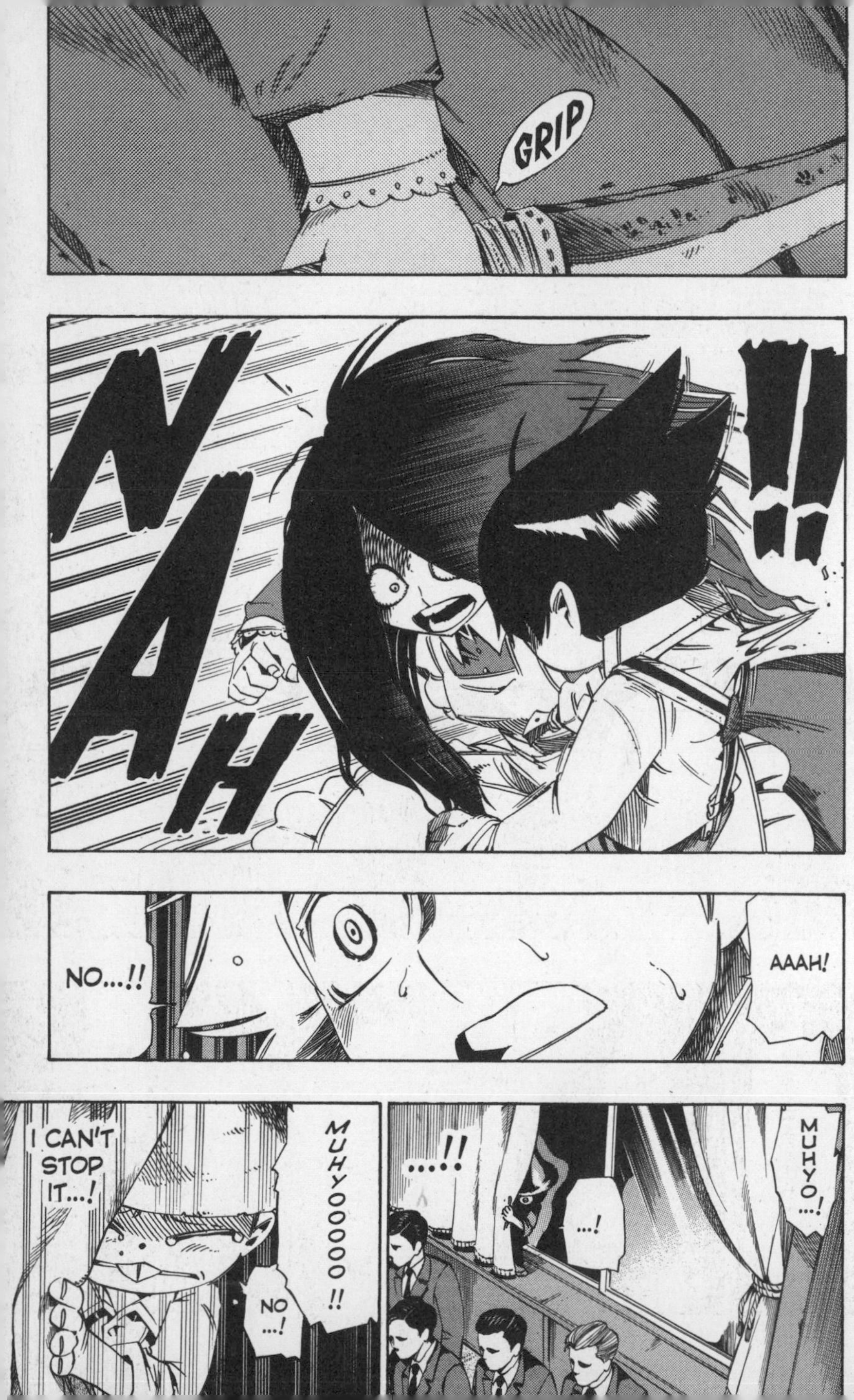
GRIP
NAAAH!!
AAAH!
NO...!!
MUHYO...!
...!!
...!
MUHYOOOOO!!
I CAN'T STOP IT...!
NO ...!

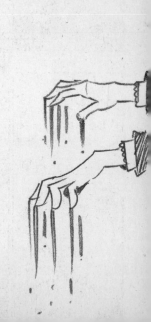

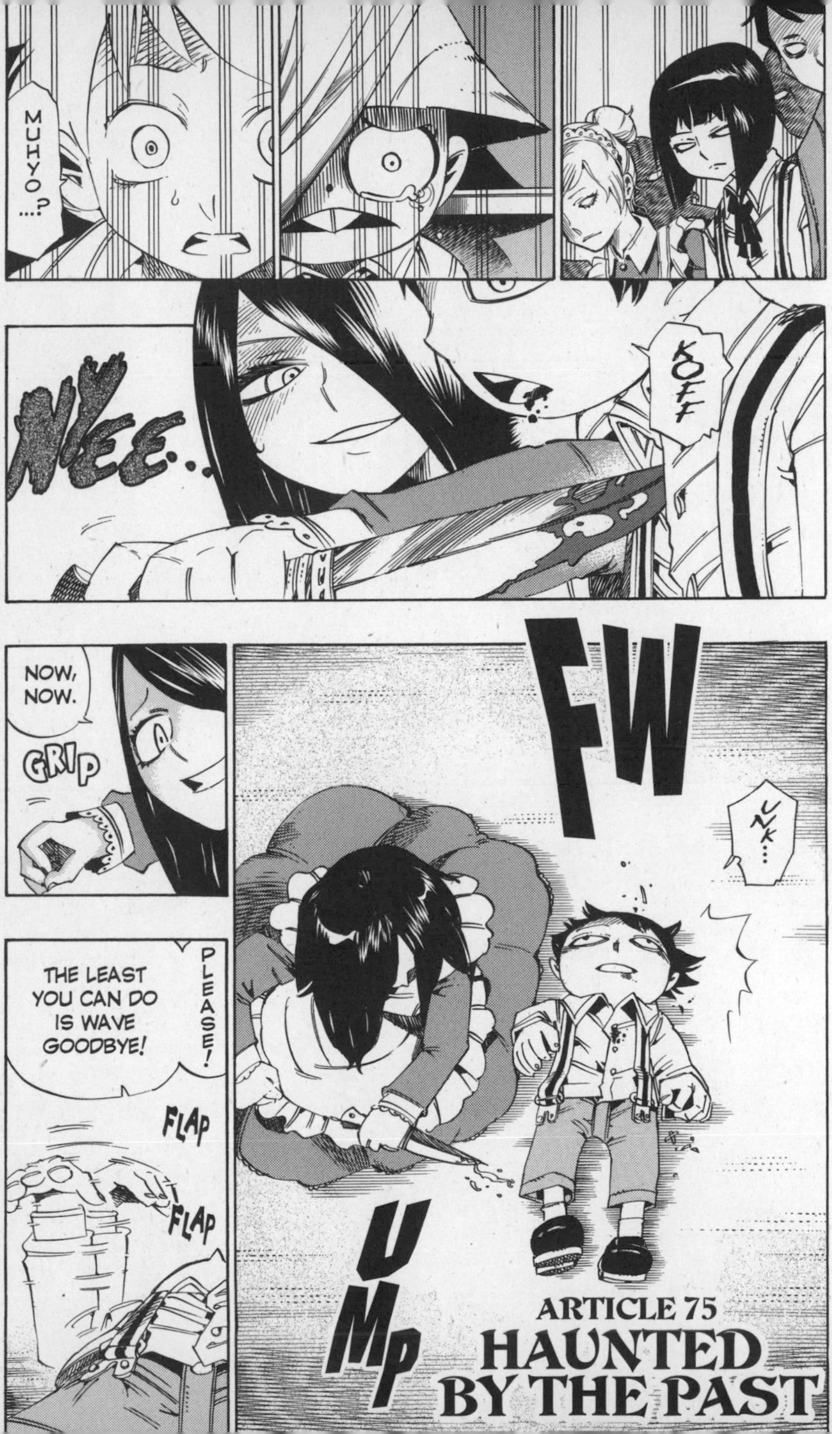
MUHYO ...?
KOFF
NYEE...
FW
UNK...
UMP
ARTICLE 75
HAUNTED BY THE PAST
NOW, NOW.
GRIP
PLEASE!
THE LEAST YOU CAN DO IS WAVE GOODBYE!
FLAP
FLAP

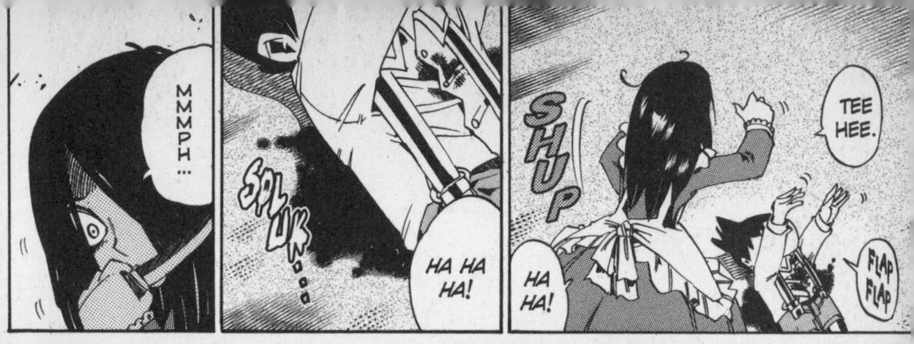
TEE HEE.
SHUP
FLAP FLAP
HA HA!
SPLUK...
HA HA HA!
MMMPH...

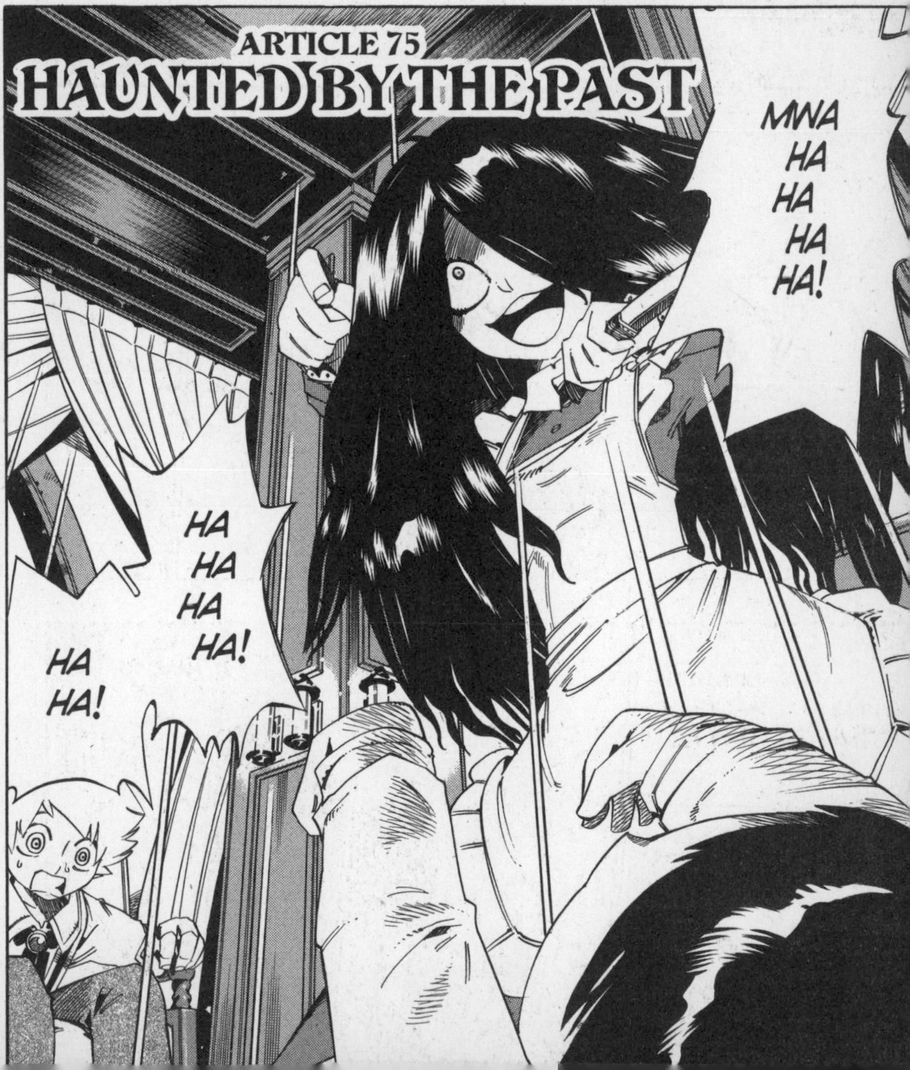
ARTICLE 75
HAUNTED BY THE PAST
MWA HA HA HA HA HA!
HA HA HA HA!
HA HA!

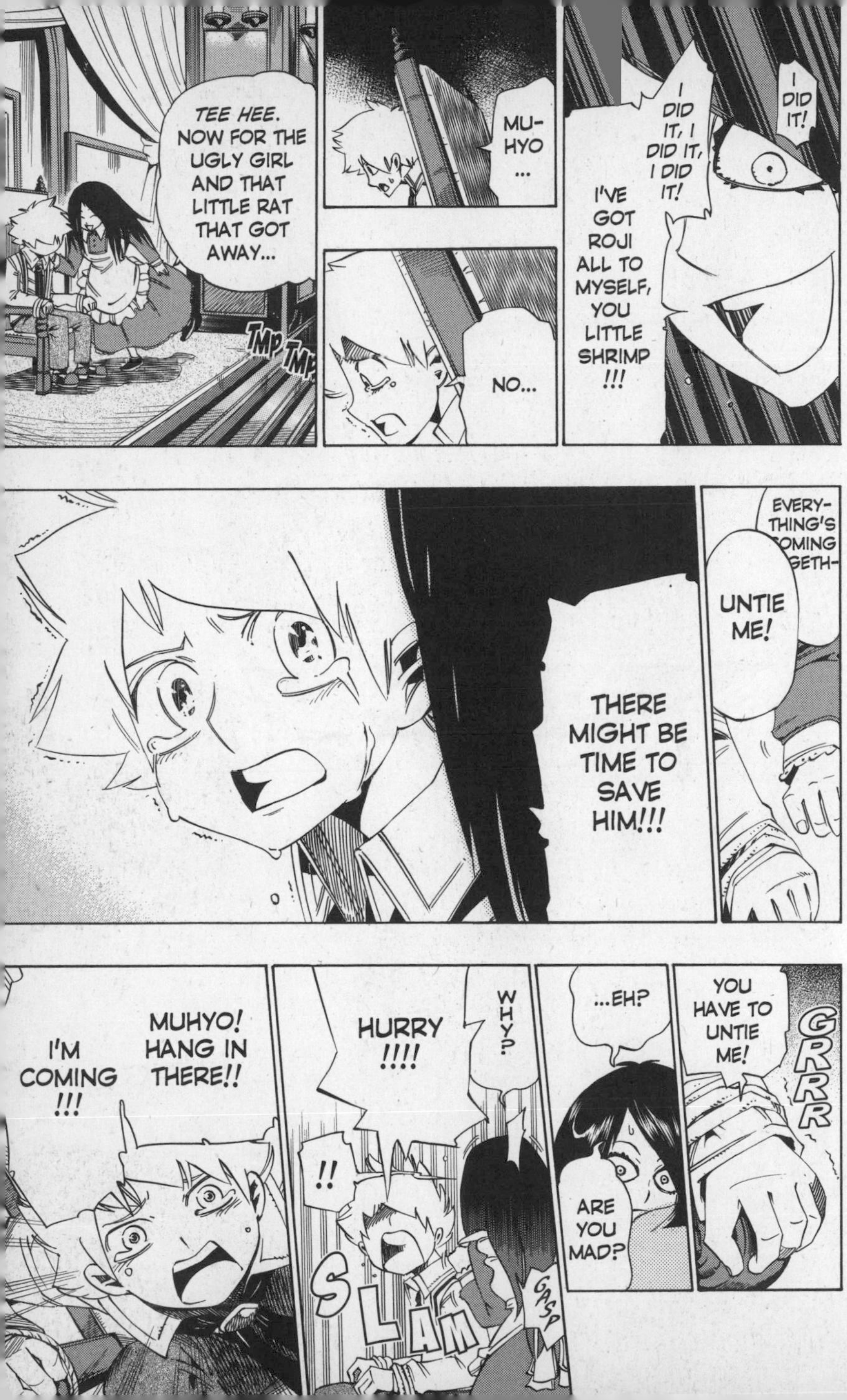
I DID IT!
I DID IT, I DID IT, I DID IT!
I'VE GOT ROJI ALL TO MYSELF, YOU LITTLE SHRIMP!!!
MU-HYO...
NO...
TEE HEE. NOW FOR THE UGLY GIRL AND THAT LITTLE RAT THAT GOT AWAY...
TMP TMP
EVERY-THING'S COMING GETH-
UNTIE ME!
THERE MIGHT BE TIME TO SAVE HIM!!!
YOU HAVE TO UNTIE ME!
GRRR
...EH?
ARE YOU MAD?
WHY?
HURRY!!!!
!!
SLAM
GASA
MUHYO! HANG IN THERE!!
I'M COMING!!!

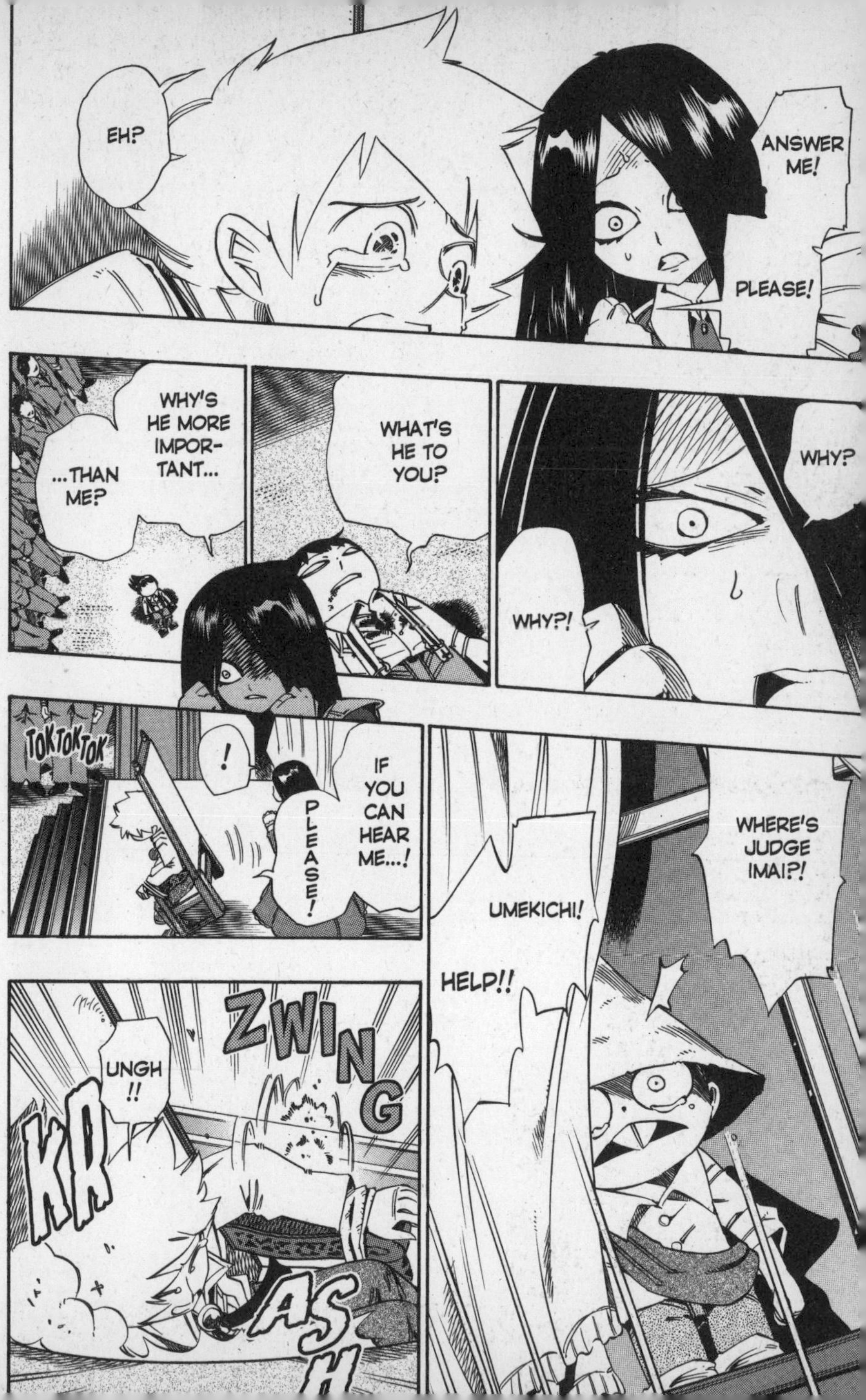
ANSWER ME!
PLEASE!
EH?
WHY?
WHY?!
WHAT'S HE TO YOU?
WHY'S HE MORE IMPOR-TANT...
...THAN ME?
WHERE'S JUDGE IMAI?!
UMEKICHI!
HELP!!
IF YOU CAN HEAR ME...!
PLEASE!
!
TOKTOKTOK
ZWING
UNGH!!
KRASH

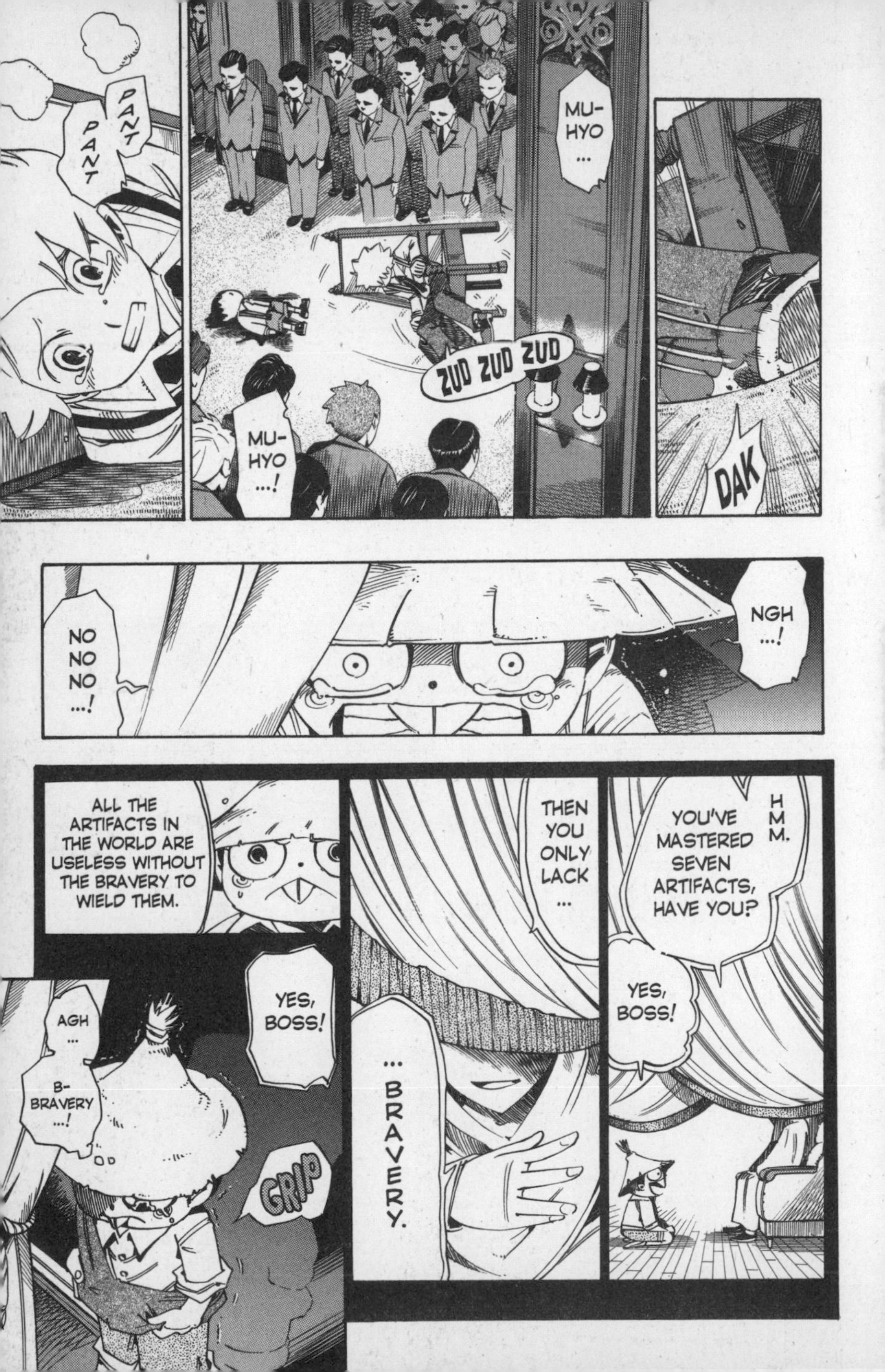
DAK
MU-HYO ...
ZUD ZUD ZUD
MU-HYO ...!
PANT PANT
NGH ...!
NO NO NO ...!
HMM.
YOU'VE MASTERED SEVEN ARTIFACTS, HAVE YOU?
YES, BOSS!
THEN YOU ONLY LACK ...
... BRAVERY.
ALL THE ARTIFACTS IN THE WORLD ARE USELESS WITHOUT THE BRAVERY TO WIELD THEM.
YES, BOSS!
GRIP
AGH ...
B-BRAVERY ...!

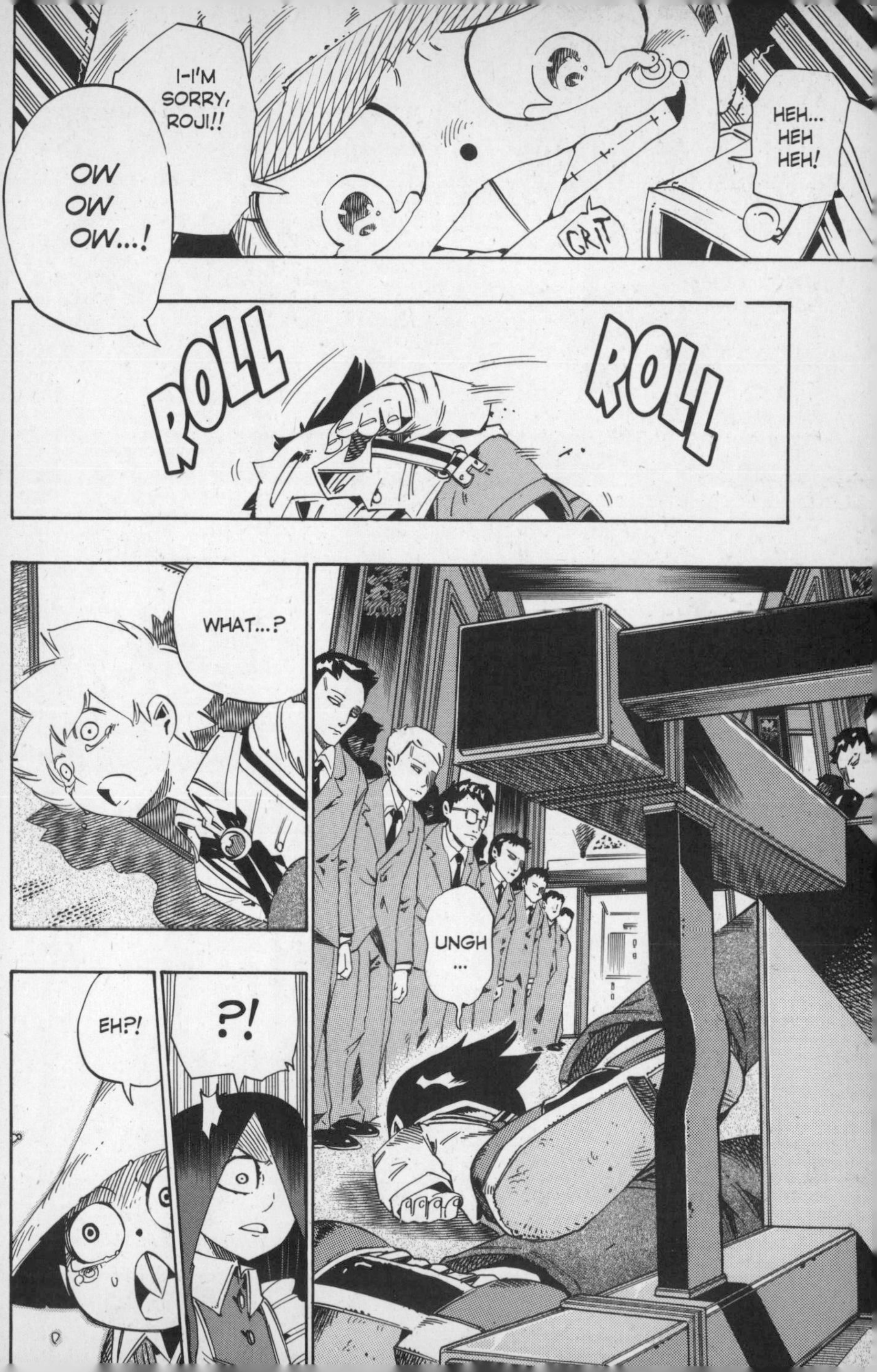
HEH... HEH HEH!
CRIT
I-I'M SORRY, ROJI!!
OW OW OW...!
ROLL
ROLL
UNGH ...
WHAT...?
?!
EH?!

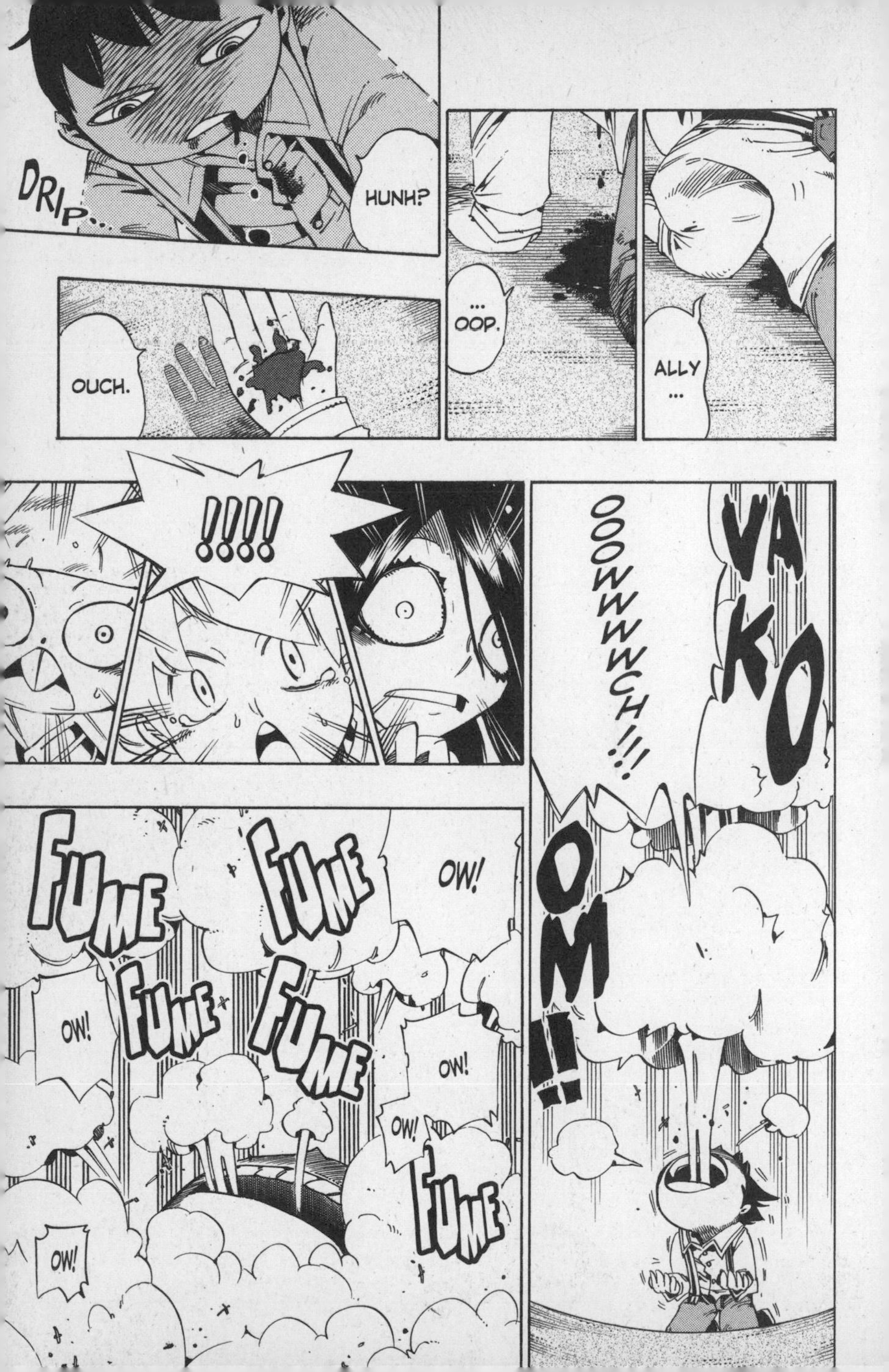
ALLY ...
... OOP.
HUNH?
DRIP...
OUCH.
VA KOOM!!
OOOWWWWCH!!!
!!!!
OW!
FUME
FUME
FUME
FUME
OW!
OW!
FUME
OW!
OW!

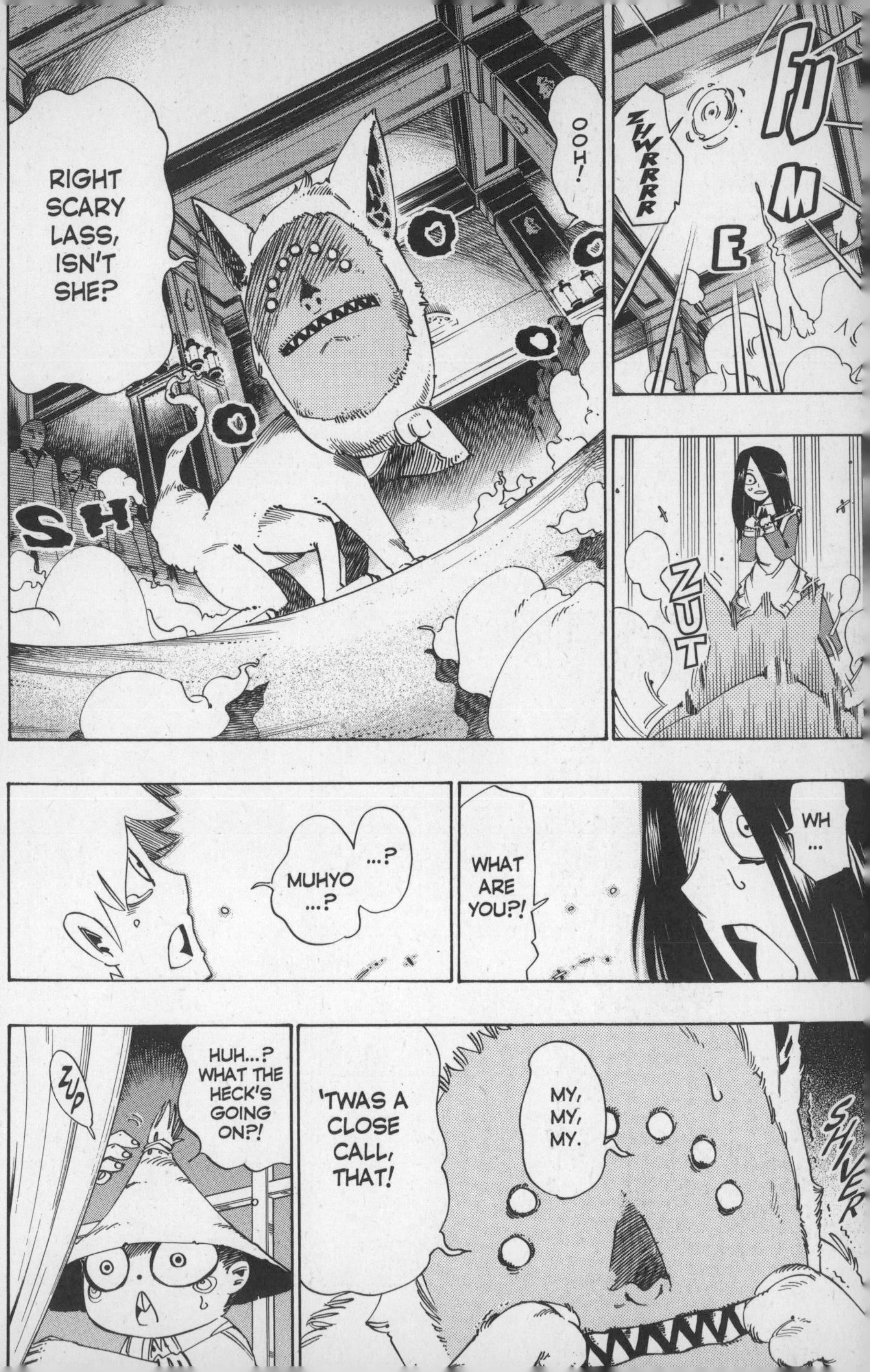
ZHWRRRR
FUME
ZUT
OOH!
RIGHT SCARY LASS, ISN'T SHE?
SH
WH...
WHAT ARE YOU?!
...?
MUHYO...?
SHIVER
MY, MY, MY.
'TWAS A CLOSE CALL, THAT!
HUH...? WHAT THE HECK'S GOING ON?!
ZUP

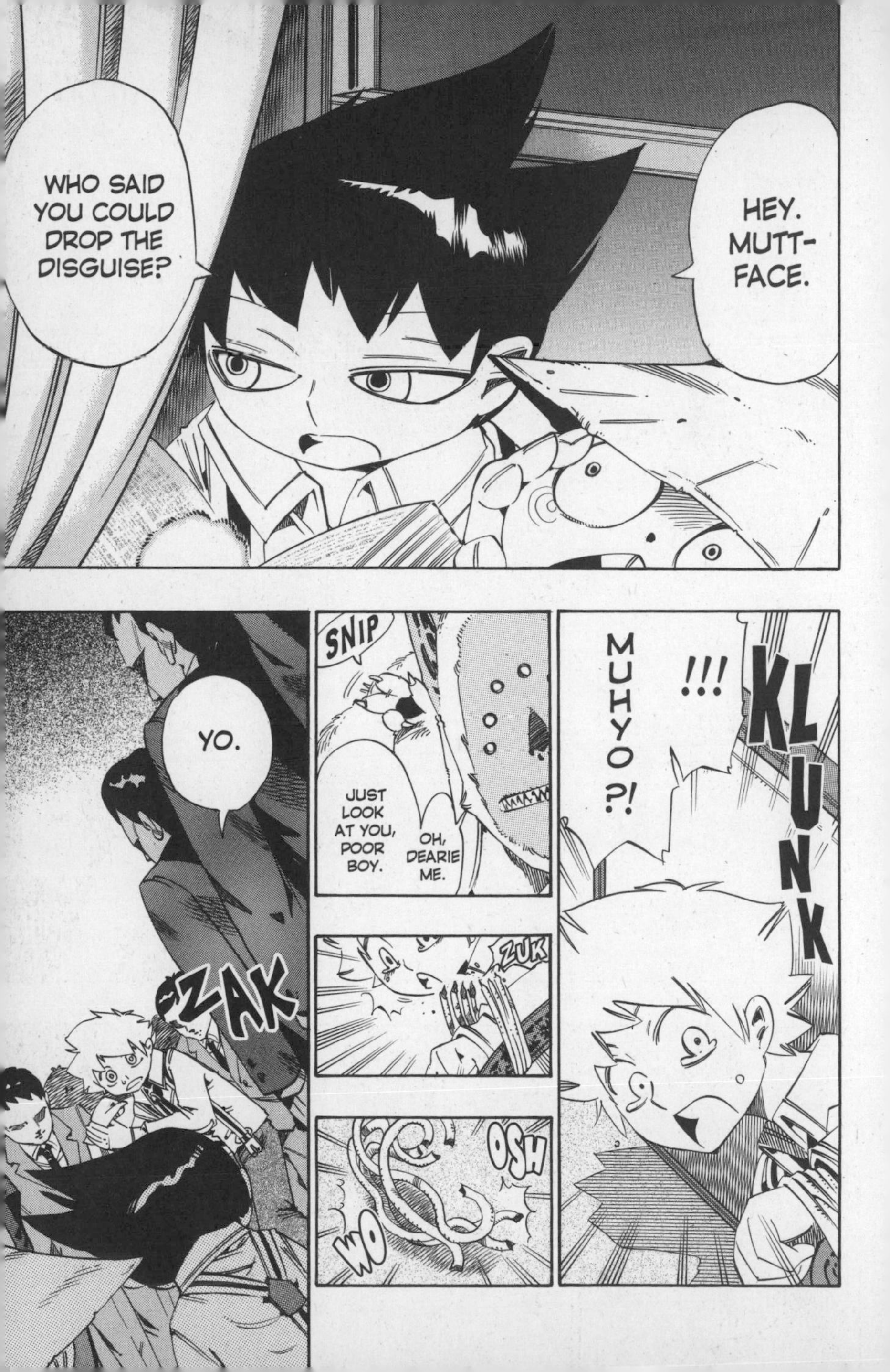

HEY. MUTT-FACE.
WHO SAID YOU COULD DROP THE DISGUISE?
KLUNK
!!!
MUHYO ?!
SNIP
OH, DEARIE ME.
JUST LOOK AT YOU, POOR BOY.
ZUK
OSH
WO
YO.
ZAK

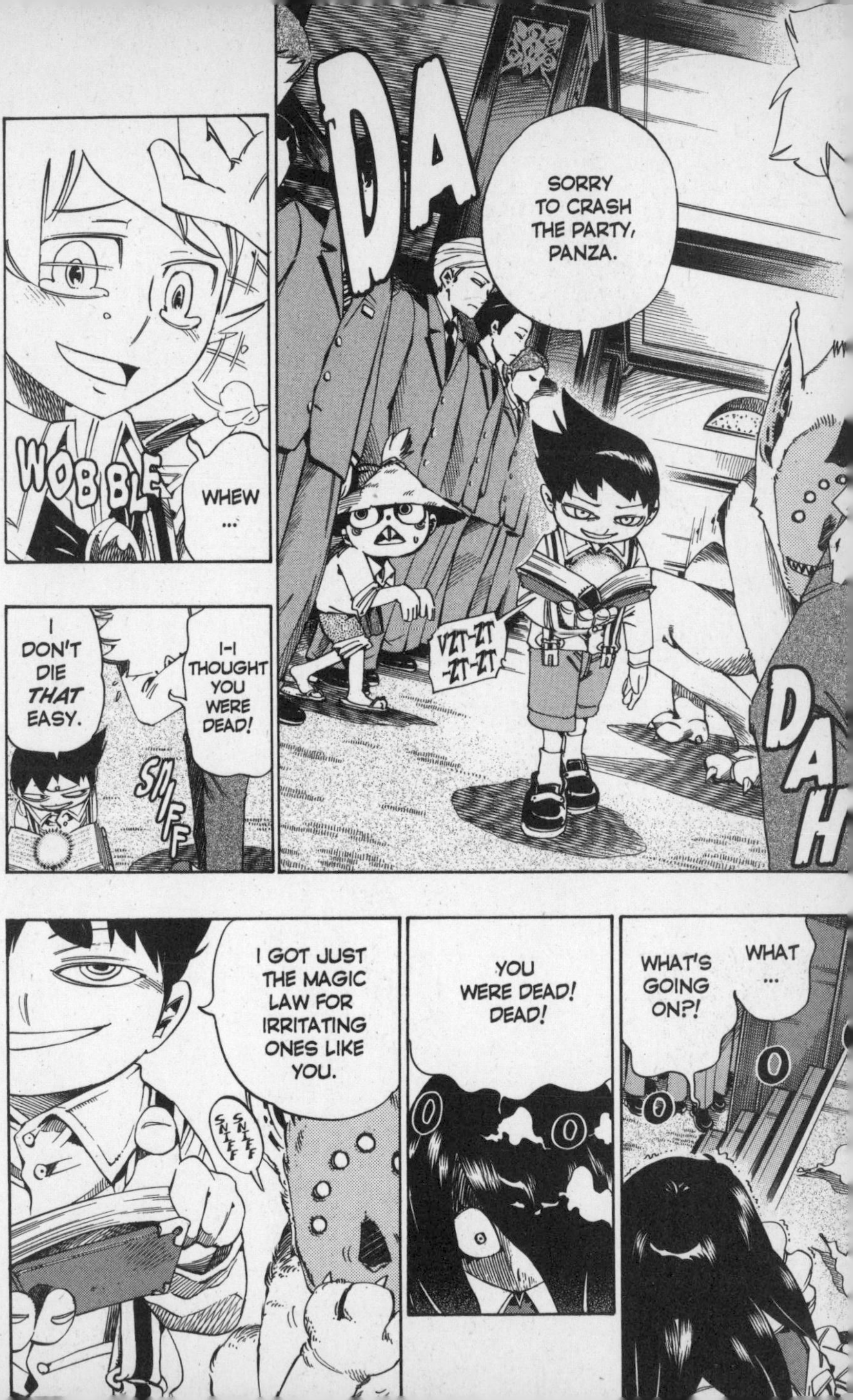

DA
SORRY TO CRASH THE PARTY, PANZA.
VZT-ZT-ZT-ZT
DAH
WHEW ...
WOBBLE
I-I THOUGHT YOU WERE DEAD!
I DON'T DIE *THAT* EASY.
SNIFF
WHAT ...
WHAT'S GOING ON?!
YOU WERE DEAD! DEAD!
I GOT JUST THE MAGIC LAW FOR IRRITATING ONES LIKE YOU.
SNIFF SNIFF

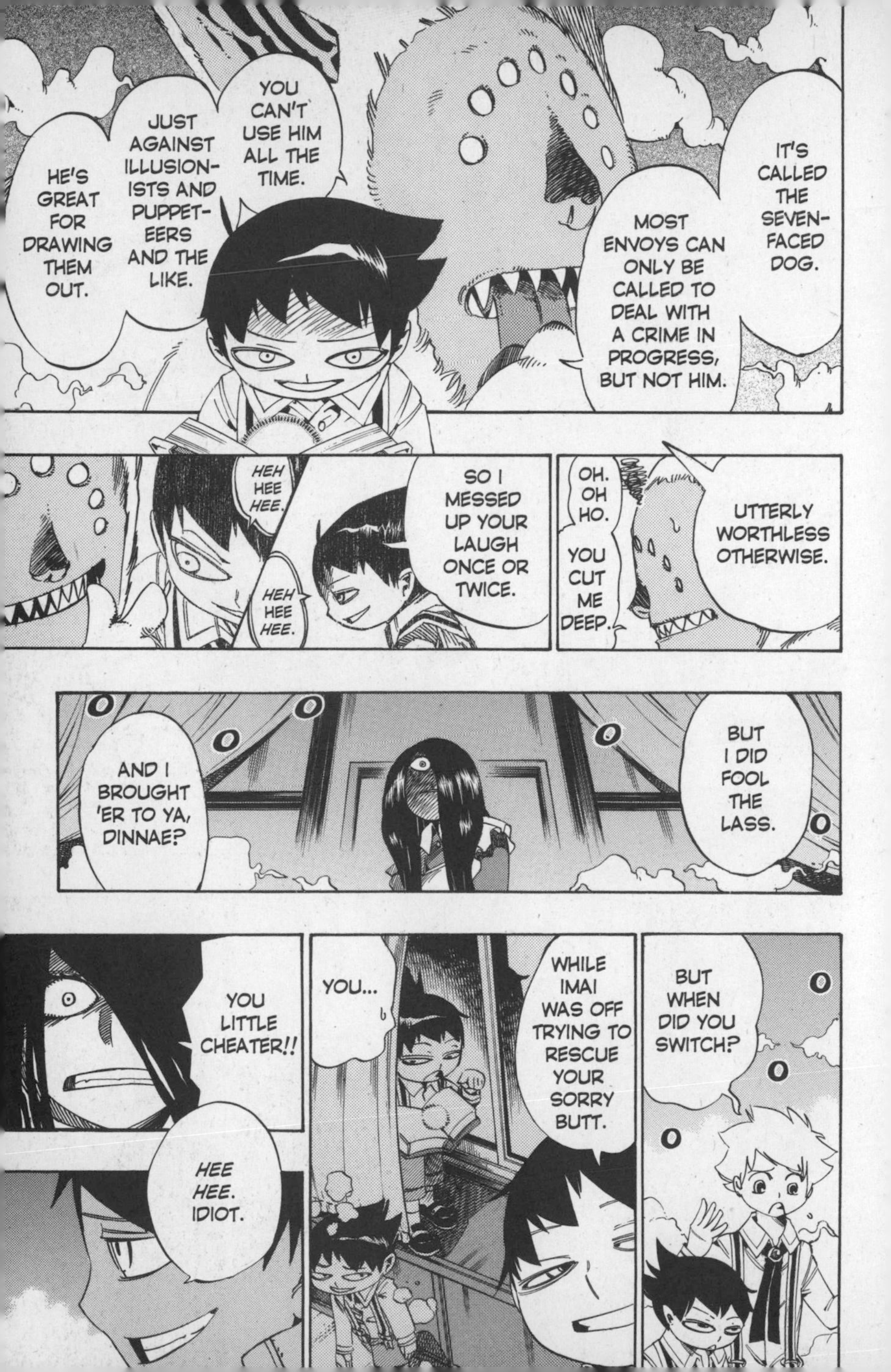
IT'S CALLED THE SEVEN-FACED DOG.
MOST ENVOYS CAN ONLY BE CALLED TO DEAL WITH A CRIME IN PROGRESS, BUT NOT HIM.
YOU CAN'T USE HIM ALL THE TIME.
JUST AGAINST ILLUSIONISTS AND PUPPETEERS AND THE LIKE.
HE'S GREAT FOR DRAWING THEM OUT.
UTTERLY WORTHLESS OTHERWISE.
OH. OH HO.
YOU CUT ME DEEP.
SO I MESSED UP YOUR LAUGH ONCE OR TWICE.
HEH HEE HEE.
HEH HEE HEE.
BUT I DID FOOL THE LASS.
AND I BROUGHT 'ER TO YA, DINNAE?
BUT WHEN DID YOU SWITCH?
WHILE IMAI WAS OFF TRYING TO RESCUE YOUR SORRY BUTT.
YOU...
YOU LITTLE CHEATER!!
HEE HEE. IDIOT.

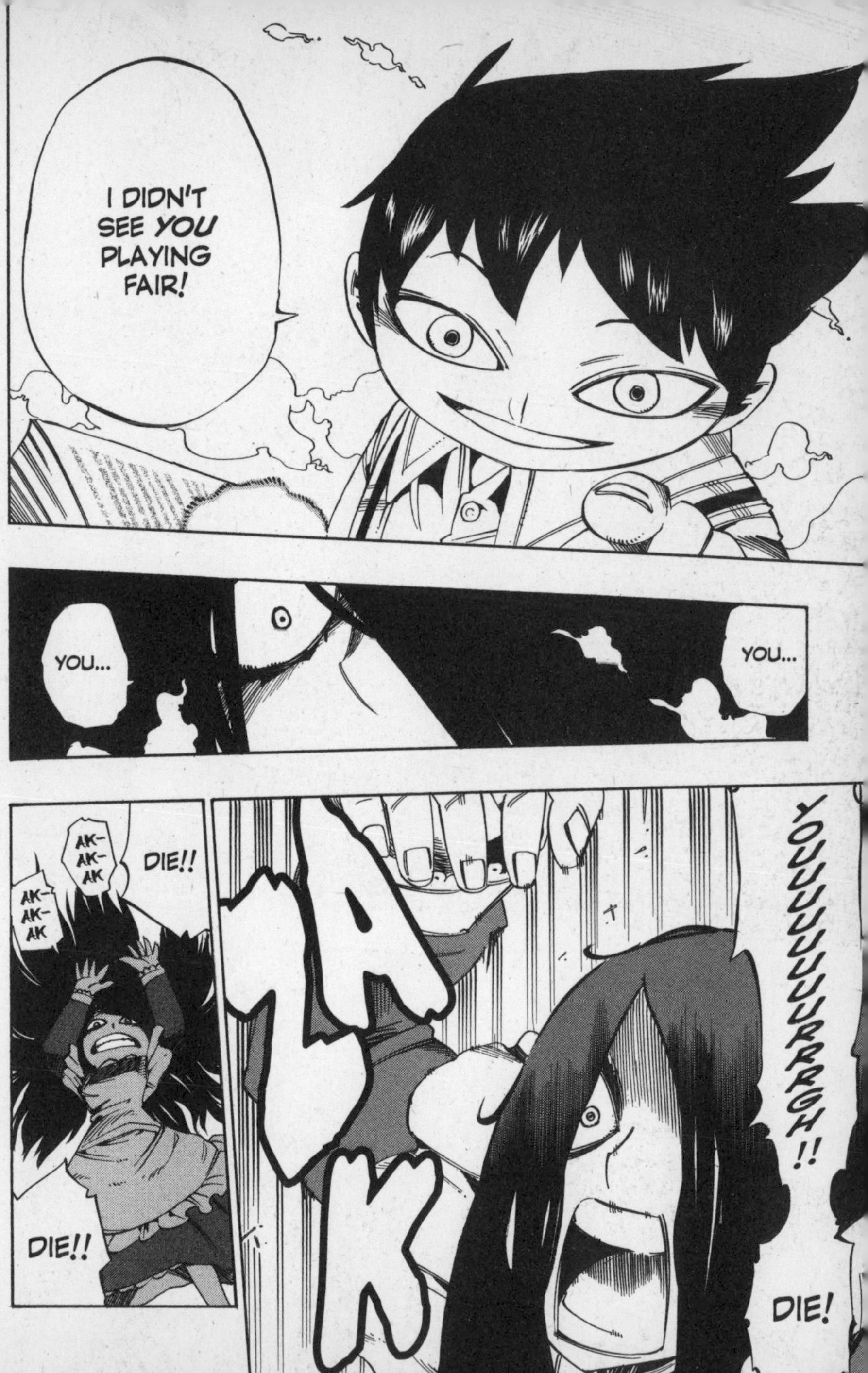
I DIDN'T SEE *YOU* PLAYING FAIR!
YOU...
YOU...
YOUUUUUUUURRRGH!!
DIE!
DIE!!
AK-AK-AK
AK-AK-AK
DIE!!

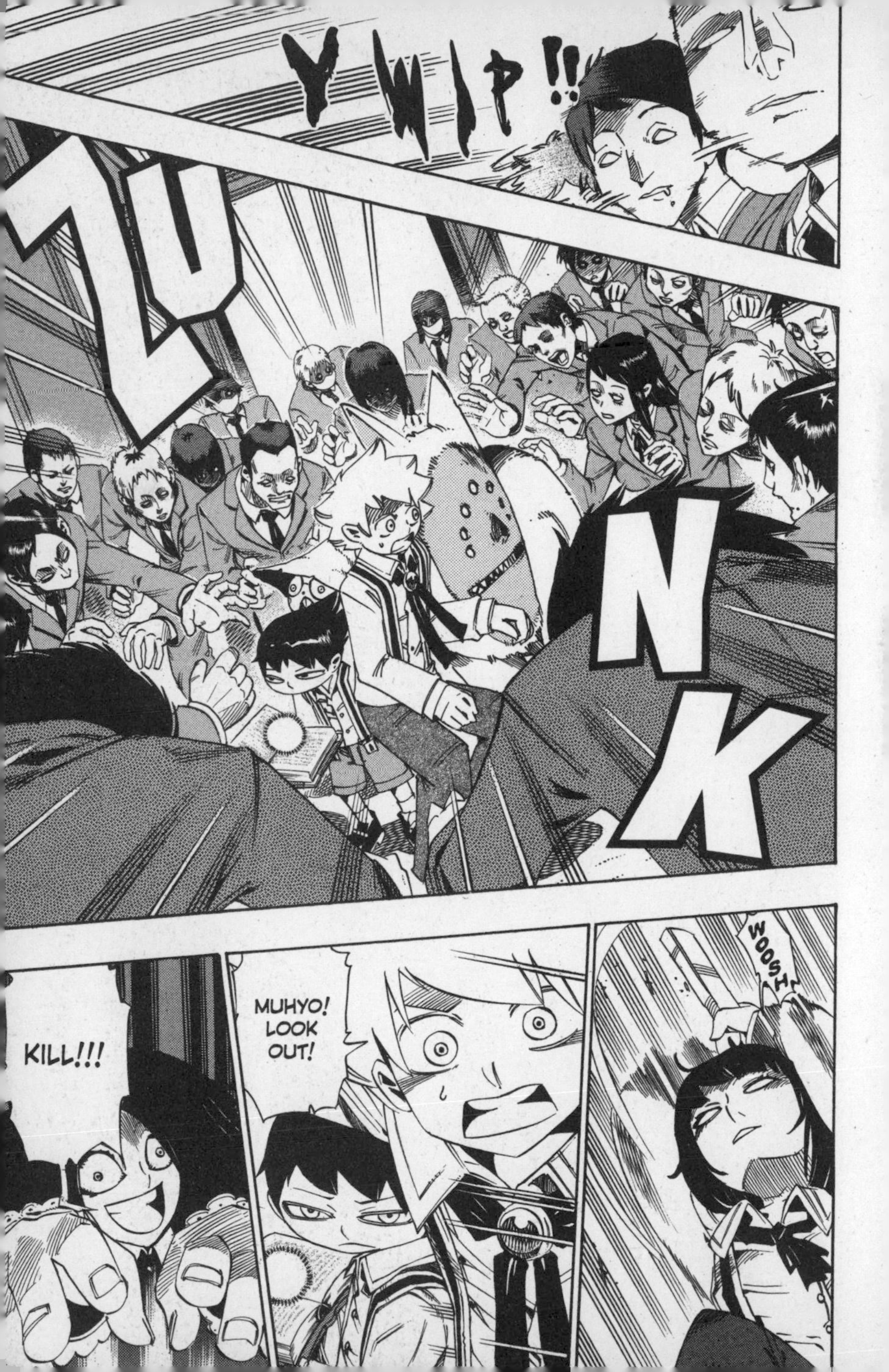
YWIP!!
ZUNK
WOOSH
MUHYO! LOOK OUT!
KILL!!!

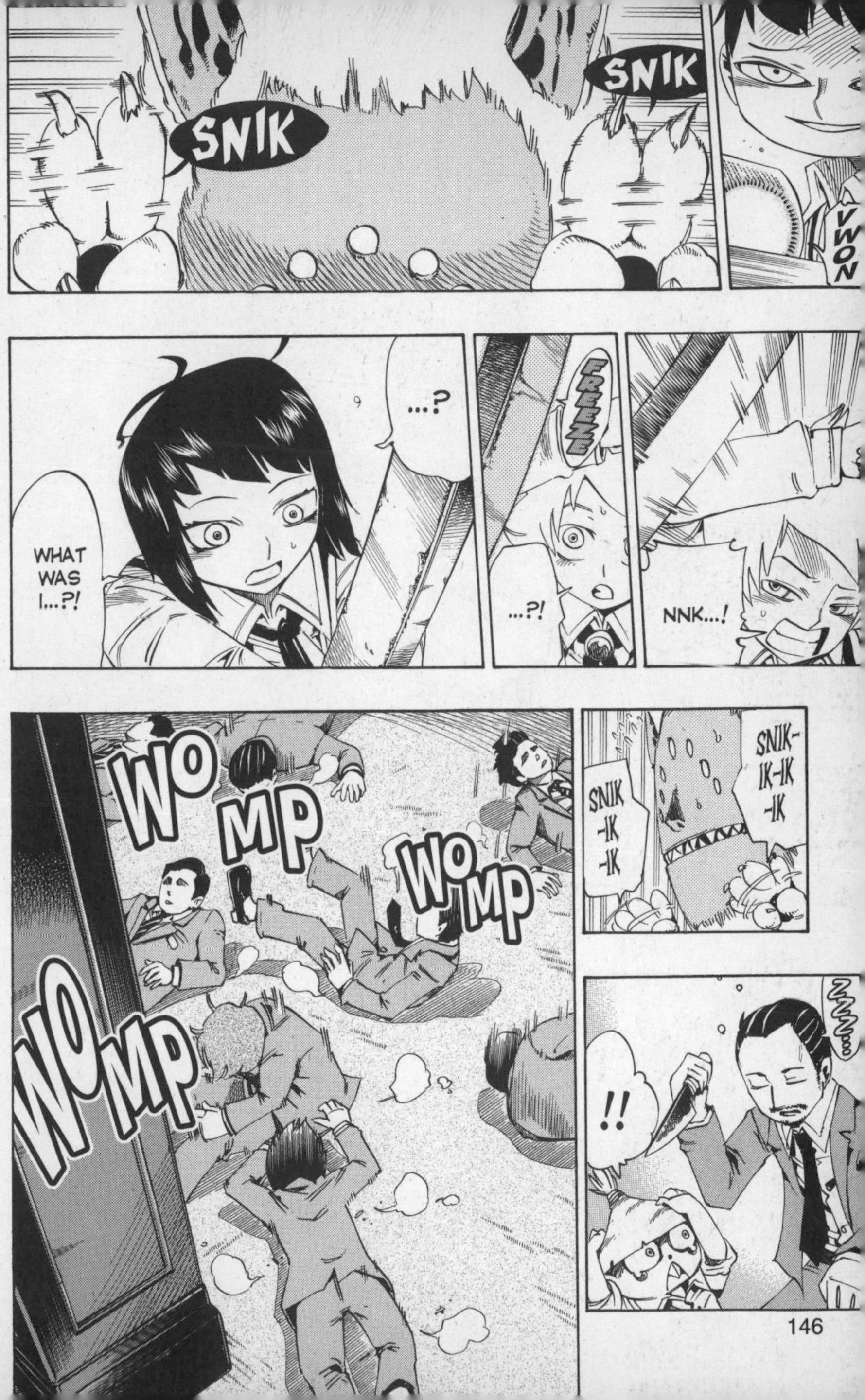
VWON
SNIK
SNIK
NNK...!
FREEZE
...?!
...?
WHAT WAS I...?!
SNIK-IK-IK-IK
SNIK -IK -IK
ZZZ...
!!
WOMP
WOMP
WOMP

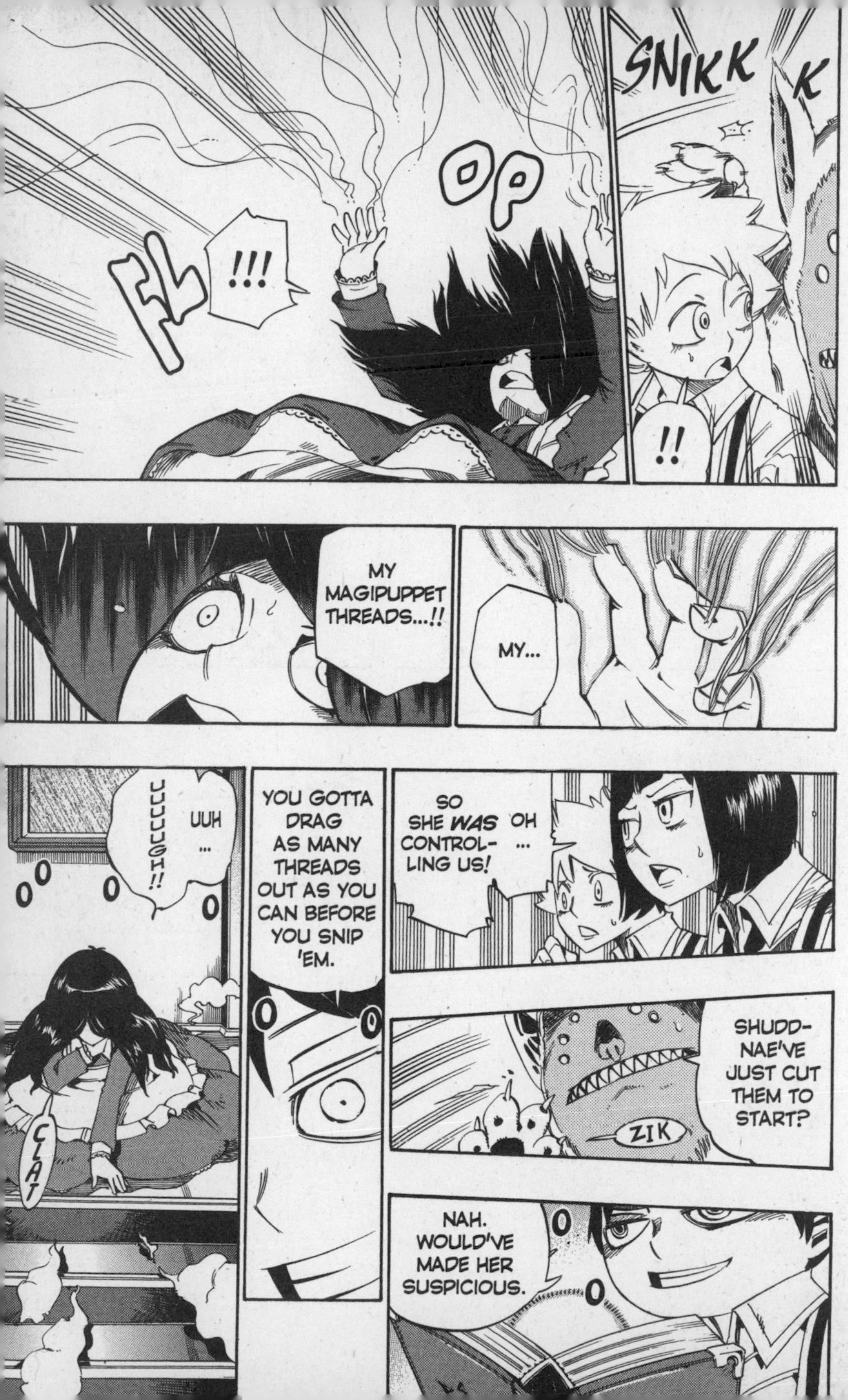
SNIKK K
!!
OP
!!!
FL
MY...
MY MAGIPUPPET THREADS...!!
OH ...
SO SHE WAS CONTROLLING US!
SHUDDNAE'VE JUST CUT THEM TO START?
ZIK
NAH. WOULD'VE MADE HER SUSPICIOUS.
YOU GOTTA DRAG AS MANY THREADS OUT AS YOU CAN BEFORE YOU SNIP 'EM.
UUH ...
UUUUUGH!!
CLAT

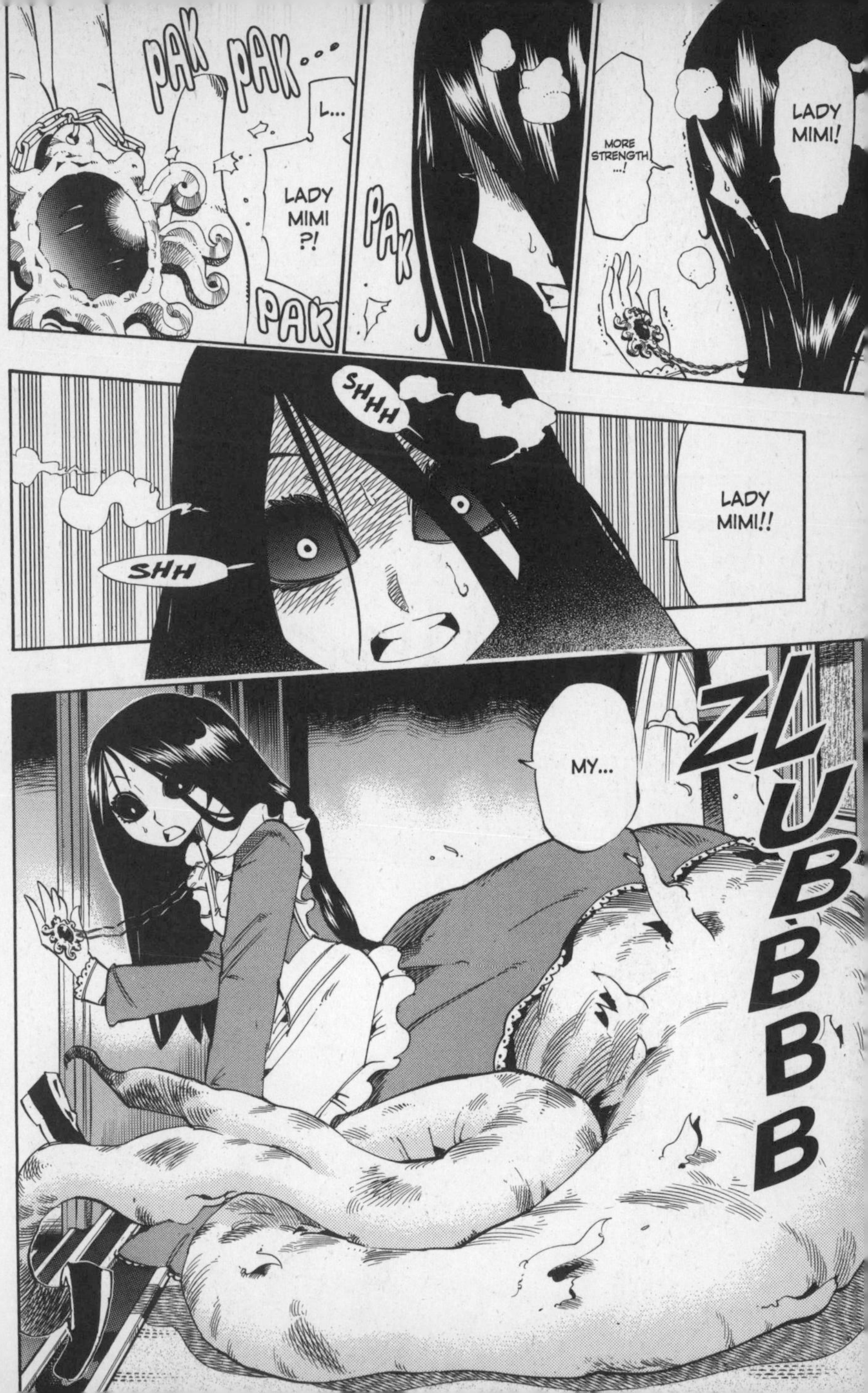
LADY MIMI!
MORE STRENGTH ...!
PAK
PAK PAK...
L...
LADY MIMI ?!
PAK
LADY MIMI!!
SHHH
SHH
ZLUBBBB
MY...

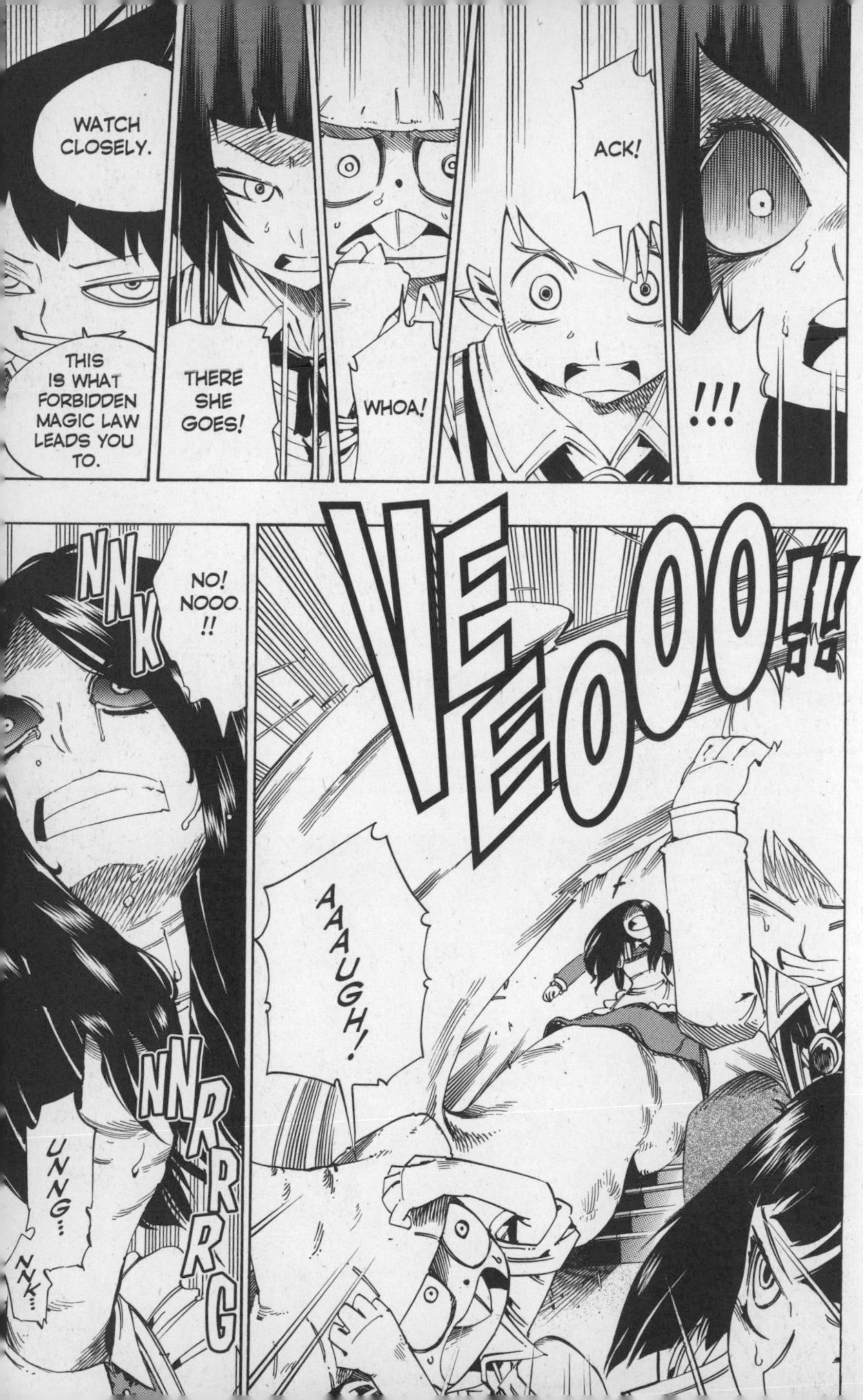
!!!
ACK!
WHOA!
THERE SHE GOES!
WATCH CLOSELY.
THIS IS WHAT FORBIDDEN MAGIC LAW LEADS YOU TO.
VEEOOO!!
AAAUGH!
NNNK
NO! NOOO!!
NNNRRRRG
UNNG...
NNK...

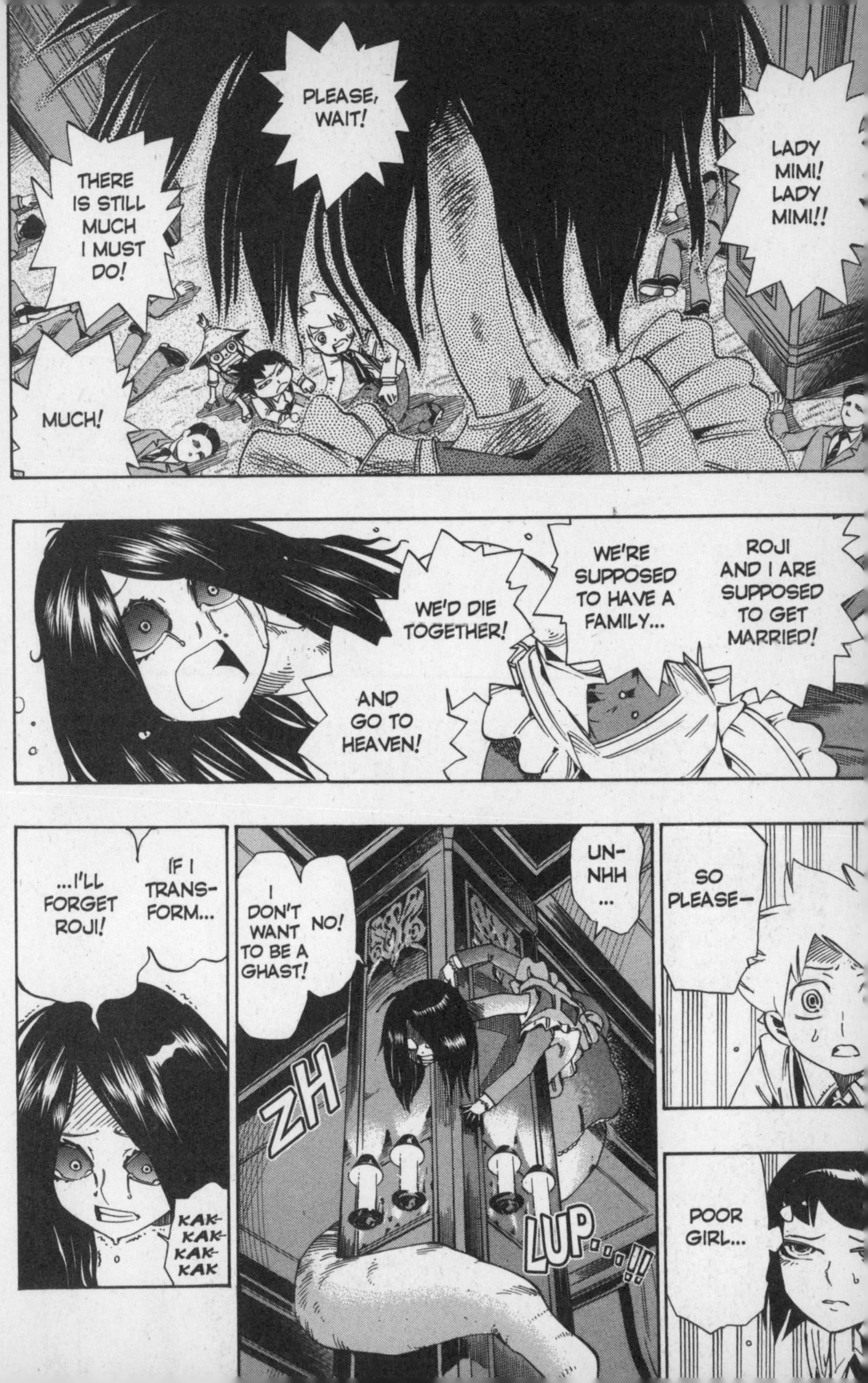
LADY MIMI! LADY MIMI!!
PLEASE, WAIT!
THERE IS STILL MUCH I MUST DO!
MUCH!
ROJI AND I ARE SUPPOSED TO GET MARRIED!
WE'RE SUPPOSED TO HAVE A FAMILY...
WE'D DIE TOGETHER!
AND GO TO HEAVEN!
SO PLEASE—
POOR GIRL...
UN-NHH ...
NO!
I DON'T WANT TO BE A GHAST!
ZH
LUP...!!
IF I TRANSFORM...
...I'LL FORGET ROJI!
KAK-KAK-KAK-KAK

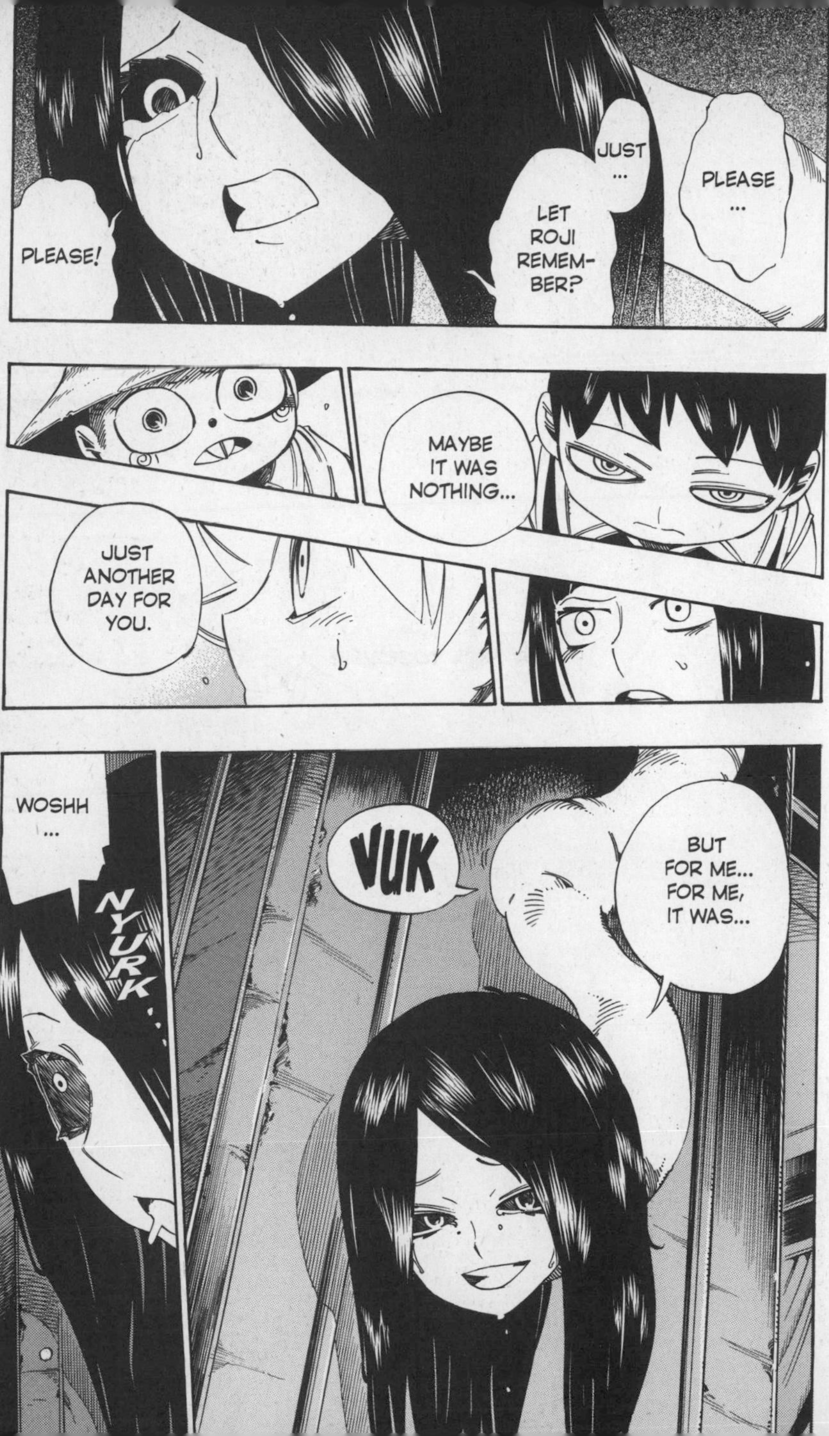
PLEASE ...
JUST ...
LET ROJI REMEMBER?
PLEASE!
MAYBE IT WAS NOTHING...
JUST ANOTHER DAY FOR YOU.
BUT FOR ME... FOR ME, IT WAS...
VUK
WOSHH ...
NYURK...

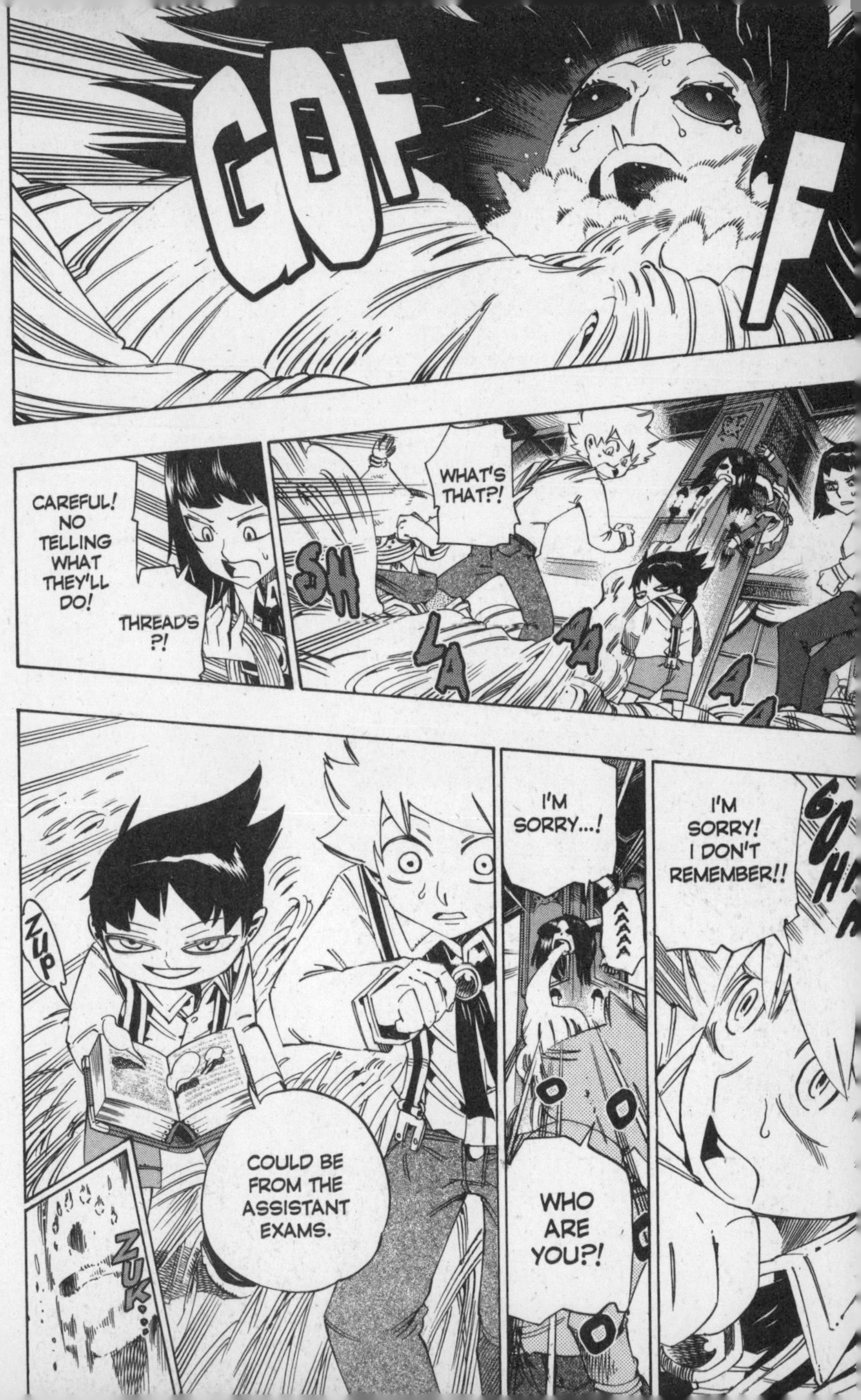
GOF
F
WHAT'S THAT?!
AA
A
A
SH
LA
CAREFUL! NO TELLING WHAT THEY'LL DO!
THREADS ?!
I'M SORRY! I DON'T REMEMBER!!
I'M SORRY...!
AAAAA
WHO ARE YOU?!
ZUP
COULD BE FROM THE ASSISTANT EXAMS.
ZUK...

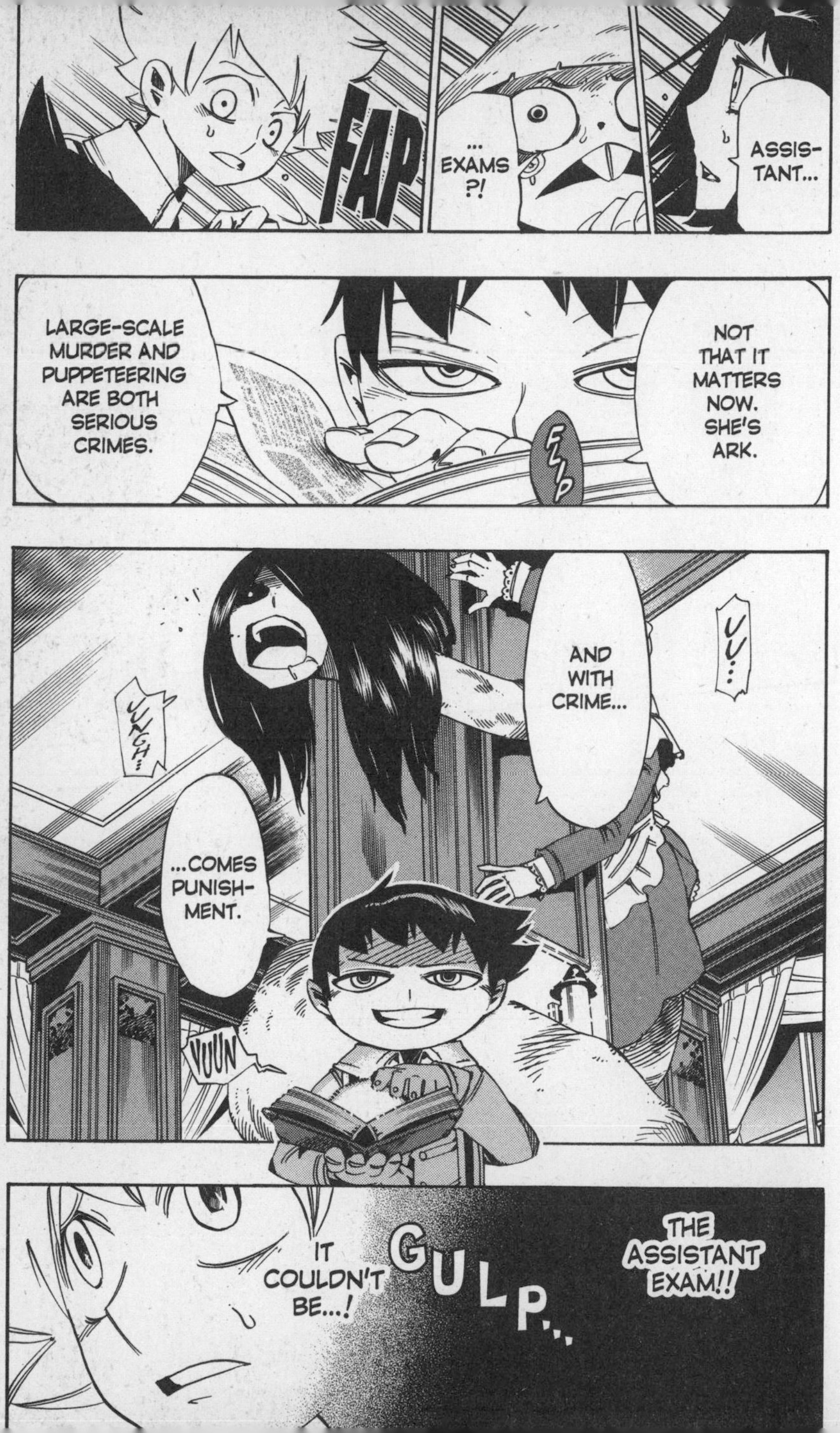
ASSIS-TANT...
... EXAMS ?!
FAP
NOT THAT IT MATTERS NOW. SHE'S ARK.
FLIP
LARGE-SCALE MURDER AND PUPPETEERING ARE BOTH SERIOUS CRIMES.
UU...
AND WITH CRIME...
JUNGH...
...COMES PUNISH-MENT.
VUUN
THE ASSISTANT EXAM!!
GULP...
IT COULDN'T BE...!

Q: I NOTICED THAT UNDER HIS COOL CAPE, MUHYO WEARS BRIGHT RED PANTS. WHY?

-M., TOKUSHIMA PREFECTURE

A: WELL, IT'S STANDARD M.L.S. UNIFORM, BUT THOSE PANTS... *WHISPER* THIS IS TOTALLY A SECRET, BUT THOSE PANTS ARE FROM THE KIDS DEPARTMENT! SEE, THEY COULDN'T FIND AN ADULT PAIR SMALL ENOUGH TO—

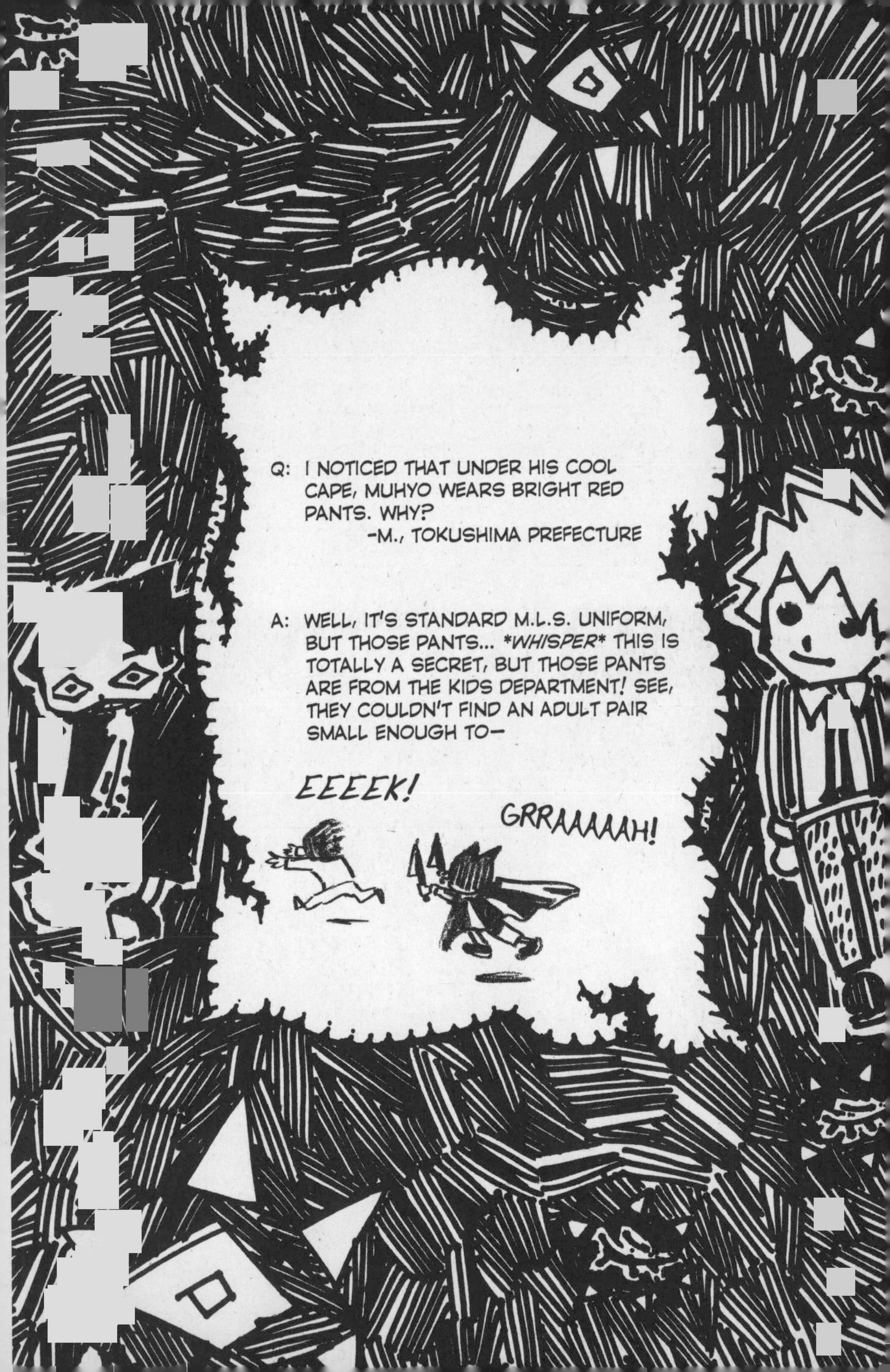
EEEEK!
GRRAAAAAAH!

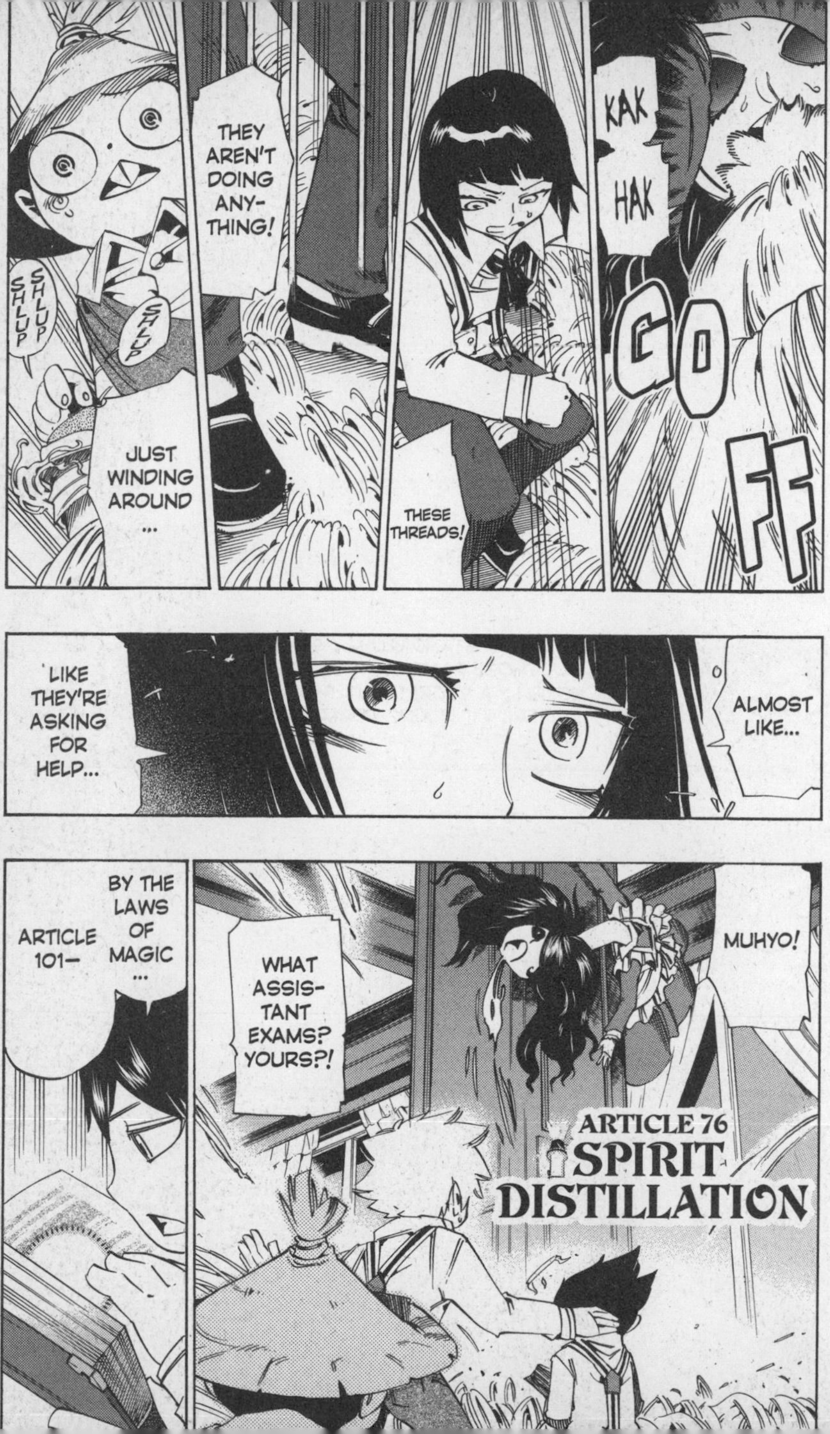

KAK
HAK
GOFF
THESE THREADS!
THEY AREN'T DOING ANY-THING!
SHLUP
SHLUP
SHLUP
JUST WINDING AROUND ...
ALMOST LIKE...
LIKE THEY'RE ASKING FOR HELP...
MUHYO!
WHAT ASSIS-TANT EXAMS? YOURS?!
ARTICLE 76
SPIRIT DISTILLATION
BY THE LAWS OF MAGIC ...
ARTICLE 101—

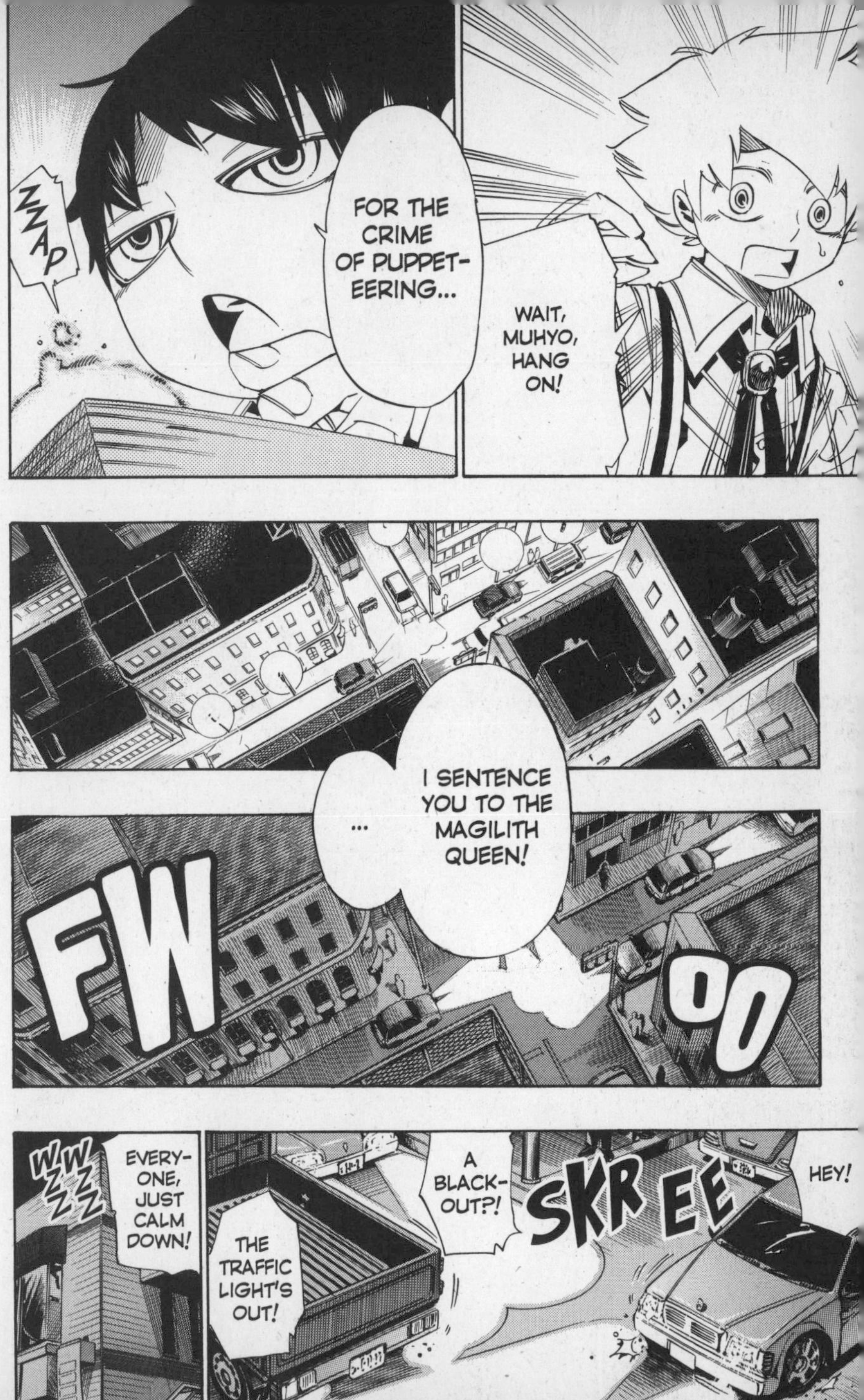
WAIT, MUHYO, HANG ON!
FOR THE CRIME OF PUPPETEERING...
ZZAP
I SENTENCE YOU TO THE MAGILITH QUEEN!
...
FWOO
HEY!
SKREE
A BLACKOUT?!
THE TRAFFIC LIGHT'S OUT!
EVERYONE, JUST CALM DOWN!
WWZZZ

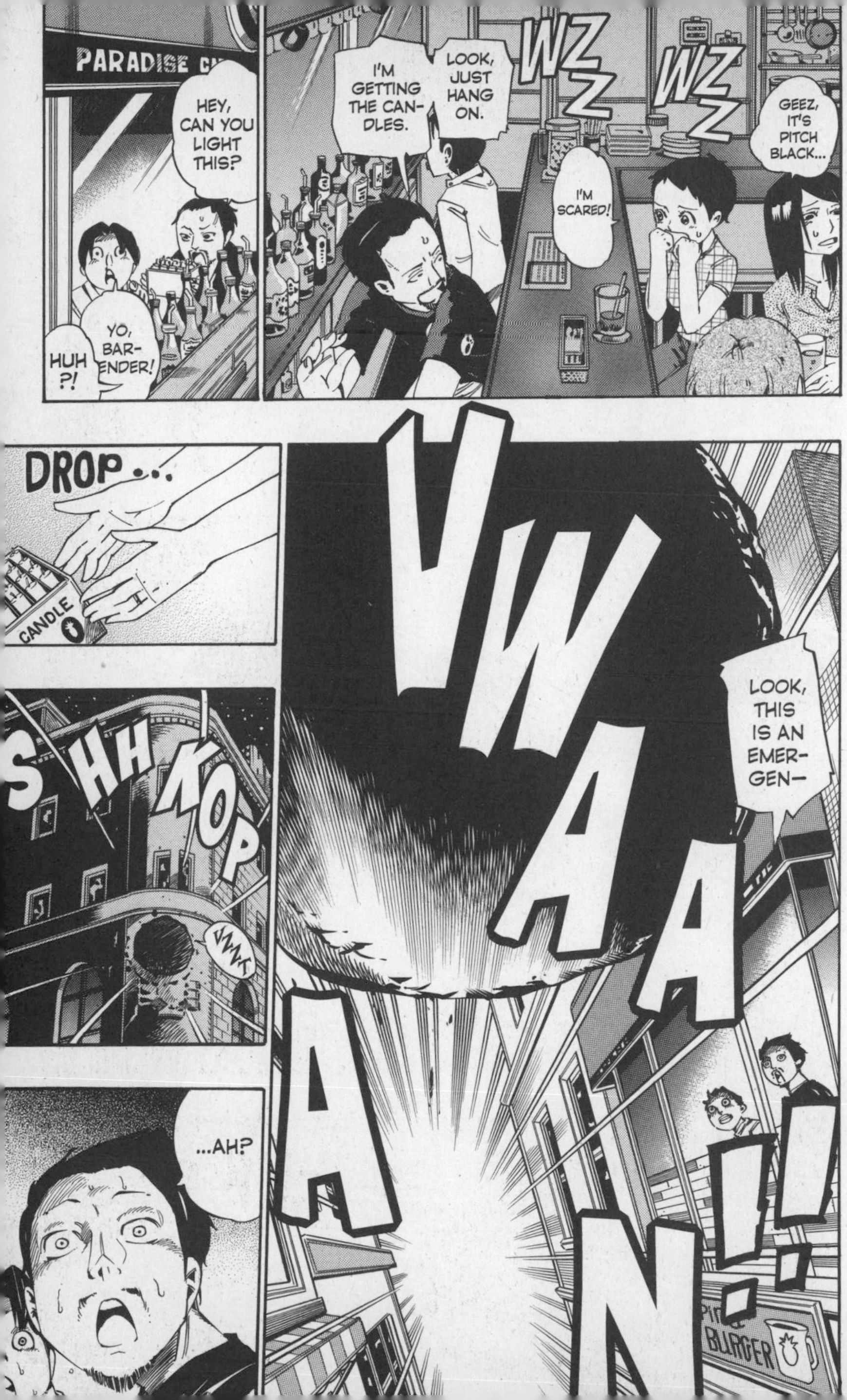
GEEZ, IT'S PITCH BLACK...
I'M SCARED!
WZZ
WZZ
LOOK, JUST HANG ON.
I'M GETTING THE CANDLES.
PARADISE
HEY, CAN YOU LIGHT THIS?
YO, BARTENDER!
HUH?!
LOOK, THIS IS AN EMERGEN—
VWAAAN!!
BURGER
DROP...
CANDLE
SHHKOP
...AH?

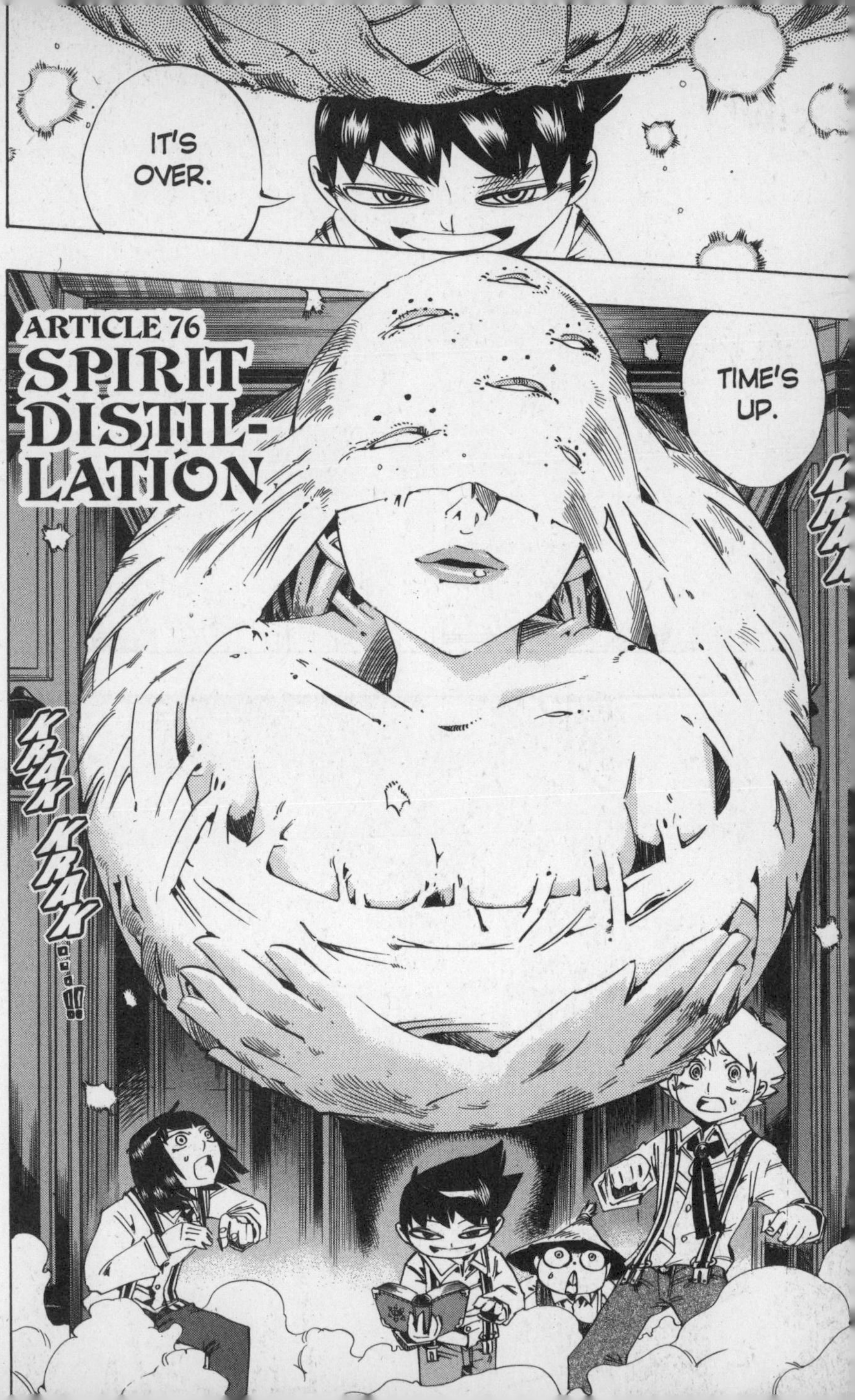
IT'S OVER.
TIME'S UP.
KRAK
ARTICLE 76
SPIRIT DISTIL-LATION
KRAK KRAK...!!

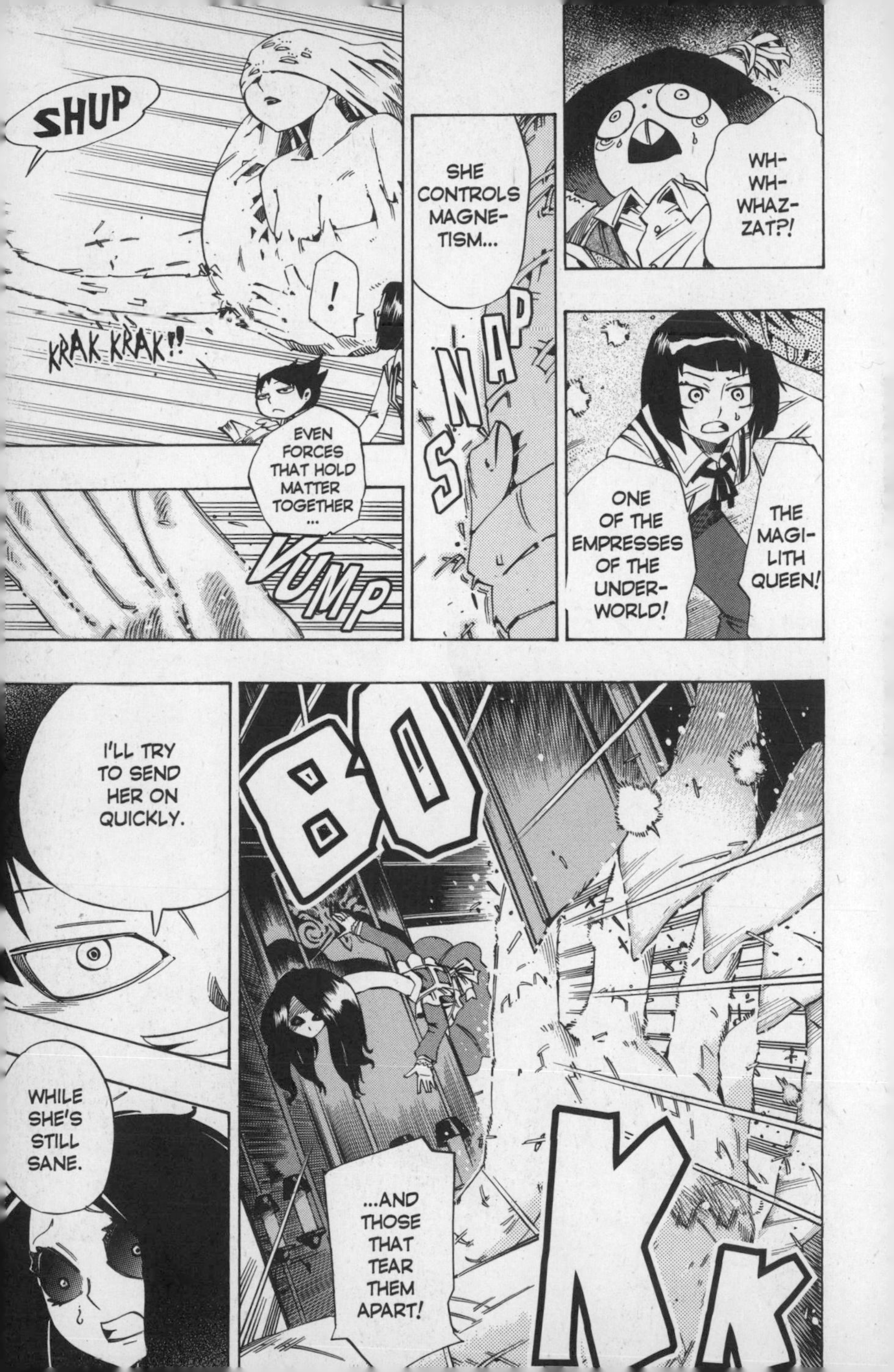
WH- WH- WHAZ-ZAT?!
THE MAGI-LITH QUEEN!
ONE OF THE EMPRESSES OF THE UNDER-WORLD!
SHE CONTROLS MAGNE-TISM...
SNAP
SHUP
!
KRAK KRAK!!
EVEN FORCES THAT HOLD MATTER TOGETHER...
VUMP
BOO
...AND THOSE THAT TEAR THEM APART!
KK
I'LL TRY TO SEND HER ON QUICKLY.
WHILE SHE'S STILL SANE.

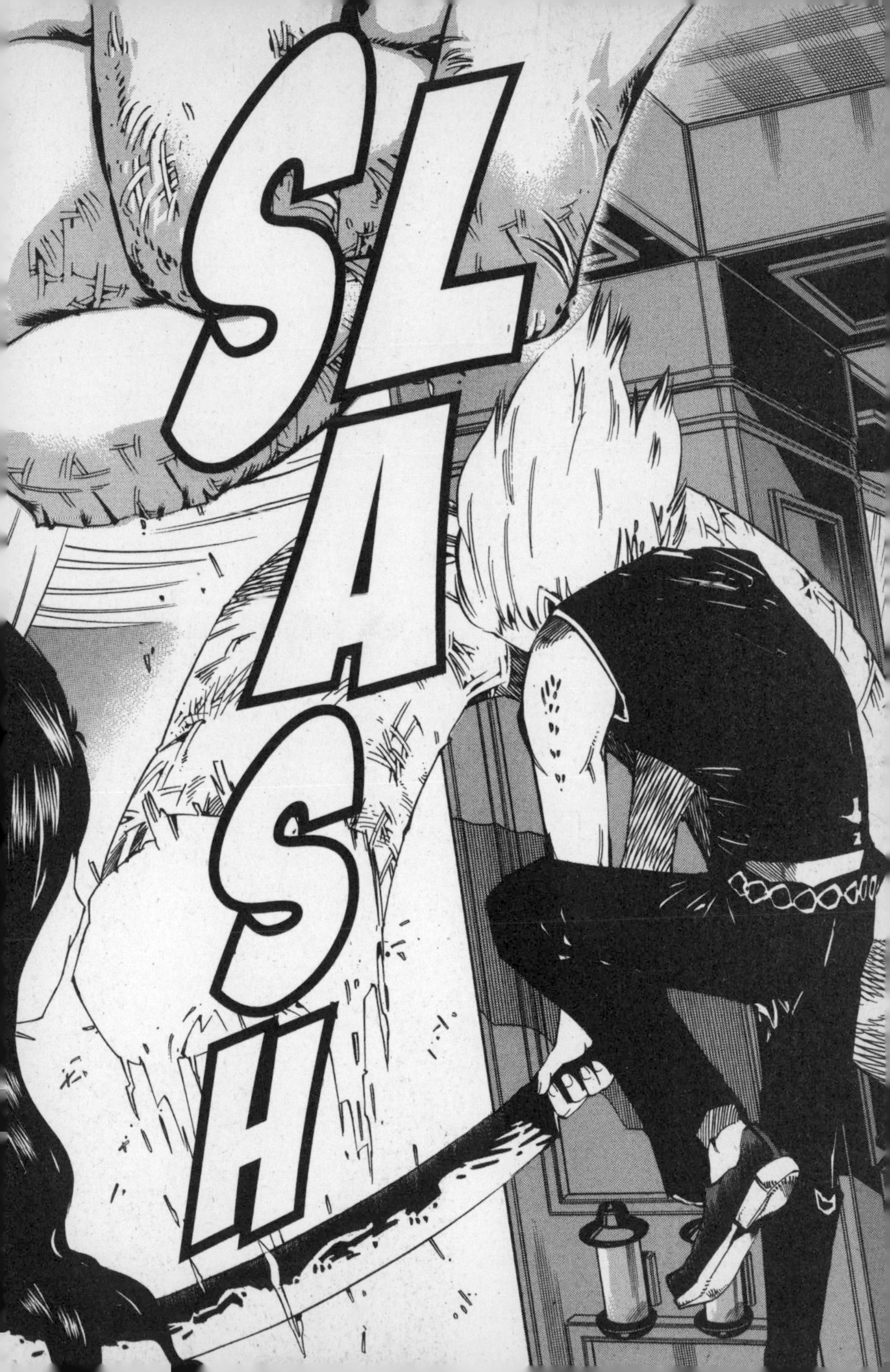
SLASH

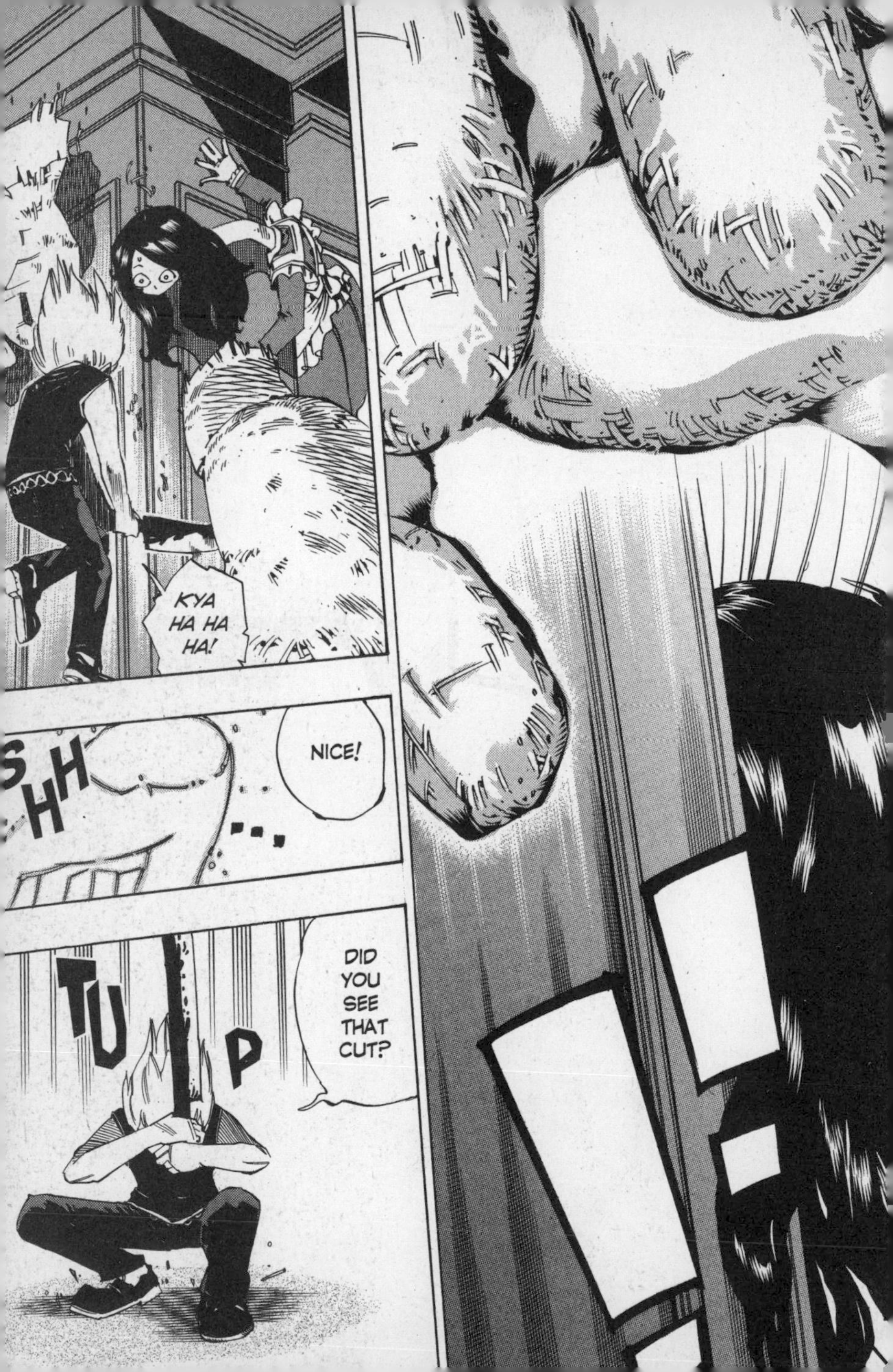
KYA HA HA HA!
NICE!
SHH...
DID YOU SEE THAT CUT?
TUP

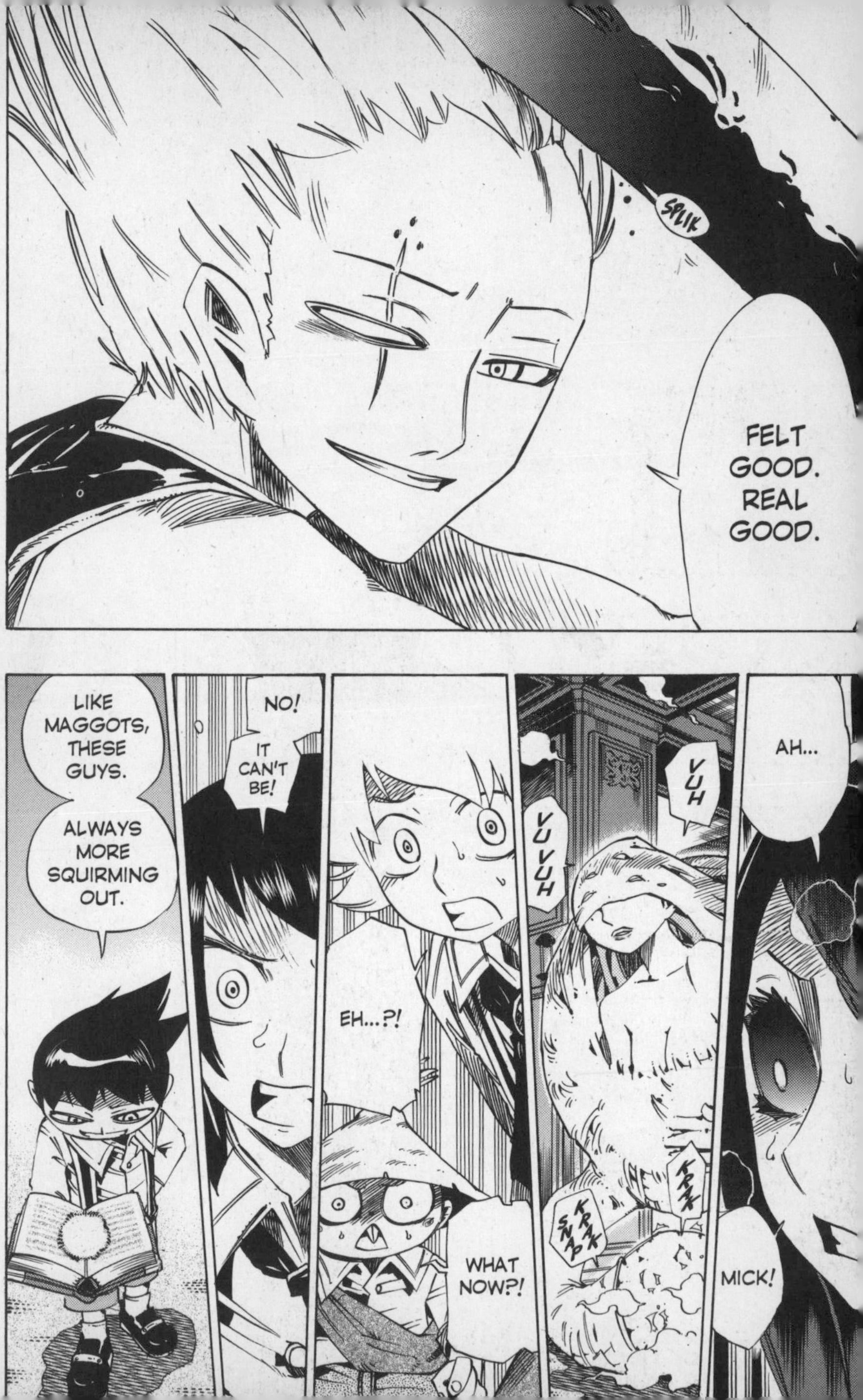
SPLIK
FELT GOOD. REAL GOOD.
AH...
MICK!
VUH
VUVUH
KRAK
KRAK SNAP
WHAT NOW?!
EH...?!
NO!
IT CAN'T BE!
LIKE MAGGOTS, THESE GUYS.
ALWAYS MORE SQUIRMING OUT.

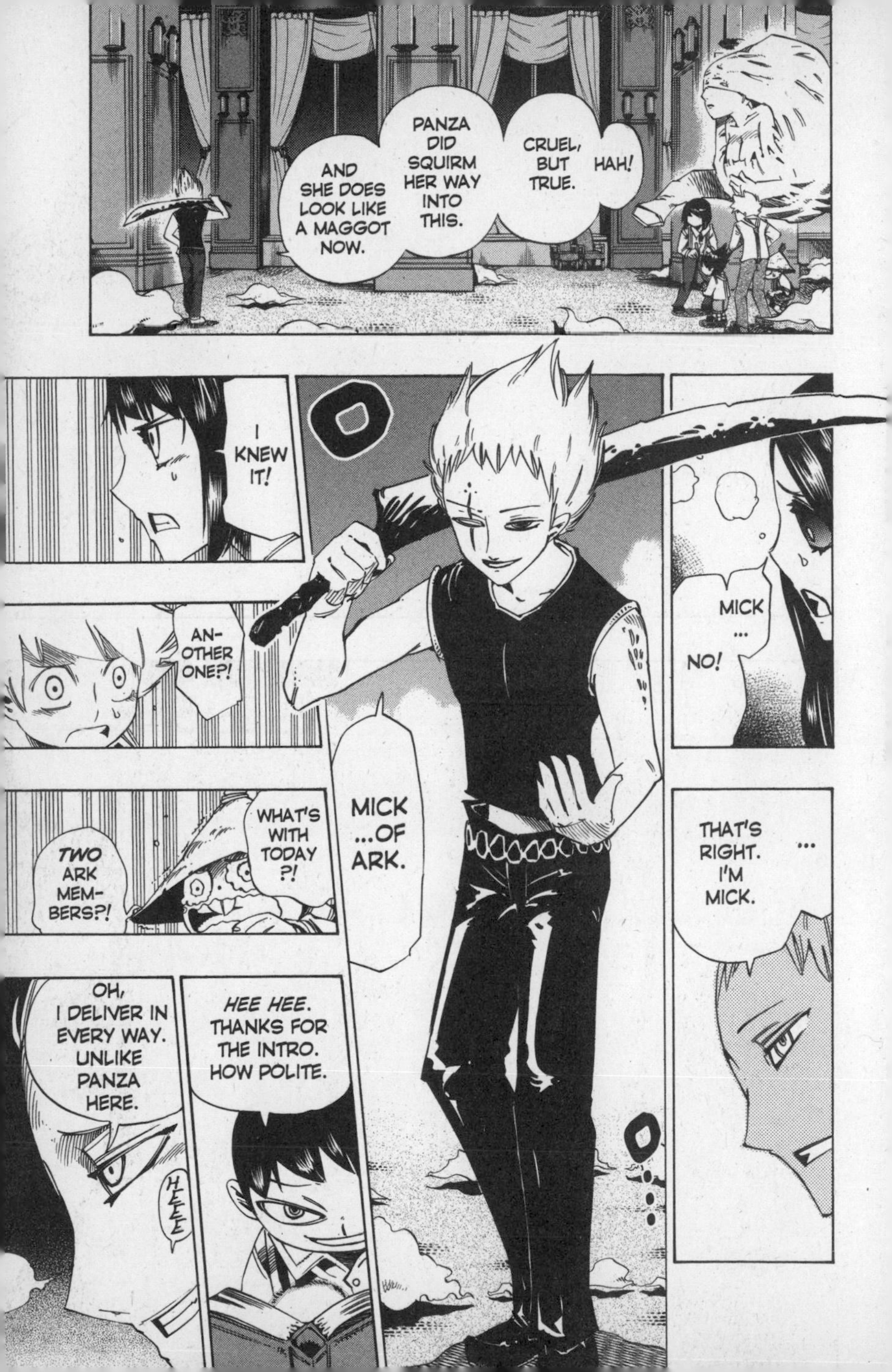
HAH!
CRUEL, BUT TRUE.
PANZA DID SQUIRM HER WAY INTO THIS.
AND SHE DOES LOOK LIKE A MAGGOT NOW.
MICK ... NO!
I KNEW IT!
AN-OTHER ONE?!
WHAT'S WITH TODAY?!
TWO ARK MEM-BERS?!
MICK ...OF ARK.
...
THAT'S RIGHT. I'M MICK.
HEE HEE. THANKS FOR THE INTRO. HOW POLITE.
HEEE
OH, I DELIVER IN EVERY WAY. UNLIKE PANZA HERE.

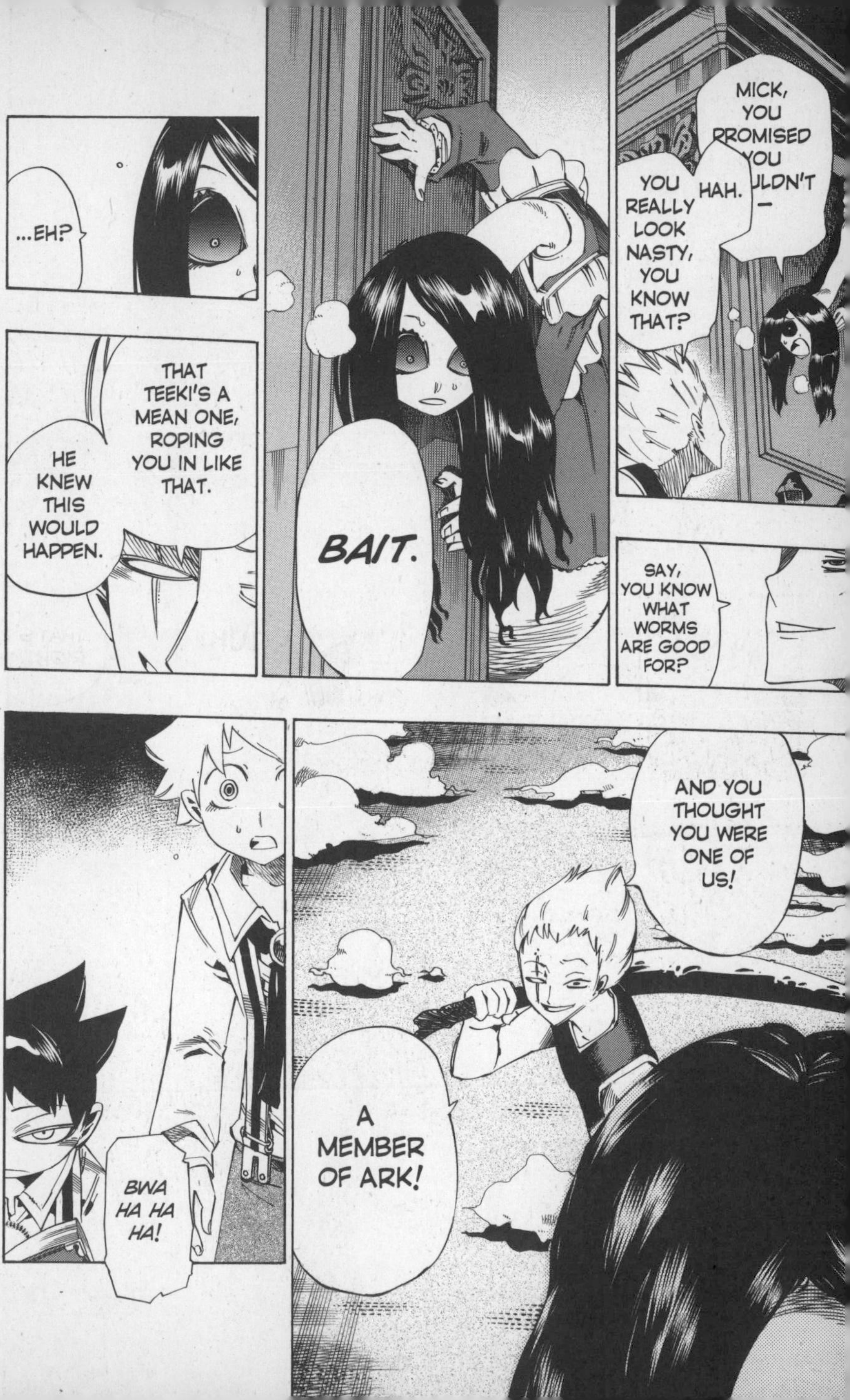

MICK, YOU PROMISED YOU ULDN'T —
HAH.
YOU REALLY LOOK NASTY, YOU KNOW THAT?
SAY, YOU KNOW WHAT WORMS ARE GOOD FOR?
BAIT.
...EH?
THAT TEEKI'S A MEAN ONE, ROPING YOU IN LIKE THAT.
HE KNEW THIS WOULD HAPPEN.
AND YOU THOUGHT YOU WERE ONE OF US!
A MEMBER OF ARK!
BWA HA HA HA!

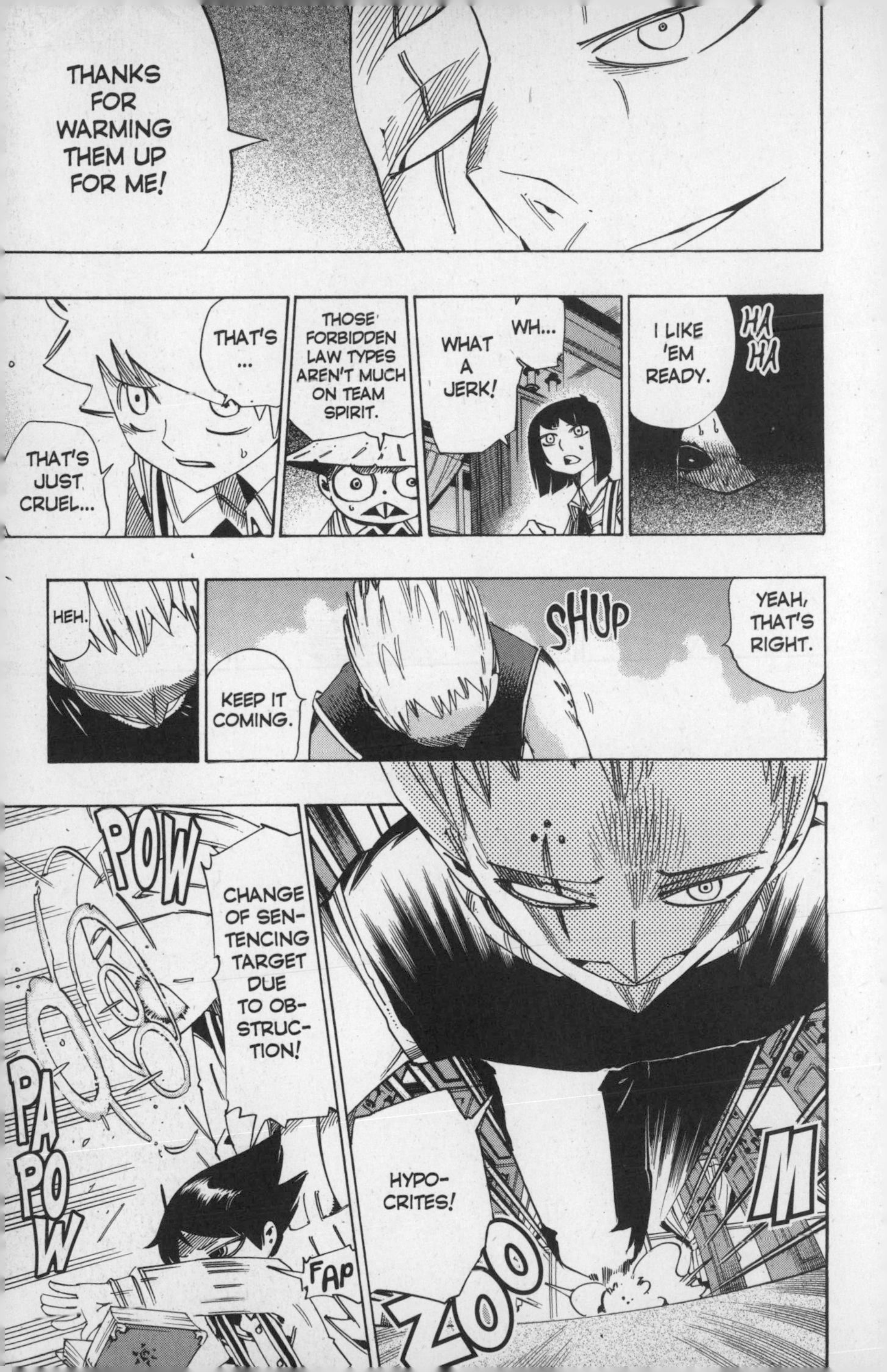
THANKS FOR WARMING THEM UP FOR ME!
HA HA
I LIKE 'EM READY.
WH...
WHAT A JERK!
THOSE FORBIDDEN LAW TYPES AREN'T MUCH ON TEAM SPIRIT.
THAT'S ...
THAT'S JUST CRUEL...
YEAH, THAT'S RIGHT.
SHUP
KEEP IT COMING.
HEH.
M
HYPO-CRITES!
ZOO
POW
CHANGE OF SEN-TENCING TARGET DUE TO OB-STRUC-TION!
PAPOW
FAP

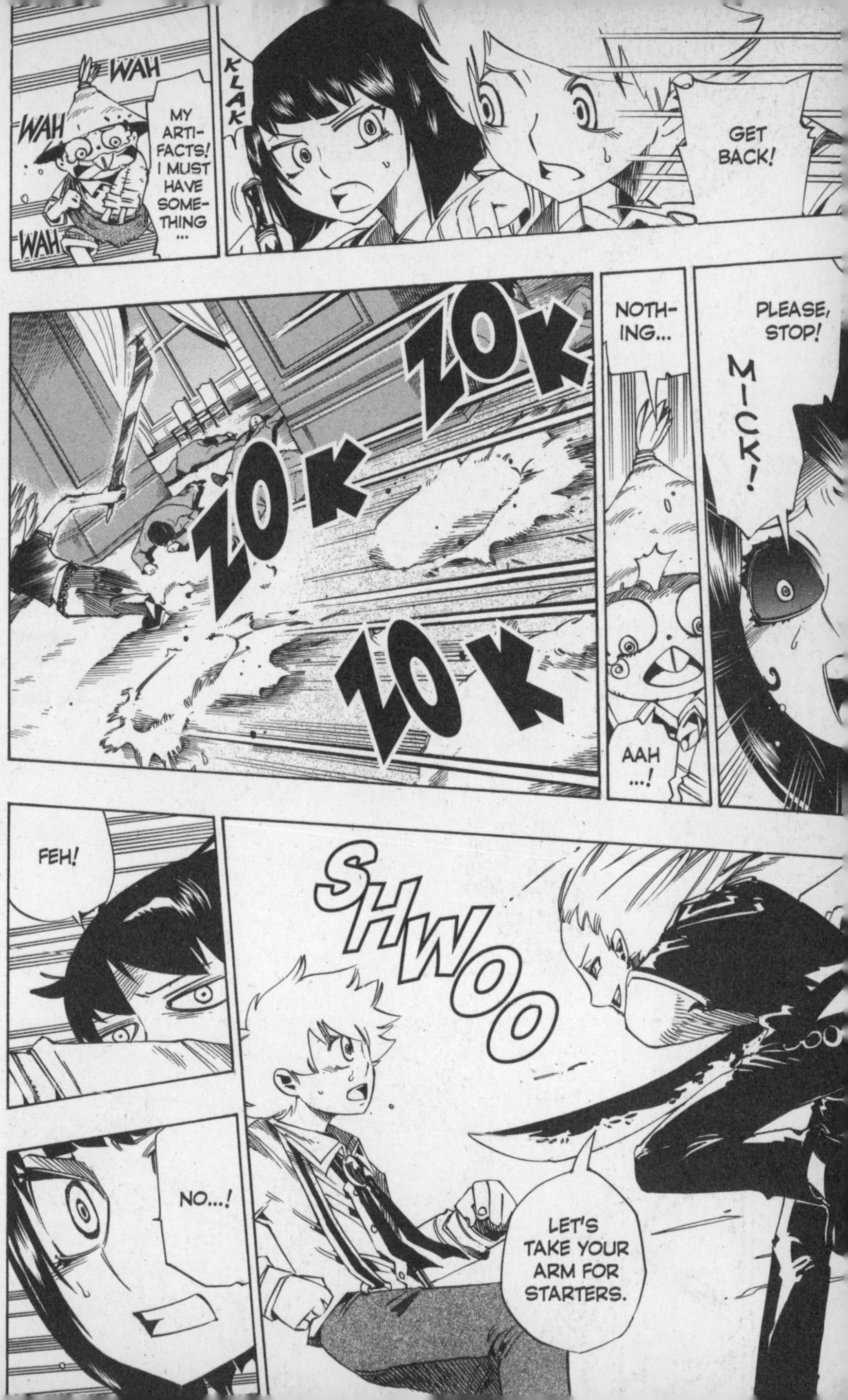
GET BACK!
KLAK
WAH
WAH
WAH
MY ARTI- FACTS! I MUST HAVE SOME- THING ...
PLEASE, STOP!
MICK!
NOTH- ING...
AAH ...!
ZOK
ZOK
ZOK
SHWOO
LET'S TAKE YOUR ARM FOR STARTERS.
FEH!
NO...!

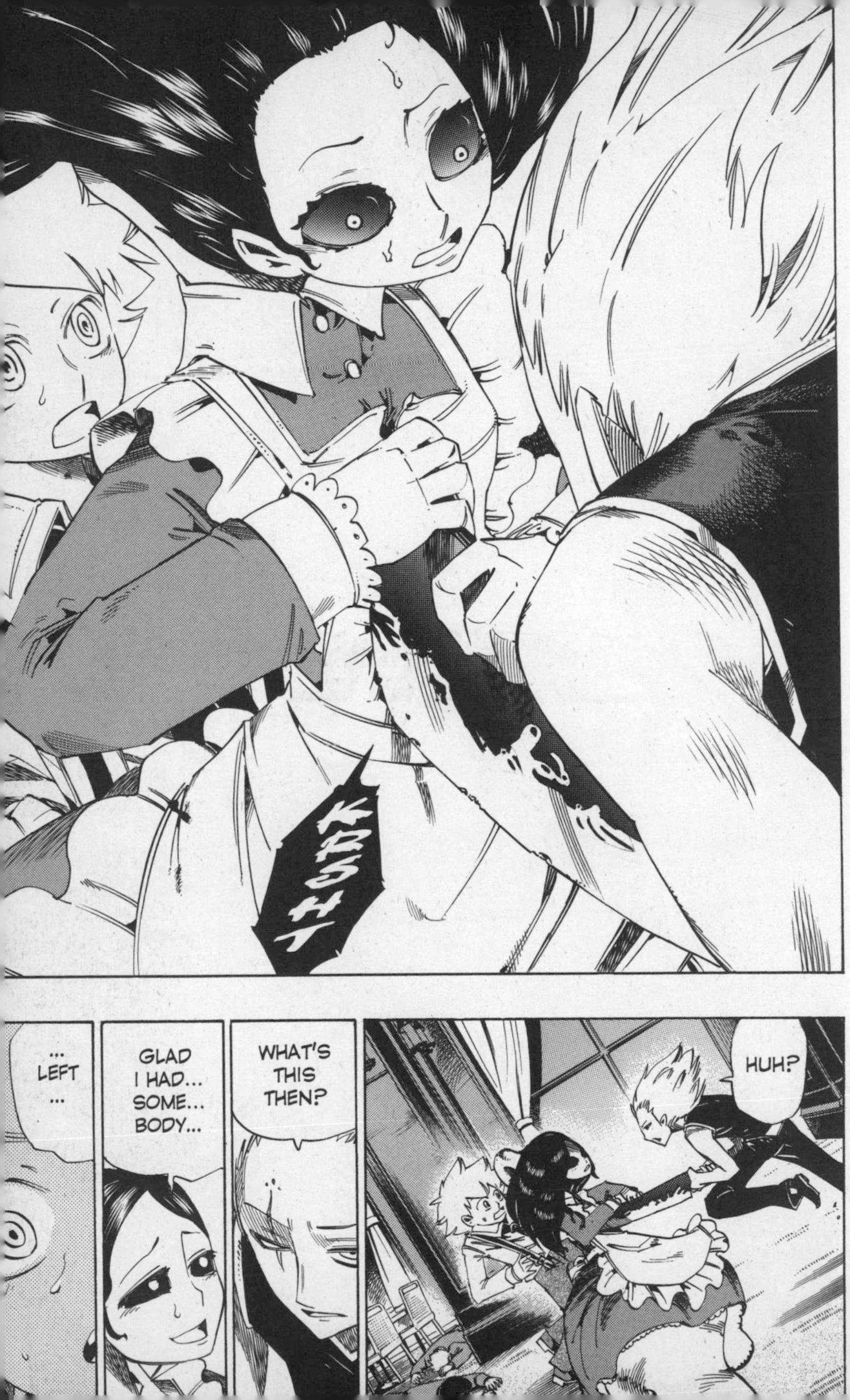
KRSHT
HUH?
WHAT'S THIS THEN?
GLAD I HAD... SOME... BODY...
... LEFT ...

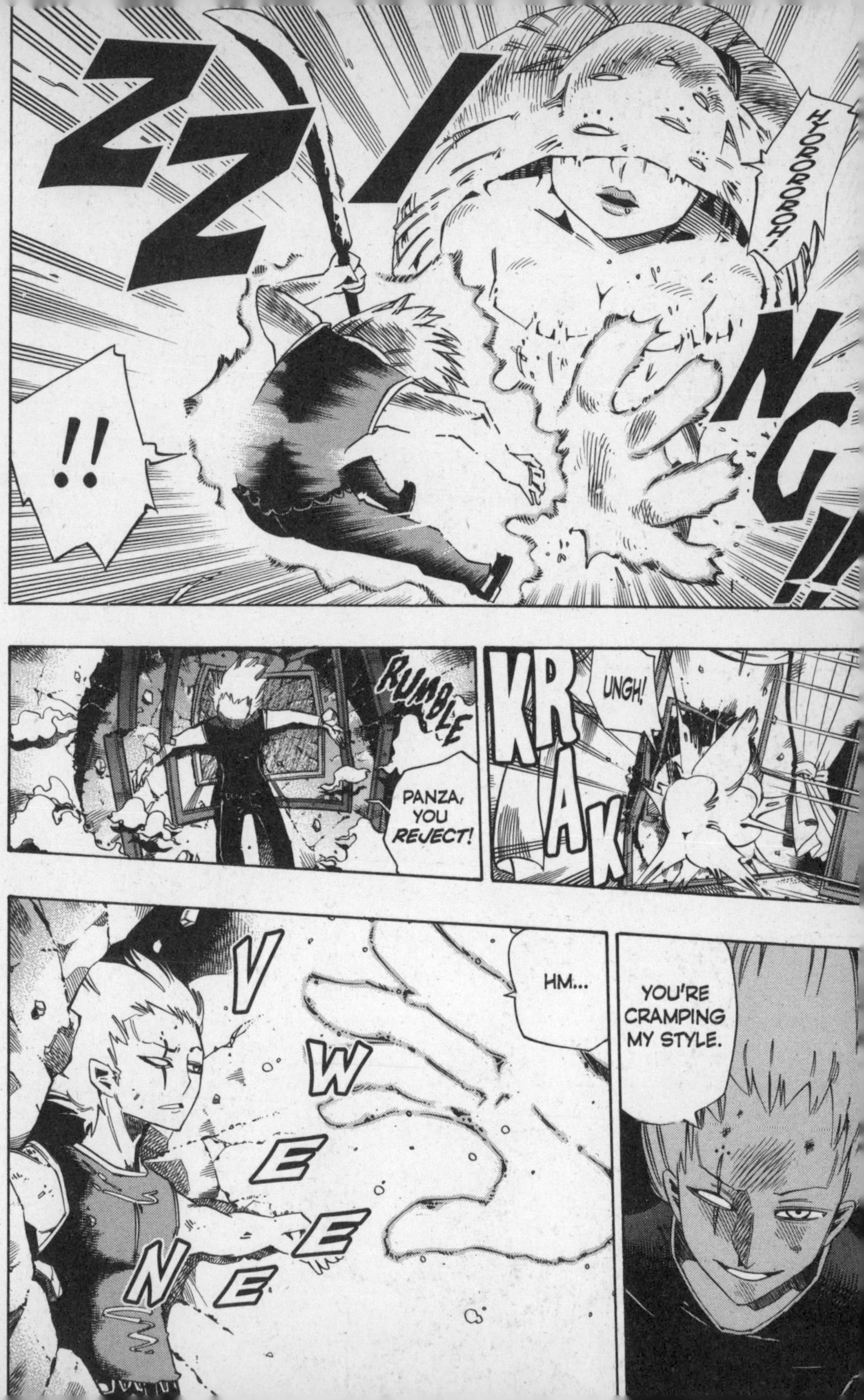
HYOROROROH!
ZZING!!
!!
KRAK
UNGH!
RUMBLE
PANZA, YOU REJECT!
YOU'RE CRAMPING MY STYLE.
HM...
VWEEEN

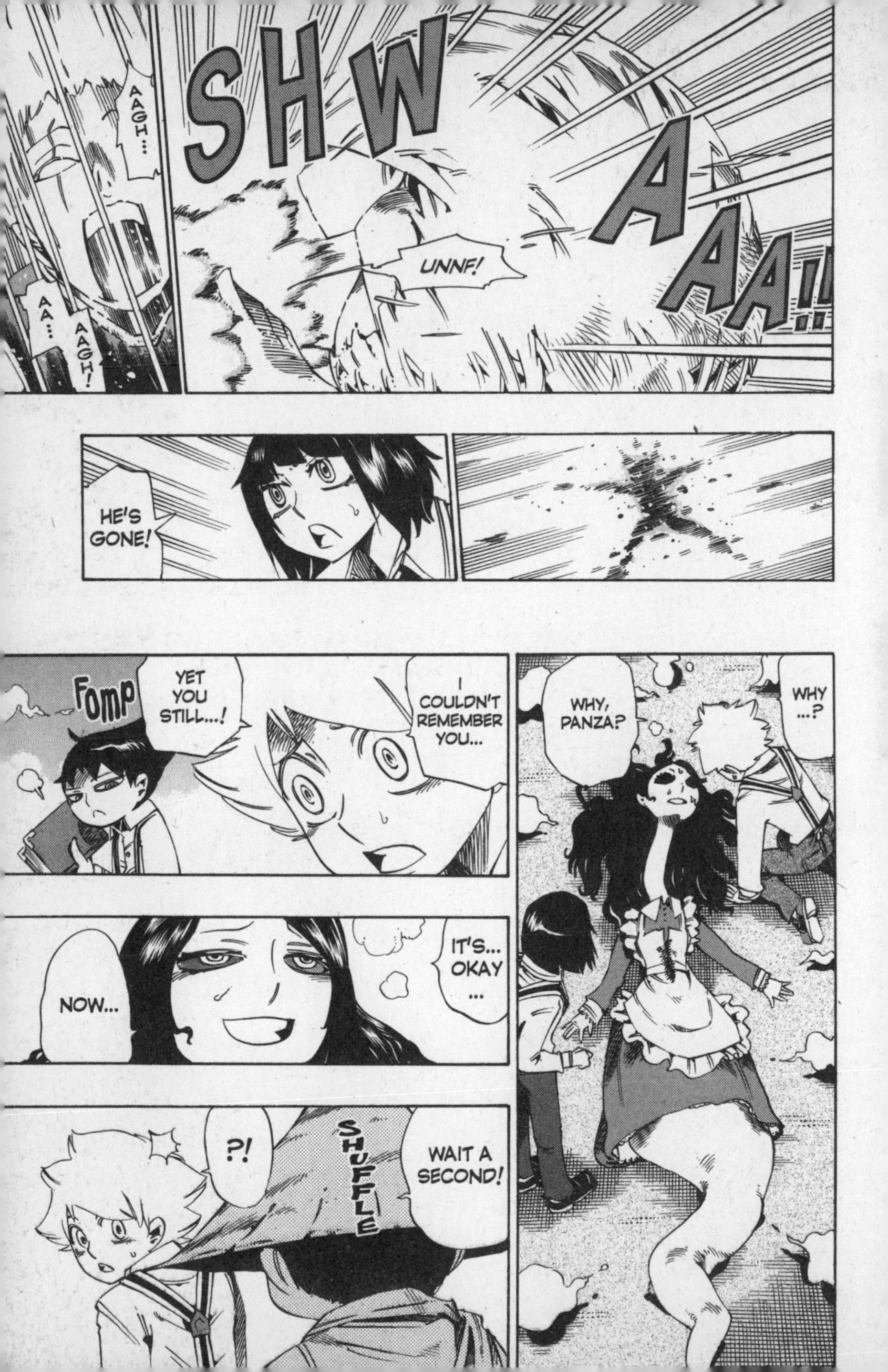
SHWAAAA!!
UNNF!
AAGH...
AA... AAGH!
HE'S GONE!
WHY ...?
WHY, PANZA?
I COULDN'T REMEMBER YOU...
YET YOU STILL...!
Fomp
IT'S... OKAY ...
NOW...
WAIT A SECOND!
SHUFFLE
?!

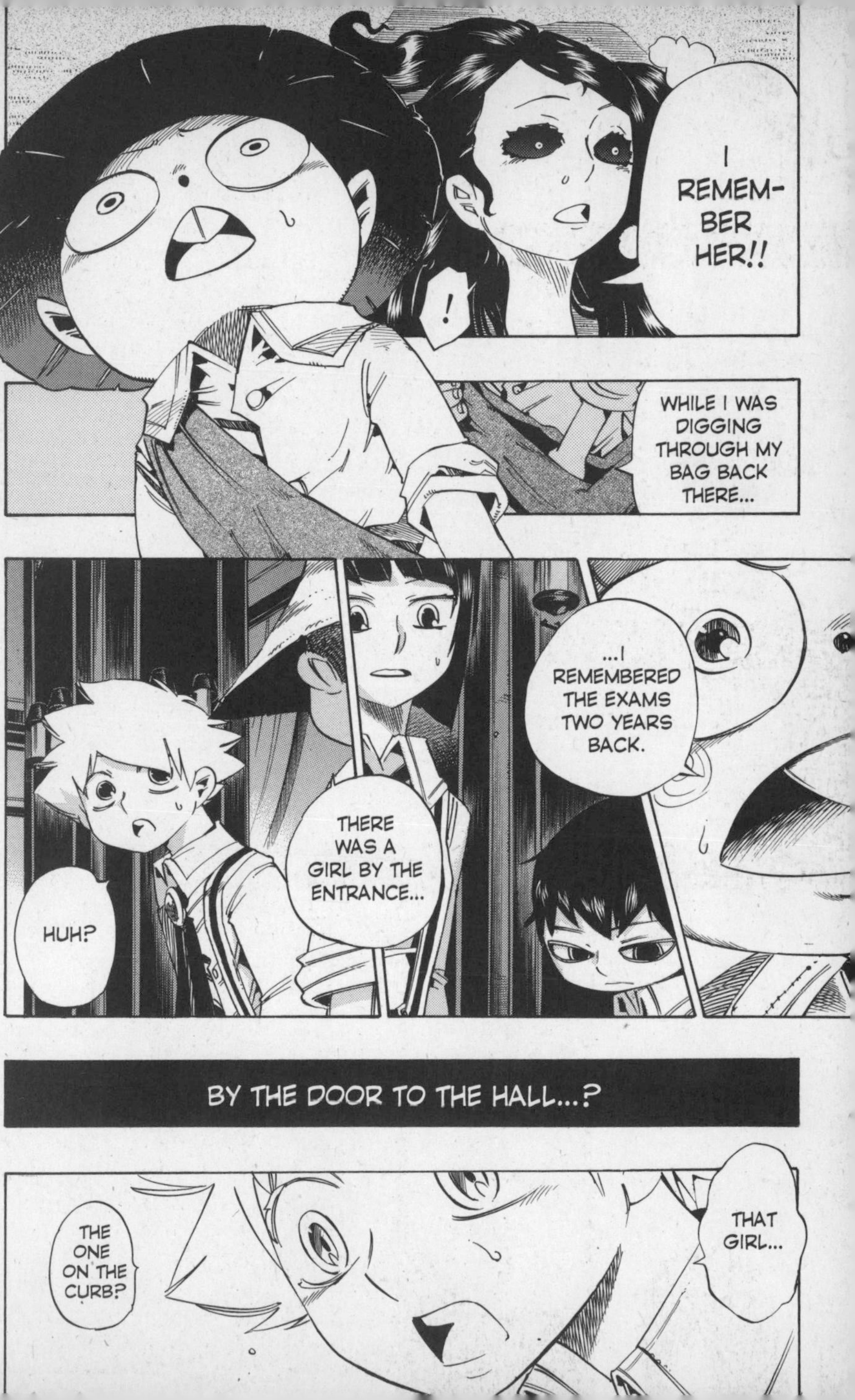
I REMEMBER HER!!
!
WHILE I WAS DIGGING THROUGH MY BAG BACK THERE...
...I REMEMBERED THE EXAMS TWO YEARS BACK.
THERE WAS A GIRL BY THE ENTRANCE...
HUH?
BY THE DOOR TO THE HALL...?
THAT GIRL...
THE ONE ON THE CURB?

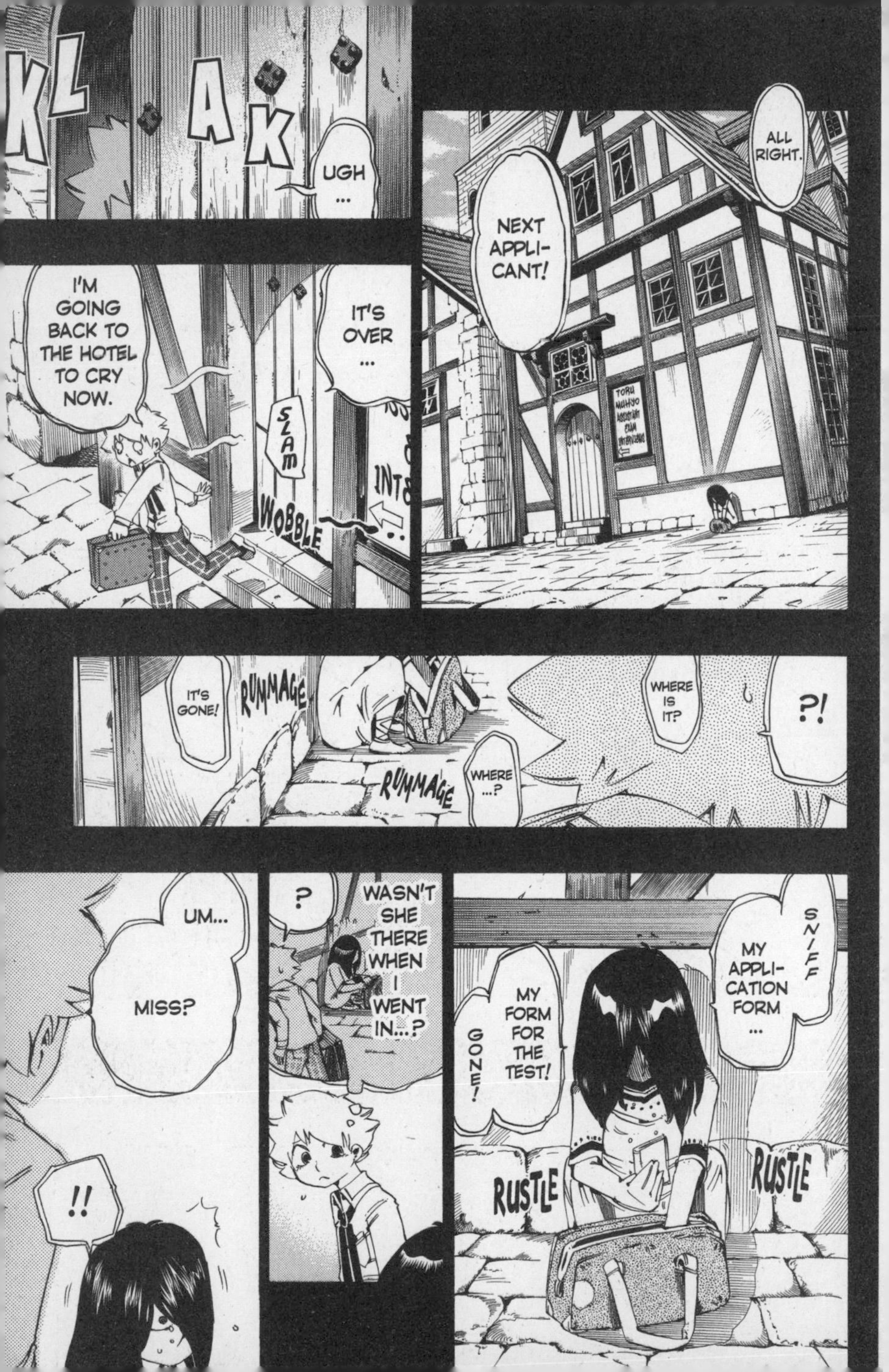
ALL RIGHT.
NEXT APPLI-CANT!
KLAK
UGH ...
IT'S OVER ...
I'M GOING BACK TO THE HOTEL TO CRY NOW.
SLAM
WOBBLE
?!
WHERE IS IT?
WHERE ...?
RUMMAGE
RUMMAGE
IT'S GONE!
SNIFF
MY APPLI-CATION FORM ...
MY FORM FOR THE TEST!
GONE!
RUSTLE
RUSTLE
?
WASN'T SHE THERE WHEN I WENT IN...?
UM...
MISS?
!!

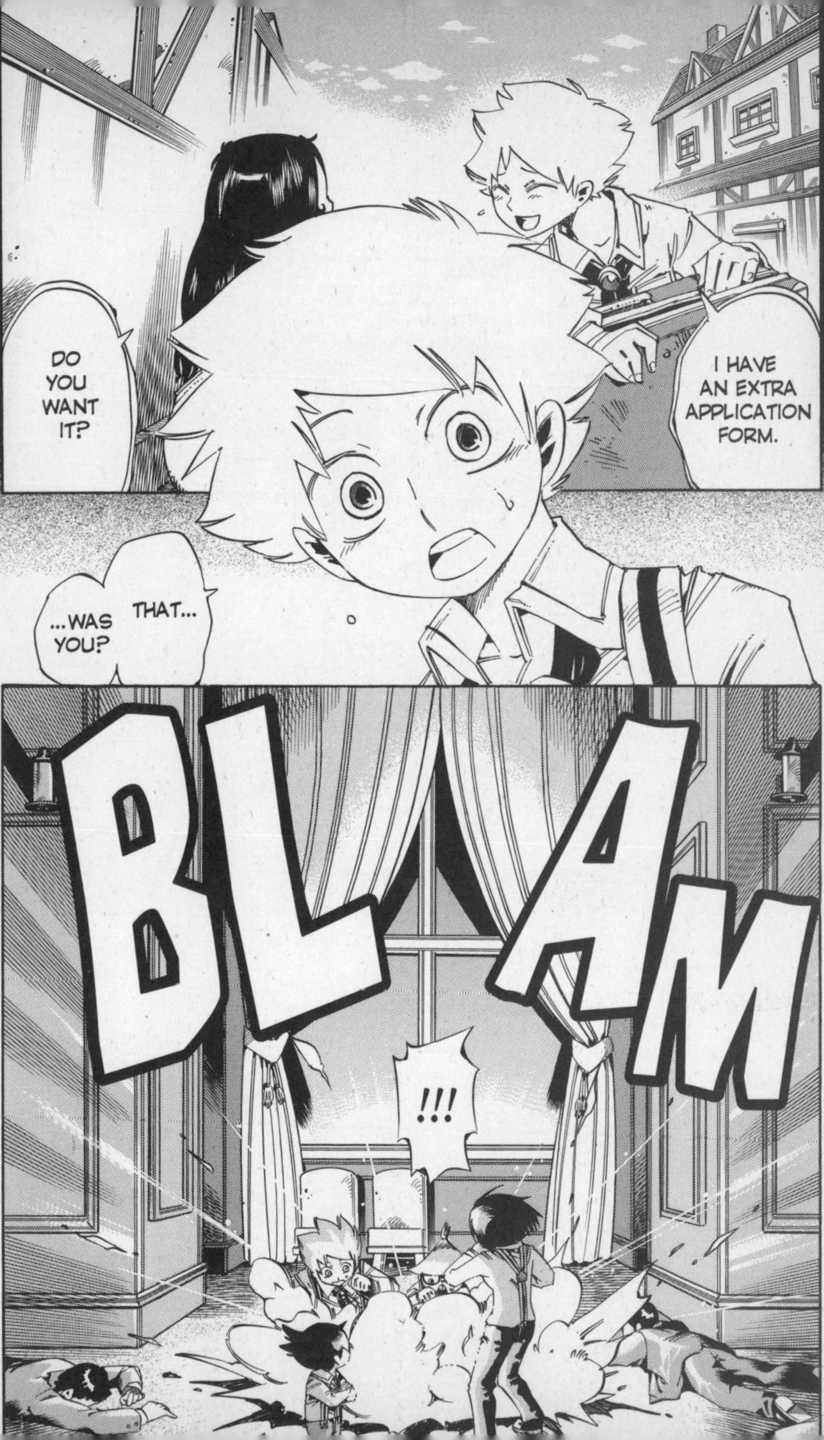
I HAVE AN EXTRA APPLICATION FORM.
DO YOU WANT IT?
THAT... ...WAS YOU?
BLAM
!!!

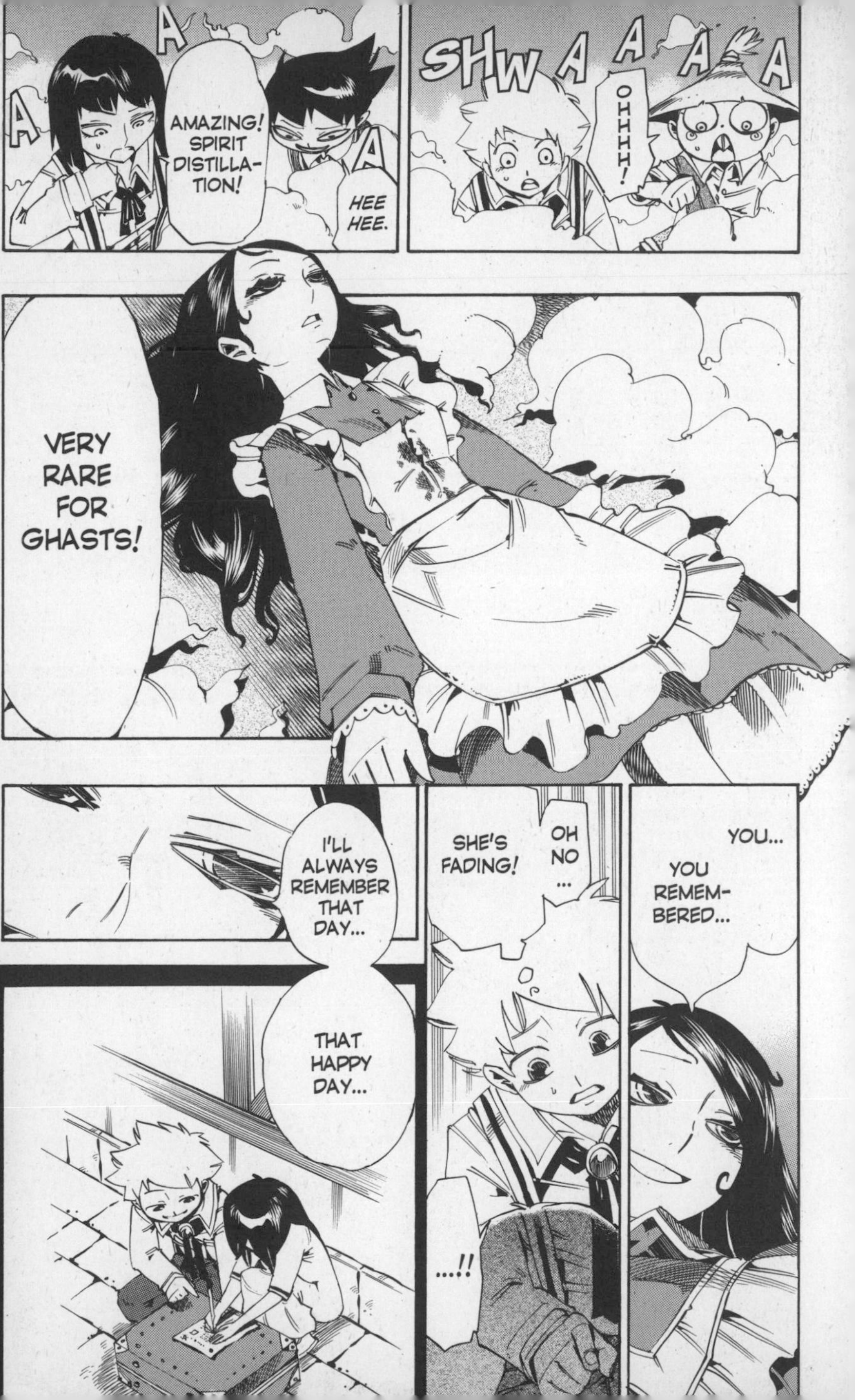
SHWAAAAA
OHHHH!
AMAZING! SPIRIT DISTILLATION!
HEE HEE.
VERY RARE FOR GHASTS!
YOU...
YOU REMEMBERED...
OH NO...
SHE'S FADING!
...!!
I'LL ALWAYS REMEMBER THAT DAY...
THAT HAPPY DAY...

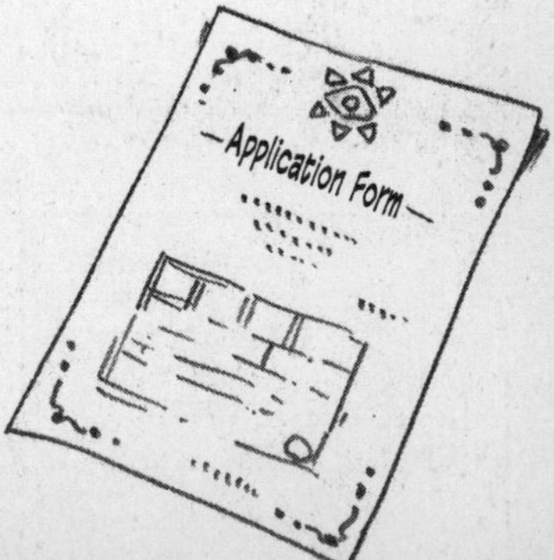
—Application Form—

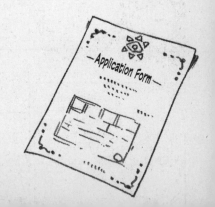

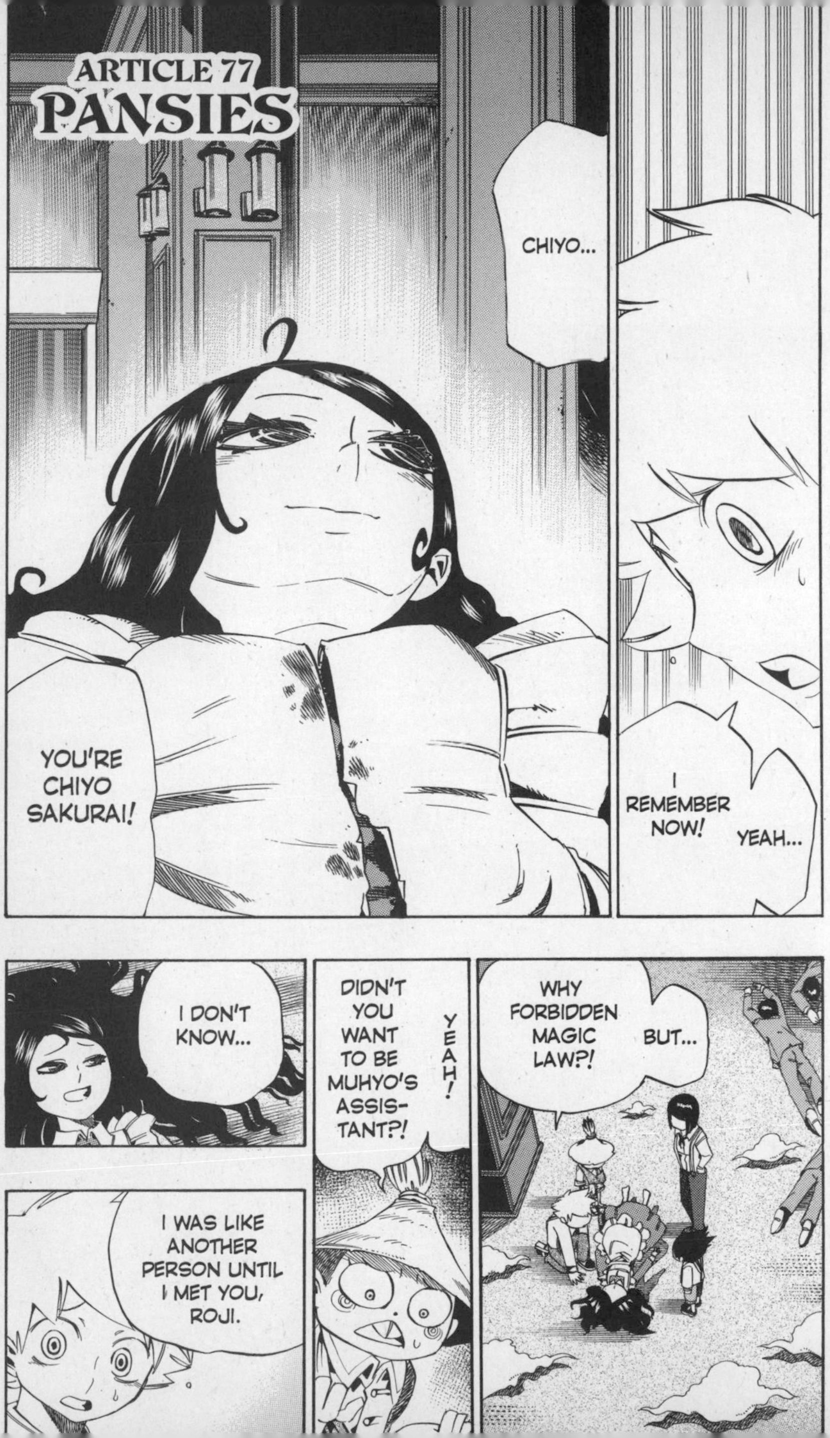
CHIYO...
YEAH...
I REMEMBER NOW!
ARTICLE 77
PANSIES
YOU'RE CHIYO SAKURAI!
BUT...
WHY FORBIDDEN MAGIC LAW?!
YEAH!
DIDN'T YOU WANT TO BE MUHYO'S ASSISTANT?!
I DON'T KNOW...
I WAS LIKE ANOTHER PERSON UNTIL I MET YOU, ROJI.

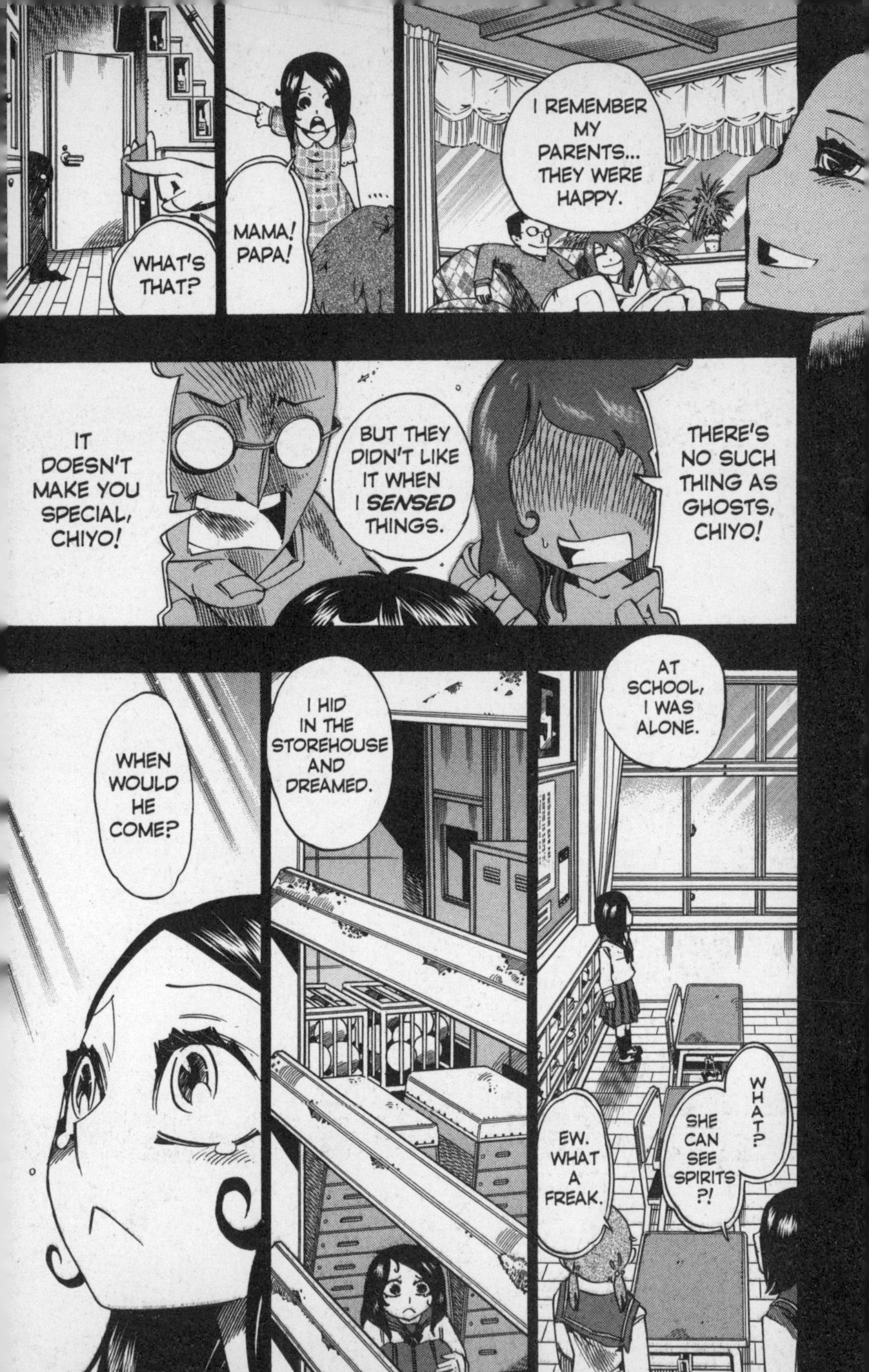
I REMEMBER MY PARENTS... THEY WERE HAPPY.
MAMA! PAPA!
WHAT'S THAT?
THERE'S NO SUCH THING AS GHOSTS, CHIYO!
BUT THEY DIDN'T LIKE IT WHEN I *SENSED* THINGS.
IT DOESN'T MAKE YOU SPECIAL, CHIYO!
AT SCHOOL, I WAS ALONE.
WHAT?
SHE CAN SEE SPIRITS?!
EW. WHAT A FREAK.
I HID IN THE STOREHOUSE AND DREAMED.
WHEN WOULD HE COME?

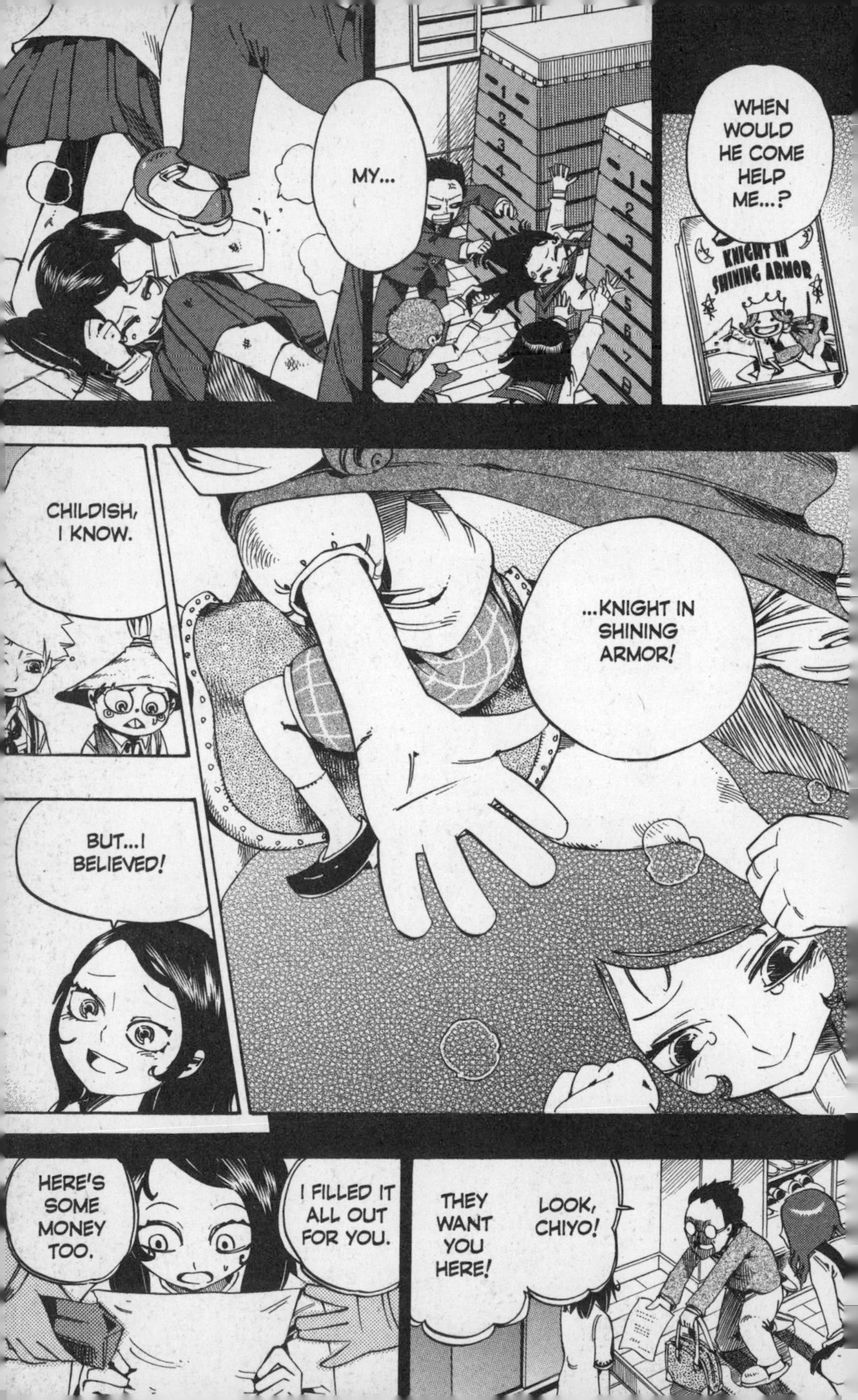
WHEN WOULD HE COME HELP ME...?
KNIGHT IN SHINING ARMOR
MY...
...KNIGHT IN SHINING ARMOR!
CHILDISH, I KNOW.
BUT...I BELIEVED!
LOOK, CHIYO!
THEY WANT YOU HERE!
I FILLED IT ALL OUT FOR YOU.
HERE'S SOME MONEY TOO.

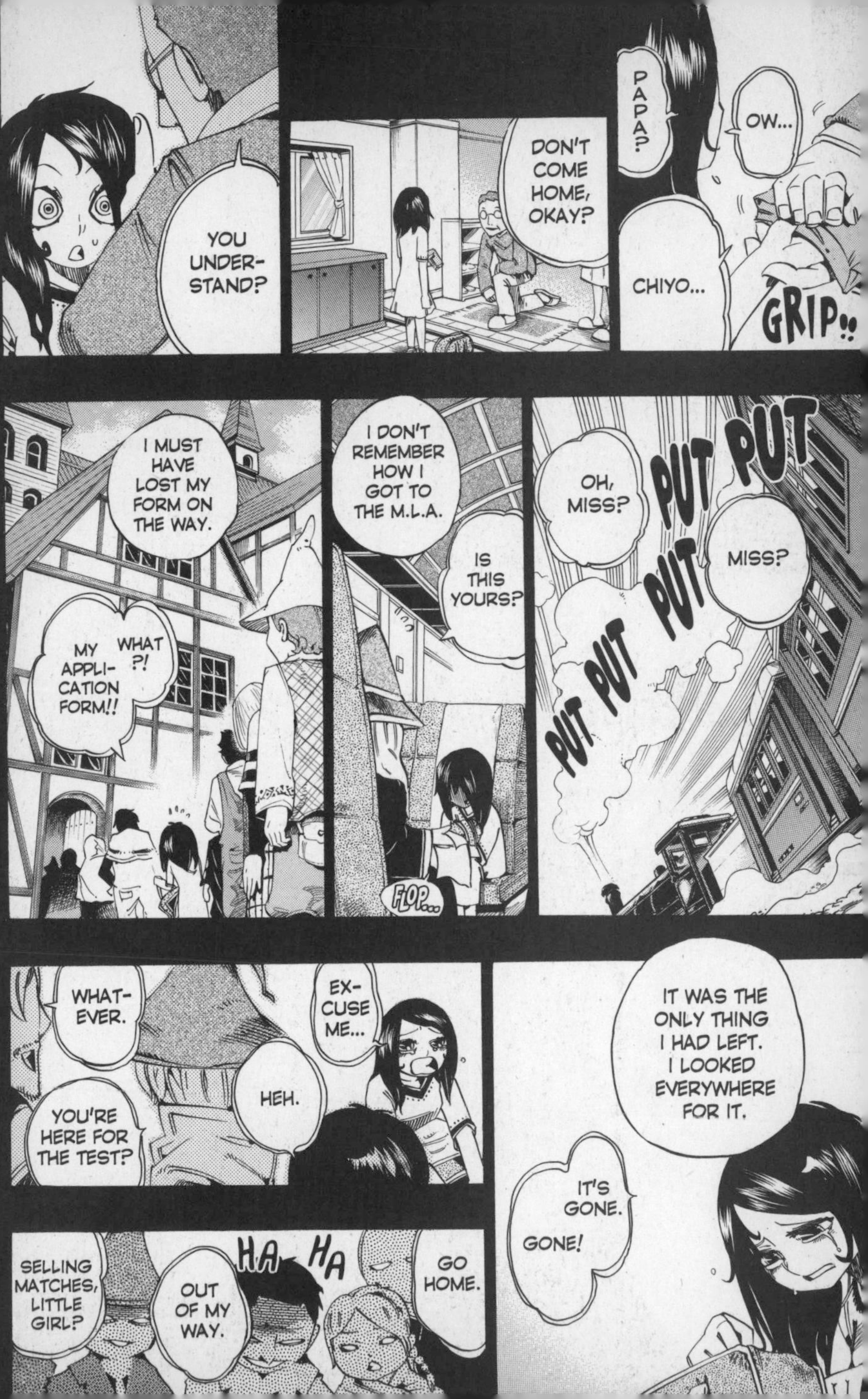

OW...
PAPA?
CHIYO...
GRIP!!
DON'T COME HOME, OKAY?
YOU UNDERSTAND?
PUT PUT
OH, MISS?
MISS?
PUT PUT PUT PUT
I DON'T REMEMBER HOW I GOT TO THE M.L.A.
IS THIS YOURS?
FLOP...
I MUST HAVE LOST MY FORM ON THE WAY.
WHAT?!
MY APPLICATION FORM!!
IT WAS THE ONLY THING I HAD LEFT. I LOOKED EVERYWHERE FOR IT.
IT'S GONE.
GONE!
EXCUSE ME...
WHATEVER.
HEH.
YOU'RE HERE FOR THE TEST?
GO HOME.
HA HA
OUT OF MY WAY.
SELLING MATCHES, LITTLE GIRL?

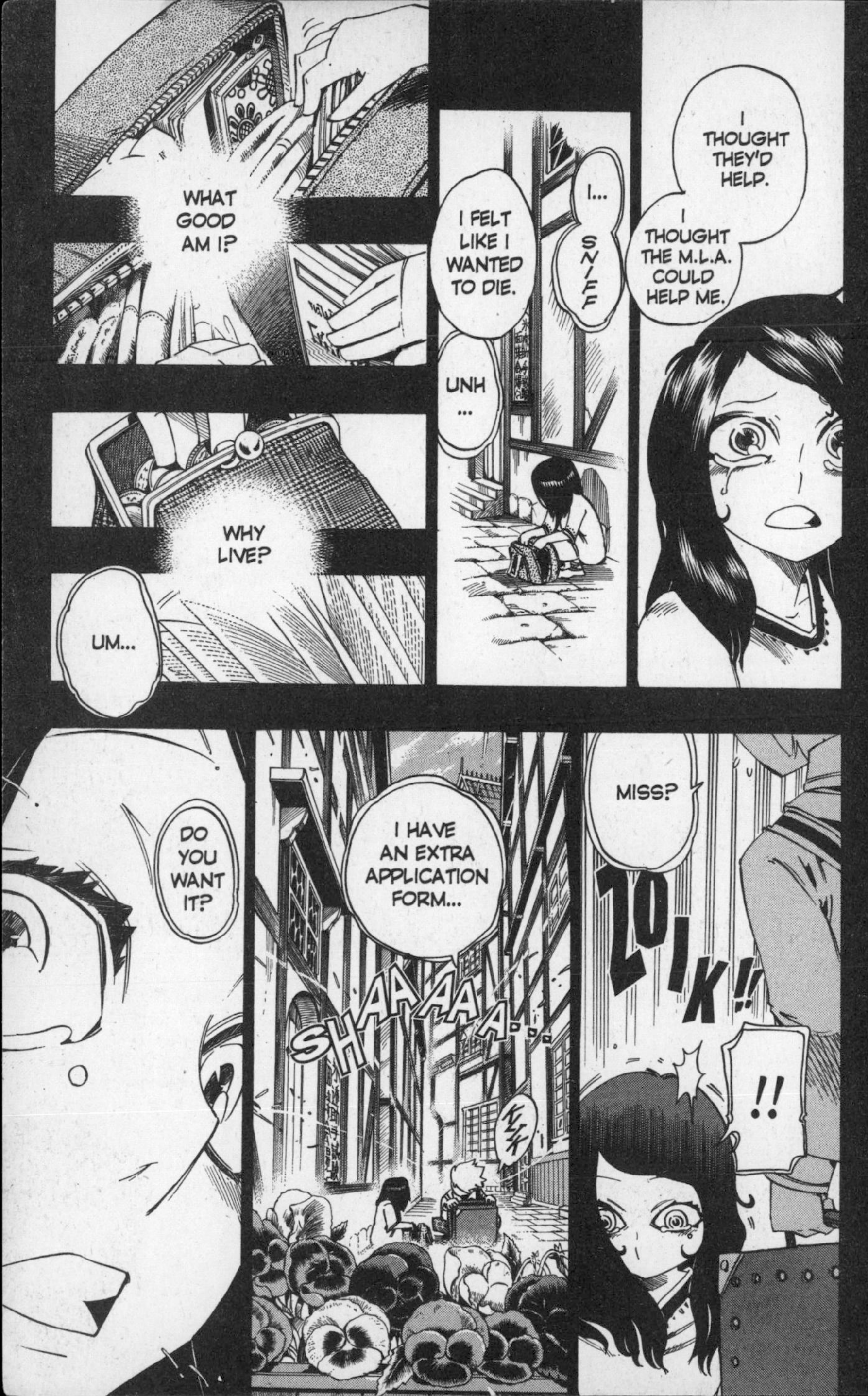
I THOUGHT THEY'D HELP.
I THOUGHT THE M.L.A. COULD HELP ME.
I...
SNIFF
I FELT LIKE I WANTED TO DIE.
UNH...
WHAT GOOD AM I?
WHY LIVE?
UM...
MISS?
ZOIK!!
!!
I HAVE AN EXTRA APPLICATION FORM...
SHAAAAA...
DO YOU WANT IT?

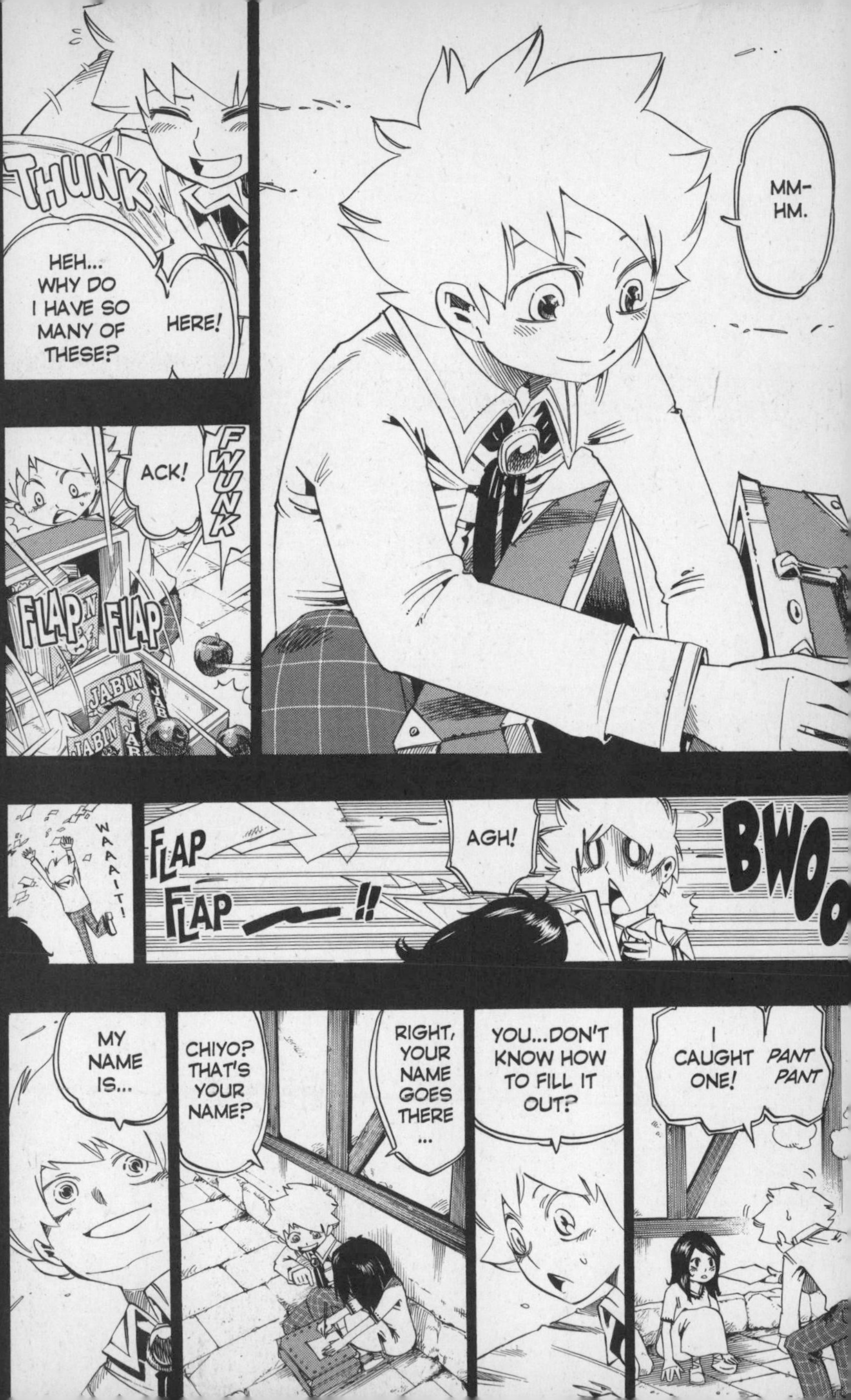
MM-HM.
THUNK
HERE!
HEH... WHY DO I HAVE SO MANY OF THESE?
FWUNK
ACK!
FLAP 'N' FLAP
JABIN
BWOO
AGH!
FLAP FLAP —!!
WAAAIT!
I CAUGHT ONE!
PANT PANT
YOU...DON'T KNOW HOW TO FILL IT OUT?
RIGHT, YOUR NAME GOES THERE ...
CHIYO? THAT'S YOUR NAME?
MY NAME IS...

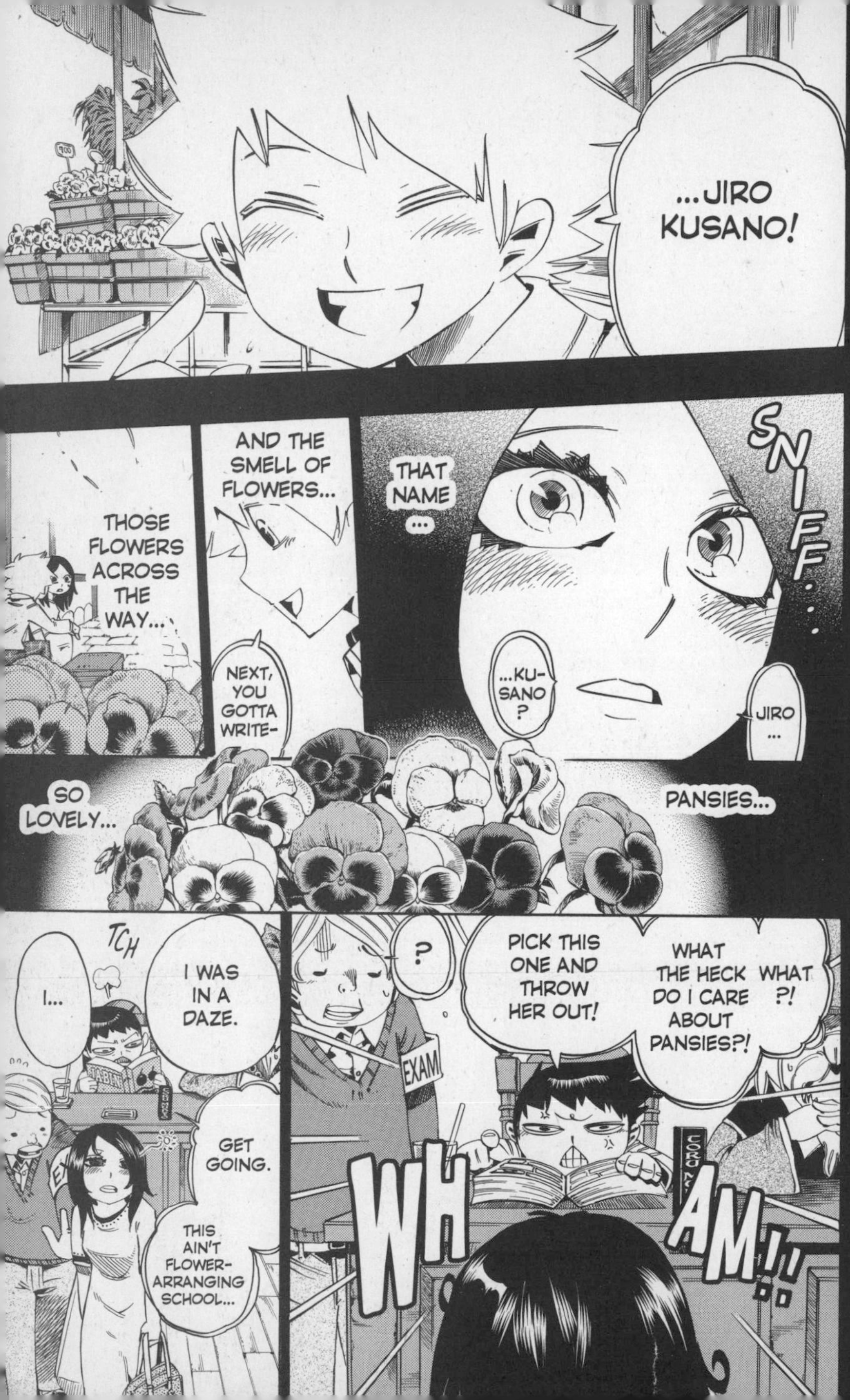

...JIRO KUSANO!
SNIFF...
JIRO...
...KUSANO?
THAT NAME...
AND THE SMELL OF FLOWERS...
NEXT, YOU GOTTA WRITE-
THOSE FLOWERS ACROSS THE WAY...
PANSIES...
SO LOVELY...
WHAT?!
WHAT THE HECK DO I CARE ABOUT PANSIES?!
PICK THIS ONE AND THROW HER OUT!
?
EXAM
WHAM!!
I WAS IN A DAZE.
TCH
I...
GET GOING.
THIS AIN'T FLOWER-ARRANGING SCHOOL...

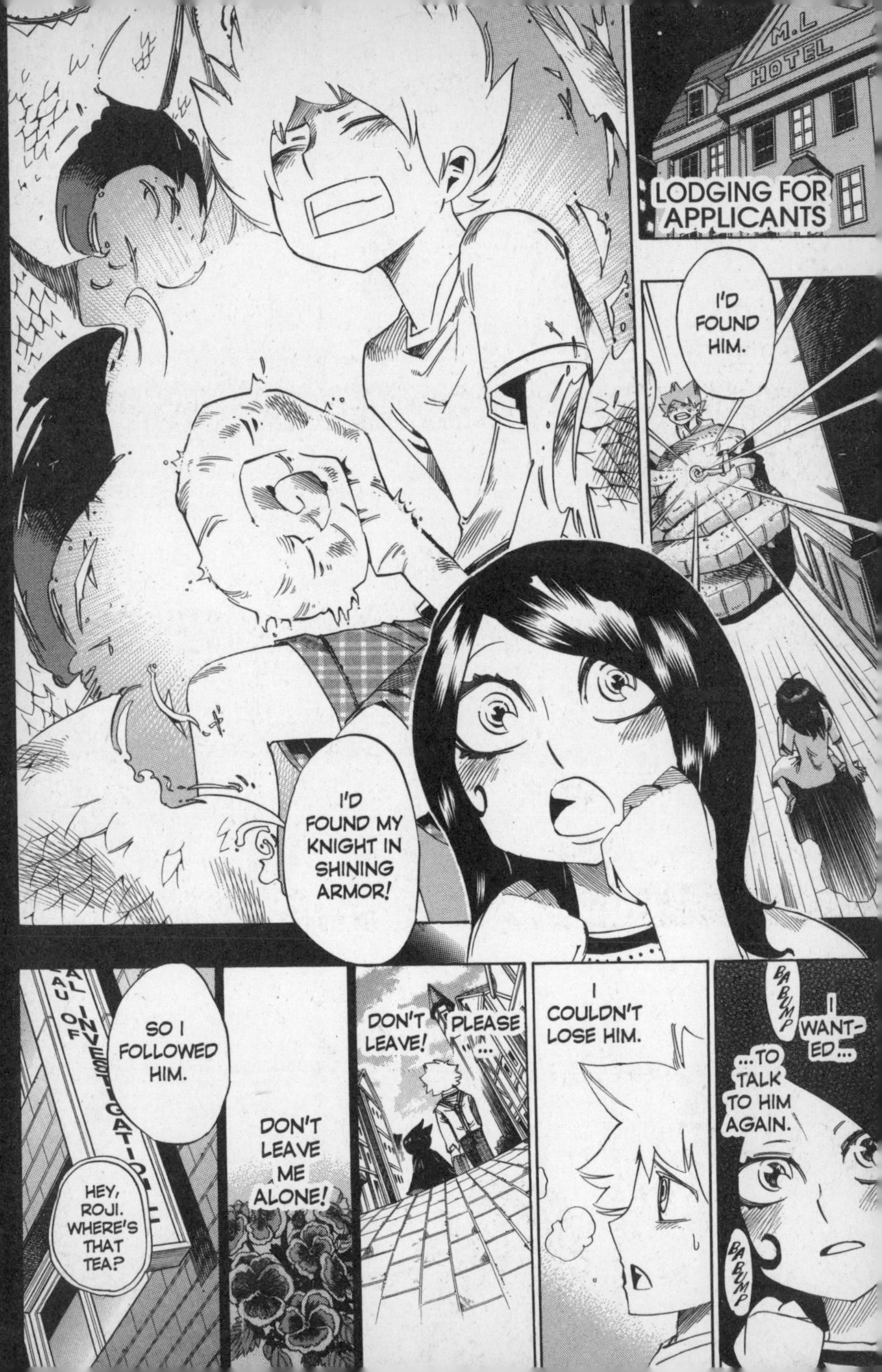
M.L
HOTEL
LODGING FOR APPLICANTS
I'D FOUND HIM.
I'D FOUND MY KNIGHT IN SHINING ARMOR!
BA BUMP
I WANTED...
...TO TALK TO HIM AGAIN.
BA BUMP
I COULDN'T LOSE HIM.
PLEASE...
DON'T LEAVE!
DON'T LEAVE ME ALONE!
SO I FOLLOWED HIM.
HEY, ROJI. WHERE'S THAT TEA?

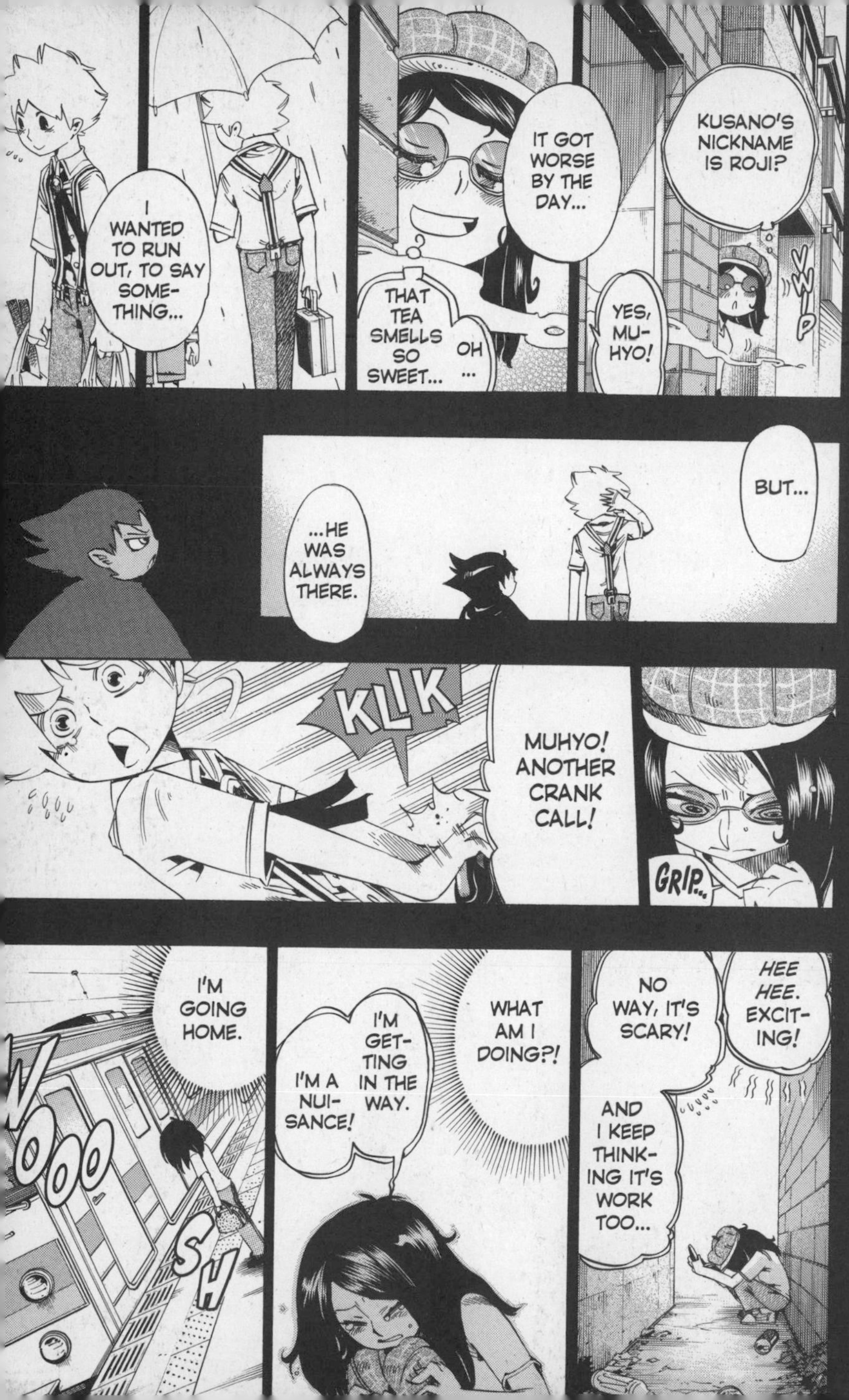
KUSANO'S NICKNAME IS ROJI?
YES, MUHYO!
VWIP
IT GOT WORSE BY THE DAY...
OH ...
THAT TEA SMELLS SO SWEET...
I WANTED TO RUN OUT, TO SAY SOME-THING...
BUT...
...HE WAS ALWAYS THERE.
MUHYO! ANOTHER CRANK CALL!
GRIP...
KLIK
HEE HEE. EXCIT-ING!
NO WAY, IT'S SCARY!
AND I KEEP THINK-ING IT'S WORK TOO...
WHAT AM I DOING?!
I'M GET-TING IN THE WAY.
I'M A NUI-SANCE!
I'M GOING HOME.
WOOOSH

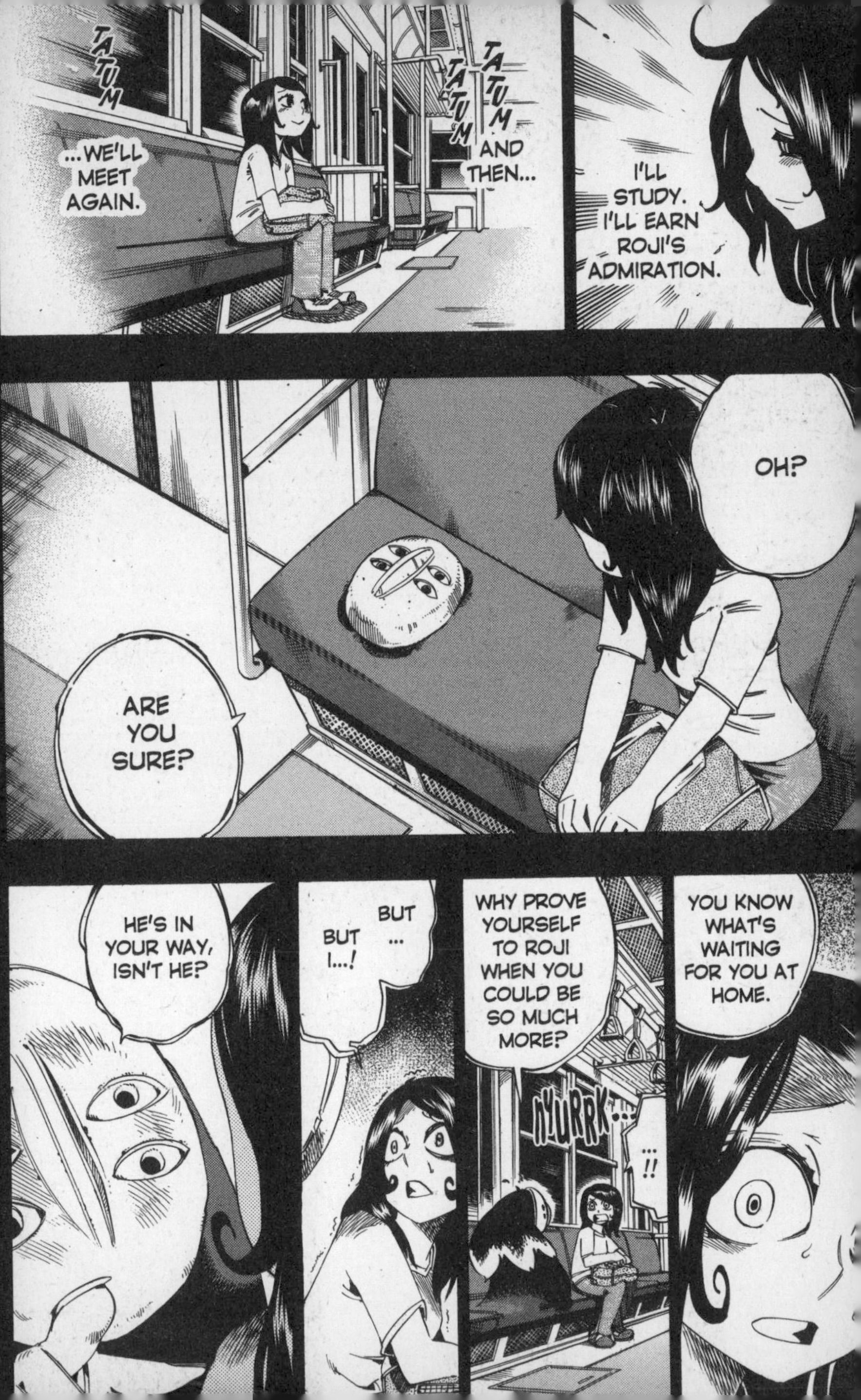
I'LL STUDY. I'LL EARN ROJI'S ADMIRATION.
TATUM
TATUM
AND THEN...
TATUM
...WE'LL MEET AGAIN.
OH?
ARE YOU SURE?
YOU KNOW WHAT'S WAITING FOR YOU AT HOME.
WHY PROVE YOURSELF TO ROJI WHEN YOU COULD BE SO MUCH MORE?
NYURRK...
...!!
BUT ...
BUT I...!
HE'S IN YOUR WAY, ISN'T HE?

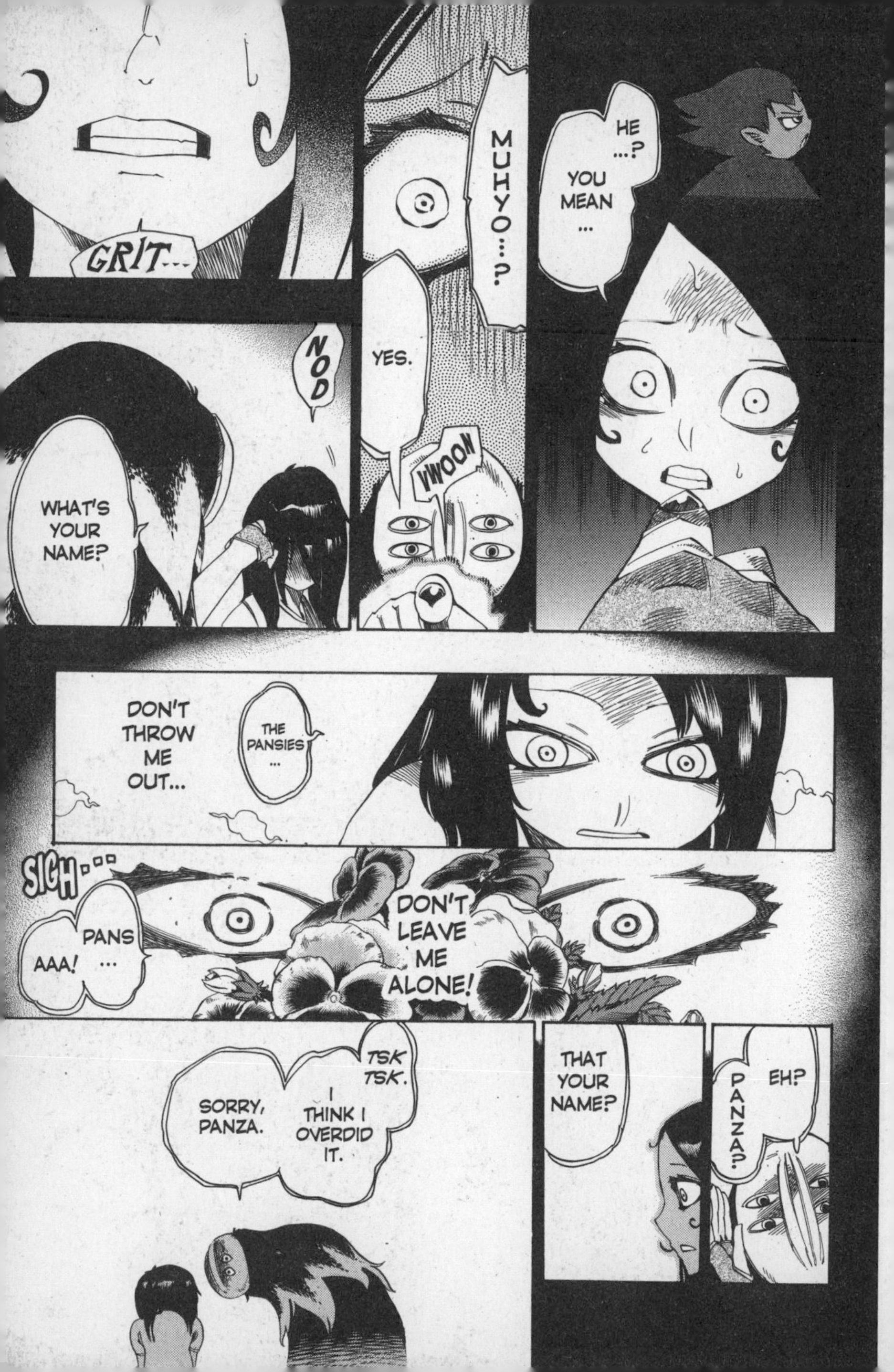
HE ...? YOU MEAN ...
MUHYO...?
YES.
VWOON
GRIT...
NOD
WHAT'S YOUR NAME?
THE PANSIES ...
DON'T THROW ME OUT...
DON'T LEAVE ME ALONE!
PANS ... AAA!
SIGH...
EH? PANZA?
THAT YOUR NAME?
TSK TSK.
SORRY, PANZA. I THINK I OVERDID IT.

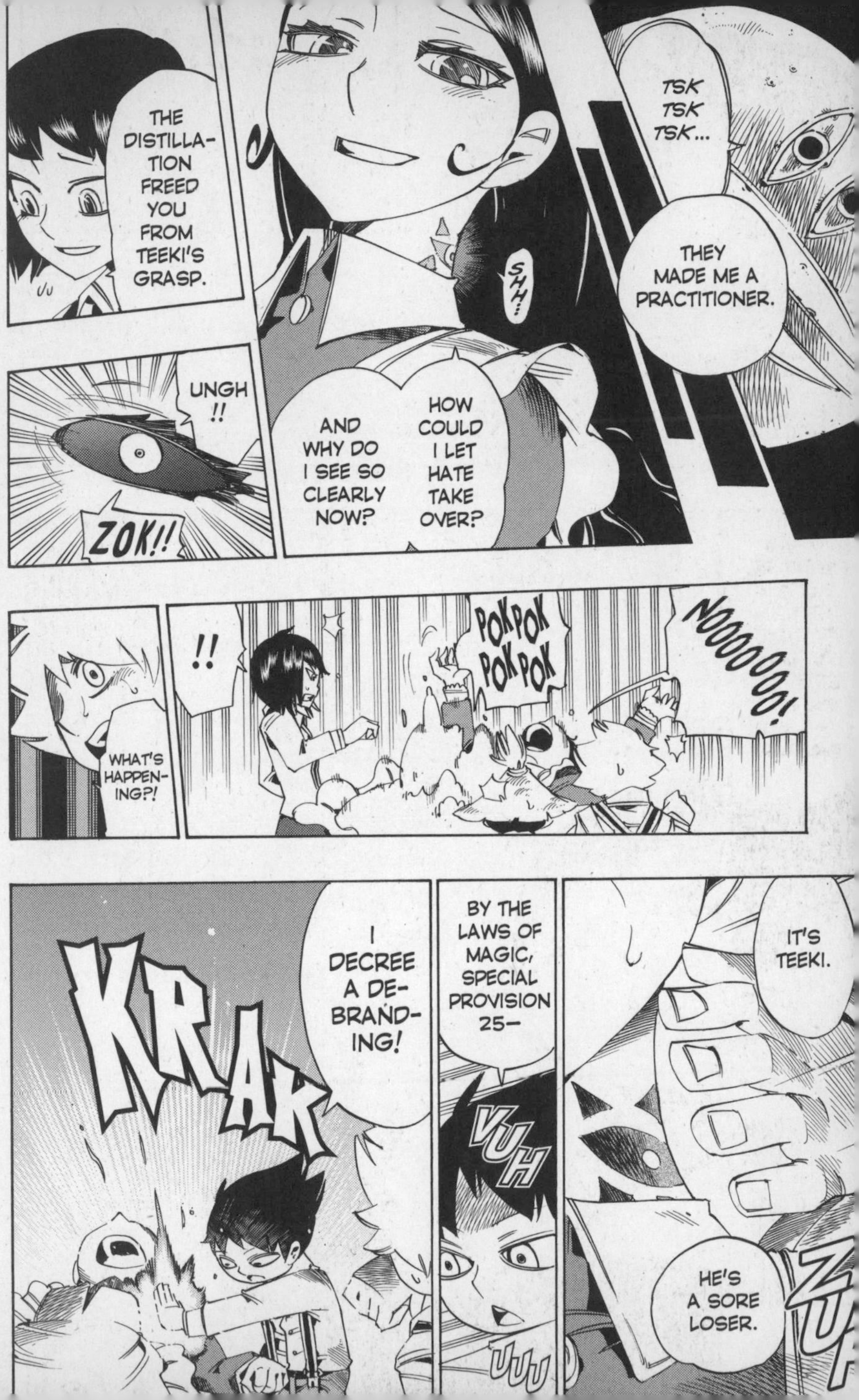
TSK TSK TSK...
THEY MADE ME A PRACTITIONER.
SHH...
HOW COULD I LET HATE TAKE OVER?
AND WHY DO I SEE SO CLEARLY NOW?
THE DISTILLATION FREED YOU FROM TEEKI'S GRASP.
UNGH!!
ZOK!!
NOOOOOOOO!
POKPOK POKPOK
!!
WHAT'S HAPPENING?!
IT'S TEEKI.
HE'S A SORE LOSER.
BY THE LAWS OF MAGIC, SPECIAL PROVISION 25—
VUH
I DECREE A DE-BRANDING!
KRAK

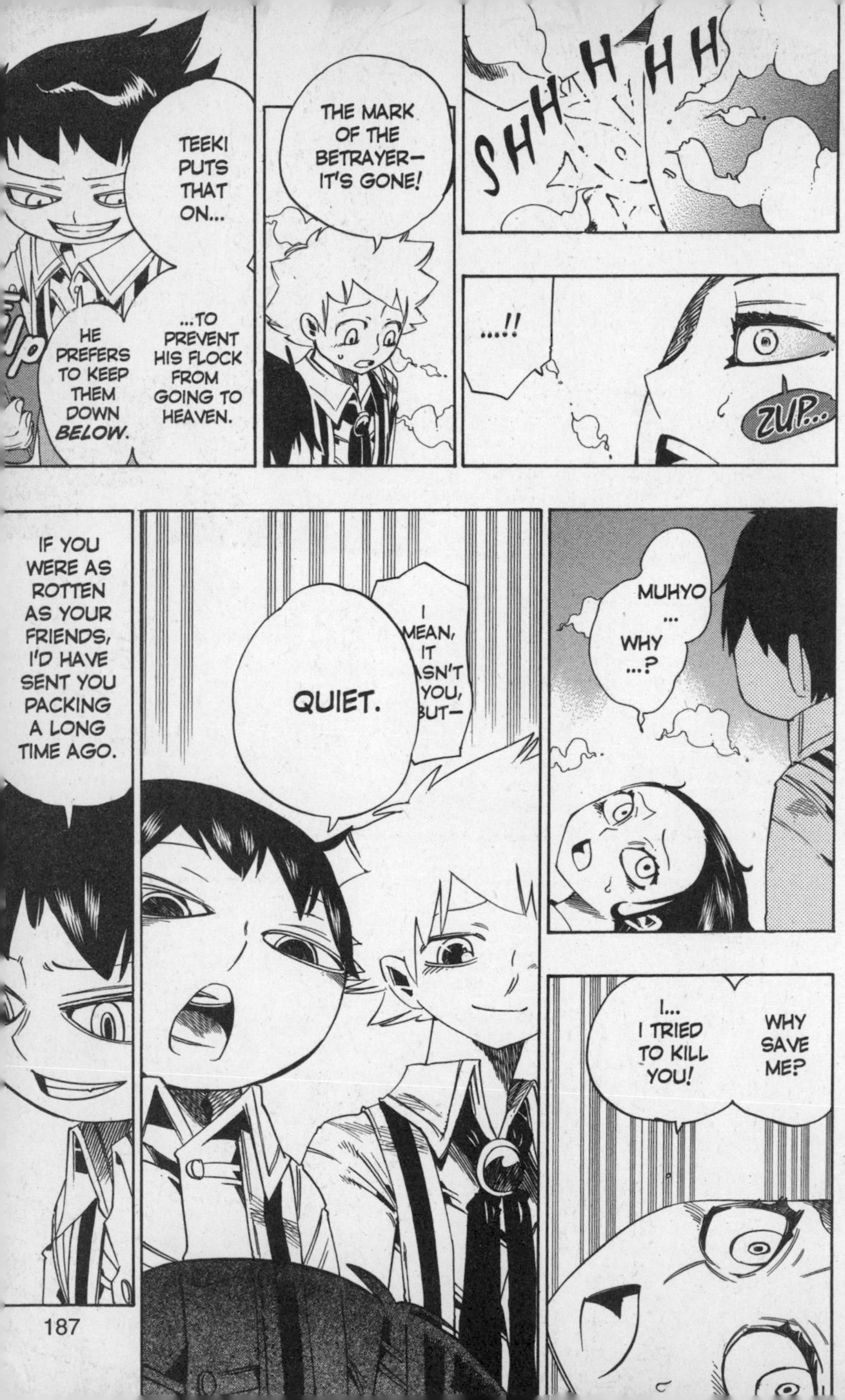
SHHHHHH
...!!
ZUP...
THE MARK OF THE BETRAYER— IT'S GONE!
TEEKI PUTS THAT ON...
...TO PREVENT HIS FLOCK FROM GOING TO HEAVEN.
HE PREFERS TO KEEP THEM DOWN *BELOW*.
MUHYO ... WHY ...?
WHY SAVE ME?
I... I TRIED TO KILL YOU!
I MEAN, IT ASN'T YOU, BUT—
QUIET.
IF YOU WERE AS ROTTEN AS YOUR FRIENDS, I'D HAVE SENT YOU PACKING A LONG TIME AGO.

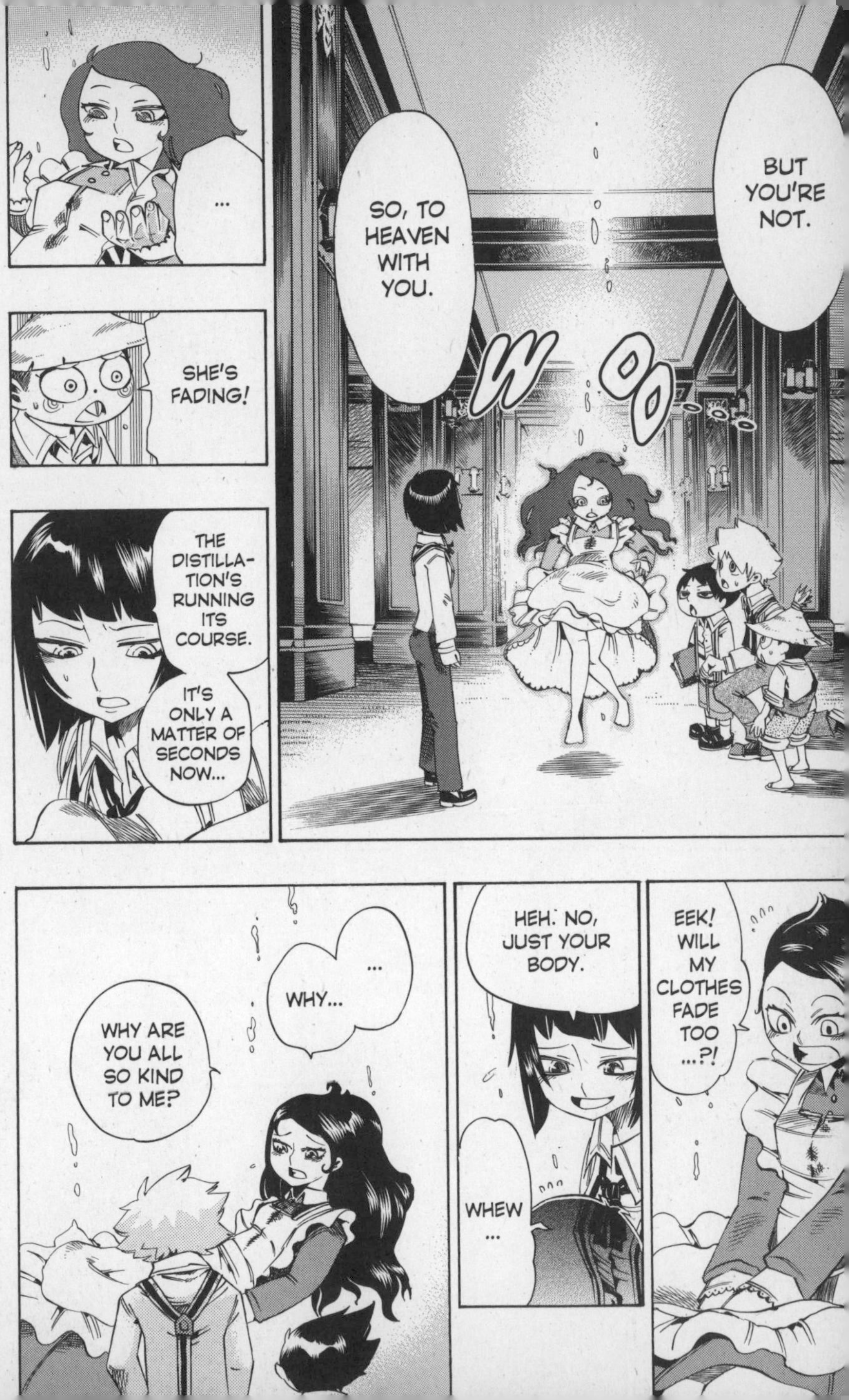
BUT YOU'RE NOT.
SO, TO HEAVEN WITH YOU.
WOO
...
SHE'S FADING!
THE DISTILLATION'S RUNNING ITS COURSE.
IT'S ONLY A MATTER OF SECONDS NOW...
EEK! WILL MY CLOTHES FADE TOO ...?!
HEH. NO, JUST YOUR BODY.
WHEW ...
...
WHY...
WHY ARE YOU ALL SO KIND TO ME?

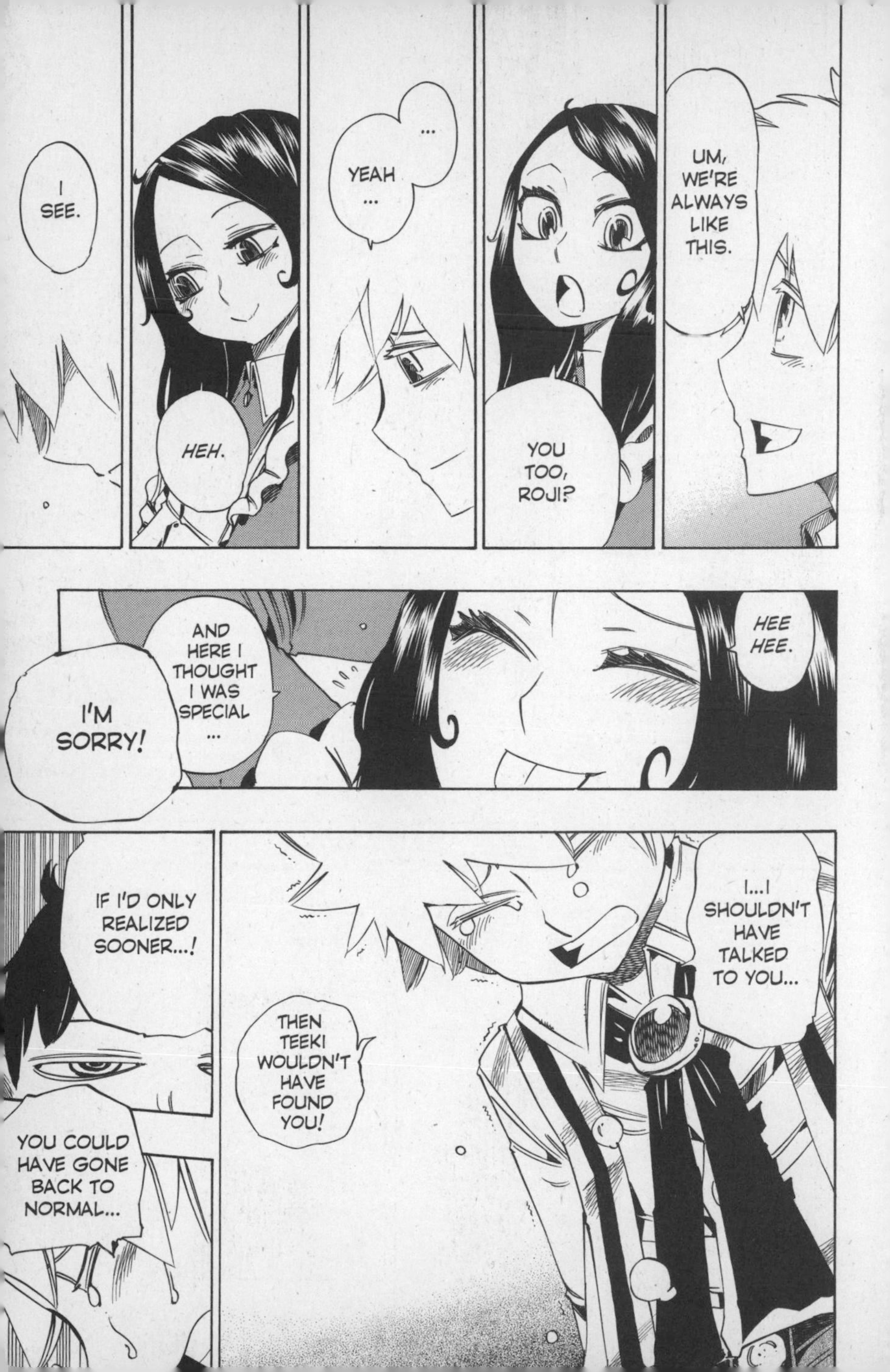
UM, WE'RE ALWAYS LIKE THIS.
YOU TOO, ROJI?
...
YEAH ...
HEH.
I SEE.
HEE HEE.
AND HERE I THOUGHT I WAS SPECIAL ...
I'M SORRY!
I...I SHOULDN'T HAVE TALKED TO YOU...
THEN TEEKI WOULDN'T HAVE FOUND YOU!
IF I'D ONLY REALIZED SOONER...!
YOU COULD HAVE GONE BACK TO NORMAL...

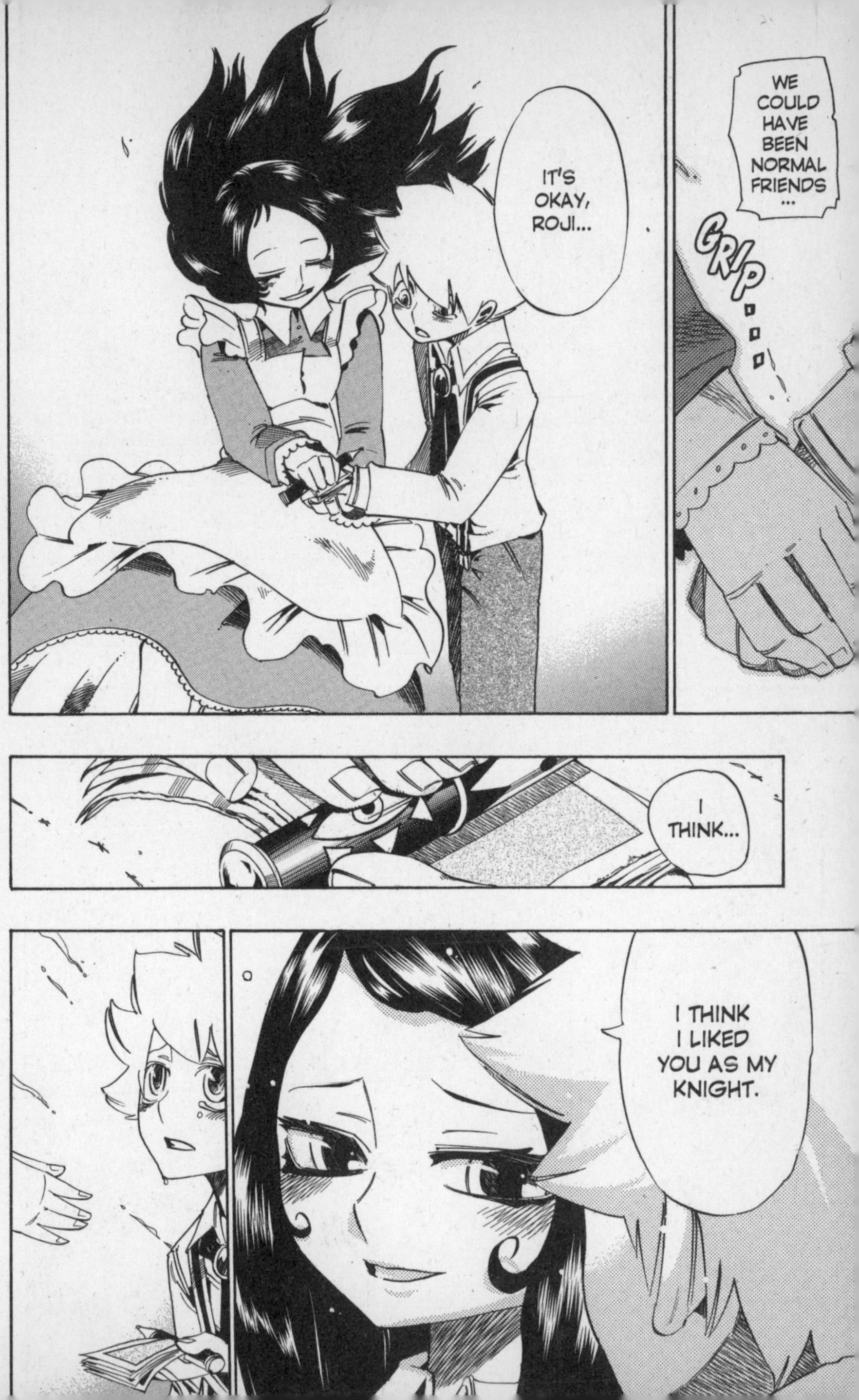
WE COULD HAVE BEEN NORMAL FRIENDS...
GRIP...
IT'S OKAY, ROJI...
I THINK...
I THINK I LIKED YOU AS MY KNIGHT.

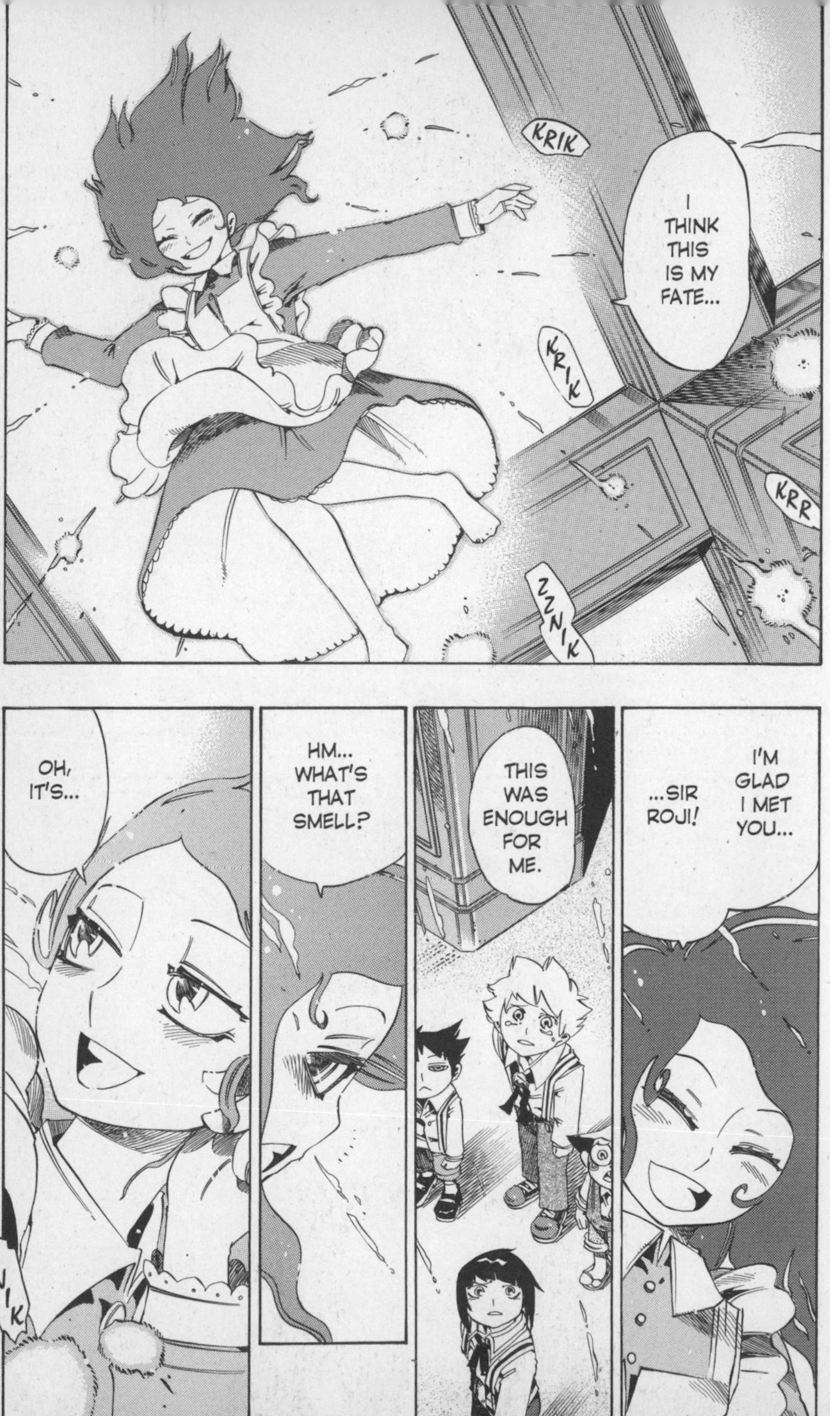

KRIK
I THINK THIS IS MY FATE...
KRIK
KRR
ZZNIK
I'M GLAD I MET YOU...
...SIR ROJI!
THIS WAS ENOUGH FOR ME.
HM... WHAT'S THAT SMELL?
OH, IT'S...
SNIK

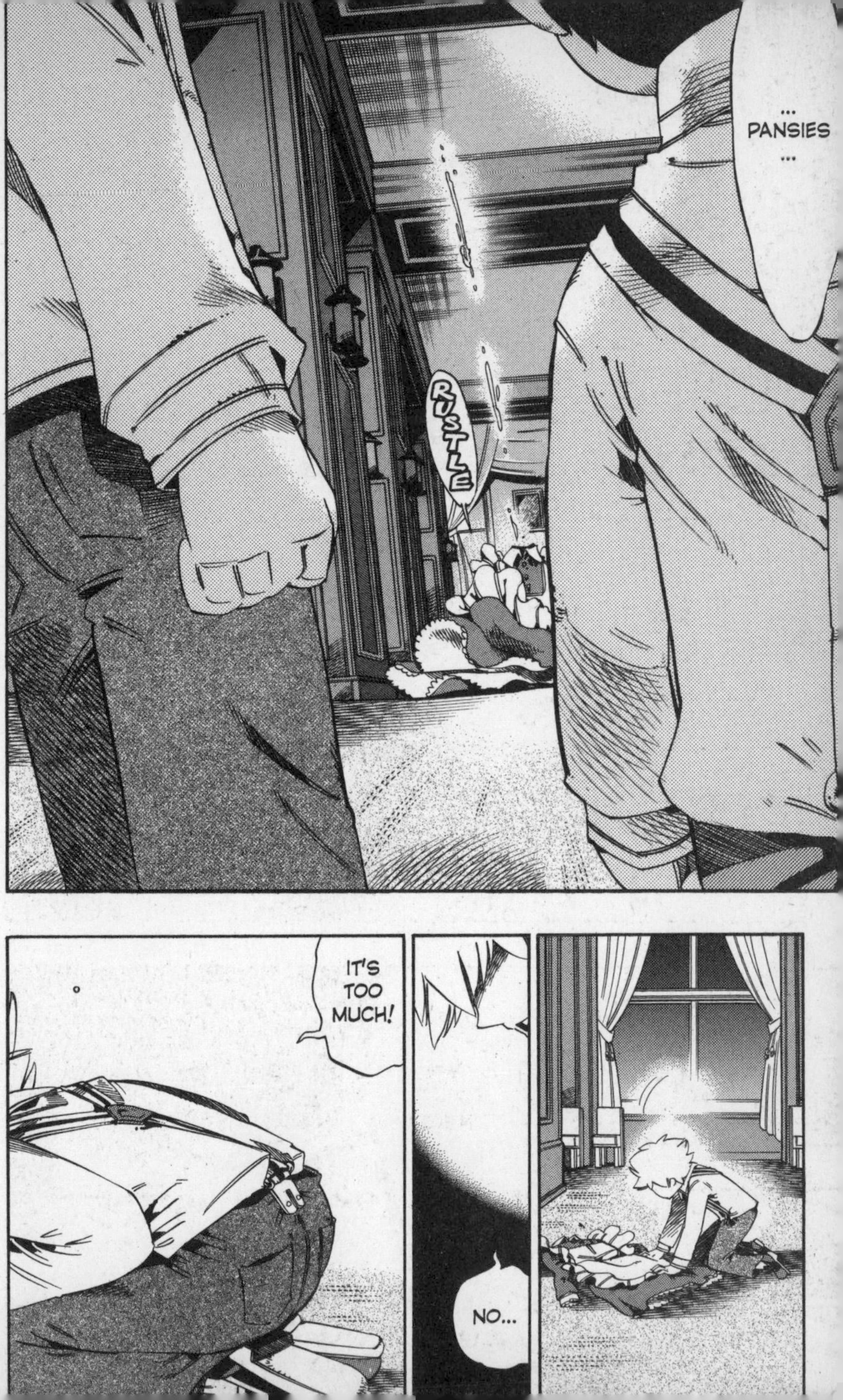
... PANSIES ...
RUSTLE
NO...
IT'S TOO MUCH!

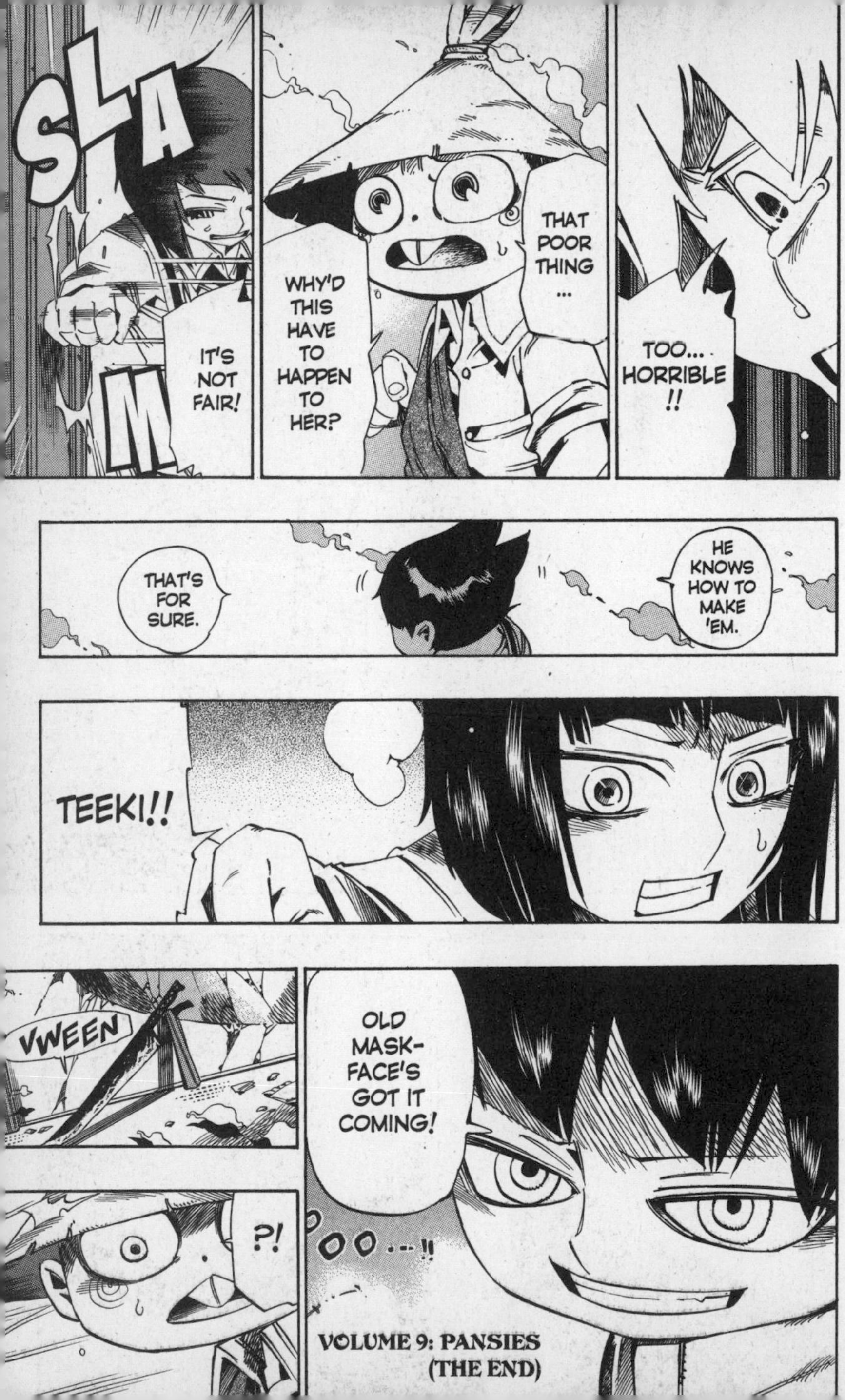
TOO... HORRIBLE!!
THAT POOR THING ...
WHY'D THIS HAVE TO HAPPEN TO HER?
SLAM
IT'S NOT FAIR!
HE KNOWS HOW TO MAKE 'EM.
THAT'S FOR SURE.
TEEKI!!
OLD MASK-FACE'S GOT IT COMING!
OOO...!!
VWEEN
?!
VOLUME 9: PANSIES
(THE END)

In The Next Volume...

Ark assassin Mick is down but not out for the count! What diabolical plan is he hatching for Muhyo and friends?

Available April 2009!

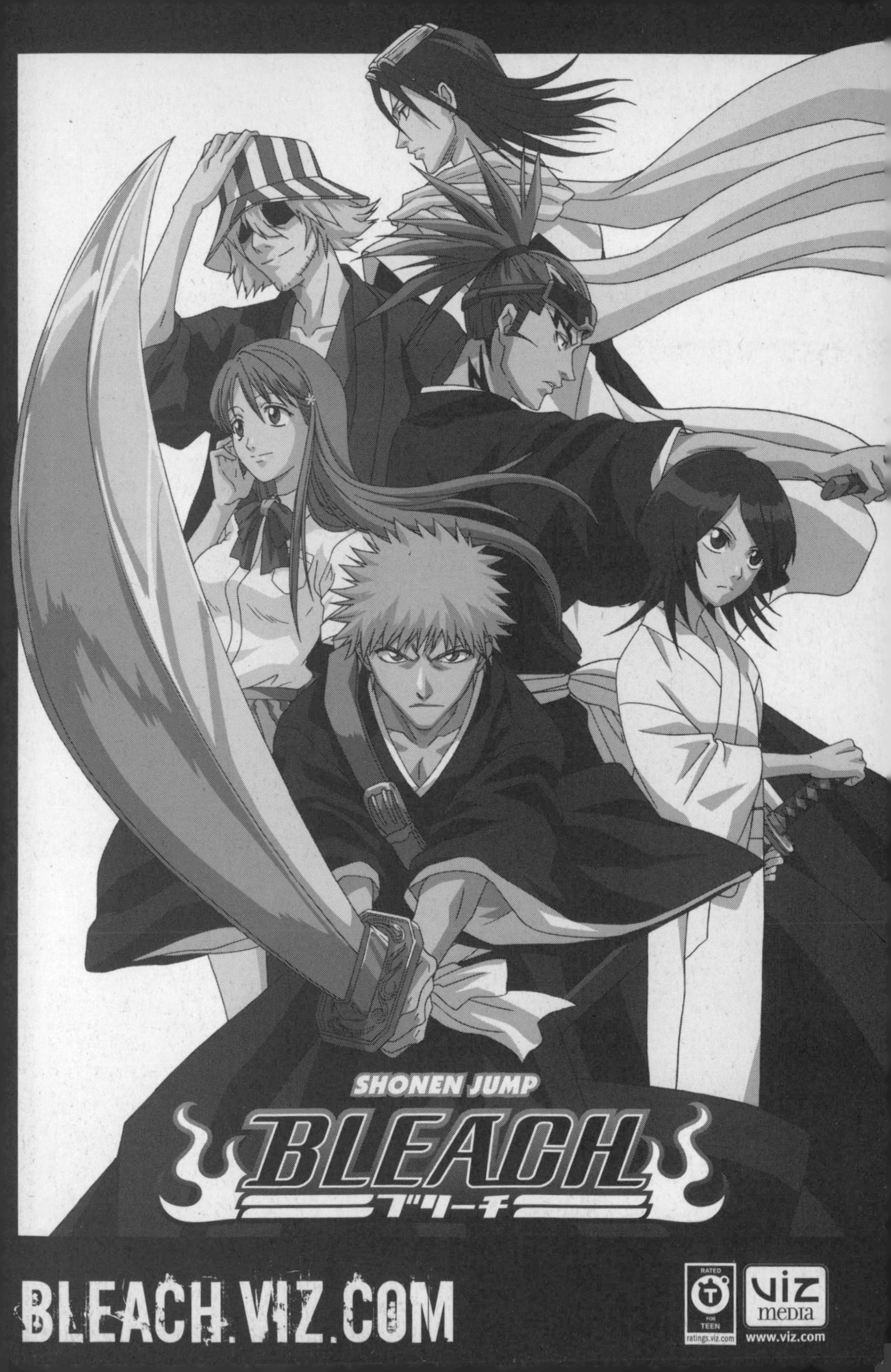
SHONEN JUMP
BLEACH
ブリーチ
BLEACH.VIZ.COM
RATED T FOR TEEN
ratings.viz.com
viz media
www.viz.com